D1225887

THE FIRE BIRD

A MEMOIR

RUSSIAN AND EAST EUROPEAN STUDIES

Jonathan Harris, Editor

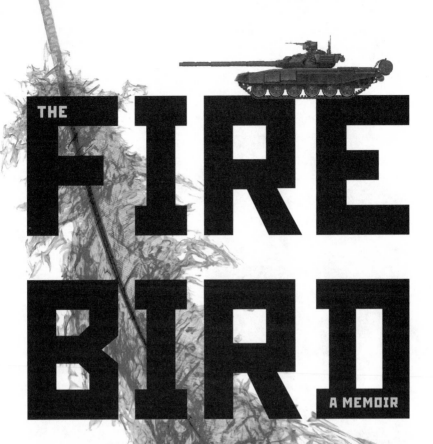

THE FIRE BIRD

A MEMOIR

THE ELUSIVE FATE OF

RUSSIAN DEMOCRACY

ANDREI KOZYREV
WITH A FOREWORD BY MICHAEL McFAUL

UNIVERSITY OF PITTSBURGH PRESS

Published by the University of Pittsburgh Press, Pittsburgh, Pa., 15260
Copyright © 2019, University of Pittsburgh Press
All rights reserved
Manufactured in the United States of America
Printed on acid-free paper
10 9 8 7 6 5 4 3 2 1

Cataloging-in-Publication data is available from the Library of Congress

ISBN 13: 978-0-8229-4592-5
ISBN 10: 0-8229-4592-4

Cover art: Alexander Popatov/Shutterstock.com
Cover design: Alex Wolfe

To Natalia and Andrei, my children

CONTENTS

FOREWORD

Michael McFaul

I FIRST MET RUSSIAN FOREIGN MINISTER ANDREI KOZYREV in 1990, when the Soviet Union still had a foreign minister of its own, Eduard Shevardnadze. I was part of an American delegation in Moscow that was conducting a workshop on democracy on behalf of the National Democratic Institute, so we decided to pay a courtesy call to this newly appointed official in Boris Yeltsin's government. Obviously, his job description at the time was eccentric. He was the foreign minister for the Russian Republic, one of fifteen republics that constituted the Soviet Union. It was the equivalent of being the foreign minister of California. At that time the fate of the Soviet Union was not certain; the job therefore of the Russian foreign minister was ambiguous.

Minister Kozyrev made a huge positive impression on me and on our delegation as a whole. His commitment to democratic reforms at home and closer relations with the West were obvious. As a PhD student at Oxford at the time, writing about Soviet and American policies toward southern Africa, I actually had read some of Andrei's written work before our meeting. Seeing opportunity in Gorbachev's policies of glasnost and perestroika, he boldly published articles repudiating the Soviet construct of "international class struggle" as the basis for its foreign policy and was especially critical of Soviet adventurism in what was called back then the "Third World." In person, he was even more impressive. He was not trying to find a third way between Soviet communism and Western democracy; he was seeking to join the West. Kozyrev embraced the audacious idea that Russians would be better off as partners of the United States and as citizens of Europe. I could trace no lingering legacy at all of Cold War thinking in his fresh, blunt, and candid assessment of the possibilities of collaboration between our two countries. I remember leaving that meeting with the following thought: if Russian Foreign Minister Kozyrev someday does become the Soviet foreign minister, we have a real chance of ending the Cold War for good.

Andrei Kozyrev, however, never became the Soviet foreign minister. Instead, he was part of a circle of other young reformers around Boris Yeltsin who helped to bring down the Soviet Union. Disillusion with outmoded Soviet ways and an emerging aspiration toward liberal-democratic ideals was their shared calling card. From the summer of 1990 until the summer of 1991, the Soviet government and the Russian government dueled over divergent visions for the future of the country. In August 1991 this standoff precipitated an inflection moment when a group of hard-liners within the Soviet government placed Soviet President Mikhail Gorbachev under house arrest and attempted a coup. Yeltsin and his supporters resisted. Kozyrev was in the Russian White House—the home of the Russian government at the time—when the Soviet Armed Forces moved to seize the building during this coup attempt. He was present when Boris Yeltsin defiantly stood on a tank to address the crowd that had gathered to support the Russian government against the coup plotters. After three tumultuous days, the coup failed and momentum for Soviet dissolution accelerated. Kozyrev then participated in the secret negotiations at Brezhnev's former hunting lodge deep in the primeval forest of Belovezha, Belarus, where the leaders of the Soviet republics of Russia, Ukraine, and Belarus agreed to secede, recognize each other's sovereignty, and dissolve the Soviet Union to form a new Commonwealth of Independent States. Instead of becoming Soviet foreign minister, Andrei Kozyrev became the first foreign minister of a newly independent Russia, a position in which he served for five years.

The first months after the failed August 1991 coup were filled with optimism, both in Russia and the West. At the time, Time magazine trumpeted, "Serfdom's End: A Thousand Years of Autocracy Are Reversed." However it may look in hindsight, this hopeful sentiment was not unusual. Leaders from the democratic world embraced the new government in Moscow, and Andrei Kozyrev was their perfect interlocutor. As someone who not only clearly identified with the reformers in Yeltsin's government but also had been educated at the Institute of International Relations—the Soviet training academy for grooming new diplomats— and held previous experience in the Soviet foreign ministry, Kozyrev had the perfect mix of skills, ideas, and experience to serve a newly independent Russia as its top diplomat at this crucial moment in history. For five years Kozyrev pursued Russia's national interest on the global stage honorably and capably.

At home, however, the transitions from communism to capitalism and from autocracy to democracy were extremely painful. During the 1990s Russians endured major and sustained economic depression, much worse than Americans experienced in the 1930s. The same White House that Kozyrev helped to defend in August 1991 was again attacked by tanks in October 1993, this time not by enemies of the Russia state but by the president of Russia himself, Boris Yeltsin. The causes of this standoff between the Russian president and parliament in 1993 were complicated; there were no white hats and black hats in this catastrophe. But tragically, if understandably, few Russians could draw inspiration about the practice of democracy from these political events, especially against the backdrop of economic collapse. These intertwined political and economic outcomes laid waste to Russia's democratic aspirations and opened a path for the eventual return of authoritarian rule.

As someone firmly identified with Yeltsin and the market reformers, Foreign Minister Kozyrev became an increasingly unpopular figure in Russia. Of course, Kozyrev himself had no direct responsibility for either the economy or domestic politics, but the reputation of everyone in Yeltsin's government at the time suffered. As he discusses in the pages of this book, Kozyrev himself became frustrated by Yeltsin's increasingly chaotic behavior, and he therefore decided to step down from his position as foreign minister in 1996 after successfully running for a seat in the new Russian parliament. As a member of parliament, Kozyrev continued to argue for closer engagement with the West. After one term he retired from political life and pursued a career in the private sector, later settling in the United States.

Kozyrev's memoir represents a significant contribution to our understanding of the first years of Russian independence. As we now move past the twenty-fifth anniversary of the collapse of the Soviet Union, US–Russian relations are at a level of hostility in some ways more intense than during the twilight years of the Cold War. This new conflict has its origins in the events of the early post-Soviet era—in exactly the handful of years that Kozyrev is crucially positioned to shed light on. He provides an account as one who witnessed, from the highest levels of independent Russia's first government, how the international conflicts contributing to this renewed East–West confrontation first took root in confusion and misunderstanding. In tracing the origins of the most intractable problems that now lay at the heart of our new confrontational era in US–Russian relations, Kozyrev reveals how in 1992 he denounced the hard-line Russian security and military forces that were fueling regional conflicts in Georgia, Moldova, Karabakh, and Crimea. These would later solidify as Putin's aggression and "frozen conflicts" on Russia's periphery today.

Through Kozyrev's eyes we see how hard-liners in Russia, who had only grudgingly accepted Eastern Europe joining Western economic institutions, balked at the prospect of these states cooperating with, let alone joining, the old foe NATO. The prospect of expanded NATO influence is what drew the first signs of outright opposition, from more than just the Communists, against Yeltsin's administration. According to Kozyrev, even honest diplomatic communications between the Yeltsin and Clinton governments failed to convey accurately either American intentions or Russian reservations during the early stages of NATO expansion, with consequences that we live with to this day and that Putin still uses to spin his dark tale of Western animosity to Russia's rightful destiny. If we ever get the opportunity to change dynamics in Russian–American relations, we should try to learn from our past mistakes. *The Firebird* provides many useful lessons.

In this memoir we also reexperience historical events with a personal, as well as a public, aspect. We see Kozyrev scrambling to contact the US White House from that remote hunting lodge in Belarus to inform President Bush of the dissolution of the Soviet Union. There is the comical description of an alcohol-fueled and nearly disastrous late-night dinner between Boris Yeltsin and Poland's president, Lech Wałęsa. And then there is the story behind Kozyrev's famous "Stockholm Surprise" speech that was designed to shock a gathering of world leaders with its (feigned) hostile Soviet-style rhetoric. These episodes and many others add fascinating highlights to a substantive treatment of the missed opportunities and warning signs of the early years of the post-Soviet era.

The Firebird is not just a retrospective memoir but also a guide to new possibilities for Russia and her foreign relations in the future. Kozyrev shows how some of the main issues of the current US–Russian conflict have their source in the earliest days of Russian independence. He also explains how Russian popular opinion and Russian leaders, particularly with regard to attitudes toward the West, are strongly linked and ultimately not to be ignored. By detailing some of the mistakes and opportunities missed by Russian and Western leaders alike, Andrei Kozyrev offers key ideas and critical insights for how to formulate a more effective policy toward Russia.

Perhaps readers of this honest, detailed, and ultimately hopeful memoir will be inspired to once again believe that democracy has not yet seen its final days in Russia.

AUTHOR'S NOTE

THROUGHOUT THIS BOOK, I QUOTE MYSELF AND others extensively. These quotes represent my best recollection of conversations and should not be considered verbatim transcripts.

THE FIRE BIRD

A MEMOIR

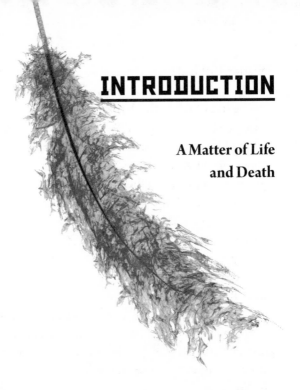

INTRODUCTION

A Matter of Life and Death

IT WAS DECEMBER 1991. I was in a hunting lodge deep in a vast forest, and I had to make a phone call that would change not just my life but the lives of millions. In a detail that might seem astonishing today—not least to younger readers—I had nothing more technologically sophisticated than an ordinary landline on which to make contact with a center of power that most of my fellow countrymen and women had viewed for decades as the enemy. Sitting on the end of the phone looking at the pine tree wilderness outside the window, I realized I was being put through, first to the White House in Washington, DC, and then to the president of the United States himself, George H. W. Bush.

I had two important pieces of news for Bush. The first was that his former Cold War opponent, the Soviet Union, was to be divided into twelve newly independent states. The second, and equally crucial piece of information was that only Russia would inherit and control the Soviet nuclear missile capability, which even today could destroy America.

Like the baby boomers in the United States, my generation in Russia felt as if it had lived permanently on the brink of annihilation. For almost half a century, both sides in the Cold War had stockpiled nuclear arsenals in an equation that had earned itself the moniker of mutual assured destruction. The acronym—MAD—felt entirely appropriate.

The story I tell in this book remains acutely relevant today, not least because MAD is still in place. Although about 4,860 miles separate Moscow and Washington, it has increasingly been observed in recent years that what happens in Russia remains vitally important for the United States (and consequently, for the rest of the world). Recent political analysis has overwhelmingly focused on Russia's online influence. Yet it should not be forgotten that it remains a political big beast by sheer virtue of its geography, since it borders America and Japan by sea, and China, Central Asia, and Europe on land. The country also possesses tremendous wealth in natural resources and human talent that shore it up as a global player even when its economy underperforms. Beyond this, Russia together with the United States, European Union, and Canada, is a key supplier and operator of the International Space Station.

When I made that phone call at the end of 1991, the death of the Cold War and the birth of a new democratic Russia seemed to promise a bright new future for both sides. That was my dream, at least. As Russia's first foreign minister (1992–96) I was in a prime position to pursue it vigorously.

Was I naive? Some critics have since made that allegation, but the truth is inevitably more complicated. I was not naive to be optimistic and, in this book, I want to explain why. I have always been, to my core, a son of my homeland. We have a famous fable about a Firebird that can bring a whole new realm of happiness once caught, despite presenting huge challenges to its captor. In my political career, I feel as if I have chased my own Firebird, believing that sooner or later the Russian people will discover the road to democracy and cooperative foreign policy.

Yet even the greatest optimist has to concede that right now it is the challenges that are most painfully evident. Today it is hard to believe just how promising the initial contacts between the United States and the new Russia were. Presidents George H. W. Bush and Boris Yeltsin signed a declaration only a month after the birth of the new state that declared, "Russia and the United States do not regard each other as potential adversaries. From now on, the relationship will be characterized by friendship and partnership." The document explicitly indicated the basis of this change: "a common commitment to democracy and economic freedom."

Progress remained rapid—at the next meeting between the presidents on June 16–17, 1992, they decided to decrease strategic nuclear arsenals by almost two-thirds. These cuts greatly reduced Russia's superiority in heavy ground-based missiles (arguably representing a destabilizing first-strike capability) and slashed the US advantage in sea-based missiles and strategic bombers. That groundbreaking arrangement was enshrined in the Strategic Arms Reduction Treaty (START II), which the two presidents signed in January 1993. START I had been signed two years earlier by President Ronald Reagan and Mikhail Gorbachev.

For the United States the era began with a decade of prosperity made possible, in large part, by the "peace dividend" that came with the Cold War's end. Russia, however, had a different fate in store. In transitioning from the Soviet system to capitalism, the Russian people were forced to endure a decade of economic turmoil worse than the US Great Depression. These years also witnessed the Kremlin's failure to cement a sustainable democratic system.

Today, the United States and Russia are, I strongly believe, engaged in a renewed Cold War. Russian aggression toward America and NATO allies in cyberspace, its support of the old Soviet client regime Syria, and its military interventions in Ukraine and Georgia are loud and clear. The repeated pronouncements of US presidents promising better relations with Russia have given little hope for real improvement. President Trump's three predecessors all came into office seeking better relations with a Russia that remained defiant. They all left office with relations worse off.

How did we get to this state? Americans and Russians are right to wonder: What happened to the early days of promise, and is there hope for better relations in the months and years to come. This book is my attempt to answer these questions.

From my position, I witnessed the early rumblings in the Russian bureaucracy of growing hostility toward Russia's new democratic order (or even disorder, as it often seemed at the time). The individuals and concepts (including acrimony toward NATO and a belief in Russia's predicament of authoritarianism in contrast to the democratic West) behind that hostility are essentially at the heart of the US–Russian conflict today. I was convinced at the time that democratic reforms and pro-Western foreign policy were linked, and that if one were to fail, both would fail. Time would prove my assumption to be correct.

Even with all that has passed, I still believe in the words I spoke when I addressed a crowd of over a million of my countrymen who turned out to protest the hard-liner coup attempt in August 1991: "I was and am convinced that a democratic Russia should be as natural an ally of democratic America as the totalitarian Soviet Union was its enemy."

My confidence in this ideal is rooted in my own background. I was raised from childhood to have faith in the Soviet system. As the situation stood I was on track for a very successful diplomatic career, but I decided to risk this to join the movement dedicated to a democratic future for Russia.

An Ordinary Soviet Boy

I was born not in Russia, but in Brussels, Belgium, and have paid a certain price for that accident of birth throughout my life. My association with Brussels—NATO's home and a perennial target of Soviet propaganda—has often raised suspicions against me, whether I've been presenting my driver's license to a cop on a Russian back road or later on in my professional life. Even in America people often wonder how a Russian minister could have been born in Belgium. The truth is my father worked in Belgium for about two years (1949–51) as an engineer with the Soviet trade mission. Three months after my birth in 1951, he returned with his family to Moscow, where I grew up. I never saw Belgium again until I was forty years old.

The story of my family could be considered the Soviet answer to the American dream. My father was the tenth child in a family of Russian peasants. The four brothers and one sister who did not die in childhood grew up strong and good-looking. One by one, they left the village for Moscow, graduated, and found jobs in the city. The brothers had good careers: two became army colonels and one a senior engineer—my father worked in the Ministry of Foreign Trade. All joined the Communist Party. The sister married a man who rose to become a factory director, and they also joined the Party. My father's side of the family always said that the Soviet system had been favorable to them.

My mother felt the same way. She was a high school teacher and also a member of the Communist Party. It was only in adulthood that I realized that December 24, the day she was born, was also Christmas Eve on the Roman Catholic calendar. Our family was not even aware that Orthodox Christmas was January 7. My father and mother did not care about religion or the church calendar. Orthodox Easter was celebrated, but only as an opportunity to feast on typical Russian holiday cuisine. My mother would always cook up a banquet and invite over as many friends and relatives as possible to share it.

As she served the guests, she would usually mention her gratitude to her late grandmother, who had taught her the recipes and passed on the tradition. In a cultural twist that I would only later appreciate as ironic, it emerged that the inspiration of this Orthodox tradition was herself the child of a provincial Jewish family. Not that this meant anything to me then. If my Christian references were almost nonexistent, so were my Jewish ones: I had never heard of a synagogue or the Torah.

It is telling that I became most strongly aware of my heritage from the reactions of others. In all my official papers, from birth certificate to passport (which in the Soviet Union indicated nationality as well as citizenship), I, like both my parents, was listed as ethnically Russian. Yet I had inherited a typically Jewish-looking nose. This prompted enemies in street fights to throw in "Jew" along with a whole barrage of other insults.

Thus, at the same time that I became aware of the element of Jewishness in my background, I woke up to the fact that it was not easy to be a Jew in the Soviet Union or the Russian Empire. Old habits die hard, and although most Russians are not anti-Semitic, I was convinced that my nose would dictate a practical limit to the scope of my ambitions. Beyond this, my parents' low status in the Soviet hierarchy made me an unlikely candidate for the elite foreign policy college, the Moscow State Institute of International Relations (MGIMO). Typically, students of my age were the offspring of high-level Communist Party, government, and KGB officials. Yet I was admitted.

After high school I briefly worked as a fixer in a giant factory. I also joined a youth performance troupe, which comprised ordinary workers like me and people with university education. We produced funny and clever stage performances that did amazingly well in competitions. The director encouraged me to apply to a good college and promised some financial support. I applied to a school that also housed foreign students. After I successfully passed the exams, the local KGB director informed me that the security clearance for access to military secrets I had gained working at the factory precluded contacts with foreigners for three years, which meant I could not accept the place. Amazingly, the officer who had attended (and, I believe, censored) performances by our troupe, felt bad for me and lent strong support to my application to the MGIMO, which at the time was under heavy KGB surveillance. Looking back, I'm surprised that he didn't try to recruit me. Thanks to him I was able to retake and pass the exams and become an MGIMO student.

Five years later I graduated with distinction and, with the help of the influential father of one of my classmates, I got a job in the Soviet Foreign Ministry.

Because my family lacked the Party connections of many of my peers, I initially lagged behind them professionally. To obtain my postgraduate diploma in history, I wrote a thesis on the mechanics of United Nations deliberations, which I hoped would help me get a position. Eventually, I had the opportunity to make myself useful by taking notes at a seminar in Moscow presided over by the USSR's foreign minister Andrei Gromyko. My predecessors had struggled mightily to write down what Gromyko said—he was ailing and spoke only occasionally in abrupt and broken sentences that often made little sense. Browsing my notes, I decided that the only course of action was to pick out key words from his inchoate rambling, and fashion them into statements that reflected what *should* have been said by a Soviet official in accordance with Party policy. After that, my career began to take off.

I managed to join the Communist Party at the age of twenty—quite an achievement, since the earliest age at which one could join was nineteen. I was very proud of this. For me, membership had far less to do with an ideology that was becoming increasingly disconnected from the reality of daily life, than a distinction beneficial for a career in the Soviet system.

The Break with Communism

I had my first taste of "enemy power" in the fall of 1975. I was assigned as a junior staff member to the Soviet delegation to the United Nations in New York. It was a turning point. I fell in love with the city and grabbed any opportunity I could to wander the streets, staring at skyscrapers, shop windows, cars, and occasionally dropping in at inexpensive Chinese restaurants. It all seemed so luxurious in comparison with the dull scarcity of Soviet life.

I soon realized that this "luxury" belonged not just to a small number of wealthy capitalists, as we were taught to believe in the Soviet Union, but to a large number, indeed a majority, of Americans. While the homeless and poor I had seen so regularly on Soviet TV existed, they constituted a small minority of the population. It was clear that even average Americans had a much better lifestyle than most Soviets could dream of in any foreseeable future. My discovery that capitalism had dramatic material advantages over socialism, in direct contradiction to what I had been taught in the Soviet Union, came as both a huge shock and a revelation. It was the first blow against my loyalty to the Communist Party.

The second was perhaps even more devastating. It was a warm spring Sunday morning and I bought a copy of Boris Pasternak's *Doctor Zhivago* in a bookshop in mid-Manhattan. I sat on a bench in the sunshine in Central Park reading until darkness fell. I then left the book on the bench, afraid to take it back to the Soviet mission where I had my room.

The book thrilled me. It was a wonderful, exhilarating piece of Russian literature and poetry. But why was it banned in the Soviet Union and its author denounced as a hostile dissident? After all, none of the main protagonists had any political views to speak of, nor did they engage in anti-communist activity. The question gnawed uncomfortably at me for days.

Gradually the answer came to me. Pasternak's crime was that the book celebrated personal freedom, the idea that a human being had the right to be independent from the state. *Doctor Zhivago* was a stark illustration of how completely that idea was at odds with the Soviet system.

That was the moment when I lost all my illusions about the political arrangements under which the people of the Soviet Union were living. I knew I couldn't defect, not out of loyalty to the system, but because of the devastating effect it would have on the lives of my relatives back home. Instead I became an "internal dissident," denying the Soviet system in my heart but never challenging it openly. I had always admired Andrei Sakharov and a few other open dissidents but felt I could not join them because of the hopelessness of fighting the system.

Gorbachev and Perestroika

When Mikhail Gorbachev came to power in 1985 and introduced perestroika, his plan for "restructuring" the Soviet economy, I saw it as a window being opened in an airless room, nothing more. I was deeply doubtful that in the long term he seriously intended to challenge and change the system.

Soon it became clear that Gorbachev wanted to renovate the Soviet system in order to make it less confrontational with the West, which would allow it to become more competitive economically. The Soviet Union had originally been conceived as economically self-sufficient. But by the 1980s, it was in increasingly poor shape and heavily dependent on exports to the West of crude oil and other mineral resources. The country was unable to feed itself, and in 1984 grain imports from the West, which had been rising since the late 1970s, broke all records. At the same time, government debt was growing dramatically throughout the decade and defense spending was being maintaining at unsustainably high levels. It was only when Gorbachev met with resistance from the Soviet bureaucracy that he resorted to the weapon it feared most: glasnost, public debate, and a relaxing of the Iron Curtain. I think he was genuinely surprised by the result. The weapon he used against his foes within the Soviet system proved to be lethal to the system itself. Communism simply could not exist without totalitarian control based on intimidation.

Since Gorbachev sought to become a respected world leader, a task force was set up in the Foreign Ministry to monitor and report to the Kremlin how the world, in particular the United States, assessed Gorbachev's domestic and foreign initiatives. My boss, Vladimir Petrovsky, led the team, and I was on it. Along with a couple of other young participants, we wrote reports intended to be as direct and honest as possible (or, more specifically, to the extent tolerated by our cautious and conservative bosses). Our recurring argument was that relaxing tensions with the West was not enough to gain real acceptance from the world's democracies. Nikita Khrushchev and Leonid Brezhnev had also tried this but were always undercut by the ugly practices of the KGB at home.

Gorbachev had to prove that his changes were genuine in order to win respect from the West, and (more importantly) a reprieve from the arms race that was bankrupting the country.

When preparations were under way for Gorbachev's major address at the UN General Assembly scheduled for September 26, 1989, our group suggested that he endorse the Universal Declaration of Human Rights (UDHR), which promoted freedom of speech.

It was a dramatic moment. Clearly, free speech was a principle that ran directly counter to decades of Soviet censorship. Gorbachev had to choose between his liberal rhetoric and his desire to maintain the Party's traditional control over society. He left the latter task to his hard-line appointees headed by the burly, bullying party hack Yegor Ligachev, who had been summoned to Moscow from Siberia for his "managerial skills." Ligachev was the designated chief ideologist in the politburo, from which the party ruled. It came as little surprise that he reportedly called our proposal "subversion with formulations." We were proud to adopt his condemnation as our slogan.

In the end, it was Foreign Minister Eduard Shevardnadze who persuaded Gorbachev to include the passage endorsing the UDHR in his UN address. Shevardnadze was another Gorbachev appointee to the politburo. Moscow gossips dubbed him "the white fox" for his vast head of gray hair and his remarkable ability to navigate the party bureaucracy while promoting detente with the West.

The argument in our group's next report was born for me ten years earlier, reading *Doctor Zhivago* in Central Park. It warned Gorbachev of the damage that would be done to his credibility and prestige if censorship continued in the Soviet Union. To our amazement, he agreed to publicly endorse the principle of freedom of speech and gave orders to curb censorship as part of his glasnost policy. We were elated: the words of the Soviet leader spoken overseas *had* to be turned into deeds inside our own country! But we were also painfully aware that Ligachev and his comrades retained powerful positions in the bureaucracy and would try to shape and limit the implementation of these freedoms.

Joining the Democratic Opposition

In the summer of 1989, I wrote an article suggesting that we cooperate with the United States instead of supporting rogue regimes like the Syrian dictatorship in the Middle East. First published in the Soviet press, the article was reported and then reproduced in the *Washington Post* and other major news outlets all over the world. This brought me my first recognition, in my own right, on the international stage and in the emerging pro-democracy movement inside the country.

Inevitably, the article came to the attention of my employer. It received harsh criticism from some senior Communist Party officials at home and from staunch foreign "comrades," notably in Cuba and Milošević's Yugoslavia. Foreign Minister Shevardnadze defied them all and appointed me to head the prestigious UN Department. As the youngest department director, I could look forward to a bright future in the Foreign Ministry of the Soviet Union.

In the summer of 1990, Boris Yeltsin won the popular election to become head of the Russian Republic's parliament. He quickly started putting together a government team dedicated to implementing reforms that could end the Soviet system. It is no exaggeration to say that Yeltsin's election set my imagination afire.

I sought an appointment as minister of foreign affairs of the Russian Republic. As a ceremonial post, with virtually no power or responsibility, it had traditionally been assigned by order of the Soviet Foreign Ministry and was occupied by aging ambassadors easing into retirement. But with Yeltsin's election, the appointment would be made by the rebellious parliament of the Russian Federation. By winning the post, I would join Yeltsin's team of reformers.

Yeltsin would later tell me there had been other candidates to choose from, including my patron Vladimir Petrovsky and Anatoly Adamishin, both highly respected and able diplomats. He had originally envisioned me as a deputy to either of them. Yet the group of democratically minded deputies who interviewed me in a preliminary hearing insisted on putting my candidacy to a direct vote at the plenary session in October 1990. The message of my presentation and my answer to the many questions directed to me was that we had to press ahead with reforms. This accorded with the beliefs of the majority of deputies to the Russian parliament. In contrast to the Soviet Union's pursuit of limited rapprochement with the West, I spoke bluntly of a potential alliance with the most developed countries of the West, and of good-neighborly relations with China, Japan, and other nearby countries that could create favorable conditions for domestic social and economic development. The answers must have impressed the deputies, as I received a majority of the votes.

Yeltsin kept me at arm's length at first, unsure of what to make of me. I don't think I gained his confidence until I organized his successful visit to Prague in the summer of 1991. His previous foreign visits, including a rather scandalous one to the United States the previous year, had to that point not gone very well. During that US trip, Yeltsin had spent far too much time with the famous American bourbon Jack Daniels, for which he had been roundly criticized in the press. So, he was horrified when president Václav Havel suggested they take a walk to a famous pub in Prague, where he and other then-dissidents used to sip famous (and delicious) Czech beers, while discussing opposition strategy. It almost cost me my job to persuade Yeltsin to accept the invitation. I assured him that Havel's invitation wasn't a reference to his drinking but a highly symbolic gesture of confidence in this new democratic breed of Moscow leaders and a vivid departure from previous Soviet officials, whom the Czechoslovaks found both boring and frightening. Following my advice simply to limit the amount of Czech nectar that he drank, the president found he had a good time in the pub. A few days later I was able to show him press clippings confirming that the pub episode had been positively received all over the world, even by the opposition press in Moscow.

Yet important as the Prague trip turned out to be, events later that summer would prove to be far more important to my country and the world.

PART I

**Russia versus the
Soviet Union, 1991**

1

The Russian White House under Siege

AUGUST 19, 1991, SHOULD HAVE BEEN A regular Monday morning, but it opened on an unexpected note. Instead of the news, all Russian TV and radio stations were broadcasting Tchaikovsky's *Swan Lake*. Audiences across the country understood at once that something serious had happened in politics. Ever since 1982, major events such as the deaths of Soviet leaders (three in the span of three years) had been announced after national broadcasting of this sort.

At age sixty, Gorbachev was on the young side and seemingly too healthy to follow his immediate predecessors. However, he was not immune to actions from Kremlin hard-liners fighting against his liberalization policies. And act they did: an announcer reported that Gorbachev had fallen ill at his state-owned dacha at a Black Sea resort. "The new Soviet leadership" in Moscow would reinstate socialist "law and order."

At the time of the announcement I was already in a car and heading to the city from my state-owned dacha in a Russian government compound about fifteen miles from Moscow. Yeltsin occupied a house around the corner from me, though he had campaigned against such perks and had gained popularity by vigorously denouncing unwarranted privileges for top officials. The compound served as a kind of out-of-office meeting place for members of the Russian government.

As I drove in, I noticed signs of unusual activity near the local traffic police station. There were armored personnel carriers, solders with machine guns, and men in gray raincoats with that unmistakable KGB look surrounding them.

"Do we go on or make a U-turn?" The driver turned to me, his face pale. I knew what he meant. Fear of the KGB's ruthless power was a key pillar of the Soviet regime.

I tried to make myself sound self-assured. "Go on, no problem," I told him. Already it seemed that this Monday morning was to be marked by encounters with what Dostoyevsky had identified as both the greatness and the darkness of the Russian soul. The Tchaikovsky music represented the pinnacle of Russia's cultural achievements, while the gray-clad men at the checkpoint evoked the horrors of the infamous Gulag Archipelago so vividly described by Alexander Solzhenitsyn. I saw before me a pivotal clash of extremes and was determined to take the right side. My Russian upbringing had instilled these kinds of literary images and moral absolutes in me ever since I was a boy.

As I returned to reality, I realized that the driver was following the usual route to the small, shabby mansion that housed the Russian Federation's Foreign Ministry, located far from the central government region. I asked him to drop me instead at the "White House," the colloquially named big white building that housed the Russian Parliament and the president's office. If anything were to happen, it would be there.

On reaching the government building at about 8:30 a.m., I teased a young policeman at the entrance in a friendly way, as I always did. "Hi, tough guy, so what's for breakfast in your handgun holder today?" He answered unexpectedly seriously: "Today it's a revolver. We are here to protect you." In numbers they represented no more than a squad and had no chance against the KGB Special Forces. Neither did we, I thought.

In the empty building I met Sergei Shakhrai, Yeltsin's key legal adviser. He had won his seat in the Russian parliament by popular vote against communist opponents. With an ironic smile, he congratulated me because the coup d'état we had been expecting from the hard-liners for at least ten months had arrived, and, of course, no preparations had been made.

"It's you who says it's a coup," I replied. "Though the plotters may be right about one thing: they *are* the new Soviet leadership." This was true—President Gorbachev had appointed the leaders of the coup only a few months prior. The head of the group was none other than Gorbachev's handpicked vice-president, Gennady Yanayev, who had been approved by the Soviet legislature only on a second vote, and only under heavy pressure from Gorbachev. The other leaders were the prime minister of the USSR and the top ministers of Gorbachev's cabinet: the heads of the KGB, Defense, and Interior (police). "If Gorbachev has fallen ill, as they claim, why shouldn't they impose law and order, even in his absence?"

"We should demand that Gorbachev speak to the public, however ill he is. If he cannot do this, it should be confirmed by the best doctors and publicly announced. Otherwise it is a coup!" Sergei declared. "I will call Yeltsin now. He is still at his dacha with a few aides. They are working on a statement condemning the coup. It's very important that when we were on the way here, the KGB stopped neither of us. I shall advise him to return to Moscow. Is there anything you would like to suggest to him?"

"I think my ministry should call the Western embassies, as well as the media, and ask their representatives to come here at, say, 10:30 a.m. By that time Yeltsin will be either in the White House or in detention. In any case, the world should hear from us and learn what is going on."

Shakhrai dialed Yeltsin's dacha and spoke to Gennady Burbulis, Yeltsin's closest aide at the time. Burbulis had been a professor of philosophy (Marxist philosophy of course, as all other schools of thought were banned) in Sverdlovsk (now Ekaterinburg), the industrial center of the Urals. It was in Sverdlovsk that both he and Yeltsin had first won competitive elections to the parliament by running *against* communist opponents. Being a man of letters, Burbulis had a better knowledge of the key democratic concepts that both of them supported but he lacked Yeltsin's charisma and ability to command big rallies. Known widely as the "Gray Cardinal," he contributed hugely, perhaps decisively, to Yeltsin's determined anti-communist stance in the critical years 1989 to 1992. Gennady was also a dear friend and mentor to me. That August morning he called back quickly. Our proposals were approved.

I immediately called my ministry and was pleased to find out that my key officers were in place and ready to do their jobs without needing explanation. It was a small staff—about sixty people. The Soviet Foreign Ministry housed thousands of diplomats and employees who were also doing their jobs, albeit working for the opposite political side.

At Burbulis's suggestion, we went to his office to meet a group of high-profile supporters from civil society, headed by the academician Yuri Ryzhov, a well-known physicist and outspoken supporter of liberalization in Russia. Ryzhov possessed both conviction and charisma, but refused later offers to serve as prime minister, claiming lack of expertise in economics. Later I succeeded in drawing him into a government position—ambassador to France—where he performed brilliantly. On August 19, 1991, he had simply walked into an empty, unguarded White House and was busy calling friends from the democratically oriented political clubs that had sprung up in Moscow in the late 1980s. And they came. Within a short time, no fewer than thirty scientists, lawyers, movie stars, and journalists had appeared. Even the world-renowned cellist, Mstislav Rostropovich, had taken an early flight back to Moscow from abroad to join the resistance. I felt encouraged and honored to be on the same side as them. The fact that these leading figures had gathered in Burbulis's office said a great deal about their faith in him, and our common cause.

Next we went to see the vice president of Russia, Alexander Rutskoi, who was checking his gun when we arrived. He told us that he was in charge of the defense of the White House against the coup plotters. Rutskoi almost matched Yeltsin for charisma and apparent determination, but his convictions were weaker, as was his commitment to (and knowledge of) civil society. Rutskoi was first and foremost a military man and a veteran of the Afghan war, for which he received the highest decoration, Hero of the Soviet Union. He first entered politics as a staunch communist and then, sensing the winds of change, broke with the party leaders to lead the so-called Communists for Reform.

Many democrats were concerned that Yeltsin had chosen Rutskoi instead of Burbulis or Shakhrai as a running mate in the presidential election campaign. I think he felt that Rutskoi would help attract parts of the broad military constituency. Unfortunately, his messy populism and habit of shouting hysterically at opponents instead of debating with them hardly endeared him to the white-collar civilian electorate and more thoughtful officers in the Soviet army. However, his bravery for the democratic side during the coup was critical and was the one important exception to his political behavior both before and after the coup.

After seeing Rutskoi, I headed to the office of the Russian prime minister, Ivan Silayev, a gray-haired man in his sixties. A former minister of aviation of the USSR, he had been approved by the Russian parliament as a compromise figure after Yeltsin's more radical candidates, including Shakhrai, had been rejected.

That August morning, Silayev did not hesitate to denounce the coup on his own behalf and that of the cabinet, which had assembled to unanimously approve a resolution to that effect. Most of the Russian ministers were Silayev's people, and his leadership was a decisive factor for them.

Before long Yeltsin's successor as chair of the Russian parliament, Ruslan Khasbulatov, arrived and denounced the coup. Khasbulatov was an ambitious middle-aged former economics professor who had become a politician. But the fact remained that neither the Russian Federation's president, nor the government, nor parliament had any power. The Soviet state still controlled everything at that moment. But we all understood that presenting a united front against the hard-liners gave us tremendous moral authority.

David and Goliath, This Time in Moscow

Standing by the window in Silayev's office I watched shiny Mercedes and BMWs—then still rare in Moscow—driving western diplomats and reporters to the entrance of the building. At first it seemed strange that they were all coming from my right-hand side as I looked out the window. Then, turning my gaze to the left, I saw the unimaginable taking shape: battle tanks were creeping in single file along the bridge over the Moscow River toward the government building. These vehicles were rare guests too. They had never been seen before in the city other than in military parades on national holidays. In contrast to those dusty beasts they were sparkly clean. Mentally it was quite a captivating juxtaposition. It epitomized the choice Russia confronted at the time and has been facing ever since: to move forward to Western-style democracy or be drawn back into militaristic authoritarianism.

The symbolism of the hard-liners' move was no less obvious. The outsized display of force harked back to the worst Soviet traditions of intimidation. It could also be taken as a signal of doggedness, and fear crept between my shoulders.

A guard burst into the room: "Mr. Prime Minister and you gentlemen, please pick up some guns from the reserve stock!"

Silayev immediately countermanded the order: "No! Our weapons should be different. We'll go to the press hall and tell the truth about what's happening to the diplomats and media representatives who have already arrived."

Walking to the Press Hall, someone recalled an old joke about a man calling the KGB to protest that his lost parrot spoke only for itself. No one laughed.

The press hall was almost full. On my way in, I saw diplomats from the Western countries. Poland, Hungary, and other Central and Eastern European nations that until recently had been in the sphere of Soviet influence were represented at the ambassadorial level. With memories of Soviet crackdowns on democratic movements in their own countries still fresh in their minds, they were quick to grasp the situation and show support.

Yeltsin read out the statement denouncing the coup and calling for Gorbachev's return, and turned to us with a question. Why had the coup plotters not hesitated to bring tanks into Moscow, and yet allowed him to hold a *press conference?* The answer was unanimous: the soldiers and officers, including the KGB agents, were reluctant to use force against the first ever popularly elected Russian leader, with an election just two months away. And, like most Russians, they were fed up with Soviet rule.

In the middle of the Q&A session, Yeltsin asked me to take over and he left the hall. In another moment CNN and the other world news outlets were transmitting video of Yeltsin shaking hands with the soldiers, climbing up on a tank, and denouncing the hard-liners. The photograph of the Russian president standing atop a tank was reproduced in news media all over the world and has become an enduring image of Russia's anti-communist revolution.

Small but fast-growing crowds began gathering around the White House in support of the revolution and the reformers. Within a few hours they had formed a full circle, a "living wall," around the building. We were winning in the court of domestic public opinion.

The overwhelming and unrestrained power of the communist dictatorship, which had terrorized Russia for more than seventy years, seemed unable to reinstate itself in the very center of Moscow. Yet the tanks were still there, and the government building was under siege. Only one telephone line connecting Moscow to the outside world was functioning. No cars were permitted to enter or leave. What we had won could be described less as a victory and more as a chance to succeed.

The leaders of the Soviet republics were silent, except for the heads of the three Baltic republics who asked the West for protection and recognition of their sovereignty. Others, as we learned later, were occupied with consolidating their power and declaring independence. The major Western capitals were very cautious in their comments.

Yeltsin dispatched his old friend Oleg Lobov to Sverdlovsk, where they had worked in the Communist Party regional department, to organize a backup office in case the coup plotters squeezed us out of Moscow. I was sent abroad with a written order signed by Yeltsin to promote the position of the legitimate president and government of the Russian Federation. No government in exile was mentioned in the document, because it could be used against us if I were detained before crossing the Soviet border. But Yeltsin believed that according to international custom, a minister of foreign affairs could, without special credentials, declare a government in exile if the legitimate government at home had been overthrown.

"Tell the officials and the media when you arrive that you have credentials from the president of Russia to set up a government in exile," Yeltsin said to me during a meeting before my departure. "So, these crazy guys here will know that even if they kill me, they will still have a big problem."

I was honored by his trust in me and told him so. I also pointed out that I didn't think the situation in Moscow would ever reach the level where it would require a government-in-exile. While prenotification of the relevant officials would be helpful, it should be kept confidential as it was important not to weaken the message of our determination to win in Russia. Everybody, including the criminals in the Kremlin, should be aware of our resolve to rescue Gorbachev and bring him back.

I mentioned Gorbachev, fully aware of what might follow and was hardly surprised by the president's emotional response. "I know that you like Gorbachev more than me. They've told me that many times. But don't forget you are going as the envoy of the Russian Federation's president and government." For a moment Yeltsin could not suppress his envy of and disdain for Gorbachev. But he quickly returned to the matter at hand. "You know, Andrei Vladimirovich, how much we count on your professionalism. I concur with making no public statements about the government-in-exile for the time being. Why should we be constantly calling for Gorbachev's return? Shakhrai started this. And I agreed to refer to Gorbachev at the press conference. But those soldiers and people downstairs couldn't care less. They support the Russian president."

"Shakhrai and I, as well as Burbulis and those people standing outside, have no illusions concerning Gorbachev," I said to Yeltsin. "We all know the difference between him and the first popularly elected president of Russia. In the West, however, many are still suffering from Gorbymania. We should come out as defenders of law and order and call Gorbachev back. That would make us, not the plotters, worthy of international support."

"You are probably right. But first we must defeat the plotters, and then see to it that Gorbachev cannot appoint them, or clowns like them, again." He was deep in thought, almost speaking to himself.

"I admire your courage, Boris Nikolayevich, and my heart will be with you."

He stood up; we embraced. This is the right person in the right place and at the right time to change history, I thought as I left his office.

"Stand by Us"

As I was waiting to leave for the airport, I called my friend Allen Weinstein, then president of the Center for Democracy in Washington, DC, and later archivist of the United States. I briefed him on the situation in Russia, and he told me of the somewhat confused and mixed reaction in the West. Allen suggested that I write a commentary for the world media. I agreed. We started to sketch out the text, hoping not to be disconnected, over the next fifteen minutes. Weinstein finalized the article, working from notes, and the following morning (August 21) it appeared as an op-ed in the *Washington Post*. It was the first direct word from the rebellious Russian White House to the American public, and its title spoke for itself: "Stand By Us."

Around midnight I left the White House. The scene that greeted me exceeded my wildest imaginings. The road leading away from the building goes along an embankment of the Moscow River, offering a gorgeous view over its broad and leisurely waters. On the opposite shore the iconic silhouette of one of Stalin's seven "wedding cake" skyscrapers rose skyward. In the park in front of it stands a huge statue of the prominent Ukrainian poet and national hero, Taras Shevchenko. The mighty bronze figure on top of the granite rock is posed taking a resolute step forward, his head bent in deep thought. It was a perfect figure for that historic moment.

On my side of the river, near the White House, thousands of people were circulating in a friendly and cheerful crowd. Guys and gals in blue jeans (made in the United States) were mingling with soldiers of the same age in military fatigues stationed near their tanks. Occasionally they would climb up on the tanks together and sit there, sharing homemade sandwiches and singing pop songs. They were simultaneously having fun and preparing to mobilize. The soldiers were waiting for orders to clarify why they had been deployed to the center of the city. Would those orders mean storming the White House, perhaps even firing into the crowd of civilians with whom they shared so much? And what about the civilians: would they commit themselves to stopping the soldiers in case of attack? The air was electric.

I called home, my wife Irina had no illusions about the dangerous situations we were in, but was calm and brave. She said that our daughter, Natalia, then eleven years old, would stay the night at the home of a classmate whose parents had offered a refuge for "our foreign minister's family." They, too, had heard the music and knew what it meant. That night, I knew what kind of people we were fighting for.

My friend and assistant, Andrei Shkurko, a young and gifted diplomat, drove me to Sheremetyevo Airport in his private car. We considered how best to avoid my being arrested by the KGB at the airport—something they would try to do, even if they had stopped short of storming the White House.

The KGB guys in Moscow were bureaucrats, we decided. They would expect me to use the VIP service and be on the flight to London, because they would certainly have intercepted our telephone conversations with the British embassy. But my ticket was to Paris, as the London flight was sold out. I decided to avoid the VIP lounge and use the regular service to France, letting the "fat major" from the KGB sit in the comfort of the VIP room and watch for the London flight. And so I did, and so he did, as I later I heard from my friends in the Soviet Foreign Ministry.

Despite having different visa and ticket destinations, I was allowed to go through the passport control checkpoint by the border guards, who happened to be sympathetic to our cause. I will always remember those guards with appreciation. A revolution begins when people in uniforms along with ordinary people get fed up with the old system. That's the critical mass that makes radical change possible.

Soon after I took my seat on the Aeroflot flight, the cabin attendant came up to me and said in a low voice, "Are you a Russian minister? We've recognized you. You are on assignment, are you not? That's what we thought. Welcome!" She hurried away with a conspiratorial look and air of triumph. In the course of the ensuing three-hour flight, I was given the royal treatment.

When the landing procedures began, the captain came to me and asked whether I expected anybody to be meeting me at the door of the plane. I appreciated the hidden meaning behind what appeared to be a simple courtesy question. According to international law, an aircraft is regarded as the territory of its flag state, the country where it is registered. Before I stepped out the door of the plane, I would still be on the territory of the Soviet Union. Thus, hypothetically, Soviet agents (especially those with diplomatic passports) could step in, push me back into the cabin and keep me there as hostage while denying access to the French authorities and demanding the quickest possible return flight to Moscow.

Apparently, the captain had heard anecdotes of this tactic used by KGB agents on would-be defectors to the West. I told the captain that I definitely did not expect to meet Soviet representatives in Paris, especially not at the door to the aircraft. But I would not be surprised to be met by French officials at the plane's door immediately upon arrival, as was the usual procedure for high-level envoys.

"Good," the captain said. "In that case we won't open the door before the French officials arrive at its threshold. If anyone else should show up"—he took a deep breath—"I think there could be technical problems with this door. It has needed repairs for a long time now, you know. But don't worry, we will do everything right!"

Again, I thought that the coup, and indeed the Soviet system, was doomed.

When we landed, a protocol officer from the French Foreign Ministry, along with a number of plainclothes officers clearly recognizable as security guards, greeted me at the door of the plane. They accompanied me during my stay thereafter.

The French officials helped with everything, from organizing meetings with ambassadors from the United States and some other countries to staging press conferences. The afternoon I spent at the French Foreign Ministry was rather frustrating, however. I felt that my interlocutors were morally and emotionally on my side, yet they were consistently evasive. I was not surprised. In coming to Paris I had no illusions: the West, however sympathetic to the democrats in Russia, would be careful not to anger the rulers in the Kremlin, no matter how deplorable they were. The fate of Russia would be decided in Moscow, not in Washington or Paris.

The French officials told me up front that at the same time they were speaking with me, a couple of high-ranking Soviet diplomats were in the room next door. That delegation was presenting a quite different assessment of the events unfolding in Moscow.

"Actually, they are all familiar faces to you, led by your former boss, Vladimir Petrovsky, Mr. Kozyrev," one of my hosts said. Petrovsky had led the "subversion by formulations" team in the Soviet Foreign Ministry. Was he ditching his principles to pursue his career now? I felt sick to my stomach. (I had the same sensation years later seeing my former deputies and friends Sergei Lavrov and Vitaly Churkin defending Putin's intervention in Ukraine as foreign minister and ambassador to the UN, respectively.) "Would you like to meet the Soviets, or would you prefer to wait an extra minute or so here while they pass through the corridor?" the French official went on.

"Actually, I would rather enjoy an extra cup of coffee here and let them leave," I said. The French official nodded understandingly. "This seems to be the only point on which you Russians have concurred so far."

But not all Soviet agents were so polite to me. When my French hosts brought me to the Hôtel de Crillon on the magnificent Place de la Concorde I received a telephone call. An artificially altered voice told me that the KGB had a long reach, even in Paris, not to speak of Moscow where I had left my family. The last point made me shiver

Back in Moscow, a fresh group of military and security forces started an offensive against the defenders of the Russian White House on the night of August 20–21. The plotters ordered tanks to move to the barricades. That action was shown live on CNN and other TV channels all over the world. I was watching and commenting on those events live all night long from the BBC office in Paris.

I pointed out the striking similarity of the scene in Moscow to that of the night assault that Soviet tanks and commandos had launched on the TV station in Riga earlier in January. I argued that the proper response from the world community to this latest assault should be the immediate recognition of the Baltic states as independent countries. My call for full recognition was only partially an emotional response to the moment: over the past eight months, the Yeltsin government had had a number of meetings with the new democratic authorities of the Baltic republics, and we knew that they would never return to the Soviet system, whatever it cost them.

Back in March, Estonia's foreign minister (later its first president), Lennart Meri, a freedom-loving intellectual, had come to Moscow, where we had signed a declaration of friendly relations between the Russian and Estonian republics. Similar agreements were then reached with Latvia and Lithuania. The documents all stipulated the obligation of the Baltic republics to protect the rights of the Russian minorities in their countries. In signing these agreements, Russia became the first to establish official relations with these new states that were once designated for Soviet rule as part of the Molotov–Ribbentrop Pact with Nazi Germany in 1939.

By the time I left the BBC's offices, the assault had evidently failed. But the White House was still under siege, protected by barricades and a living wall. Things seemed at a standstill, but I was able to reach Yeltsin's office by phone, and his aides sounded upbeat.

That third day also marked a clear turning point in the world attitude toward the events unfolding in Moscow. President Bush and the leaders of other Western countries had telephone conversations with Yeltsin and issued public statements rebuking the coup plotters.

In Paris, I had warm and friendly meetings with the foreign affairs minister, Roland Dumas. I was also received by the French president, François Mitterrand and enjoyed his high-style polite and seemingly aloof intellectualism even if initially it felt cold and somewhat arrogant. Yeltsin could never overcome this barrier, and Mitterrand, perhaps suspecting deep-seated populism and earthiness in the Russian, made little effort to help him. They were too different. In conversations with me though, which the French president granted every time I was around, he revealed compassion as well as a deep interest in history, especially Russian history. His initial acceptance of the coup was apparently prompted by the traditional obedience of Russian people to their authoritarian rulers. Later he was elated when such tradition was broken in those August days. In Paris I also met the US Ambassador and was invited to make a speech at the forthcoming meeting of the NATO foreign ministers, scheduled for August 23, in Brussels. On the evening of the twenty-second I flew to the capital of Belgium. It was my first visit to the city of my birth, since I had been taken to Moscow at the age of three months, and the hosts kindly showed me the hospital where my mom had given birth.

Early on the morning of August 23, I received a call from a friend in the Russian White House saying that the coup attempt had been defeated. Yet again I had been given a new life in Brussels, but this time I stayed only three hours instead of the three months I had been there after my birth. My mission seemed to be over, and I informed my hosts of my desire to return home.

While preparing to leave for Moscow, I first met with the Belgian foreign minister and then with the US secretary of state, James Baker. The next morning's papers carried a big photograph of Baker and me embracing and smiling happily for reporters. Baker was holding his hand high and giving the victory sign.

I was impressed by Baker's knowledge of Soviet socioeconomic problems and his genuine desire to help solve them. I suggested that a new partnership be developed between Russia and America. As to the fate of the Soviet Union, I said, it now depended on the willingness of Gorbachev to part ways with his communist friends and on his and Yeltsin's ability to rise above their ambitions and work together on meaningful political and economic reforms. I felt deeply skeptical on both points but did not share my misgivings with Baker.

This much was true: a unique historic opportunity was at hand.

Citizens of the Free World

On returning to Moscow, I went immediately to a rally of a million people on the Manezh, the vast square near the Kremlin. Speaker after speaker called for reforms to guarantee that there would be no return to the past. I was pushed to the microphone. By that time in my life I had had some experience speaking at rallies, but nothing like this! When you see an ocean of faces looking at you and waiting to hear from you, it becomes difficult to formulate any thoughts. It is also quite difficult to control your voice so as to be heard without shouting. I did grasp that like the other speakers, I was expected to speak of a wonderful future and about what should happen, rather than to address the reality of the moment.

"Citizens of the free world! Today we earned the right to call ourselves and to be called free. We've just defeated a brutal attempt to throw us back to the humiliating position behind the Iron Curtain. There is no more and will never again be a free world somewhere outside and a different world inside here. We will learn to live in the same free world as other people do.

"In foreign policy, democratic Russia should be as natural an ally of the democratic United States and other Western countries as the totalitarian Soviet Union was their enemy.

"Clearly, it will take time and hard work to implement this vision of a new Russia. But we must stick to our course and not compromise our principles."

A storm of applause followed each of my sentences.

After the rally, I walked the few blocks to the parking lot in the company of Western and Eastern European ambassadors and a few reporters who had also attended the gathering. They wanted to know how much would actually depend on the Russian government. Gorbachev remained the president of the Soviet Union, and the Soviet Foreign Ministry still reported to him. Other governments would have to take them and only them as counterparts.

"From now on," I answered, "Gorbachev and Yeltsin will work together, and their teams and we will follow suit." I hardly believed my own words as I spoke them.

After the rally I rushed to the White House and to Yeltsin's office. He rose from his armchair in the far corner of the room and embraced me.

"I told you it wouldn't be long," he said. He quickly got to the point: "We need to think of strong moves now to consolidate our leadership in foreign policy."

"Speaking of strong moves, I think there is one . . ."

At this Yeltsin lifted his hand quickly and his expression became almost wily. "I know what you are going to propose. In Paris you offered full recognition of the Baltic states."

"You read my mind, Mr. President, as always."

"Some foreign policy experts," he continued, trying to sound stern, though clearly enjoying himself, "think that was too much to promise without consulting the president."

"I simply spoke my mind—knowing, though, that the Russian president, in contrast to the Soviet one, would be strong enough to take this step."

How nice, I thought to myself. Those "some" are back at it. And now they are reporting on me—disparaging my moves as too quick and painting me as insubordinate. I felt that their true target was my pro-Western policy, which they hoped to change by getting rid of me. Thus, the bureaucracy strikes back.

"Now, Andrei Vladimirovich," Yeltsin admonished, his bass roaring triumphantly, "please do what the president instructs you to do! In an hour I expect the representatives of the three Baltic republics to come to this office." He paused to see the effect of his declaration on me. "Yes, I've invited them in order to announce the official recognition by the Russian Federation of these republics as independent states. Please get everything necessary ready and come back with the representatives."

That was one moment in which I simply adored him.

I rushed to telephone my deputy, Andrei Kolossovsky. Kolossovsky was a gifted young diplomat with calm manners and strong convictions. He had followed me in abandoning a promising career in the Soviet foreign service and joining the Yeltsin team. He had been on vacation abroad when the coup began and, against my recommendation to stay put, had returned to Moscow on the first flight on August 19. "Hello, boss," I heard Andrei's voice from behind me as I held the phone. He was smiling. I was always happy to see him. His humor, intelligence, and manners were like a breath of fresh air in those corridors.

"Hi. Being your boss is like a mission impossible. So, it's not for me. But I have good news for you. Even a mister know-it-all like you would be surprised by the assignment we've just gotten from the big boss."

"I think I'm here to report to you that the assignment you refer to was fulfilled a minute ago. Three draft decrees by the president of the Russian Federation announcing the official recognition of the three Baltic states are in this folder. The representatives of those states are waiting in the reception room. The media is getting ready to shoot photos of the historic event."

The Baltic representatives felt that something very important was coming. We entered the president's office together. Yeltsin stood up and showed Andrei and me to our places beside him. His tone was solemn: "Distinguished representatives, I invited you today to announce that the president of the Russian Federation has decided to officially recognize Lithuania, Latvia, and Estonia as sovereign and independent states. I will now sign the corresponding decrees and give copies to you."

He went to his desk and slowly signed each page. This habit of signing decrees on the spot, in the presence of officials and journalists, and the slow, solemn movement of the pen were characteristic of him. He also showed everybody his pen.

"This is the pen with which I signed the decrees and documents against the coup. I am using it now to sign the recognition papers. You can appreciate the symbolism," Yeltsin declared. He was a man of high drama. He liked to perform history. This was a moment when he did it well, and I admired him for it.

A ceremony that was both solemn and emotional followed. One after another the representatives spoke of the historic importance of this decision for helping the Baltic states build new democratic societies with equal rights for all who lived there—Balts, Russians, Jews, and all others.

"What effect will this act of recognition have on Gorbachev's position?" a Latvian diplomat asked.

"If he has any brains he will immediately follow suit. Otherwise the Soviet Union will once more be just trailing in the wake of the events," Yeltsin replied bluntly.

In the next few days there was an avalanche of recognitions. Country after country made official statements. The Soviet Union's recognition did not arrive until two weeks later on September 8.

The next morning, August 25, the parliaments of the Soviet Union and the Russian Federation assembled in a joint session to condemn the coup attempt. From the podium of the parliamentary assembly hall, Yeltsin held up a draft decree banning the Communist Party of the USSR and declared he had already signed the document. After a standing ovation, he asked whether Gorbachev would change his mind and sign it too. Gorbachev was obviously hesitant, but Yeltsin took his arm, led him to the center of the stage, and asked him to sign on the spot, which Gorbachev did, to a burst of laughter from the audience. The whole gathering, including the signing episode, was carried live on state television.

Two days later I was summoned to the prime minister's office for a short meeting of the cabinet. Almost all the ministers were given new assignments. Some were to replace their Soviet Union counterparts, who had lost credibility and position after supporting the coup. Some, including me, were given new addresses to house their offices and staff.

The Ministry of Foreign Affairs of the Russian Republic was now assigned to the building that only a day before had been occupied by the International Relations Department of the Communist Party. At the entrance police cadets sternly demanded my ID, but on seeing it saluted enthusiastically. For me, taking over the offices of the former communist stronghold was invigorating, but also a bit surreal. For generations of Soviet citizens the huge gray building near the Kremlin had been a special landmark associated with the menacing omnipotence of the party. Small wonder that everyone who had entered those doors did so trembling. Now I walked through empty corridors and rooms. Documents that had been top secret only few days earlier were now discarded like autumn leaves, useless, turned into refuse by the winds of history. It was the final coda of a long saga. For more than seventy years, the Soviet communists had spent millions of dollars and immense efforts to stir up revolutionary movements all across the globe. At the beginning, they seemed to genuinely believe they were helping the poor of the world fight for freedom and equality. Yet first Stalin and then all his successors cynically used communist parties and revolutionaries worldwide as their own fifth column proxies in the global confrontation with the West. Some of those organizations in the third world evolved into terrorist groups; some were that way from the beginning.

I knew the place well, since I had served there for six months as an intern before graduating from university. I had been interpreting for visiting English-, Spanish-, and Portuguese-speaking "brother" communists, mostly elderly functionaries. I felt good helping guests from the Portuguese colonies in Africa: Angola, Mozambique, and Guinea-Bissau. Most of them were younger and passionate, fresh from the battlefield and devoted to their independence movements. It was a prestigious assignment, but not the most celebrated: the children of the party bosses generally preferred internships in Soviet embassies in Western countries. During the time I was there over the next four months of 1991, foreign and Russian visitors often asked me for a sightseeing tour of the building.

Just a few days after the successful end to the coup, President Yeltsin vanished from public view. I had no access to him, but one of his personal assistants who had worked with him for a number of years told me not to worry: Yeltsin was just following his usual life pattern of falling into a depression and withdrawing following an outburst of energy during a crisis. Later Yeltsin told the press that he had been on vacation for about three weeks in the southern resort of Sochi on the Black Sea and showed us pictures of himself playing tennis on a sunny court.

He remained largely inactive in public for a few weeks after his return. Apparently, like Gorbachev, he had no clear vision of what needed to be done to complete the transformation from the Soviet system. One thing was clear—these two men could not work together. They were more interested in their personal struggle for power against each other. That was the level of leadership we had after the long devastating decades of communism.

Did We Actually Defeat the Coup Plotters?

Following the failure of the August coup, I had no illusions that it would be easy for democracy to replace the fallen communist regime. In the absence of strong leadership from either Gorbachev or Yeltsin, the momentum crucial for reform began to slow, and the mood of society grew less optimistic.

One central issue was that the fate of Russia was intrinsically tied up with that of the KGB. The core cadres of the KGB had long since abandoned communist ideology as a useless anachronism. In fact, many in the organization dreamed of getting rid of the party high priests, blaming them for the state's technological and economic backwardness. Ready to change the red communist flag to a nationalist Russian flag, they were prepared to accept some market reforms and even liberal ones, as long as they retained control behind the scenes.

I once asked Yeltsin why on the last day of the coup he had stopped thousands of protesters from taking over the KGB headquarters, and blocked Russian democrats who sought to follow the example of other Eastern European democracies in denouncing and dismantling the Soviet-era secret police and banning its former agents from public service.

He replied: "The KGB is the only organized state structure left by the old regime that works. Of course, it was criminal like everything else, but if we destroyed it, we would have risked unleashing total chaos." I had an opposite opinion but kept it to my self.

I had two more memorable conversations shortly after the coup's failure. A real Soviet dissident, a human rights activist who had recently served five years in a KGB labor camp, visited me. I can still see his striking eyes and pale face (he could have been anywhere between thirty and sixty years old), even though I cannot recall his name. "You have to agree that the recognition of the Baltic states and the decree banning the Communist Party of the USSR are the only two achievements proportional to the great opportunity and the thirst for change that was in the air after the defeat of the coup," he told me. I did not dispute the words of my guest. He had a point and in any case deserved attention and respect. "Yeltsin," my visitor went on, "was good to stand against the coup, but protected the KGB. When he gets what he wants, the real power, he won't use it for building the democratic and market institutions needed to transform the country. You—Shakhrai, Burbulis, the young people in the Russian leadership—should select a new leader and demand that Yeltsin resign."

"It's really too much of a task for me," I replied. At the time, his suggestion smacked of a second, if softer, coup attempt, I thought defensively. But at the back of my mind I knew that he was right in his assessment of Yeltsin, and that if we failed on the essence of his demand in the long run, we would be defeated.

The other conversation I had was with my mother. She had a heart attack on the day of the coup and I was trying to cheer her up by reassuring her about what had been achieved. "We won an important victory. This country will never be the same totalitarian monolith it was for seventy years. There is a good chance to transform it into a modern society."

She had her doubts: "You've always lived in a world of illusions. There were some expectations that things would improve after the defeat of the coup. But those are quickly vanishing. Folks are standing in even longer lines for food than before. And speaking of you, you've stirred some very troubled waters. You will face much tougher resistance to what you are standing for. More than once this country has rejected change and its advocates. There are simply too many people now in power who want to hold on to it at all costs—besides that, the inertia of ordinary people who are used to hating and fearing everything new and bright is too strong."

"Believe me," she continued, "Yeltsin is a mixture of both those breeds, and that's the secret to his staying in power thus far and to his survival in the future. I know his type from my youth, when I was one of the young party activists. His agenda is very different from yours and your kind of people's. He is just using you in his power struggle, and he will soon throw all of you away. But I see that you will not turn back. So just be careful and remember your family."

I recall both these conversations every August on the anniversary of the defeat of the coup attempt.

Every year the Russian press also covers the anniversary of the coup, but in a more and more skeptical and reserved way. On the tenth anniversary of the August coup, a US correspondent, Peter Baker, interviewed the commander of a Soviet battalion that had been sent to attack the Russian White House, but instead had used its arms to protect the democrats on the street: "What was lacking? Why did it happen this way?" he complained. "It is hard to say that there wasn't enough courage to bring things to the end. We wanted more and envisioned more, especially in the economic field. The main thing is that the same people remained in power—the people who used to work in the party apparatus."

None of the coup plotters had to live in seclusion or face a life of shame: they were all granted amnesty in February 1994 as part of a sweeping resolution by the new parliament, the Duma. Their leader, Gennady Yanayev, presided over a well-to-do foundation. His team member, Vasily Starodubtsev, was governor of the Tula region. One of the plotters headed a party. Another chaired a Duma committee. A key plotter, KGB head Vladimir Kryuchkov, could be seen on national TV participating in the inauguration and other prestigious events of President Vladimir Putin's public career.

Sometimes I ask myself whether I would have stood up against the coup in August 1991 had I been able to foresee the future. My answer is yes.

The defeat of the coup attempt was the highest moral and political point ever reached by the Russian people. It demonstrated their democratic potential and thus established an important historical precedent. And it set the stage for what was to follow: The official, irretrievable end to the Soviet Union in the weeks and months ahead, and the birth of a new Russian state on the uncertain road to democracy.

2

A New Russia Is Born
from the Flames

AFTER THE DEFEAT OF THE AUGUST COUP the Soviet president and government quickly started to lose power. Yet the opposite was happening in the constituent republics that had rushed to establish self-rule. The Soviet state was visibly coming apart, creating enormous uncertainties, risks, and opportunities and requiring politicians to make difficult, even momentous choices. It would have been simple for me to claim that the affairs of the republics were internal Soviet issues as long as they were parts of the Soviet Union, and to stay away from the difficult problems they represented. Yet I believed that my responsibilities as foreign minister covered all external concerns of the Russian Federation. I chose this interpretation because I wanted the process of establishing new relations between Russia and the other republics (whether they chose unity with Russia or independence) to be peaceful, amicable, and based on international law.

The Borders of Russia

One reason for the coup was hard-liner dissatisfaction with the draft of a new Union treaty that the heads of the republics and Gorbachev intended to sign on August 20, 1991. The plotters rejected the treaty as too weak in assuring the center's power and their own position at the top. As a result of their exploits, they destroyed both. In fact, I would go as far as to say that they blew up the Soviet Union.

Even before the coup, the governments of the fifteen republics held much more legitimacy in the eyes of the population than the Gorbachev central administration. Direct popular elections for the executive and legislative branches—even though still within the Soviet framework—took place in the republics for the first time ever in 1990–91. Gorbachev himself had never risked direct election to the presidency of the Soviet Union and remained appointed to that post by the discredited Soviet legislature based on the Communist Party recommendation. Capitalizing on the weakness of the center, especially after the coup attempt, the newly elected authorities started to act like the governments of sovereign states.

It is worth recalling that the Declaration of State Sovereignty of the Russian Soviet Federative Socialist Republic separating it from the Soviet Union had been almost unanimously approved by the republic's parliament in June 1990. Yet the parliament was far from unified politically.

Democratically oriented deputies constituted about 50 percent of the parliament. They voted to approve the document on state sovereignty so as to do what the Gorbachev central government of the Soviet Union refused to do with the Russian Republic: break the Communist Party's grip on power, and institute private property and freedom of the press. Their strategy was to achieve their reforms in the Russian Republic, which technically constituted the vast majority of the Union's territory, population, and economy. In doing so, they would drag along the rest of the republics on the road of change, and hopefully preserve a union between them on a new, democratic basis.

The communists and nationalists, on the other hand, saw the declaration of sovereignty as a stepping-stone to Russian statehood and greatness. They believed that Russia, as a major part of the Soviet Union, was subsidizing the poorer republics. With the "resurrection" of the Russian state, they intended to reverse this perversion of "empire" and make the provinces serve the metropolis instead of the other way around. In their view, the Russian Federation should also restore to Russia various territories that had historically belonged to the Russian Empire, as well as certain new ones that were now heavily populated by ethnic Russians. The Crimean Peninsula, which had been transferred to the Republic of Ukraine by the Soviet authorities in 1956, met both criteria and was at the top of the nationalists' wish list. In fact, it was the pursuit of that idée fixe that, more than anything else, scared and held other nations back from joining any new union.

The democrats argued that the danger and futility of such ambitions were vividly demonstrated by events unfolding at that time in Yugoslavia, which was also a multinational socialist state. Slobodan Milošević's government in Belgrade had chosen the path of brutal violence to forge its dream of replacing communist Yugoslavia with "Greater Serbia," in the process triggering bloody wars with its neighbors. In a sense, it was a blessing for Russia that the Yugoslav tragedy had started to unfold before our eyes just a few months earlier. By the time we had to decide how to handle the breakup of the Soviet Union, the lesson was painfully clear. I for one was haunted by the Yugoslav nightmare and vowed it would not be repeated in Russia.

Most of Yeltsin's aides, including myself, wanted to peacefully transform the Soviet Union into a loose federation (such as the United States or Germany) or a tight confederation (such as Switzerland or the United Arab Emirates) that would preserve a united state. The Russian Republic had to play a decisive role in that processes, but only as an integrator of equal participants—primus inter pares—clearly and resolutely rejecting any imperial ambitions. Yet our chance to do so disappeared in early September with an ill-advised comment from a member of Yeltsin's administration.

President Yeltsin's press secretary, an advocate of liberalization inside Russia, Pavel Voschanov, said in an interview that the non-Russian republics might face powerful demands to change their borders in favor of Greater Russia had they moved to independence. As soon as I learned of this, I hurriedly sent Yeltsin a memo pointing out that not only the borders between the Soviet republics, but indeed all the existing borders in Europe and elsewhere had been drawn arbitrarily, and there would be no end to the arguments and counterarguments for or against keeping or changing them. Millions of people of not just Russian, but also Ukrainian and Kazakh descent were living in large neighboring areas near their namesake republics. There could never be a perfect line that would satisfy the claims of all ethnic entities should they start to argue over territory. Therefore, disputes over territorial claims would automatically lead to conflict and war.

The only practical solution was to stick to the principle of the inviolability of frontiers enshrined in the Helsinki Final Act signed in 1975 by all European nations, the United States, and Canada. The Soviet Union was also a signatory to this document, and any successor state to it should be bound by its conventions. The decision had to be made once and for all time: the Pandora's box of potential territorial claims among the former Soviet republics must never be opened. The possibility of entertaining such claims had to be excluded from our government policy.

Moreover, immediate harm was growing with every hour that passed without an official rebuttal from Russia. For that reason, the memo concluded, the Ministry of Foreign Affairs of the Russian Federation would issue a formal press release making it clear that Voschanov's statement did not represent the position of Russia—it reflected his private opinion alone. The Russian president and government adhered firmly to the principles of the Helsinki Act, in particular to the principle of the inviolability of frontiers.

The ministry had only two cars. I sent one to Yeltsin's office in the Russian White House with the memo and the other with the press release to a friend in a news agency, who immediately published it. In acting this way, I took the risk of speaking for the president before his approval, but I thought it worth taking. Had Yeltsin decided otherwise, I would have resigned and challenged him publicly on that matter. Thank God, it did not happen that way. When asked later about the borders by a news correspondent, he said simply, "Russia stands for Helsinki and for the inviolability of frontiers."

The damage, though, had been done. The Russian Foreign Ministry's press release was just two hours later! The Voschanov statement circulated before our rebuttal, and precipitated outrage in the republics, especially Ukraine, which denounced Russian imperial ambitions and threats in an official statement.

In my discussions with the parliamentary deputies and in public interviews I elaborated on the subject of borders. The issue could be addressed between neighbors, but only after the establishment of political equality and voluntary integration (or reintegration) based on economic interdependence. There were good historical examples in Europe. In 1956 the Saar region, a cause of bloody wars for centuries before, was transferred from France to Germany after the population voted for it in a referendum. But this happened only because the two countries were mature democracies and close allies, and the referendum was held after exhaustive free and fair public debate. My position, which seems ironic now, was that one day we might be able to revisit the fate of, say, Crimea, but only if today we focused on building democracy and friendship in both countries and avoided creating hostility by making territorial claims.

Along with hints of territorial claims, the most important reason that it proved impossible to preserve a single state from the ruins of the Soviet order was a failure of leadership. Gorbachev and his team were unable to adapt to change on this issue and many others. Yeltsin too hesitated for months to take a leading role, partly out of fear of being accused of undermining Gorbachev and destroying the state, and partly because he lacked a plan of his own.

Once in a frank conversation with Yeltsin, a foreign visitor pointed to a growing sense of irresponsibility on the part of the Soviet government. If the Soviet government was no longer seen as representative, the passive leadership of the Russian Federation was not credible either. Yeltsin answered that Gorbachev kept promising to do something but did not, and at the same time reacted jealously to all Yeltsin's initiatives. "So, don't push me!" Yeltsin shouted angrily. He was obviously irritated and wanted to brush off the annoying problem and anyone who mentioned it to him.

Listening to this exchange, I thought that the Union was doomed by these two formidable leaders clashing in Moscow: aggressively competitive, professionally jealous, incredibly wary of each other's ambitions and power, and perpetually at loggerheads.

My Covenant with the President

It was only at the end of October that Yeltsin began to act decisively. He told a reporter that the Soviet Foreign Ministry should be transformed into a center to coordinate policy, while the authority of the Russian Federation Foreign Ministry (and, by implication, that of the other republican ministries) should drastically increase. I quickly called my colleagues in the other republics, and their response was quite positive. It looked like one last chance to salvage a unified post-Soviet federation. Needless to say, the Soviet Foreign Ministry flatly rejected the idea.

I tried to reason with my former boss, now number two in the Soviet Foreign Ministry, Vladimir Petrovsky, whom I had carefully avoided meeting in

Paris during the coup. Arguing in support of Yeltsin's proposal, I indicated readiness to yield my own position as Russian foreign minister to someone from the Soviet ministry so that they could continue to occupy the most important chair in the new structure. As for me, I could go as ambassador to the United States or some other country.

A few days later, talking to Yeltsin, I could sense his uneasiness and irritation with me. When I asked him whether I had done anything wrong, he suddenly exploded. All his life, he said, those closest to him had inflicted the deepest wounds. He had never expected betrayal from me, especially in such a time of trouble.

My obvious surprise temporarily derailed his tirade, for it was clear I had no idea what he was talking about. He had received word, he said, from the top people in the Union's Foreign Ministry that I was asking them for an ambassadorial post to the United States. When I told him his contacts had failed to explain certain critical details and the very special context of my alleged request for an ambassadorship, he exploded again. This time he was indignant about his contacts' malicious misinterpretation of my words and their ugly attempt to set me up and discredit me.

I said: "Boris Nikolayevich, let me be frank with you. I did not come to the Russian Federation's government to forge a diplomatic career. On the contrary, I left one of the brightest careers in diplomacy for political reasons. I see you as the true leader of democratic change and I want to help achieve it. That's why I will always be loyal to the first freely and popularly elected president of Russia. If I ever feel like resigning or changing my position for some reason, I will come to you and tell you about it straightforwardly—and I will move only with your consent. If you want to transfer me or fire me, just tell me, and I will accept it without a problem. In this historic transformation, everybody is replaceable except the elected leader, and he should have the freedom to maneuver."

"Khorosho, OK," he replied. "Let it be a covenant between us—you tell me first and I will tell you first." We shook hands on it. He liked gentlemen's agreements of this type and handled them somewhat theatrically. Our agreement held fast for the best part of six years. It buoyed me in times of enormous political pressure, when the media and the corridors of power were full of gossip that I had just been fired or was about to be fired. In fact, many of my colleagues in the government only learned of their dismissal from the morning papers.

Government of Reform

Yeltsin's new decisiveness extended to the economic sphere. He proposed and received approval from the Russian parliament to appoint a "government of reform." At Burbulis's suggestion, he appointed a group of young economists, led by Yegor Gaidar.

Yegor was in his mid-thirties. At first glance he looked like a typical overweight nerd immersed in academic research. So, many people erroneously suspected him of being divorced from the day-to-day reality of the current economy. His elite background—both his grandfather, father, and even father-in-law had been famous Soviet writers—and complex, erudite manner of speaking contributed to that impression. Soon after his appointment to the government, he visited a factory in an effort to sell his policy of radical reform. Answering the workers' questions about rising prices and his religious beliefs, he talked at length about a "curve of inflation expectations" and defined himself as "agnostic," without any further explanation. No wonder the workers were perplexed. Gaidar proved to be a devoted reformer and political fighter, but always inhibited both by his bookish appearance and his difficulty in communicating with wide public.

Most of Gaidar's appointees in government vastly underestimated the importance of political backing for economic reforms and behaved as technocrats with sweeping authority to fix a problem. They rarely deigned to give much explanation to the public, or even parliament. They were generally supportive of my efforts to open to the West, but they regarded the other republics as an economic burden and a impediment to the speedy progress of a more developed Russia. From day one, they faced strong resistance from an entrenched bureaucracy and a growing alienation from the ordinary people.

Creating a Commonwealth: Belavezha and Beyond

In October Gorbachev also made a move aimed at breaking the political deadlock. He organized a new round of talks with the presidents of the republics on the subject of forming a new union, but on his old terms. On November 25, Yeltsin declared that the time for forming a federal state had passed—in that he had the support of the heads of the other republics. Then Yeltsin made his most important political argument: there could be no federation or confederation without Ukraine. A direct popular vote on whether to become independent or remain in a union was scheduled in Ukraine for December 1. No decision could be made before the vote results were in.

By the morning of December 2, we knew that the outcome of the Ukrainian referendum had exceeded all expectations. Even though one-third of Ukraine's population consisted of ethnic Russians living in industrial areas neighboring and closely integrated with Russia, more than 80 percent of the entire population cast votes in favor of independence.

I was glad Ukraine had rejected the old system, which was thus dead. But there could be no new union, Soviet or not, without Ukraine. So, an answer to the simple question—what would happen next to the homeland in which we lived?—would be needed before its disintegration became uncontrolled, chaotic, and potentially violent.

By lunchtime I had sent Yeltsin a draft statement recognizing the will of the Ukrainian people to create their own independent state and expressing Russia's readiness to establish new interstate relations with the nation. The statement was immediately approved by Yeltsin and published as the official position of the Russian Federation. Since I knew Yeltsin was receiving advice against this from other quarters, I was gratified by his resolute and speedy reaction. He had a true instinct for making the correct historical call.

Some years later I asked Leonid Kravchuk, president of Ukraine at the time of the referendum, what might have happened had the Russian Federation denounced the independence vote and thus given the Soviet government a free hand to crack down on the "Ukrainian revolt."

He had been concerned, he said, and appreciated Russia's positive stance, but had ruled out any possibility of a crackdown. The Ukrainian resistance would have comprised not just unarmed peaceful protestors, as happened in Moscow. By that time more than 90 percent of the entire armed forces personnel on the territory of the Ukrainian Republic had formally sworn allegiance to Ukraine. The top commanders were loyal to the Ukrainian government and the popularly elected Ukrainian president. "Had the Soviets tried to use force, we would have answered with armed force!" he said. "We would have had no other choice."

We began looking for ways to engage Ukraine in an arrangement that would replace the Soviet Union. A direct official negotiation would have drawn enormous press attention and limited the room for maneuver and an exploratory exchange of views. Even choosing where to have a meeting precipitated some tension. Kravchuk likely would have been reluctant to come to Moscow because it could have been seen as a summons by big brother. Beyond this, he could not negotiate with Yeltsin in Russia while ignoring Gorbachev in the Kremlin. If Yeltsin were to go to Kyiv, the Russian press would interpret it as a sign of Moscow's weakness. So, the best choice would be a "casual" unofficial encounter between Yeltsin and Kravchuk in a third location.

A good opportunity for that came during Yeltsin's previously scheduled visit to Belarus, neighboring both the Russian Federation and Ukraine. As Yeltsin had previously visited Ukraine and Kazakhstan and had signed bilateral treaties of friendship and cooperation with them, it seemed long overdue to do the same with Belarus.

Stanislav Shushkevich, the chairman of the Belarusian parliament, and Vyacheslav Kebich, the prime minister agreed to invite Ukraine's president, Leonid Kravchuk, to spend a weekend together with them and Yeltsin. To underscore the unofficial nature of the get-together, the decision was made to hold it in Belavezha, a hunting resort near Belarus's capital city of Minsk.

On the Russian side we developed a flexible "scaled-down" approach, in which Russia would first try to achieve the tightest form of federation with Belarus. These two states would then jointly engage Ukraine, loosening, as needed, the proposed form of integration to a confederation or, as a last resort, a commonwealth. In any case the central and unified control of nuclear weapons, wherever they were located, should be maintained. To avoid the appearance of a Slavic-only club, the three republics would propose forming a new union to all the other republics.

The debacle that ensued in Minsk almost put an end to our hopes for a new union of any kind.

We arrived in Minsk early in the morning and, after a wreath-laying ceremony at the Tomb of the Unknown Soldier commemorating our shared victory over Nazi Germany, we went on to the parliament building. Yeltsin's solemn address to the special plenary session of parliament, shown live on Belarusian TV, was filled with declarations of friendship between the two peoples and references to glorious episodes in their shared history.

Yeltsin was in peak oratorical form. More than once his speech was interrupted by ovations.

Suddenly I caught a worried look from Burbulis. Yeltsin had pointedly pushed aside the prepared text of his speech and said he had secured a special present for our Belarusian brothers.

Burbulis and I looked at each other and shrugged. We knew only too well Yeltsin's predilection for unscripted and generally ill-advised improvisation.

"As you know," Yeltsin continued triumphantly, "the president of Russia now has offices in the Kremlin, not just the president of Soviet Union. And which one of them is a guest is a state secret."

These words had a mixed effect. They attested to the further weakening of the disliked Gorbachev and the Soviet central bureaucracy. Yet another inescapable interpretation was that the old Soviet center would soon be taken over by the new Russian authorities, and the Soviet diktat replaced with a Russian one.

The audience remained calm and waited for his next words.

"In the Kremlin archives I found a document, centuries old, that I will now hand over to you. It might help you start your own state archives. This is a decree of one of the Russian czars. It testifies that for centuries Russia exercised a sincere brotherly attitude toward Belarus." With that Yeltsin turned to his assistant who handed him an ancient deed with the sprawling signature of a czar.

The deputies were perplexed but ready to accept the surprise politely.

Yeltsin evidently expected a much more enthusiastic response to his great personal gesture. For additional impact he started reading the document aloud, stumbling over the Old Slavonic language. He could barely follow the meaning of the words. But it soon became evident that the decree celebrated the victory of Russian troops over the army of a Polish-Lithuanian alliance, which in those days combined the territories of present-day Poland, the Baltics, and Belarus. Moreover, the czar, in celebrating the victory, promised never again to leave Belarus unprotected and ungoverned by the Russian Empire.

An angry uproar erupted in the hall. Some deputies stood up in their seats, loudly demanding an explanation. With difficulty, Shushkevich quieted the audience sufficiently to allow the president of Russia to finish his speech.

That was the beginning of the end of the intricate plan to use the summit in Belarus as a starting point for creating a new union.

When later that day we asked Shushkevich whether we could count on his support for our first proposal, to preserve the Union but on a new democratic basis, he said only that he had persuaded the parliamentary leaders to refrain from making comments to the press, and the national TV station not to rebroadcast Yeltsin's speech.

The next day at the hunting lodge, Shushkevich kept his thoughts to himself while Ukraine's president Kravchuk flatly rejected our proposal to form a federation or confederation with Russia. Even our third proposal, to form a close alliance (something like NATO but with much better integrated armed forces and with all the nuclear weapons under unified command) plus a common market, was met negatively.

That night at dinner, Burbulis went out of his way to defend the idea of at least some unity. He recalled Rudyard Kipling's words, "We are of the same blood," and, after noticing they had some effect, returned to them. Yegor Gaidar stressed the benefits of economic interdependence, and I pointed out that the nuclear armed forces could not be divided without prohibitively high internal and external risks. We undertook to draft an agreement together with colleagues of other delegations overnight, to be reviewed in the morning by the presidents.

The Russian writing team—Yegor Gaidar, Sergei Shakhrai, and I—and the Belarusian foreign minister Piotr Kravchenko did the actual job of drafting a framework arrangement.

Kravchuk's aides declined to sit down with us. They were afraid to be drawn into drafting a document that might commit the Ukrainian Republic to a new union. But hour by hour they would pass by the cabin where we were working and chat with us casually, asking how the document was coming along.

We started by listing things that should stay as they were, especially the centralized control of the nuclear arsenal, as well as open borders for population on all sides and economic cooperation. The main difficulty was that the declaration had to announce the termination of the Soviet Union as a state and as a member of the international community. At the same time, the three republics were to proclaim themselves as sovereign states and full participants in international relations.

I thought that such a statement could not be made in Belavezha because not all the members of the Union were present. I believed that we could only draft a treaty that was acceptable to the three republics present, before appealing to the remaining republics to meet at a conference and join us.

Shakhrai nixed my approach as being too fraught with future risk and insisted on the right of the three republics to dissolve the Union straightaway. He offered a logical argument based on history. Four sovereign subjects had created the USSR in 1922: the Russian Federal Republic, Belarus, Ukraine, and the Transcaucasian Federation. Since the Transcaucasian Federation had ceased to exist, the three remaining republics had the legal authority to revise their previous decision and to take action.

That night history played one of its most spectacular and mysterious tricks. We had read the story of the republics being sovereign states and voluntarily uniting in the USSR in our school history textbooks but had taken it as just another fairy tale of yore adored by Soviet propaganda. Everybody knew that the Soviet Union had been put together and always ruled as a centralized state by the iron hand of the Communist Party, KGB, and the army. All of a sudden, the old fable came back to lay the basis for real action. So, history changed its course.

We finished the draft at dawn. The Ukrainians perused the text and indicated that they considered it acceptable. They said, however, that they would present the text to the Ukrainian president as a draft composed by the other two delegations. Their extreme caution underscored the delicate nature and fundamental difficulty of the task before us.

The next day the close circle of the presidents and their prime ministers, as well as Burbulis from the Russian delegation, went over the draft. Their most substantial alteration was the name of the new entity: the designation "Commonwealth" that we had proposed was expanded to the "Commonwealth of Independent States" (CIS). Once that was settled, the document was agreed upon.

A short signing ceremony took place in the afternoon. The mood was upbeat and businesslike. When the ceremony was over, the leaders decided to call Gorbachev and inform him of what had happened. I suggested making a call to George H. W. Bush as well.

"Why?" one of the participants asked. "We must concentrate on the internal reaction. The hard-liners in Moscow could characterize what we've done as high treason. And the Americans are in favor of preserving the status quo—the Soviet Union."

"Yes, the Americans are for the Union because they fear destabilization. Like us, they fear the terrifying example of the bloody civil war in Yugoslavia," I replied. "Above all, they are concerned with what happens to the nuclear missiles targeting them. So, our decision today to peacefully replace the disintegrating Soviet Union with the Commonwealth of Independent States and to keep the Doomsday machine under unified control is not only salvation for us—it's also good news for them. Yet they might be offended receiving this information not from us but from the morning papers—not least because those reports could be inaccurate. We should not risk a nuclear crisis."

It was agreed to make two calls. Shushkevich, as host of the gathering in Belarus, was to talk to Gorbachev. Yeltsin, as the successor head of the nuclear command center in Moscow, was to talk to Bush.

Shushkevich quickly picked up the receiver of a phone with a direct line to the Kremlin. It had been installed in the hunting lodge years ago for the convenience of the Communist Party bosses who liked to fly in from Moscow to shoot bears and reindeer on weekends. A metallic-sounding voice answered, saying that President Gorbachev would be notified of the request for a conversation, and advised Shushkevich to wait not far from the phone.

I was asked to establish the connection with the US president. Luckily, in my notebook I found a number for the State Department in Washington. A receptionist answered and quickly pointed out that it happened to be late Sunday afternoon and she was not in the mood for stupid jokes.

"Please, hold on!" I shouted. "I am calling from the Soviet Union on behalf of the president of Russia, Boris Yeltsin, and it is vital that he speak to President Bush! Just let me explain!"

I took a deep breath and tried my best to explain that Russia was no longer the same as the Soviet Union and the difference between the two presidents: Gorbachev, whom she had heard of, and Yeltsin, whom she had not. After a thorough interrogation, she connected me to somebody else. It took more than thirty minutes before I reached somebody who sounded like he had the authority to arrange a top-level conversation. But a simple and quite reasonable question—how to call me back when President Bush was ready to speak by phone—nearly derailed the whole effort.

"I am sorry; we are not actually calling from Moscow." I tried to sound relaxed and self-assured, though I was close to panicking. I knew that Yeltsin's bodyguard had sent the housekeeper away and that nobody else in the house knew the phone number for the lodge.

"It is a somewhat remote place," I pleaded, "and I am afraid it would take time to find out the area code and the number itself. Could you please hold on so that we don't lose the connection?"

"Have I heard you correctly, Mr. Kozyrev, that Mr. Yeltsin was having a historically important meeting with the other leaders . . . in that area. . . . What did you say its name was?"

"The meeting started two days ago in Minsk, the capital city of the Belorussian Republic," I replied. "Later the leaders decided to spend the weekend in a more casual environment, and now we are in a hunting resort near Minsk, in the Belavezha Woods."

"And that's where they've just reached an agreement to replace the USSR with something else, and it is so important that Mr. Yeltsin should urgently brief President Bush. Is that what you are saying, Mr. Kozyrev?"

"Yes, exactly. I know it sounds bizarre, but that's what it is—history in the making, if you will excuse the expression."

"OK, I will instruct the operator to hold on until I brief the president. I'll get back to you as soon as possible."

A few minutes later the two presidents spoke.

That was the first crucial call to be made. The one to the Soviet president, protected by bureaucrats with steely voices, came second. Later, Gorbachev and the opposition media portrayed the sequencing as proof that the Belavezha group was unpatriotic and subservient to the United States. These false accusations contributed to Yeltsin's subsequent hypersensitivity toward Russian public opinion and to any hint of American superiority, even in procedural matters.

When he first got on the phone, Yeltsin suddenly seemed a little overwhelmed. We could hear him starting every sentence with the Russian version of "Deeply esteemed Mister President Bush!" A former provincial party apparatchik with limited foreign experience, that peculiar mixture of centuries-old mistrust and awe of the West, not rare among Russians, was deeply ingrained in his mind.

"Call him George. You have met before. The tone of this conversation should be a little friendlier and more human," I kept whispering to Yeltsin. "You sound so tense and formal that the guy might get scared. You are not asking for something terrible. Rather, you are briefing a friend on an important move and counting on his understanding."

The advice appeared to help. Swiftly changing his tone, Yeltsin began again. "Dear George, it is a difficult but inevitable decision we made to change the Soviet Union to a new commonwealth of states. I wanted to be sure that when it is publicly announced, it would not come as a surprise to you. We count on your understanding and will stay in touch."

On that note, Bush also started to sound more relaxed. "Yes, Boris, I know it's hard. You should find the best solution in accordance with the will of the people who elected you. I appreciate your call and wish you and the other leaders there all the best. I'm glad you feel like treating Gorbachev right. Yes, let's stay in touch."

The signed document establishing the commonwealth was in effect a death sentence for the Soviet Union, the largest country on earth and our fatherland. It was an emotional moment for us. Yet we knew it was inevitable, and we had done our best to avoid a much more disastrous outcome. Moreover, we were cautiously optimistic about the potential of the Commonwealth.

Yet we knew there were strong opponents of reform. They were somewhat weakened and demoralized, but still ubiquitous. It was far from clear who would ultimately have the upper hand. On the flight back to Moscow, when someone jokingly suggested taking bets on the chances of our plane getting shot down on the order of a hard-line general commanding an antiaircraft unit near Moscow, no one accepted the challenge. The hostility we faced then and in the future was real. However urgent the need for reform was, and however fervently we pursued that course, the personal and political risk we voluntarily faced was never far from our minds.

When our return flight landed in Moscow, it was very reassuring to see the minister of defense of the Soviet Union Marshal Yevgeny Shaposhnikov among those in the welcoming group of friends and colleagues. The participants in the Belavezha meeting had taken care to appoint Shaposhnikov commander in chief of the newly created Unified Command of the Strategic Forces of the CIS, and it was in this capacity that Shaposhnikov welcomed Yeltsin and all of us at the airport, pledging allegiance.

What if he had chosen to arrive with a squad of commandos, in his capacity as minister of defense of the Soviet Union, to arrest a group of people who had just signed an agreement to break up the Soviet state?

Shaposhnikov had not participated in the opposition movement nor was he known as a reformer. He was just an honest officer with sound judgment who recognized that the Soviet Union was doomed by history. I had met him two or three times before and was pleased by his decency and open-mindedness. Russia was fortunate to have this man as head of the armed forces at that crucial moment.

A few months later Yeltsin appointed General Pavel Grachev, a former paratrooper, to the Defense Ministry of the Russian Federation. Like Vice President Rutskoi, Grachev was a decorated Afghan war veteran.

Grachev also had a taste for bureaucratic intrigue and material gain, unlike Shaposhnikov. I suspected he harbored his own ambitions for high office. He sensed and exploited Yeltsin's ego and, like me, being a generation younger than our boss, perfectly played the role of admiring student. He even called him "father" at private gatherings. At friendly dinners Yeltsin many times told me as well as some of the other usual invitees, including Grachev, how he valued the young paratrooper who became his unchallengeable favorite. He spoke of how, in June 1991 Grachev had welcomed Yeltsin and treated him with dignity when the newly elected president of Russia had visited a paratrooper brigade under the young general's command. Moreover, Grachev had refused to attack the White House on August 19, despite an order from his superior officer in Moscow to do so. (On another occasion, Grachev clarified this story, and said that he had demanded a written order instead of just an oral command, and declared that he would have carried out the attack had that written order ever been issued.)

Grachev's appointment made him Shaposhnikov's boss. Soon the latter felt so uncomfortable in the new command structure that he left the armed forces and joined senior management at Aeroflot. As a lifelong air force officer, it was a natural move for him.

On my return to Moscow, I plunged into activities on three fronts. One front comprised the media, which were the first to get the text of the agreement, as we had faxed it from Balavezha to Interfax, a news agency. The second front, of equal if not greater concern, was the Russian parliament, to which that same day we sent an official letter containing the text of the agreement and a request to ratify it. Forming the third front were the heads of the other republics, to whom we dispatched an invitation to join the commonwealth. All of them sought information and clarification as to what had happened in Belavezha, but the preliminary response was generally encouraging. For months there seemed to be universal recognition that the Soviet state, headed by Gorbachev and resistant to change, was on a dangerous slide to disaster and that this slide had now been stopped. Most expressed relief and the hope for a new beginning.

There was also considerable confusion, especially about the nature of the new alliance. Some thought that it contained enough common spheres of authority—such as the unified command of nuclear forces, single currency, open borders, and coordination in foreign policy—to make a new union state. Gorbachev contributed to this misperception. He remained in the president's suite of offices in the Kremlin and, in a desperate attempt to bolster his position, even reappointed Eduard Shevardnadze as foreign minister of the Soviet Union. He was evidently counting on the high prestige in foreign and domestic politics that the minister had won from 1987 to 1991. Shevardnadze had sought cooperation with the West but was constantly pressured and hounded by hard-liners in government. When I came to say good-bye in October 1990 after becoming foreign minister of the Russian Federation, I could sense how lonely and haunted he felt. Just two months later he publicly warned against the looming effects of the hard-liners and resigned from Gorbachev's cabinet.

Shevardnadze's eleventh-hour return to the post of Soviet foreign minister in December 1991 was a mystery to me. Could he not to see that the Soviet Union was going down? I asked him about it later when he became president of Georgia. He told me he was unable to refuse a plea from Gorbachev, an old friend.

However, the majority of those who took the CIS for the new union state saw it merely as a mechanism that would switch out Gorbachev and his people and replace them with Yeltsin and his. Some insisted that the new state or a group of states was based on the pan-Slavic idea, and would thus exclude the Central Asian and Caucasian republics of the former Soviet Union. All those misinterpretations were dear to communists and nationalists and immediately created trouble, both domestically and internationally.

We explained that the commonwealth was not a state. At Ukraine's insistence, the very next line in the document stated that all the activities of the organs of the former Soviet Union should be immediately terminated. The line right after that stressed that the new commonwealth would have no features of a new state. Moreover, in order to overcome the suspicions of the other member states that nothing would change in Moscow, the agreement specifically stated that the new coordinating institutions would be located not in Moscow, but in Minsk, the capital of Belarus. That the new group of states had gathered on a voluntary nonethnic, nonreligious basis, and that it was open to other republics to join. In fact, the president of Kazakhstan Nursultan Nazarbayev had been invited to Minsk and Belavezha from the very beginning. He promised to come but chose not to appear there, in an attempt to keep open his political options, since Gorbachev had offered him the post of prime minister of the Soviet Union.

All that was clear from the text of the agreement, yet we had to repeat it over and over—not only to the press but also to representatives of the other newly independent states and the diplomatic corps.

Getting the Approval of Parliament

The agreement reached at Belavezha still faced its most important hurdle: ratification by the Supreme Soviet, the parliament of the Russian Republic. It was a fraught moment, politically and historically. If the result were negative, Yeltsin's legitimacy as president, entrusted by the people of Russia to lead the country into an independent future, would be seriously undermined, with unpredictable results. Moreover, since Russia was the most powerful republic, the fate of the whole post-Soviet space was up for a vote.

Most deputies seemed to understand the gravity of the situation. Nevertheless, the final resolution was preceded by three hours of statements, questioning, and heated debate.

In a brief but powerful opening statement Yeltsin made it clear that the alternative to the commonwealth was an accelerating and potentially disastrous process of uncontrolled disintegration of the Soviet Union. He referred to previous attempts at the federation, then confederation of sovereign states; but with the passage of time, the best form of integration that could now be achieved was a commonwealth—and parliament should not let this opportunity slide. He described the CIS as offering a promising framework for cooperation and for the reintegration of the newborn states on a solid basis of equality and free choice.

Yeltsin's statement set a positive and upbeat tone for the whole proceeding. Other speakers followed. When my turn came, I presented additional arguments for what I deeply believed to be the right course and I fielded many questions.

Two of those questions touched on matters of particular importance to me as foreign minister and to the vitality of the CIS among modern nations. One dealt with the international legitimacy of the commonwealth and its prospects. That gave me an opportunity to inform the deputies and the media, abundantly present in the hall, that the European Community and the United States had accepted our explanations and welcomed the formation of the CIS as an expression of the free will and legitimate choice of the peoples of the former Soviet Union.

The second major question concerned the potential future development of the CIS. I told the deputies that the relationship between Russia and its neighbors would depend on them, the elected representatives of the Russian people. If they stuck to domestic reforms and to a policy of respect and equality regarding the newly independent states, they would make Russia an attractive partner in the process of reintegration. On the other hand, if the reforms in Russia failed, then the commonwealth would be weak. Old-style Moscow would hardly draw in the other new states. Since deputies had already endorsed a course of reforms, I saw a bright future for the commonwealth.

The proceedings concluded with an almost unanimous vote in favor of ratification of the Belavezha Accords. It was an overwhelming endorsement of the will to end the epoch of the Soviet Union and set the stage for a new democratic Russia. A little later the deputies unanimously voted to change the official name of the country from the Russian Soviet Federative Socialist Republic to the Russian Federation, or Russia.

Ukraine's agenda was to make clear that the end of the federal structure was absolute. It also wanted to stress the inviolability of its borders. These principles were formulated in amendments to the Belavezha Accords and attached to them in the act of ratification passed by the Rada, the Ukrainian parliament, on December 12, 1991. The same thing happened, albeit less emphatically, during the ratification procedure in the Belarusian parliament, where the neutral status of Belarus was also emphasized.

Thus, all the signatories of the Belavezha Accords ratified it through democratic parliamentary procedures. A few days later Kazakhstan proclaimed its independence and took the lead in convening a summit meeting of all the former Soviet republics in its capital city, Alma-Ata.

On December 21, the heads of newly independent states signed a protocol in Alma-Ata that made all of them members of the commonwealth established by the Belavezha Accords. The Alma-Ata Protocol finalized the dissolution of the Soviet Union and marked the start of a new era in the history of the former republics that had gained independence. In a signal departure from both Russia's historical precedent and the ongoing bloody conflict raging among the territories of former Yugoslavia, not only was the change in status achieved without armed conflict, the newly independent states voluntarily chose to form a new cooperative alliance among themselves.

Only Georgia declined to participate. Its nationalist leader, Zviad Gamsakhurdia, insisted that the independence of his state needed no confirmation and that the CIS represented too great an integration with Russia and the other former Soviet republics.

Successor States and Legal Issues

All the republics were eager to cement their newly achieved independence. This was partly a reaction to confusing signals from Moscow. These were coming not only from Gorbachev but also from Yeltsin who publicly boasted many times about taking control of central power structures in Moscow and, in particular, of the "nuclear attaché case," the device to authorize the use of nuclear weapons in case of emergency that was always carried by two officers who followed the president of the USSR everywhere. Yeltsin evidently could not wait to take the attaché case and the glamorous president's office space in the Kremlin from Gorbachev. He dreamed of it as a symbol of power, almost as young boy dreams of wearing a necktie as a symbol of being an adult.

The democrats suggested that Yeltsin take an office in the Russian White House, which had become a symbol of democratic resolve and victory over the old guard. The Kremlin could then be allowed to become exclusively a national historical monument, open to the public and free of government offices. In Yeltsin's utter rejection of such proposals I sensed his deep-seated and overwhelming lust for power, including the trappings of the office that Gorbachev once held. It worried me a lot. I knew that this could grow like a cancer and devour the fragile embryo of democracy.

Watching the power intrigues in Moscow, Kazakhstan's Nazarbayev and other leaders absent from the Belavezha gathering did not want to be taken for granted. Though no one challenged the substance of what had been agreed, they expressed unease with what they considered the secondary role offered to their countries because of the fact that they had not been part of the initial decision to terminate the Soviet Union.

Pressed with the demand that equality be provided from the very beginning, I recalled that Poland had been absent from the ceremony of signing of the Charter of the United Nations and only joined that body about a month later. Yet Poland was counted among the initial signatories and founding members of the world body by the consent of the other participants. This "Polish precedent" was used in forging the agreement that every republic that already had jointed or would in the future join the CIS would be considered an initial and founding member, with equal rights. The heads of all interested republics would have a special summit soon to sign a protocol of adherence to the commonwealth, and that would be regarded as an integral and equal part of the Belavezha Accords. These steps cleared the way for the other republics to accept the Belavezha Accords with pride and dignity.

Two questions concerning Russian relations with the world outside the CIS loomed large in my mind during preparations for the Alma-Ata summit, because the answers depended on reaching an agreement with the former Soviet republics. How would the Soviet Union's international heritage, namely, the status of a great power bearing the obligations of a nuclear state and holding a permanent seat on the UN Security Council, be transferred to Russia? Soon, after the Belavezha Accords were signed, I called the US secretary of state Jim Baker and the foreign ministers Douglas Hurd of Great Britain and Roland Dumas of France to brief them on the event.

All agreed in principle that the nuclear obligations and the UN status should pass to Russia in an orderly way with the consent of other succession states, the former republics of the Soviet Union, and the UN member states. Legally, all republics had equal rights as heirs of the former Soviet Union and would have been able to divide up its assets and liabilities, either by mutual consensus at a diplomatic conference or through an international arbitration process. The ramifications of trying to apportion the former single entity's legal obligations, treaty memberships, and UN seat and parcel them out in equal measure to the successor states caught me on the back foot. And apparently my interlocutors felt the same way.

The British had developed expertise in solving the legal puzzles surrounding issues of succession, since they had had to tackle very similar problems when first building and then taking apart their empire. A few days later Douglas Hurd outlined in a telephone conversation the concept of a "continuation state," by which Russia, as one of the successor states, could simply assume the Soviet Union's treaty obligations and diplomatic functions, including membership in the UN and on the Security Council. For that, no formal decision of an international conference was needed. If all the CIS countries approved one way or another, the concept should work nicely for Russia. In practice, the procedure boiled down to a technical change of nameplate at UN conferences and Security Council meetings and Russia's assumption of the Soviet Union's diplomatic ties, embassies, and so on. But it was critically important that no great power challenged this status in the early days.

Yeltsin agreed to seek continuation-state status for Russia, and we set about working with the US, French, and British foreign ministers to bring it to fruition. We also needed the approval of, or at least not rejection from,

China, the only non-Western permanent member of the Security Council. I met with the Chinese ambassador and assured him of our determination to seek the best possible good-neighbor relations with his country and asked for his support or neutrality on the succession matter. Somehow, I believed that China would not create a problem, and indeed the response from Beijing was quick and consensual.

The success of our efforts hinged in large part on the UN secretary-general-elect Boutros Boutros-Ghali and the outgoing head of the UN, Javier Pérez de Cuéllar, who gave the order to change the nameplate on the Soviet seat in the UN Security Council to that of the Russian Federation. In a reversal of the usual situation, it was one of those rare moments in history when the fate of a great power depended on the office of the secretary-general. Normally, the top UN official depends on the great powers, the permanent members of the UN Security Council, which have the power of veto over his appointment. The same could be said of the role of the permanent representative of the Soviet Union to the UN, Yuli Vorontsov.

Diplomats are totally dependent on their governments, which can fire them at any moment. That day Vorontsov could either have blocked the Russian Federation's efforts to become the Soviet Union's continuation state or, conversely, could have "fired" the Soviet government from the world organization, which he did. A seasoned diplomat, he picked up on the idea easily and creatively when I briefed him by phone. With that change of nameplate, Vorontsov took the seat of the Russian Federation and spoke at a UN Security Council meeting as permanent representative of the Russian Federation instead of the Soviet Union, executing the change easily, as if it were a small matter. (Had he declined to do so and challenged the change, the question of the succession would have become an international problem.) Soviet ambassadors all over the world soon followed Vorontsov's example, and the Russian Federation smoothly took its rightful place as a great power.

In the meantime, we had to seal Russia's status as a continuation state with the approval of the CIS. At the Alma-Ata summit the republican leaders, now heads of independent states, had to handle all matters related to succession. They decided to do so at a strategic session just among themselves, and rather quickly ratified decisions, previously agreed on by experts, to establish the most important organs of the commonwealth, including the Councils of the Heads of States and Heads of Governments and the Joint Military Command of Strategic Forces. The documentation on strategic forces confirmed that the practical control and servicing of all nuclear weapons, wherever they were situated at that time, would be exercised by Russia and directed from headquarters in Moscow.

For the most part, however, the attendees were discussing urgent economic matters and they invited their prime ministers to join them. All the states were in bad shape. They were stunned to realize that the Soviet government had no financial or gold reserves and a huge international debt. The principals at the meeting decided it would be most practical for Russia to service the whole debt of the USSR, and in exchange to receive the majority of Soviet assets. The details were to be worked out in further deliberations. In this way all the republics avoided being placed in default on some percentage of Soviet-era debt, which meant they were free to engage in the international finance and trade vital for restarting their ruined economies.

Only limited support staff—the restrictions applied to ministers as well—had access to the conference room in which that top-level meeting took place. Two or three times my Russian colleagues and I were called on to provide explanations and statistics that could only be known by those who had access to Soviet databases from Moscow.

I took advantage of one of those summonses and asked Yeltsin to raise the issue of the permanent UN Security Council seat. We had discussed it before, and he was well aware of its potentially troublesome nature. He shrewdly brought it up right after the emotional discussion of the impoverishing financial legacy of the Soviet Union.

He pointed out that in order to overcome that crippling legacy, the republics had to support each other both domestically and in their multiple relations with the outside world. By joining the world financial institutions, especially the International Monetary Fund (IMF) and the World Bank, the newly independent states could borrow on international markets. Of course, it would be important to seek membership in the UN as the most prominent organization of sovereign nations.

In that connection Yeltsin recalled that Ukraine and Belarus had been among the founding members of the UN from the start. The other republics, including Russia, would have to apply for new membership. But the idea that Russia was not a member of the UN while Ukraine and Belarus were struck everyone as so incongruous that they were inclined to accept any reasonable solution to the problem. And Yeltsin offered that.

Let's agree, he proposed, that Ukraine and Belarus should leverage their member status in the UN to help others join the organization as soon as possible. In saying that, he stressed the privileged position of the two states and invoked a kind of moral responsibility on their part to help the others, rather than putting a burden on them. As for Russia, he went on, it could undertake the responsibility of continuing to observe the obligations of the former Soviet Union stemming from international treaties, including the UN Charter. Thus, it would also continue membership in the world body. That implied no bias against the other newly independent states, each of which was an equal and unchallengeable successor of the Soviet Union.

The proposal quickly gained support as offering an easy and harmless exit from an awkward situation. But we were not yet out of the woods. Normally, someone pointed out, the experts would have prepared a draft document formalizing the decision, and the document would have been read and discussed. In that eventuality, I knew, it surely would have met with resistance from the Ukrainians and the Belarusian foreign minister, Piotr Kravchenko, who could easily haggle over the wording of any document for hours, which would have meant no approval before the conclusion of the summit. The bosses were tired and the hour was late.

Yet I myself saw that the late hour could offer us an advantage. I whispered to Yeltsin that a draft decision concerning the UN did exist, although it had not been distributed earlier along with the other decision documents. It was a concise half-page text that could easily be read aloud and approved by acclamation. Yeltsin's reaction was swift—drawing on his natural flair for improvisation, he announced that I had prepared the text appropriately, but that I had erred in not printing enough copies in advance, for which he, Yeltsin, now had to apologize. Even so he believed that a mistake made by his foreign minister should not stop the heads of state from making the correct decision.

Yeltsin sounded so irritated by my alleged mistake that he seemed ready to fire me on the spot. The gamble paid off—no one wanted trouble, and I was well-known by and on good terms with many in the room. Furthermore, they wanted to end the day with a positive move in the international sphere, especially since their domestic affairs were in such bad shape. So it was quickly agreed that the lack of paper copies was not a problem, and the document I had prepared—which was very concise and clear—was approved after it was read aloud.

Immediately after the meeting the Ukrainians and Kravchenko tried to persuade their bosses to challenge the resolution as having been improperly prepared and presented. But dinner was being served, and the principals were in the mood to celebrate, not argue. Most important, the leaders of the newly independent states recognized that the decision to make Russia the continuation state to the Soviet Union and for Russia to take the permanent UN Security Council seat was the correct one. The weight of history alone made this appropriate, both within the newly established CIS and on the world stage.

On December 23, the European Union and the entire international community welcomed Russia as a continuing state, expressing their intention to maintain friendly relations. In line with what we had requested, the EU and the United States also signaled their readiness to recognize other former Soviet republics as soon as those states "presented guaranties" of adhering to democracy, protecting the rights of minorities, upholding the nonproliferation of nuclear weapons, and respecting the inviolability of frontiers.

First Steps in Foreign Policy

As foreign minister I was able to see firsthand how leaders around the world viewed the Russian transition with hope. It was quite evident on Yeltsin's trip to Italy on December 17. The trip had been planned long beforehand, but suddenly it had become the first foreign visit by the president of the Russian Federation as the head of an independent state. Yeltsin was greeted as the respected leader of a great country determined to move forward with reform. Few protocol details needed changing, and none in the Declaration of Friendly Relations, which was signed by the presidents of Russia and Italy. At that time, Washington and many other Western capitals were still negotiating with Gorbachev and his Foreign Ministry. Our trip spoke volumes about the sagacity of the Italian diplomats and politicians, who foresaw well in advance with whom they would be doing business in Moscow.

The beauty of Rome's historical architecture captivated Yeltsin, who had worked in the construction business. Our Italian colleagues constantly referred to the democratic reforms in Russia as a way of breathing new life into Russia's enormous cultural and spiritual heritage as part of European civilization. During one short walk in the center of Rome, Yeltsin and I discussed how false the Russian nationalists were in their theory that Western-style democracy damaged the cultural identity and uniqueness of nations.

We also paid a visit to Pope John Paul II, born Karol Józef Wojtyła. Yeltsin expressed deep respect for the pontiff. As we were leaving, the pope shook our hands in farewell and also tried to add a personal gesture toward each member of our small group. When he came to me, he held my hand in his hands, and looked into my eyes, repeating a few times in Russian, "I know, I know... God bless you."

The day before we departed for Italy, on December 16, Yeltsin signed a decree stipulating that the Russian Federation's ministries, including mine, were to take control of all Soviet ministries still in operation. From that day on, Gorbachev and his few aides still sitting in their Kremlin offices represented all that remained of the Soviet empire. From Rome I placed a call to Eduard Shevardnadze, the outgoing Soviet minister of foreign affairs. He was packing up his personal things and just about to leave. "Tomorrow," he said, "you must come and run the ministry." I expressed my gratitude for his contribution to changing the foreign policy of the Soviet Union to one that was more open to the West and to the international community in general. Shortly after he left the ministry he went to Georgia, which was in the throes of civil war, to become president of that state. I admired his courageous decision. He could easily have chosen a different life, say, that of a professor, either in Moscow or in the West.

My return to the big Foreign Ministry building, after more than a year of being isolated and feeling constantly under pressure, was rewarding. I had taken the risk of walking away from a promising career in that skyscraper, which had been built in the same year I was born, at the apogee of Stalinism. I had chosen instead to go to a small, creaky house, drawn by the powerful idea of helping turn the final page on that epoch. Often, as I passed by, the act of gazing up at the windows of my former office had made me look deeply into my soul. Yes, I missed the comfort of a top position in a powerful institution and the professional satisfaction that had come from practicing diplomacy at the UN, the mecca of world diplomacy. But not for a single moment, even in the tense early morning hours of the day of the coup, did I have second thoughts.

I knew the ministry from the inside and fully realized the magnitude of the difficulties awaiting me there. The major problem was the legacy in the minds of many diplomats of the deceptive simplicity of a world divided into "us" in Moscow and "them," our enemy in the West. In between lay a global battleground on which the Soviet diplomats had to act as the motherland's champions. As a member of the Belavezha group that had toppled the Soviet Union and pushed for alliance with the West, I would as a matter of course meet animosity.

At first, most of the democrats recommended breaking up the structure and firing most of the personnel of the ministry. I believed I should not be guided by revenge. The Soviet diplomats were career professionals and fluent in foreign languages. Replacing them would not be easy. They had been my colleagues for many years, and I owed them a chance. When I briefed Yeltsin on my decision, he halfheartedly agreed with the prophetic words: "It's your choice. If you regret it later, there won't be anyone else to blame."

I summoned the upper echelon of the ministry personnel and told them that the time of uncertainty and being pushed onto the wrong side of history by hard-liners, as we had been during the coup, was over. Now we all had the opportunity to provide our professional services to a democratic Russia, and our former enemies, the Western democracies, were to become new friends. We also faced the unprecedented challenge of establishing diplomatic ties from scratch with the former Soviet republics, which only yesterday had been part of the Ministry of the Interior; today they were the concern of the Foreign Ministry. I offered an accelerated career path to those diplomats wishing to switch to this challenging new field.

On December 19, NATO opened its ministerial meeting, intending the next day to establish the North Atlantic Cooperation Council (NACC) to promote cooperation with the Soviet Union and Eastern European countries. While welcoming the idea, we felt it necessary to make clear both the transition to the Russian Federation and our approach to NATO. That day Yeltsin signed a letter addressed to the secretary-general of the alliance. It opened with the assessment that deep reforms in Russia had created unprecedented opportunities for mutual trust with NATO based on common values. That statement alone was a signal departure from the traditional Soviet stance—namely, that both sides of the Cold War were equally responsible for changing their policies. Now we recognized that Moscow had to choose democratic values, after which one could expect Russia to stop confronting NATO and, as a result, NATO to cease confronting Russia.

"Today we do not ask for Russian membership in NATO, but regard it as our long-term political objective," Yeltsin wrote, in one of the first political declarations of new Russia.

Yet again, a great historic moment was accompanied by a moment of absurdity. The text of the letter given to the press contained a technical error: the word "not" was left out of the English translation. This meant that it read, "Today we do ask for Russian membership in NATO but regard it as our long-term objective." We issued a correction, but the mistake served to draw additional attention to the document and its meaning—which, in essence, was the same with or without "not."

The next day the letter was given to NATO by Russia's ambassador, Nikolai N. Afanasyevsky, who had previously represented the Soviet Union. Amazingly, Western diplomats seemed to be so ill-informed about developments in Moscow and hypnotized by Gorbymania that the ambassador's acting in the new capacity mesmerized them. "Before the four-hour meeting was over," the *New York Times* reported, "Mr. Afanasyevsky stunned the foreign ministers by announcing that his country no longer existed, and that he had been ordered to strike all references to the 'Soviet Union' from the final communiqué, which had already been distributed to the press."

The NACC was a provisional answer to the aspirations of those post-communist countries that had seen NATO as a symbol and guarantor of the defeat of the communist domination of Europe and expressed a desire to join the alliance as soon as possible. In the NACC they saw something that was partly a substitute and partly a prep class for membership, since NATO countries could neither admit unprepared applicants nor close the door on the new democracies forever.

US secretary of state James Baker paid a visit to Moscow on December 20. Oddly enough, he spent roughly equal time talking separately to Gorbachev and Yeltsin who was already the only real power in town. Baker assured the Russian president of NATO's readiness to meet Russia halfway in the search for common ground for cooperation and promised to continue the discussion of proper moves with other NATO member states. Yeltsin and I spoke with Baker about Russia's determination to lead the CIS on a path of democracy on the basis of the Helsinki principles of the inviolability of borders and territorial integrity, of development of a market economy, and of integration with the West and its impressive international institutions, such as the IMF, the World Bank, and NATO. Yeltsin also assured Baker that he would control the attaché case with the nuclear codes and be the civilian commander in chief, while Yevgeny Shaposhnikov would command the Commonwealth Strategic Forces. The Americans agreed that the Soviet Union's nuclear weapons should remain under the control of one country—which could only be Russia. Nuclear nonproliferation was identified as a shared priority. Most immediately it meant persuading the other three republics with nuclear weapons on their territory—Ukraine, Belarus, and Kazakhstan—to get rid of these arms as soon as possible. Baker intended to stress this point to those states and did so in Kyiv after departing from Moscow.

First Aid

The winter of 1991–92 promised to be hard. The former republics had to face the empty warehouses and larders left by the corrupt Soviet government. Street protests in December 1991 underscored how much the populations of the newly independent states were suffering, and how much they expected of their governments under the new system.

We were glad, then, when Baker offered an outright injection of aid to tide people over the winter.

The humanitarian assistance provided subsequently by the United States and other Western economies was indeed impressively generous—but the effects of that aid rarely reached ordinary citizens, including my family and friends. Stories of corruption and diversion of aid in Russia began appearing in the media. The situation seemed merely a continuation of business as usual. Nothing changed when the Russian authorities took over. The Russian Foreign Ministry received daily updates from the Western embassies in Moscow describing chaotic aid distribution and the questionable behavior of Russian government agencies in charge of receiving the aid and transferring it to people.

On the basis of that information, we prepared a number of reports on aid distribution and failure, which I gave personally to Yeltsin, Burbulis, Yegor Gaidar, and the top parliamentary leaders. Yet the problems continued, highlighting the real weakness of the government's operational performance.

It was this that created an opening for Ruslan Khasbulatov, the new leader of parliament, and the Russian Federation's vice president, Alexander Rutskoi, and his office to demand supervision and operational management of the aid distribution. The government rejected both demands, pointing to its prerogatives as the executive branch in the power structure. All sides used the media to exchange accusations of special corrupt interests behind the position of adversaries.

The political dividing lines quickly became more pronounced. The democrats tended to defend the government against even justified criticism and a reasonable amount of parliamentary control. The conservatives adopted an accusatory line and began consolidating around the offices of the leader of parliament and the vice president.

The corrupt bureaucracy, once entrenched in the Soviet system and now seamlessly shifting into the new Russian system, easily manipulated the new bosses, exploiting these vulnerabilities and divisions. To many it was repugnant to hear a department chief who just a few months earlier had held a Communist Party card report on his efforts to introduce new market-oriented mechanisms in his area of responsibility. Such free-market fighters often had relatives holding a minor position in parliament while business partners headed up private companies with exclusive contracts to distribute foreign aid.

The more the veteran bureaucrats regained their influence, the more they were drawn to Russian nationalistic rhetoric. Some government agencies began responding to accusations of mismanagement of foreign aid by insisting that the lion's share of the blame lay with the West itself. They asserted that donors were proclaiming their generosity while failing to provide meaningful assistance.

But the Russian bureaucracy was primarily angered by the demands of Western donors that the end users of aid be identified. Though that was an appropriate precaution, the bureaucrats argued that it introduced an artificial delay, and that food and medical supplies were past their expiration dates by the time they arrived in Russia. Disposing of such items meant that the auditing agencies could not account for their whereabouts, they claimed. No doubt they were also sold through private firms, which were not subjected to close inspection.

It should also be noted that large amounts of supplies did reach the right people, mostly through nongovernmental organizations or direct local contacts. In some cases, this aid played a very important, even vital role in helping the people of the former Soviet republics survive the winter of 1991–92. Many years later, I met doctors and schoolteachers in my constituency in Murmansk and elsewhere in distant regions of Russia who expressed gratitude for American, German, and other Western aid in the early 1990s. Yet large-scale bureaucratic mismanagement and corruption, followed by a malicious propaganda campaign, considerably spoiled the public image of Western humanitarian assistance.

In response to the reports my ministry issued on choke points, loss, and diversion of aid supplies, some agencies began accusing the ministry of defending the West instead of defending Russia's interests. These accusations were transmitted to parliament and immediately used by the political opposition to publicly attack the Foreign Ministry and me personally. Of course, the real target was the policy of cooperation with the West and the pursuit of Western-type reforms in general. From then on, the corrupt bureaucracy promoted through parliament and the press claimed that Yeltsin and I had made political concessions to the Americans in return for largely rotten humanitarian supplies.

I protested to Yegor Gaidar, first deputy prime minister, and his aides about the false and politically dangerous nature of that demagoguery, which originated in government departments under their oversight. Unfortunately, Gaidar was preoccupied with the urgent problems of a collapsing economy and with introducing macro reforms on an unprecedented scale, so no meaningful corrective measures were taken. The economists in government, I felt, lacked political seasoning. As good technicians, they sought to apply pure economic theory to the task of reforming society and underestimated the importance of political strategy and the dissemination of correct information. That arrogance gave the opposition free rein to portray the reformers as pro-Western and unpatriotic.

On December 26, I went to the Kremlin on a business matter. As the car was crossing the square in the middle of the old fortress, my aide drew my attention to the roof of the presidential building. In place of the Soviet red banner with its mortar and sickle, the Russian tricolor was floating in the breeze. That meant Yeltsin had been installed in the presidential offices. I joined him there, and we raised a glass to the end of the tortuous process of saying farewell to the Soviet Union and its last leader, and to the dawn of a new era.

On December 30, 1991, the first regular meeting of the CIS countries was convened in Minsk. The new headquarters did not yet have adequate room and technical support for eleven top-level delegations. Some rules and procedures were devised on the spot, adding to the general confusion. But the predominant spirit was of a new beginning and a new cooperation. The major institutions of the Commonwealth were inaugurated, and decisions made that aimed at political, military, and economic cooperation among the CIS countries. These were mainly declarations of intent, but since they were adopted by consensus of the top leadership of the new governments, there was a promise of serious follow-up.

I made it home in time to attend a New Year's Eve performance of *The Nutcracker* at the Bolshoi Theatre with my family. I looked at the ballet while at the same time watching my eleven-year-old daughter out of the corner of my eye and sharing in her excitement. The Nutcracker and his companions had a terrifying fight with the dark forces of the Mouse King, but in the end, they won. The victory came as a result of their courage and enthusiasm, but also with the help of a fairy with a magic wand. I had a childish feeling of living vicariously through that story and was optimistic about the upcoming year. Yet I couldn't help thinking that nothing less than a magic wand would be needed for us to win the more difficult fight of implementing the promise of a new day in domestic and foreign policy.

PART II

Climbing a Steep Slope,
1992–1994

ALAS, I HAD NO MAGIC WAND. On the contrary, we faced a steep learning curve for bringing about positive change in Russia led by the president. My colleagues and I had to work on a strategy to forge a new path for Russia in the realm of foreign policy. The foreign policy I wanted to pursue consisted of four main pillars. The first was the creation of a favorable environment for democratization and market-oriented reforms in Russia, which entailed the second pillar, developing good relations with neighboring states in a belt around Russia. The third pillar was integrating Russia into the community of the most developed democratic states of the Northern Hemisphere, usually called Western countries (though for Russia, Canada, the United States, and Japan are eastern neighbors). The fourth pillar was the maintainenance of mutually beneficial relations with all other countries. This was the set of policies I had presented to the parliament of the Russian Federation in October 1990 and won approval for. It was also the policy framework on the basis of which the president reappointed me as foreign minister of independent Russia. I did my best to help Yeltsin negotiate this increasingly daunting learning curve, until he changed course.

The urgent task for Russia was to overcome the legacy of perverse development under the so-called socialist system that the Soviet Union imposed on large parts of Eastern and Central Europe. In foreign policy terms this task meant forming new relations with other countries that had been freed from that system. In many aspects it amounted to shaping the future of Russia itself.

In 1992 the Russian Federation emerged as an independent state along with fourteen sovereign states on its borders. The three former Soviet republics on the Baltic Sea—Estonia, Latvia, and Lithuania—had gained their independence in September 1991 and were embraced by northern Europeans as determined applicants to the club of Western democracies. The other new states signed in to the Commonwealth of Independent States, including five in Central Asia: Kazakhstan, Kyrgyzstan, Tajikistan, Turkmenistan, and Uzbekistan; three in Easten Europe: Belarus, Ukraine, and Moldova; and three in the Transcaucasus: Armenia, Azerbaijan, and Georgia, which joined the CIS later. The direction they would choose was far from clear.

3

Cooperation with the Post-Socialist States

DEVELOPING A FRAMEWORK FOR COOPERATION WITH THE newly independent states presented formidable challenges. All of them strove to eliminate any reminders of dependency on the imperial center but at the same time sought new modes of collaboration, being strongly connected by humanitarian, cultural, and economic ties. Both in Moscow and in the respective capitals there was little opportunity for analysis as we pushed forward into an unknown future. First and foremost, it was vital to prevent the post-Soviet states from turning against one another, echoing the horrible disaster playing out in Yugoslavia, a scenario that would be amplified by the added potential for a nuclear war. Second, we tried to shape new forms of cooperation in as many fields and as strongly as possible.

The establishment of the Commonwealth of Independent States (CIS) provided the cornerstone of our efforts to turn potential conflicts into opportunities. This was largely achieved through several bilateral and multilateral treaties and declarations signed in 1991 and 1992, as the heads of state and their ministers came together to discuss their concerns, as well as through the numerous nontreaty meetings in 1992 that cemented personal relations and increased familiarity with and transparency about major problems. In this way the political aspects of building relations with and among the CIS

countries were supported by organizational forums, which in turn strengthened personal ties and recognition among leaders.

Even so, on the political front, the Foreign Ministry faced absurd charges
that it was neglecting the newly independent states in its obsession with the
West. The charges were mounted by the opposition, which sought a neoim-
perialist policy and, finding that one was not forthcoming, dismissed the new
foreign policy as weak and ineffectual. Part of the media also failed to view
relations with the former republics in the context of foreign policy, preferring
instead a notion of the "near abroad" states. This appellation, which became
popular around 1991, was seen by those countries not as a benign reflection
of their ties to the Russian people but as a denial of their full independence
by Russian imperialists—as indeed it was. I avoided using the label as much
as possible.

The difficulties we faced in implementing the new foreign policy were not
just political but also logistical. No one from the old Soviet Foreign Ministry
specialized in newly independent states. Up to that point, matters pertaining
to the Soviet Union's constituent republics had fallen under the aegis of the
Communist Party apparatus.

Maybe, we thought, some individuals with knowledge of the former republics could be found among the party bureaucracy. Slightly reluctantly, we
offered positions to a few of them, but they turned us down. Most had joined
business or research institutions and disliked the new direction of Russia's
foreign policy anyway.

Eventually I asked a democratically oriented member of the parliament,
Feodor Shelov-Kovedyayev, to take the position of first deputy foreign
minister to handle relations with legislators and the former Soviet republics.
Shelov-Kovedyayev always emphasized his independent-mindedness and
self-assuredness, even in his manner of dress. Watching the crowd of parliamentarians, one could not miss a tall figure in a colored jacket, contrasting
the multitude of baggy Soviet-style black and gray suits. He even wore a bright
bow tie, something Soviet cartoonists had always used to some someone
out as foreign. (A reluctance to put on a bow tie was one reason that Yeltsin
initially declined to wear a tuxedo for official ceremonies.) Representing the
parliament, Feodor had accompanied Yeltsin to Kazakhstan in August 1991,
and I had noted his sound judgment on relations with neighbors. During
the August putsch he was to be found among the other democratic deputies
defending the Russian White House. At first Yeltsin was reluctant to sup-

port his candidacy because Feodor was not trained in diplomacy, but when I pointed out that there was no career diplomat with expertise in dealing either with parliament or with the other republics, Yeltsin agreed to back him. Shelov-Kovedyayev proved to be instrumental especially in the initial and most difficult period of 1992.

It was he who undertook the task of organizing from scratch a CIS department in the ministry and recruiting diplomats to serve on assignment to the newly independent states. That was a tough proposition. We needed the best people to engage the new and somewhat fragile governments of the CIS countries on matters pertaining to a shared future, including such critical issues as security, peacekeeping, and managing a common currency, but traditionally, assignments to Western countries had been regarded by Soviet diplomats as the most prestigious and the best paying, too. The practice up to that point was that "Westerners" received their salary in the hard currency of the country of service, while those posted to Eastern European countries were paid in the soft currency of the socialist economies. In a typically perverse Soviet manner, the communist diplomats had privately preferred "enemy" countries rather than Soviet allies even as they vehemently argued for the opposite. This entrenched attitude did not change even when the need for duplicity disappeared. The new policy openly recognized reality: the West was more developed and enjoyed a better standard of living. Russia should build strategic partnerships and alliances with it and undertake the internal reforms necessary to catch up to the West so that not only diplomats, but all Russians could enjoy a Western way of life and hard currency. At the same time, relations with the CIS countries were no less vital, and diplomatic service on that track was no less prestigious. Quite a few former Soviet diplomats did not welcome the change in tenor, however, and still privately preferred to serve in Western countries.

We offered accelerated promotion and other incentives to the young diplomats who volunteered to go to the CIS countries, and by midsummer had a working structure with a good staff to address the challenges of the post-Soviet space. Yet Feodor seemed irresistibly drawn to other Western directions of policymaking, particularly the sessions of the disarmament committees, which were held in Geneva. I offered him a week in Geneva in the spring so that he could gain an idea of how established international bodies worked, and he soon became a frequent visitor there. This came to the attention of the press and Yeltsin, who asked me about it. I referred to the ministry's need to acquire international experience to apply to problems in the CIS, but even to me that reasoning sounded unpersuasive, and matters snowballed from there. The problems were exacerbated by the second assignment in Feodor's portfolio, managing relations with parliament, where the opposition attacked the ministry precisely on its handling of CIS issues. Although the attacks were politically motivated and ginned up as part of a larger power struggle, it was difficult to argue with the many parliamentarians who felt that the frequent trips to the West of the first deputy foreign minister distracted him from both contacts with parliament and the CIS, and the president soon fired him. On my initiative a veteran diplomat, Anatoly Adamishin, who had been the Soviet Union's ambassador to Italy, replaced him, doing the job more professionally if with less passion and political vigor.

On January 8, 1992, the foreign ministers of the CIS countries gathered in Moscow to follow up on the issues discussed and decisions made at the December summits. Over the next twelve months this type of collective ministerial meeting took place more than twenty times. There were also six meetings of heads of state and countless conferences involving ministers of defense, finance, economy, and education. While few of the dozens of resolutions passed on cooperative engagement were realistic and even fewer were implemented, the frequent contacts and declarations of good intentions helped build a tight network of personal ties and led to smaller-scale arrangements that were successfully implemented and did much to promote mutual trust.

Almost all the heads of state knew each other from Soviet times, when they had met in the corridors of the Communist Party headquarters in Moscow. That shared background created a peculiar sense of comradeship even though it was underscored by old rivalries and scores yet to be settled.

While some republican leaders seemed more than willing to continue the old Soviet game of extorting subsidies and economic concessions from "Big Brother" Russia, they had also not forgotten their humiliating subjugation and were eager to reject strong coordinating institutions. The failure to build such institutions right from the start, though perhaps unavoidable, in light of all that had passed, contributed significantly to the failure of the reform movement and to the subsequent fate of the republics.

Yet some decisions were of historic significance. The most important ones related to unified control of the armed forces inherited from the Soviet Union. This helped prevent chaos as the new states took control of the old military structures on their territories and created new national armed forces.

Russia also gradually took under its flag some military installations and forces outside its borders in areas of civil and ethnic conflict in Tajikistan, Georgia, and Moldova. If it had not done so, those troops, flatly defying the local government and remaining loyal to a nonexistent Soviet Union, could have become leaderless and thus extremely dangerous in an unstable environment.

Although the new Russian commanders—initially former Soviet commanders who agreed to recognize the new authority in Moscow—could be biased and unable to stop corruption, they also provided a degree of discipline and most of the time avoided getting involved in fighting. Some units under the Russian banner did play a constructive role in stabilizing conflict situations and protecting civilians, as did 201st Army Division in Dushanbe, Tajikistan, during the civil war there in 1992–93.

Preventing the former Soviet troops and the new national armies from being drawn into local hostilities was of immediate concern to the CIS. The CIS countries undertook a mission of stopping and preventing those "mini-wars" through a united effort, which was an enormous step toward constructive cooperation. At a March 20 summit in Kyiv an agreement was reached to set up a corps of military observers and collective units for peacekeeping operations on CIS territory. A set of guiding principles was drawn up that was consistent with the UN Charter and practice—yet another indication of the readiness of the new leaders to respect standards of international law. Even though in practice, joint peacekeeping operations mostly boiled down to providing a CIS top-off to Russian operations, since the other member states faced difficulties contributing troops and money, they played an important role in making mandates and missions more balanced and international than they would have been otherwise. In a different development, on May 15, 1992, the presidents of nine states signed the Tashkent Treaty, aimed at establishing a collective security system.

Strengthening the legal basis of the CIS and its institutions was another ongoing concern of the CIS. By the end of 1992 the heads of states had succeeded in creating a charter for the CIS drafted by foreign ministers. This fundamental document defined both the major goals of further integration and the mechanisms for attaining them. It was signed at a summit of CIS countries on January 22, 1993. The CIS Charter formed the basis for the Treaty on Creation of an Economic Union, signed by the heads of state on September 24, 1993, and for a document establishing the Interstate Economic

Committee, which was signed in October 1994. Thus, considerable positive
diplomatic and basic legal work were done, and a degree of cooperation was
achieved in many fields.

Maintaining a common currency, however, was one goal that could not
be sustained. Although most CIS countries had agreed to do so initially, their
very different developmental trajectories and Russia's astronomical inflation
in 1992–93 proved to be insurmountable barriers. Nonetheless, striving to
strengthen integration, Yeltsin frequently urged the republican leaders to stay
in the ruble zone, even as the Russian financial authorities were scheming
to get rid of their weaker partners, which they regarded as dead weight. The
problem of the uncontrolled distribution of rubles by the other CIS countries
also introduced chaos in monetary matters. Over the course of 1991 and 1992,
one by one the new states introduced their own currencies. The controversial and disorderly manner in which the common currency of the ruble was
abolished dealt a major blow to ambitions aimed at preserving a high level
of economic integration and cementing mutual reliance in planning future
development.

Nuclear Nonproliferation and the Ukrainian Knot

While wrestling with the unprecedented task of restructuring relations
among the former Soviet republics in the new cooperative framework of the
CIS, we had to face the question of what to do with the strategic nuclear
arsenal of the former Soviet Union, which was now spread among four states,
Ukraine, Belarus, Kazakhstan, and Russia. Each of them commanded more
nuclear power than France, Great Britain, or China.

During intensive multilateral and bilateral discussions in the first few
months of 1992, we ironed out the technical aspects of a new arrangement
for the control and possible use of nuclear weapons. The black attaché case
with the nuclear codes would remain with the president of Russia, who would
consult the heads of Belarus, Kazakhstan, and Ukraine in case of an alert. In
principle, all three non-Russian states accepted the obligation of ridding their
territory of nuclear weapons and joining the Treaty on the Non-Proliferation
of Nuclear Weapons, signed by a majority of UN member states in 1968. Most
important, all three agreed to be nonnuclear states in accordance with the
Non-Proliferation Treaty. Also, all agreed to move the tactical nuclear weap-

ons to Russia immediately and to begin doing the same with the strategic missiles and bombers.

Belarus was the first to step up to the plate, signing the respective agreements and undertaking practical measures to remove the nuclear weapons and strategic materials from its territory. Kazakhstan followed suit after two to three months of hesitation, which was prompted in part by President Nazarbayev's ill-calculated idea to try to bargain either with Russia or the United States for some political or financial gain for giving up the share of the Doomsday Machine on Kazakh territory. Hesitation and bargaining dominated the Ukrainian approach, and the issue of demilitarizing its Soviet-era supplies became woven into a knot of other intractable problems in Russian–Ukrainian relations.

In October 1991 the Russian vice president Alexander Rutskoi had gone to Kyiv to negotiate the price of Russian natural gas exports to Ukraine, and through Ukrainian territory to the West and Turkey. On that visit he also claimed Russian control and ownership of the Black Sea fleet, based in the Crimean Peninsula, and, indirectly, Russian sovereignty over the whole region.

When the authorities in Kyiv pushed back strongly, as expected, Rutskoi publicly warned them against stubbornness in dealing with Moscow, which had nuclear weapons. Ukraine's answer to such attempted blackmail was that it too had nuclear weapons and would defend its borders by all means. Since that unhappy episode in rude diplomacy, the two issues, the possession of nuclear weapons and the matter of Crimea, became linked in the minds of Ukrainian politicians, reducing to a minimum their cooperation in the sphere of nuclear weapons containment. Rutskoi's statement was the first threat to the prospects of a smooth denuclearization of Ukraine and the establishment of friendly Russian–Ukrainian relations. But the real knockout blows were inflicted by two similar resolutions claiming Crimea for Russia that were passed by the Russian Federation parliament, in April 1992 and again in March 1993. Each time, despite firm denials of territorial claims by the Russian president's office and the Foreign Ministry, Ukraine's parliament redoubled the force of its public rebuttals. These incidents were followed by a hardening of the positions of Ukrainian diplomats at the negotiating table and a freeze on working on the future of nuclear sites. The Russian ability to deal with Ukraine was effectively crippled, and Moscow turned for help to the United States.

Aggregating all Soviet-era nuclear weapons under Moscow's control and command was in the interest of international community, in accordance with the principle of nuclear nonproliferation, and we had to work together to solve it. The key lay in the hands of the "nuclear club"—the United States, the United Kingdom, France, and China. Alongside them we coordinated the effort to denuclearize Ukraine and Kazakhstan. That was a high priority in my meetings with the US secretary of state Jim Baker, the UK foreign secretary Douglas Hurd, and the French foreign minister Roland Dumas, who visited Moscow during January 1992. It also dominated my private meetings in New York at the Jubilee session of the UN Security Council, which for the first time in fifty years included heads of states and governments. I spoke with the foreign ministers of all the members of the nuclear club, who promised to make it clear to the newly independent states that abandoning the nuclear option was a prerequisite for further relations with the great powers. China's position was of particular importance for its neighbor, Kazakhstan.

A further step was taken in May with the active participation of US secretary of state Baker at a meeting of the Conference on Security and Cooperation in Europe (CSCE) ministerial meeting in Lisbon. The foreign ministers of all three republics signed an agreement to become nonnuclear states. At the same time, an international effort was launched in Lisbon to keep the former Soviet nuclear scientists busy in Russia and other CIS countries so they would have fewer incentives to work on contracts for countries such as Iraq or Iran. It was dubbed the "KGB initiative," named after Kozyrev, Genscher, the foreign minister of Germany, who suggested the name, and Baker.

In this way a solid international foundation was laid for successful resolution of the delicate and vital problem of preventing the proliferation of nuclear weapons after the dissolution of the Soviet Union.

This process culminated in Budapest on December 5, 1994, when the Russian Federation, the United States of America, and the United Kingdom signed the Budapest Memorandum on Security Assurances. These documents provided security assurances to the three countries in exchange for their accession to nonproliferation. By the end of 1996, all nuclear weapons had been removed to Russian territory. Thus, the three former Soviet republics lived up to their obligations under the Memorandum. Unfortunately, this would prove not to be the case with Russia, which in 2014 annexed Crimea, which, at the time the Memorandum had been signed was part of the Ukrainian territory. Article 1 of the Budapest Memorandum demands that Russia "respect Belarusian, Kazakh and Ukrainian independence and sovereignty and the existing borders."

Eastern Europe: The Bridge Concept

Crafting new relations with the Eastern European states that until lately had been within the Soviet sphere of influence was of special importance for new Russia. It was of key importance to define the nature of those relations—in that sense, the process, like so much else connected to the former Soviet space, was as much a matter of foreign policy as it was of domestic policy.

Since they were only recently liberated from the Soviet camp the former socialist countries of Eastern Europe were more sensitive to developments in Russia than were their Western neighbors. Their leaders were grateful for Gorbachev's policies of perestroika and glasnost in the USSR, which had helped break the back of the communist regime in their countries and opened the way for liberation. Yet they were also aware that Gorbachev had not dismantled the sturdy pillars of the Soviet system, such as the Communist Party itself, the KGB, and the military-industrial complex, and that, though deposed, Gorbachev continued to pledge allegiance to socialism.

In practical terms, in the final years of the Soviet Union, the Eastern European countries suffered from a disruption of economic ties with the Soviet Union, which amounted in some cases to the lion's share of foreign trade. This trade was not easily replaced. These weakened economic ties stemmed in part from Moscow's policy of punishing the former satellite countries for radically switching geopolitical orientation. Almost all those nations expressed a desire to join the European Community (now the European Union) and NATO as soon as possible. Under Gorbachev's new thinking, the punishment for such defection no longer entailed the use of military force, as had happened in Hungary in 1956 or Czechoslovakia in 1968, but it was still sufficient to restrain the Eastern European states in their search for new relations with the West. As the democratic movement in Moscow gained strength during the course of 1991, they cautiously looked to reviving relations with Yeltsin's government on a new basis.

I regarded the new European democracies as natural allies in overcoming the Soviet legacy and building a new society. In foreign policy terms they were the best candidates for erecting a bridge from the CIS to the West.

They would be fastest to democratize and to introduce market reforms, and in that sense, they could lead the way for Russia. This bridge strategy proved productive. Its long-term success, however, would require the new Russia's unreserved condemnation of the Soviet past, something strongly desired by the governments in those countries. Understandably, they wanted the old practices of the Soviet Union to be publicly repudiated by Moscow.

In 1991, when the Russian Federation was still part of the Soviet Union, the newly elected president of Czechoslovakia, Václav Havel, was the first foreign leader to invite Yeltsin on a visit with a protocol equal to that usually provided to heads of independent states. This first official visit, carefully prepared as a historic encounter of Russian democrats with their allies and predecessors in Eastern Europe, was a significant foreign policy achievement for the reformers in Moscow and for Yeltsin personally. Boris Pankin, the Soviet ambassador to Prague, acting on his own and risking the wrath of Gorbachev and the Soviet ministry, accompanied Yeltsin, which helped make the visit look more official. Yeltsin used the visit to unambiguously condemn the Soviet intervention in 1968, when tanks rolled into Wenceslas Square, putting an end to the Czechoslovak government's liberalization reforms and the Prague Spring.

In April 1992 Havel came to Moscow on a return official visit. A treaty of friendship and cooperation was signed that referred to relations of equality between the two countries based on freedom of choice and shared democratic values. Again, and this time in writing, the 1968 intervention was deplored as an unjustified use of force, inadmissible in international relations. The withdrawal of Soviet armed forces from Czechoslovakia was confirmed and the related financial and material matters were dealt with. As in other similar cases, Russia was returning camps and buildings occupied by the Soviet army while the other side agreed to help with an orderly evacuation.

The treaty signed with Havel, an outstanding democrat and widely respected figure, provided an introduction for Yeltsin to a club of democratic world leaders and laid a solid basis for a new opening with the Eastern European states. It was also immediately challenged by the opposition in parliament under the pretext that it went too far and could lead to legal claims of reparations from other Eastern European countries. That possibility, however, had been anticipated and carefully avoided in wording worked out with the Czechoslovaks, who understood that the new Russia—while recognizing its historic responsibilities—could not become a scapegoat for the communist Soviet Union. In a brief chat that we had outside the main action of the summit, Havel explained to me the main reason for his desire to join NATO in his distinctive concise, simple, but insightful way: "I just want to join the Western democracies full-scale. Don't you?" I did.

In the same fashion as with Havel, a new treaty of cooperation that included strong but legally nonbinding language condemning the Soviet intervention was signed during Yeltsin's visit to Hungary in November 1992. I was impressed by his willingness to make symbolic gestures of departure from the Soviet legacy. The Russian president went to the grave of Imre Nagy, a Hungarian liberal prime minister whose attempts to free Hungary from the grip of the Soviet Union had been repressed by the Red Army during the October 1956 revolution. Nagy himself had been executed, and Yeltsin laid a wreath during an official ceremony. He also apologized for the invasion and handed over documents from the Communist Party and KGB archives related to it.

After the formal events he spoke to the press, and his spontaneous remarks conveyed emotional outrage over the Soviet Union's brutality and injustices. Only later it occurred to me that with his straightforward rejection of Russia's communist past on his trips abroad, Yeltsin may have been trying to compensate for what he was about to do to the democratic movement in Russia. For the communist and "centrist" opposition had finally wrung concessions from him, which he would announce at the upcoming parliamentary congress on December 10, when he would also fire his first deputy head of government, Yegor Gaidar.

This was particularly ironic because it was in Hungary that the Gaidar government had started to demonstrate some efficacy in foreign economic affairs. During Yeltsin's visit the total amount of the Russian debt to Hungary was agreed on as $1.7 billion and a repayment model was set up. Half of the payment would come in the form of military hardware, including spare parts for Soviet weapons being used by the Hungarian army, and settlements were reached on the provision of other material goods and energy. This agreement cleared the way for the reactivation of economic ties between the two countries, and Russian–Hungarian trade quickly rebounded. The Hungarian diplomats were among the best in East Europe. I maintained a friendly rapport with the Hungarian foreign ministers Géza Jeszenszky and later László Kovács, who played instrumental roles during the Budapest summit conference of the CSCE not only in strengthening the international body but also in helping myself and the US secretary of state Warren Christopher reach an important agreement on a number of issues, including the famous Budapest Memorandum of 1994.

Until the controversy over NATO expansion—the inclusion of Eastern European states as new members—overshadowed Russian relations with Eastern Europe in 1994, the main problems in those relationships were in the economic sphere. The emerging Russian private business sector was more interested in selling oil and other mineral resources to the West for hard currency than in trying to restore cooperative ties, which in many cases had been built on administrative-political decisions dictated by the desire to keep the Eastern European countries within the sphere of Soviet influence and uncompetitive in open-market conditions. Clearly, the new economies forming on both sides of the divide were looking not backward, to barter arrangements and cumbersome currency rates, but ahead, to participation in Western European markets with hard currency and quality standards. Russia and its former socialist partners had to undergo deep internal market-oriented reforms over an extended period before sizable economic ties could be developed on the new basis. The same applied to the rest of the former Soviet republics, where the change was deeper and more painful.

Unfortunately, political and managerial mistakes rendered the transformation even more difficult. With the happy exception of Hungary, slowness and inefficiency in the financial and economic branches of the Russian government and some of the Eastern European governments proved major stumbling blocks to increasing trade with the other republics, which had been damaged in the late Soviet period. Moreover, with the loss of Yegor Gaidar, the Russian economic authorities largely changed from a cadre of young reformers to veteran bureaucrats under the leadership of Prime Minister Viktor Chernomyrdin, and Russia gradually returned to its old habits of punishing pro-Western regimes and favoring neo-Soviet regimes in Eastern Europe and in the post-Soviet space of neighboring countries. Different financial and trade instruments were brought to bear for this purpose, even if the results were deleterious to Russia's own interests—and they were always counterproductive in the long run.

For all these reasons, an agreement settling the debt issue with the Czech Republic was reached only in May 1994, three years after Havel's visit to Moscow. Even more striking was the delay in reaching an agreement with

Bulgaria. The president of Bulgaria, Zhelyu Zhelev, came to Moscow on an official visit to the Russian Federation in October 1991. Since it was not a visit to the still extant Soviet Union, he did not meet Gorbachev, but he and Yeltsin signed a declaration of cooperation that established full diplomatic relations with Russia. The treaty of friendship was concluded in August 1992 at the summit in Sofia, but an agreement settling Russia's small debt of $100 million was reached only in May 1995. The Polish president Lech Wałęsa and Yeltsin signed a new treaty on friendship and cooperation in Moscow in May 1992, but the mutual debt claims waited three years for resolution, when they were simply written off by agreement of both parties.

I had anticipated a gap between political and economic improvement—in which foreign policy would normally precede foreign economic policy—but did not expect it to be so striking. My concept was that once foreign policy had opened the door to better relations, trade and investment would follow. And the Russian Foreign Ministry did its job, proving there were no insurmountable obstacles preventing Eastern European countries from being the good friends of a democratic Russia and a bridge to the West. However, there were many internal political impediments to realizing economic change. A favorite canard of Russian neo-Soviet politicians is that the Eastern European countries cannot be friendly to Russia on a voluntary basis because they look to the West, not the East. When Russia was looking to the West too, which to my mind was in that country's best interest, the Eastern Europeans were not turning their backs on Moscow. On the contrary: they were politically ready to work together, benefiting from economic cooperation, which expanded as market reforms took hold.

In reality, it was Russia that turned its back on those countries, at the same time that it turned its back on the West and revived the image of NATO as an enemy. I remain convinced that sooner or later Russia will again start looking to the community of the most advanced European nations, where it belongs, and will be able to draw on the reservoir of goodwill embodied in the treaties we signed in the early 1990s.

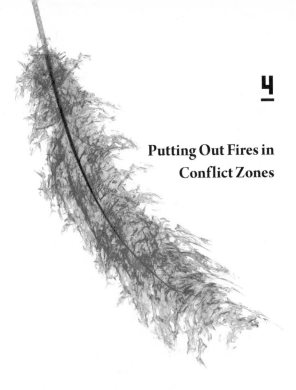

4

Putting Out Fires in Conflict Zones

AFTER THE BREAKUP OF THE SOVIET UNION we succeeded in preventing Russia from conducting military conflict with any of the newly independent states, but some of the latter could not achieve the same within their own territories.

Armenia was almost at war with Azerbaijan over a contested region. Georgia, Moldova, and Tajikistan had been embroiled in internal clashes. All those conflicts threatened to escalate into open warfare with potentially disastrous consequences for the broader regions bordering Russia. All conflicting parties wanted Russia's help in solving their problems.

Russia for its part had to take these troubles seriously. Until very recently, each of the newly independent states had been united under one national banner. Large numbers of ethnic Russians lived in these new states—and the negative consequences of internal conflicts in the former republics could well flow freely back into Russian territory. The Soviet republics had had no border guards or checkpoints between them, and after independence we had no time or resources to remedy that situation. In 1992 thousands of refugees entered Russia from Azerbaijan and Tajikistan. Criminal gangs that typically flourish in war-ridden zones also gained free passage into Russia. This inflow worsened the socioeconomic situation in neighboring Russian regions that had already not been particularly prosperous under Soviet rule and were now struggling to adjust to a new economic system. The humanitarian tragedies that always accompany civil war were perhaps an even greater problem. Russian public opinion was extremely sensitive to the carnage going on next door. It would have been suicidal for any government of Russia to remain above the fray.

These regional conflicts, closely tied to the destiny of Russia itself, were viewed differently by different political forces in Moscow. The opposition wanted Russia to take sides and stir up hostilities in accordance with the old imperial strategy of divide and govern. On the flip side some, including radical democrats, suggested isolationism. Both options were immoral and unrealistic. Russia was strong enough to influence those regions, but it could neither have control over the conflicts nor prevent the spread of their damaging spinoffs. It was in Russia's interest to help nations on its border to gain stability and preferably travel together with Russia on the path of reforms and integration into the community of democratic countries.

So, I had no choice but to dive into the muddy waters of ethnic and civil disputes. I sought to offer Russia's services as an "honest broker," while carefully exercising Russian political, diplomatic, and economic influence in trying to move the opposing parties in the civil wars toward a peaceful solution, or at least to an end to the killing.

Nagorno-Karabakh

At the beginning of 1992, the bloodiest and most internationalized conflict was well under way in Nagorno-Karabakh, a region in eastern Azerbaijan populated mostly by Armenians. They were fighting the Azerbaijanis, or Azeris, either to gain independence or to have the opportunity to join neighboring Armenia. The fighting, which had started in 1988, ramped up after Armenia and Azerbaijan became independent states. By 1992 the conflict threatened to escalate into open war between the two states and push hundreds of thousands of refugees from both sides into Russia. Further complicating these matters, both sides had influential lobbying groups in Moscow.

One of my first moves as foreign minister was to invite the foreign ministers of Armenia and Azerbaijan to Moscow and try to jump-start peace talks. The result was encouraging. In a joint communiqué issued on February

20, 1992, after a long and heated meeting, the foreign ministers of Armenia, Azerbaijan, and Russia called on the conflicting parties to immediately stop fighting and start peace negotiations.

On March 10, we met again in Brussels at a conference of the North Atlantic Cooperation Council, a forum for discussions between NATO and other European states, including the former Soviet republics, where we confirmed the joint communiqué of February 20.

Later that March, as the fighting continued, I decided to go to the Karabakh conflict zone to meet the leaders of the fighting forces face-to-face and learn more about the situation on the ground. We communicated with Armenia, Azerbaijan, and local commanders to get the permits for the trip, and on April 2, after a long flight with two or three stopovers, I finally found myself walking down the central avenue of Stepanakert, the capital of Nagorno-Karabakh, accompanied by my four bodyguards and ten fighters with machine guns from Nagorno-Karabakh's military force.

This was a new and shocking experience. I had never been in a war zone before.

The small town looked dead and haunted: deserted streets, houses turned into rubble. As we approached the ruins of the city hall, people started coming out of nowhere, their faces gray from deprivation and from hiding in underground shelters. One boy almost ran into me. He was apparently blinded by the bright sun and in a euphoric state. I asked him in Russian why he was so excited.

The boy looked at me with his big black eyes and shouted, "Since Kozyrev has arrived, there will be no bombing!"

I relayed the incident to the then leader of Nagorno-Karabakh, Artur Mkrtchyan, who met me in the city hall.

"What on earth justifies all this human suffering?" I asked him. "Isn't it high time to negotiate a cease-fire? I think I could help with that if you are interested."

He said that the Azeris would kill those civilians, including the children, if they could only lay their hands on the place. The only solution for Nagorno-Karabakh's people was to fight for their independence from Azerbaijan. And if Russia wanted to help those children, it should join the fight on the side of Armenian combatants. As a first step, Moscow should officially recognize the independence of Nagorno-Karabakh, thus setting an example for other members of the international community.

I appreciated this straightforward articulation of his position and decided to reciprocate in the same manner. Independence was not a realistic aim in the foreseeable future, I told him. To pursue it in an uncompromising way as an immediate and only target would mean endless war and suffering for the people on both sides of the firing line. The conflict could not be solved by military means alone. And Russia would not be drawn into the conflict as a participant.

The proposals I had to offer him had been coordinated with the foreign ministers of Armenia and Azerbaijan and backed by the Conference on Security and Co-operation in Europe (CSCE). They boiled down to suggesting that both sides undertake to resolve their long-standing differences through negotiations and in the meantime to stop the fighting.

Mkrtchyan was not prepared to countenance any proposal right away. Instead he introduced another argument to shore up his demands. For Armenians, he said, it was natural to consider Moscow an ally and protector because most Armenians, like most Russians, belonged to the Orthodox Christian faith. Armenia bordered Muslim Turkey and Azerbaijan. Its only Christian neighbor was Georgia, which had also sought Russia's help against Muslim invaders. A related historical argument was Nagorno-Karabakh's status as a Russian protectorate before the formation of the Soviet Union.

This kind of reasoning had considerable traction among the pro-Armenian community in Moscow, which included not only nationalists and imperialists but also outstanding figures in the Russian democratic movement such as Elena Bonner, the widow of Andrei Sakharov, and the ethnographer and activist Galina Starovoitova. Many Russians toyed with the idea of Nagorno-Karabakh becoming a protectorate, even though it was obvious that the moment Nagorno-Karabakh separated from Azerbaijan it would be absorbed into Armenia because the secessionists were closely intertwined with the power circles in that country.

I told Mkrtchyan that those historical ties between our countries should convince our friends to welcome Russia as an honest broker and listen to our advice, which was based on deep sympathy.

To be sure, back home I was also under pressure from the Azeri side. Moscow was a battleground of lobbies representing different parties to the ethnic conflicts raging in the former Soviet republics. In trying to draw Russia to their side they resorted to means beyond persuasion. My journalist friends told me there were unofficial prices for newspaper articles or TV programs arguing in favor of one side or the other.

At that meeting in Stepanakert's ruined city hall in the middle of the war zone I told Mkrtchyan that I fully sympathized with the quest of the Karabakh Armenians to be protected from any type of discrimination and to have autonomy. That right should be clearly recognized and probably even guaranteed by a third party, which could be the United Nations or a group of neighboring states, or even Russia alone. As to full independence for Nagorno-Karabakh, those who wanted it should be patient and wait to see whether the issue could be raised and resolved in a peaceful and democratic environment in accordance with the principles of the CSCE.

We spoke first in the presence of my assistants and armed men from the Armenian side. Everyone sat on half-broken chairs around a big rectangular table in a room with cracked windows and bullet-scarred walls. Mkrtchyan spoke very loudly, repeating his unrealistic demands and apparently turning a deaf ear to anything I said.

When he invited me to continue the discussion in his private office—a reasonably well-appointed room, in which we were served tea in small, elegant cups—his demeanor changed. We talked alone for almost an hour, with Artur mostly listening and asking questions in a soft voice. At the end I asked him outright whether he was in control of the situation politically and militarily. He looked startled, as if I had read his thoughts, but quickly pulled himself together. "Of course, I am in control. I am a political leader and the military forces abide my political decisions." After a pause, he added, "You know, these people are tough-minded fighters." Later I heard this kind of song in every conflict zone not only within the former Soviet Union but also in Serbia and Bosnia.

When we shook hands good-bye he gently pulled me aside, embraced me, and said quietly, "I promise to think over what you have said and will give you a better answer later." We agreed to stay in touch. I felt personally drawn to him and often recalled our meeting with hope.

A few weeks later Artur was killed.

There was more bloodshed on the battlefield, too, which was exacerbated by an influx of mercenaries and adventurists from Russia. The path for Armenian and Azerbaijan leaders to a cease-fire was crooked and strewn with obstacles. It was only gradually that they began to understand and accept the limits to what was realistically attainable. I held dozens of meetings in Yere-

van, the capital of Armenia, in Moscow, and in Azerbaijan—the other party
to the conflict, where I flew next. In one particularly hair-raising incident,
my helicopter had to evade ground fire that was directed at us while en route
from a point somewhere between the warring factions.

The first stop was Susa, a small township near the front line mostly
populated by Azeris. It was like rewatching the same horror movie: women
and children with frightened eyes emerging from cellars, rubble and broken
windows. Even the stories of atrocities sounded familiar, but this time the
Azeris were the victims.

My visit to the war zone helped me put together a detailed picture that
subsequently proved to be typical of conflicts all over the former Soviet space.
First, the conflict had deep roots in the long history of interethnic animosity,
which had been intensified by the Soviet habits of intolerance and the use
of force. Second, it could be solved only by the parties directly involved and
would require compromise. Third, the road to compromise was blocked lo-
cally by the military commanders who were running the show far more than
the politicians were. Fourth, those commanders tried their best to get support
and supplies from the Russian military units located in those republics, and
they occasionally succeeded.

All this strengthened my conviction that Moscow should not try to
repeat the Soviet attempt to interfere with an iron fist to pacify the conflicting parties. Intervention of that ilk had proved short-lived and ultimately ineffective for the Soviet Union. Following the same script would
be both practically unfeasible and politically disastrous for Russia. It would
be even worse for Russia to take up the cause of any one side. I reported
these conclusions to Yeltsin and publicly defended them in Moscow and
elsewhere.

Though nobody ever challenged them on rational grounds, my conclusions provided grist for the mills of the imperialists and the ethnic partisans,
who hated the concept of impartiality. They tried to portray it as equivalent
to abandoning Russia's "best friends," their clients. At the same time, they
insisted, without evidence, that the West was helping the opposite side. From
there it was a small step to conclude that Russian impartiality amounted to
nothing less than yielding to the West, and for this I was roundly attacked.
I was fortunate that my position as foreign minister enabled me to block
many—but as it turned out far from all—attempts to push through biased
decisions in the Kremlin and in the ranks of the Russian army to provide

military support to one side of a conflict or the other in order to radically change the balance of power.

From the conflict zone I flew to Baku, the capital of Azerbaijan. The religious argument was brought up again, though this time I was warned of the danger of the Armenian call for an Orthodox brotherhood in arms, of which the Azeris were fully aware. The Azeris pointed out that Russia had about 20 million Muslims, almost 20 percent of the population, and added that Moscow should also be careful not to alienate the Asian republics of the CIS with their predominantly Muslim populations. For the good of the broader region, everyone should strive to avoid anything resembling a Christian crusade so as to avoid provoking a militant Islamic response from an Islamic, but secularly governed, Turkey or from radical Iran.

Those were serious arguments, and I relayed them to Yeltsin and to the Russian journalist who accompanied me on my visit to Azerbaijan.

The talks in Baku were particularly tough. My hosts felt humiliated by defeat on the ground and planned revenge despite the chaotic political and economic situation in Azerbaijan itself. Warmongering had usurped governance.

Oddly enough, it was the leftover Soviet bureaucracy, so often a source of trouble in Russia, that appeared to be the main hope for stability and an eventually more reasonable approach to the Karabakh issue. As it happened, Heydar Aliyev, a tall, corpulent man with gray hair and stately manners soon took power in Azerbaijan. He was a veteran Soviet apparatchik and a former member of the leadership of the Communist Party of the Soviet Union, seasoned both in political maneuvering and grandstanding. Aliyev gradually but steadily consolidated control over the country. Step by step, he introduced more balance, restraint, and continuity into both the formulation and the execution of Azerbaijan's foreign policy.

Once Aliyev seemed to have cemented his power base, I invited him and Robert Kocharyan, then the leader of Nagorno-Karabakh and later president of Armenia, to talk face-to-face. They both chose Moscow as the best place for the meeting, which was to be strictly confidential. It was preceded by careful preparations, with the aim of avoiding the general rhetoric and recriminations that usually accompany meetings of conflicting parties so that the two leaders could get to the point as quickly as possible.

I held a brief fifteen-minute talk with each of them separately. Even in a private setting they played their roles perfectly, one presenting himself as a wise and serene political mogul and the other as a young, honest and straight-forward freedom fighter. The best dramatic actors I had seen in theaters were no more than pale shadows beside the real-life characters on display in that secret location in Moscow.

Then a protocol officer invited the two leaders to a tearoom, where we all met together. After a brief introduction I excused myself and left them alone. When their one-on-one meeting was over I again had a short talk with each of them separately. They declined to share much information about their discussion or to sign any document. Yet when I shook hands good-bye, both of them looked more than just formally grateful and more than diplomatically satisfied.

A temporary cessation of hostilities was declared but almost immediately violated, with each side blaming the other. This pattern of developments on the ground was repeated many times in the following years. And every time a cease-fire was violated, both sides redoubled their commitment to a military solution. The stumbling block to achieving a permanent cease-fire was the request by the conflicting parties for an international peacekeeping force to guarantee the cease-fire—a request I supported, but one that turned into a bone of contention between the West and me.

The Nagorno-Karabakh conflict was and is affected by broader international factors. The region has been burdened by centuries of fighting and rivalry for domination by outside powers. Competition for its oil resources and Islamic extremism cast a shadow over the area, stirring up anxiety and suspicion.

While Russia had an indispensable role to play in a region of vital interest to it, as a country, we could not try to keep Nagorno-Karabakh confined to our backyard or seek to exclude other countries from involvement, politically or economically. It would be both unrealistic and burdensome. Rather, the constructive involvement of and investment by the West could help stabilize the region and provide good economic partners. It was far better than our taking sole responsibility over an area of poverty and religious and political tensions on Russia's southern border.

Endorsing this more internationalized view, Russia first provided a limited number of peacekeepers to safeguard the cease-fire, and the CIS agreed to join the effort. Yet the contingent remained small. A larger force and a wider international effort were clearly required. We supported the parties to the conflict who wanted the UN Security Council to undertake the task. Yet the

United States and other Western countries thought that the problem should be addressed by the CSCE.

With the West unwilling to share the burden of peacekeeping, any concerted effort to solve the conflict was crippled. There was considerable diplomatic rivalry among the various countries that wanted to strengthen their influence in the region and score in public opinion as peacemakers. The conflicting parties exploited those divisions, playing outside powers against one another and extracting from them political and economic favors.

The Russian nationalists portrayed the diplomatic rivalry as proof that the Western countries wanted to push Russia out of the Transcaucasus in order to take over the oil fields on the Azeri shores of the Caspian Sea. On the other side of the coin, some Western strategists who saw nothing but the oil and geopolitical interests of the West started to accuse Russia of neoimperialism and argued for excluding Russia from the region. Both positions were dangerous and unrealistic.

I once arrived at a CSCE ministerial meeting only to learn that the Western diplomats had declined even to mention Russia and the CIS in the draft of the final document on the peace process in Karabakh. I spoke about the matter with some Western ministers, who should have been above such treachery. I reminded them that Russia had played a crucial diplomatic role in bringing the conflicting parties together to search for a peaceful solution and that the West had declined to authorize a UN peacekeeping force. Attempts to isolate Russia would only serve the interests of the Russian imperialists, who challenged the policy of partnership with the West.

There could be no consensus on the final document without a clear recognition of the positive role of Russia and the CIS in the Karabakh peace process. All other parts of the document had already been agreed on, and the Western delegations complained that I was creating the only impediment to a successful outcome of the conference. I pointed out that the adoption of an unfair document would be counterproductive for both the Karabakh peace process and the future of the CSCE. After some delay, a compromise text was adopted in which Russia and the CIS were properly mentioned.

A required multinational peacekeeping force arrived only in March 1995. The Russian-brokered permanent cease-fire held for years to come, and the peace talks between Armenia and Azerbaijan, mediated by the Organization for Security and Co-operation in Europe and Russia, continued. The points agreed on by the conflicting parties during the talks in 1992–94 are still the cornerstone to any peaceful settlement of the conflict.

Tajikistan

One of the most demanding hot spots was Tajikistan, which had imploded before the collapse of the USSR. The Tajik communist leader Rahmon Nabiyev refused to reform the government of his republic, and in doing so had isolated himself both from countrymen and from the general trend among Soviet republics. The heads of the local communist parties of neighboring Uzbekistan and Turkmenistan in 1991 managed to take the office of president of their respective countries through the ballot box. Once in office, both consolidated their power, largely by swapping Marxist slogans for nationalistic rhetoric. Next door in Kyrgyzstan, Askar Akayev, a liberal professor, won his presidential election and tried to introduce more liberal reforms.

Nabiyev's rule in Tajikistan ended in a dramatic confrontation. He had very limited coercive force without direct support from Gorbachev, who at that time controlled police and the army all over the Soviet Union. But the opposition felt encouraged by liberal pronouncements in Moscow. Thousands of people gathered in the main square of the capital city, Dushanbe, in the spring of 1992 to demand Nabiyev's resignation to be followed by free elections. The rally continued for days and eventually brought down not only the old ruler but also the very foundation of civil order and the last remnants of respect for the constitutional process.

I first flew to Dushanbe during the street protests. Meeting with the last Soviet head of the republic was like revisiting the Kremlin of the late Leonid Brezhnev. Nabiyev was fully convinced that he was the last bastion of Soviet rule, battling heroically to staunch the flood of irresponsibility and disorganization unleashed in Moscow thanks to Gorbachev's sloppy management. "There is no democratic movement with any roots or influence in the republic," he told me. "Those whom you know as Tajik democrats are intellectuals living in Moscow and publishing liberal articles in Russian newspapers. They have just come here recently to try to repeat what was done back there, ignoring the striking differences in the social and political environment. If, or rather when, I vacate power, they too would be swept away by totally different forces. What you see out there"—he pointed to the window that looked out on the square, boiling with an angry crowd—"is no more than a mob. They were stirred up by democrats, but are now already led by dark forces, in particular Muslim extremists sent and financed from abroad. That is who will run the show after the so-called democratization."

His diatribe ran together all the standard pretexts used by every communist bureaucrat unwilling to vacate his seat at the top. "Your problem," I thought, while listening to my host, "is that you are as outdated as the old Soviet limousine I took from the airport." The mention of Muslim extremists, though, was different from the standard leftover Soviet propaganda. I asked him to expand on this point a little more, but was again disappointed, as his information seemed distilled from the communist press. I also met with some leaders of the democratic movement. It was a breath of fresh air. We spoke the same language and dreamed the same dreams of a new, open, and dynamic Tajik society after liberation from Soviet orthodoxy.

Unfortunately, it soon became clear that those dreams of democracy would prove to be the furthest removed from reality of anything I heard during my first visit to Tajikistan. In 1992–93 I flew to that country almost ten times, significantly more often than to any other. And the gloom-and-doom prophecy of the old Soviet leader turned out to be the most accurate.

When I next arrived in Dushanbe, the large crowd I had previously seen in the main square seemed only a dim memory of a past golden age. The city had become a war zone. The airport had been seized by Russian troops to keep it in minimal operating order. There were fresh bullet tracks on the walls and machine-gun fire could be heard not far from where we landed.

I could not believe that the capital city of one of the former Soviet republics had become a battleground and I defiantly refused to go to the town in an armored personnel carrier offered by Russian troops. On my request, in the nearby garage, they found the old Soviet limo previously provided to me by the Soviet autocrat Nabiyev.

Tajikistan was descending into the chaos of civil war, and the process of disintegration and nonstop violence looked more and more like a repetition of what was happening in neighboring Afghanistan. Both countries lacked a central national authority recognized as legitimate by the many rival military commanders and politicians, all of whom only represented particular ethnic, regional, or clan interests. Those leaders were building up their own armies and forming unstable coalitions to fight for spheres of influence. Afghanistan was a major source of drugs, weapons, and other criminal traffic, which could be stopped from entering Russia only at the old Soviet border with Afghanistan. That border zone now belonged to Tajikistan, which was patently unable to control it.

Under such circumstances, it was Russia's responsibility to stabilize Tajikistan and, in the meantime, take control of its border with Afghanistan. Every provisional Tajik government asked Moscow to do so. On each visit to Tajikistan I would go to the border to inspect a checkpoint and talk to the servicemen. It was a real war zone. I witnessed more than one exchange of gunfire, saw fresh signs of fighting, and heard reports of casualties on both sides.

Once, while walking from one barracks to another in the territory of the Russian checkpoint, I overheard the sound of a piano accompanying a child's voice singing. A music class was under way in a small school a few hundred feet from the front line! From then on, I always went to schools to talk to the children and teachers, usually the wives of the officers. I admired those people. "Seeing you means we are not forgotten," a teacher told me.

On another occasion while at a checkpoint I received a radio communication from a stronghold about fifteen miles down the river dividing Afghanistan and Tajikistan. An Afghan commander was asking to see me to confirm an agreement he had negotiated recently with his Russian counterpart to stop fighting each other and join the effort against smugglers and terrorists. Agreements of this type were signed every now and then, covering different sections of the river and sometimes remaining in effect for a considerable time, thus saving lives. The commander was known to be influential over a large area, and an agreement with him was worth pursuing. I took a helicopter and flew to the meeting.

It was a breathtaking experience! The sunlight reflecting off the surface of the river directly beneath us made the scene surreally bright. Our course followed the blue ribbon below and threaded its way between the high mountain walls on either side. On the left was Tajik, on the right Afghan territory. I clearly saw one or two small Afghan villages and, every two to three miles, strongholds with artillery and antiaircraft guns sitting on the slopes.

"Don't worry, Mr. Minister, I fly this way once in a while and know every turn and altitude. So, it's safe enough," the pilot, a tiny man with a deep tan and the typical modest air of an old Russian soldier, said.

"I can see that you are a real master. We are moving as gracefully as those birds," I answered. "My question, though, is whether they"—I gestured toward the Afghan mountains—"know that we should be safe."

"They have a communication system. It is bad, but it works. Like today, we always inform them that our flights mean no harm, and they promise not to do any harm to us either. Of course, with these people one can never be sure of anything, but the much bigger risk comes from the Afghan and Tajik fighters, who might be on our side of river. There are groups that have just violated the border or are about to do so. They might not have any information about us, or they might be very angry with us. That's why I always keep the helicopter in the middle. And I prefer to use a light machine, like the one we are in now, rather than one of those heavy armor-plated monsters. They look threatening. But this 'butterfly' is all windows, all glass. They can see there are no weapons and only four people on board. So far so good."

That was as much assurance as he could offer, and he did so with a guilty smile.

The more demanding question, as my thoughts returned to the conflict, was this: Why not try to negotiate an agreement for joint control, or at least for relaxation of tensions along the border, not only with local commanders but also with whatever authority there was in Kabul, the Afghan capital? Russia had inherited the embassy there—an office building and two or three apartment houses occupying a block in a prestigious region of the city. An ambassador with a small staff could not negotiate much. They would need help at the political level to be recognized as different from representatives of the Soviet Union, the former enemy of today's Afghan authorities.

I asked my staff to start preparations for my visit to Kabul.

Trying to Get Help from Tajik Neighbor Afghanistan

There was one more reason for going to Afghanistan: rescuing the POWs (prisoners of war) who had been left behind in Afghanistan by the retreating Soviet army. According to different accounts, a few hundred remained. Returning them was an important humanitarian task that had been addressed by Soviet and then Russian diplomats and a couple of nongovernmental organizations.

In practice, there was little to nothing anyone could do. First of all, there was no entity, or perhaps too many, on the Afghan side to negotiate with. Two rivals, President Burhanuddin Rabbani and Prime Minister Gulbuddin Hekmatyar, headed the internationally recognized government. Each had his army, and occasionally they fought each other. When asked about the POWs, the government would say there was no single place where the prisoners were held. Rather, they were dispersed and held in custody by local commanders, who in turn would swap Russian for Afghan POWs, who, they claimed, were still being detained somewhere in Siberia. The Russian military and police flatly denied that claim.

Allegedly, some Afghan field commanders had exchanged a number of Russians for ransom money paid privately by their relatives and friends. Mostly, though, they claimed that no POWs remained in Afghanistan. According to them, the few Russians who survived had in the past two or three years voluntarily remained in Afghanistan, converted to Islam, and even changed their names. They had no interest in going back to Russia.

We did eventually succeed in negotiating the return of a few people to Moscow. Vice President Alexander Rutskoi welcomed them at the airport with lots of media present and claimed their return to be exclusively his personal achievement. In part I let him do it because I did not want to go to the ceremony. My intuition did not fail me. After Rutskoi had given the returning soldiers a fatherly embrace and almost shed a tear over their successful escape from prison, they informed the journalists on the scene that they had become faithful Muslims and wanted to go back to their new homeland, Afghanistan.

Nonetheless, the POW problem was front and center on the public radar and required extra effort, if only to be sure that everything possible was being done to resolve it. The Afghan government was aware of the political heat the issue generated and exploited it as much as possible to squeeze concessions out of us. Rabbani promised our ambassador that if I made an official visit to Kabul, my plane would carry back the remaining POWs, at least four people.

The first stop on our flight to Kabul was Tashkent, the capital of Uzbekistan. This country plays a key role in Central Asia. Ethnic Uzbeks constitute a majority in the northern regions of Tajikistan and Afghanistan, and in both countries, they form very influential communities. In Afghanistan there has always been a "Northern Alliance" of one form or another, a kind of state within a state with its own military forces armed with tanks, artillery, machine guns, and other material left behind by retreating Soviet troops. It was commonly believed that the Northern Alliance was receiving substantial support in money, ammunition, and spare parts from Uzbekistan and the other newly independent states.

In Tashkent, I had a private dinner with President Islam Karimov, who seemed to feel forgotten by Yeltsin and left to deal with regional challenges alone. That was partly true: the Russian president had no taste for diplomacy in the former Soviet space. He would not spend time seeing each head of a newly independent state privately, and preferred to meet them in a group at CIS summits, where he would spend extra time with the presidents of Ukraine and Kazakhstan.

This irritated the other republican leaders, especially Uzbekistan's president. He was actively competing for regional leadership and needed recognition from both the authorities and the media in Moscow.

I went out of my way to assure Karimov that Yeltsin did value relations with Uzbekistan, counted on the wisdom of its president, and stood ready to help overcome the problems posed by the turmoil in Tajikistan. We agreed that both Russia and Uzbekistan had a vital interest in stopping the war. I promised to coordinate our steps with him in the region and not to undertake anything that could damage Uzbek interests there. He assured me of reciprocity and of his commitment to respect the territorial integrity of Tajikistan. Although there were some lapses from that understanding on both sides, it proved indispensable in stabilizing the area.

Boarding the plane in Tashkent the next morning, I shared a memo I had received from our embassy with my chief bodyguard, Anatoly, and the pilot. The memo spelled out a specific warning: contrary to its usual route, on nearing the Kabul airport the plane should strictly avoid flying over the tallest mountain. That summit was now a stronghold of troops fighting our host, President Rabbani. Though we had cleared plans in advance with Rabbani's men, they were of course unable to coordinate with the opposition groups, and we risked being fired on.

A short while later I was awakened by shouts. I found I was lying on a huge sack of meal, where I had been solicitously covered with a piece of sacking. The big cargo plane was full of meal sacks, which we were carrying as humanitarian aid to Afghanistan. The rest of my party—two or three diplomats and the same number of journalists, who had been selected by lottery—were sitting on the bags at the back of the aircraft. From my privileged position in the corner of the pilot's cabin I saw the white face of the captain and my chief security officer shouting into his ear and emphatically pointing to something out the window. I jumped up and looked out. We were right over the tall mountain, and a number of Afghan fighters had begun firing their machine guns in our direction and uncovering green bags that looked suspiciously like Stinger antiaircraft missile holders.

"That used to be our stronghold on this summit. They cannot shoot at us!" the pilot kept repeating, his gaze fixed on those Afghan fighters in bewilderment.

"We have no troops in Afghanistan anymore, you idiot!" Anatoly shouted.

"Captain, just do something before they shoot us down!" I said as loudly and as forcefully as I could. "Remember the memo: Hekmatyar's men occupy the positions our troops used to have."

In a moment he became fully alert. As he told us later, he hadn't paid much attention to the memo. What could diplomats add to his experience of years flying back and forth from Afghanistan under wartime conditions? Yet under stress, he acted brilliantly. He was a great pilot. The plane went down like a rock, escaping fire, and landed safely. The Afghan officials welcoming us on the ground could hardly conceal their stunned amazement at that dramatic arrival. I vowed always to read embassy cables carefully in the future.

The Russian embassy was in surprisingly good condition, in contrast to the partially destroyed city. There were only a few other embassies in Kabul, and the number of those was shrinking daily as fighting inside and around the city intensified. I met briefly with the embassy staff and was deeply impressed by the prevailing businesslike mood, similar to that of the border guards. Then I went to the presidential palace to see Rabbani.

The streets were dirty and bumpy, surrounded by one- or two-story buildings, most of them damaged by artillery and gunfire. They were full of people, and the place looked like any poor Asian township. One strikingly different feature, though, was the presence of as many armed men as street merchants.

"These central streets are fairly safe," the ambassador was saying as we slowly moved along, followed by curious looks. "We are lucky to have this old but still good working Mercedes. It is armor-plated, and the windows are bulletproof. So far, thank the Lord, we have never been fired on in the car."

At that very moment through the window of the car I caught sight of a boy about twelve or thirteen years old sitting on the ground, forgotten in the middle of the multitude. He was holding an antitank grenade rifle that he had just loaded with a grenade. He raised his eyes with a bored expression that immediately changed when he spotted the shiny Mercedes in the middle of the dusty road, with no other cars in sight. The boy jumped up and, standing on his feet, made a special effort to mount the weapon on his shoulder and point it at the car. For a second our eyes met, and I read in his the simple joy of being a mischief maker able for a moment to play with the toys of older kids and imitating them.

Could he have pulled the trigger? Yes. Why didn't he? Nobody knows.

As the car passed, the boy apparently forgot about it, put the rifle on the ground, and started to look around for somebody. Soon I lost sight of him.

"Did you see the little rascal?" I asked my bodyguard, who was in the front seat.

"Yes. I was hoping you'd missed it. There was nothing I could have done. I noticed him too late, when the rifle was already on his shoulder. My first impulse was to jump out of the car and pull the weapon from his hands, but then I realized it would be too risky. He could have pulled the trigger out of fear of being punished."

"I cannot agree more. I am sure it was best to keep quiet. Do you think we would have been protected by the armor of the car?"

"No way. This projectile easily penetrates any tank's armor plates and burns everything inside with a hell of a fire." I wondered later whether the child had grown up to join the Taliban or al-Qaeda, or whether perhaps his choices took him to the other side, to join the forces fighting alongside the American coalition.

President Rabbani looked and spoke more like a university professor than a head of state or a politician. He was soft-spoken, thoughtful, and forthcoming. This was particularly striking in that chaotic and war-dominated environment. He promised to help stabilize the situation in Tajikistan and reiterated his agreement to free four POWs that afternoon.

My afternoon meeting with Prime Minister Hekmatyar yielded the same promises and assurances. His was a different character: pushy, authoritarian, combat-oriented. En route to his mountain stronghold, some distance from the city, we witnessed explosions of artillery projectiles on a hillside quite near our car. The prime minister said that unfortunately, accidental shooting was not rare in Afghanistan ever since the Soviet invasion. The retreating Soviet army had left ample weaponry, and many more people now knew how to use it.

We went directly to the airport from the meeting with Hekmatyar, and by five o'clock were ready to take off. The Afghan officials said they expected the POWs to show up at any minute. They asked our pardon for the inconvenience and thanked us for our understanding, attributing the delay to the poor road conditions. They repeated these polite remarks every ten minutes. Then a messenger from Rabbani came to inform us that the four POWs were on their way to the airport and that the president's commitment to let them go with me was ironclad.

At 6:30 p.m. the pilot informed us that if the plane did not take off right away, it would be too dark to risk the flight. I decided to stay overnight in Kabul and depart early the next morning. The Afghan officials swore that the POWs would certainly be at the airport by that time. All those promises proved hollow. At noon the next day our plane took off with no POWs on board. And nothing changed dramatically on the Tajik border. The Afghan leaders I met either were liars or could not deliver—probably both.

I was deeply concerned by what I had seen in Afghanistan. In meetings with my American counterparts, I repeatedly urged them not to abandon the country they had helped resist the Soviet intervention. There were too many armed extremists and too much anxiety left in the region after the Soviet defeat and the subsequent withdrawal of American support. In my speech at the 47th Session of the UN General Assembly in September 1992, I urged that the UN address the Afghan situation. My message fell on deaf ears. The following year at the 48th Session I said in relation to Afghanistan that the UN could not "leave millions of people who live there face-to-face with the epidemic of ethnic, clan, and religious extremism." But it would take the tragic events of September 11, 2001, to awaken the international community to the dangers brewing there.

Yet while Russia was not able to act alone in Afghanistan, we had no excuse for playing a passive role in Tajikistan.

Back to Tajikistan

The new leader of Tajikistan, Emomali Rahmonov, who later took over in Dushanbe and changed his Russified second name to the more Tajik sounding Rahmon, often told me that my visit to Kabul was very helpful. He also went there to see Rabbani and returned with many promises. He insisted that he would not have had as warm a reception had the Afghan president not remembered me as a "good friend." At that time Rahmonov had very limited, if any, political experience. I think in Afghanistan we both learned a lesson.

I first met Emomali Rahmonov in Kuliab, an important trade and administrative center in a region south of Dushanbe. I went there to see a Russian military camp that had found itself in the middle of the fighting. Rahmonov had made his name as the young and successful director of a big collective farm and had become known more recently as a political activist advocating the restoration of law and order, which, he said, was his best memory of Soviet times. Rahmonov held somewhat conflicting views of the extremists fighting in his land, describing them both as terrorists who used primitive means to kill people—catapults, Molotov cocktails, boulders—and as "Islamists" who enjoyed unimpeded access to sophisticated weaponry and support from foreign countries. Most often he seemed to favor the second view, which was endorsed by the Russian troops who also detected the hand of foreign instructors and mercenaries, allegedly Wahhabis with roots in Saudi Arabia, to whom they attributed the horrible atrocities being committed against POWs and civilians.

Rahmonov told me a story that I had already heard from Russian officers, about one Sangak Sofarov. It sounded like the fairy tale about a hero who comes out of nowhere to save his country from a dragon. The dragon, meaning the Islamists, also came out of nowhere, as nobody could clearly say what their origin was and who exactly their supporters and suppliers abroad were.

Later I learned that Sangak and his aides had spent years in jail on criminal charges. They claimed to be political prisoners who had been freed when the previous regime fell. Sangak established a populist movement advocating the brotherhood and equality of the Tajik people and the reunification of Tajikistan with Russia.

In that war-torn country, this simplistic but nostalgically reassuring message, combined with Sangak's demonstrated ability to fight and win, quickly earned him both popular support and the sympathy of the Russian military. At that moment, Sangak's forces had just started to beat back the Islamist forces. It seemed they would finally squeeze them out of the country altogether and into the territory of Afghanistan.

I agreed with Rahmonov's suggestion that we should go to an area of intense fighting to get a feeling for what was happening on the ground. In fifteen minutes, our helicopter landed not far from a village, and from there we went in an old and noisy Soviet-made military jeep. I asked the driver to stop at several points so that I could speak with people on the road, a way of ensuring that I heard from a cross-section of the population and not just a selected group of representatives.

I heard the same story from all sides: the Islamists, who insisted on a strict interpretation and implementation of Sharia law, had imposed a reign of terror. All were unanimous in their admiration for "Grandpa Sangak," as everyone called him.

We passed a couple of young girls, about the age of my daughter and wearing the same Soviet school uniforms. They were walking along the street, chatting and giggling, seemingly oblivious to the fresh signs of killing and fighting all around them. They were a little scared at being stopped by two cars with half a dozen armed men but calmed down when they saw the Russian uniforms. I approached them alone and asked how life under the previous regime had been. "You mean, under the Islamists?" they queried, and said it had been just awful. They had been told to stay home and to follow rules considered outdated and too strict "even by Grandmother's standards." Their mothers, the girls went on, were also afraid that they would be locked up in their homes and compelled to live "wrapped up in black."

"Today," they reported, interrupting each other, "our parents said that it is safe to wear these skirts and to go to school again. All that is thanks to Grandpa Sangak. He is so sweet. We want to be with the Soviet Union, with Russia."

"Grandpa Sangak" came to greet us at the train station, a sturdily built man in his late sixties with long gray hair and a resolute manner. He expressed deep gratitude for the "special honor" of meeting me and for the "indispensable help" of the Russian troops in "restoring law and order." I noticed that he spoke remarkably good Russian, with almost no accent or grammatical errors. He introduced himself as a former teacher and political dissident.

Rahmonov addressed him with respect, adopting the Asian formulations a younger man would use in the presence of a wise patriarch. Sangak recommended Rahmonov to me as a "gifted and promising young man." He was sure that the liberation from the "Islamists' intervention" was within reach and spoke of his plans to restore the country and as much as possible the Soviet Union. Later, Rahmonov described Sangak as a local commander who had become a symbol of the people's desire to get rid of Islamists rather than as a political figure.

I never saw Sangak again. His "liberation army" was growing fast and winning one battle after another. But soon after the war was basically over, Sangak was killed under unclear circumstances—as rumor had it, in his headquarters by his own aide.

Soon thereafter Rahmonov led the liberation forces to final victory and went to Dushanbe as a national leader. His ties to the Russian military commanders during all that time were very strong. He became a personal friend of the Russian defense minister, Pavel Grachev, who visited Tajikistan right after I left to see "the rising star from a collective farm." He shared my assessment that there was no alternative candidate for national leadership able to unite the country.

The next time I visited Tajikistan it was a noticeably different place. People on the streets looked more relaxed and occupied with their normal affairs. The old Soviet parliament—the only legitimate power structure on a national scale, recognized as such even by the opposition, if only because there was nothing else—was able to meet in the central city hall. That had not been possible for months for the simple reason that the deputies were afraid to travel to the capital. They overwhelmingly voted Rahmonov into power and called for preparation for new elections.

From then on, the main concern was to persuade Rahmonov to move gradually from authoritarian rule, perhaps necessary in wartime, to a normal political process and eventually to national reconciliation. About a year, later talks between the government and the opposition started. Rahmonov won the popular vote and became president of a country with a political system not much different from that of its Central Asian autocratic neighbors.

Yeltsin did not appear to follow events in Tajikistan closely, though Grachev and I regularly reported to him on what we were doing and hoping to attain. It took us some effort to persuade the president to give Rahmonov a short audience during a CIS conference, after which more cordiality was evident. Rahmonov, much like the Belarusian leader Alexander Lukashenko, another young newcomer to the club of post-Soviet heads of state, intuitively found a way to win Yeltsin's heart. They treated him almost as Rahmonov had treated Sangak Safarov, referring to him respectfully as "father" in private.

Moldova and Georgia

While walking through a Russian forward post on the Tajik–Afghan border one day in April 1992, I overheard news from Russia on a local radio station that made me even more nervous than being in a war zone. Unable to reach

Yeltsin by phone, I sent him a message through the military communication network. I then asked my aides to prepare the jet to fly from Dushanbe directly to Kishinev, the capital of Moldova. The matter was urgent.

According to the news reports, Vice President Alexander Rutskoi had recently visited Transnistria, a region in the Republic of Moldova with a predominantly Russian population. During his visit, he had called on, even ordered, the Fourteenth Army of Russia, which was stationed there, to fight on the side of the separatist government of a self-proclaimed Russian Transnistrian Socialist Republic.

I defined my mission in Moldova as firefighting. Above all, it was vitally important to persuade the troops to stay in their barracks and to remain neutral and out of politics. We also had to try to push the parties involved in the local conflict toward settling their differences peacefully and in a way that respected both the rights of the Russian population and the integrity of the Moldovan state.

In Kishinev, I had a brief, tense discussion with top government officials. I told them that despite the difference in emphasis and tone between Rutskoi and me, the message we both carried was clear: Transnistria, which was mostly populated by Russians, should be given real autonomy. The use of Moldovan armed or police forces to install direct control by the central government had to be officially rejected and previous attempts to do so deplored. The officials with whom we spoke basically agreed to these points but couched their acceptance in somewhat ambiguous terms.

The nationalist government of Moldova was not prepared to part with the simplistic idea that it had a right to establish absolute rule everywhere and by any means since it had won the elections.

Most of the Moldovan elite were obsessed with the desire to prove their independence from Moscow. If they had to have an ally, it should be Romania, a Western neighbor that spoke the same language. Had Romania been a highly developed country, Moldova would doubtlessly have pushed hard for a merger. But after the new Moldovan leaders visited their Western brother, they cooled on the idea. "That is not the West we have dreamed of," one of them told me. "We would rather stay independent."

The difficult talks in Kishinev were downright reasonable compared to what awaited me in Tiraspol, the largest city and administrative center of Transnistria.

As our helicopter approached the airport, what I saw out the window alerted me instantly. The main square was full of people waving Soviet red flags. They were mostly women—angry women, I was told when we landed.

My small entourage—two assistants and two bodyguards—was met by a platoon of soldiers, headed by a colonel, with suspicious looks and a bare minimum of official courtesy. The colonel introduced himself as the acting commander of the Soviet Fourteenth Army, then said it was not the best of times to come to Tiraspol because of high tensions. He could probably manage to keep us safe in the airport for about half an hour while we waited for the representatives of the government of Transnistria to arrive for a talk. After that, he thought, it would be better for us to leave.

"Thank you for coming to meet me, officer," I said, controlling my voice. "Now listen carefully to my order. You are to summon the officers of the Russian—remember to say it loud and clear, the *Russian* Fourteenth Army— to the club in one hour's time to have a meeting with the minister of the Russian government with extraordinary powers from the president of Russia. You will also telephone Mr. Smirnov, the so-called president of the so-called Transnistrian Socialist Republic, and tell him to wait for me somewhere near the Russian army's headquarters. I will receive him after the meeting with the officers. Is that understood?

"Now I will go to the square and talk to the people there. It seems that the local chiefs are looking for trouble—big trouble, Goddamn it!" These last words I addressed to my entourage, but loudly enough that the officer could hear them.

"Roger, sir. Everything will be done, sir," the officer said, and saluted.

It took twenty minutes to drive to the center of the city. I got out of the car a few steps from the crowd. There I spotted the colonel speaking agitatedly with my chief of security.

"He is a good man," Viktor said, taking me aside so that nobody could hear us. "He made the phone call from his car. They are deeply sorry. They will do as you say, but they strongly advise, indeed beg you, not to go to this rally. There are about four hundred women here. Many of them are angry. A few days ago, Rutskoi told them that you and the other democrats in Moscow had betrayed them. It is an extremely dangerous situation. Mobs like this can easily become aggressive. If that happened, we would not be able to do anything."

"I know. Wait for me here. I will just talk to them. Otherwise those red-brown bastards"—communists and Nazis—"both here and in Moscow will think they can scare me." I replied.

"Of course. We will go with you." Viktor said in his soft voice and with his usual friendly smile, but with ironclad resolve. We had first met in the besieged Russian White House. Viktor, a seasoned KGB officer, had voluntarily gone there to show support, and we had since become friends.

The sea of women parted, clearing a path for us. They were impressed by the very fact of my coming there. At the same time, I felt the electric sensation of prejudice and hatred ready to discharge in an unpredictable way. An older woman in the crowd shouted out to me. "Why have you come? Why are you walking along with no machine-gun-armed bodyguards like Rutskoi had a few days ago? Do you think you are welcome here?"

Like many in the crowd, the woman was brandishing a pole that resembled a spear, to which a red flag was attached. Viktor was following her every move. We were all familiar with the communist hoodlums' habit of using flagpoles as weapons.

I was desperately thinking of an example to follow. In *Doctor Zhivago* an official lecturing a mob was killed. "Let he who is without sin cast the first stone." The frayed Gospel passage from a book I had accidentally received in a swap as a teen had always stayed in my mind, just like Zhivago. "Yes, say something dramatic first, and then reason with them if you want to stay alive," an inner voice told me.

I jumped up onto the four-foot-high podium, gently but resolutely pushing aside an agitator. I gathered as much air in my lungs as possible and tried my best to make my voice heard by everyone.

"Women, most of you are mothers. I challenge anyone of you who is ready to send your children to fight in a fratricidal war to raise your hand now!"

For a moment they seemed startled. Everyone was looking around to see the result of the vote. No hand went up. The same woman who had addressed me with the questions interrupted the silence, her voice less hysterical, but still excited: "Girls, listen, girls! What are we doing really? Let's listen to him. He has a point."

Expressions changed. Aggression and rage were giving way to soul-searching seriousness and attention. All eyes were on me.

"I am not alone on this trip. I have brought a delegation from Moscow to Transnistria. The experts will work to prepare proposals that will help you." I knew that the provincial people were afraid of being forgotten and would be relieved at not having to undertake radical actions while the experts were busy working on their problems. "I have come to this square because it is important for me as a special representative of Russia to see you and to know what you are thinking. As for guards, I have plenty of them, but I've left them out there. They are waiting to accompany me to the front line. I don't need them here to talk to ladies. So please, feel free to talk to me. You—yes, you, Grandmother! Tell me what we should do for you. Don't everyone speak at once! I won't be able to answer everybody at once. Let the grandmother speak!"

My idea was to break up the crowd and remind the women that they were not a mob but individuals. I also knew they would show a degree of respect to an older person and quiet down enough to let her speak.

The older woman hesitated out of shyness and appeared to be collecting her thoughts. Then, encouraged by her neighbors, she began by saying she was impressed that the foreign minister would come from Moscow to listen to her and other simple ordinary people. Getting more and more emotional, she said that nobody wanted hatred and war, and ended by expressing the hope that I would help restore the peace.

The activists in the crowd didn't like that. They began shouting that Moscow had abandoned the Russians in Transnistria and that Russia should intervene to crack down on those bloody Moldovans. But the mood of the women had changed. More wanted to speak, and other voices called for silence so that they could be heard.

One of them mentioned her son and expressed concern that he might be going to war and be killed. By then I felt that the crowd was prepared to listen to me, and I took advantage of it.

"Thank you, ladies! I have learned a lot! I see how you feel. My mother, an ordinary schoolteacher, feels and speaks the same way back home. The person who just referred to her son said what is on everybody's mind. The Russian mother has spoken! All politicians must heed this. We, the Russian government, will make them listen, whoever they are, in Kishinev or elsewhere. I promise you that. Just give me a mandate to act. Please, raise your hand, anyone who doesn't want their Russian boys, including those Russian boys who serve in the Russian Fourteenth Army, to be pawns in a fratricidal war!

"Which of you is prepared to let us stop the warmongers on both sides, if need be by using the Fourteenth Army to keep them apart? Who wants the irresponsible politicians to be stopped? In a word, raise your hands, those who want peace now!"

The improvised vote was unanimous.

"OK—it's clear. I will tell Yeltsin and the government back in Moscow. We will not let you down or leave you alone with your problems. Your problems are our problems. Your will is our will. I will tell the officers of the Russian Fourteenth Army now, and they will act resolutely as a peacekeeping force. In accordance with your mandate I will also have a very tough talk with the leaders on both sides of this conflict. I had one yesterday in Kishinev. I am going there again after the meetings here. My message to all of them is crystal clear: they have no choice but to reject the violence altogether and start negotiations for peace. In this they can count on Russian help. Otherwise they will face Russian anger!

"Thank you! God bless you, our mothers and sisters!"

Leaving, I ran the same gauntlet on which I had entered, but this time accompanied by applause and smiling faces.

News about the outcome of the meeting went before me, clearing my way. It was a vitally important victory for my authority and probably my life.

I knew, though, that one more political battle still lay ahead, a battle for hundreds of souls witnessed by hundreds of eyes. I needed to bring the officers on side, turning the Fourteenth Army from a dangerously destabilized potential combatant in a civil war into a stable and evenhanded peacekeeping force.

That could not be achieved by raising my voice. Tough talk had worked with the colonel, who happened to be a sympathizer and just needed confirmation that the democrats could assert themselves if need be. But the officers were at a crossroads and had to choose sides. They were dangerously close to a civil war—and worse. The Soviet Fourteenth Army was equipped to play a strategic role in case of conflict between the Soviet Union and NATO. Its mission was to push through and fight in West Germany. This amount of power, had it fallen into the hands of neo-Soviet imperialists, would have been sufficient to threaten neighboring Romania (Russian communists were accusing that country of wanting to annex Moldova) and Ukraine (branded by communists as the major troublemaker responsible for breaking apart the Soviet Union).

The good colonel met me when I emerged from the human gauntlet on the square. An intelligent man in his forties, he was making every effort to calm his subordinates while his commander, a two-star general, was in Moscow. With limited and irregular financing from Russia, he was dependent on the local leaders of the minority Russian enclave to feed his troops. The lack of guidance from Moscow, compounded by a weakened chain of command, meant that unusual decision-making powers now rested with a cadre of mid-ranking officers normally responsible for helping commanders of large units to keep morale up and address administrative issues.

When we entered the Fourteenth Army officers' club, the acting commander ordered, "All rise! Attention!" The officers got to their feet somewhat slowly. Expressions of exhaustion, uncertainty, and irritation showed on their faces—but also sharp interest. This was their second political meeting in a week. Rutskoi had just told them, in effect, that I and the other young democrats in Moscow were cowardly traitors. Now the devil had dared to come and showed no fear—and he insisted on talking to them, to the officers, rather than to the commander alone. What would he say?

I decided to lean in.

"Officers, I know what kind of lies my political opponents have told you about me and the democrats in Moscow. They say that we betrayed the Soviet Union, the state you swore an oath to, and now are betraying Russians in the newly independent states, in particular in Moldova. You think it is true."

The audience burst into an uproar. The reaction was both mixed and emotional.

"OK. Some of you think it is true. Or perhaps, you don't think exactly that way but you have doubts. The problem we face here in Transnistria illustrates the trouble we had in the Soviet Union. These types of interethnic conflicts have been with us all along, but they were like water under a layer of ice. That ice was the fear of repression from Moscow. That's exactly the remedy our critics offer again, and now they want you to scare everyone back to the collapsed system. And what if people resist? Would you fire on them?

"They say that you have to protect the Russians here who are fighting against the Moldovan police on the other side of the river. And what about the Russians living in Kishinev and elsewhere in Moldova? What if they become the scapegoat for your actions? Will you occupy the whole country? Every step will mean more bloodshed in a fratricidal war. There are no easy answers to complex problems. There are no military solutions to political issues of this kind."

I could see that the majority of them were receptive to this thinking. They recognized what should not be done, but they also could not just turn aside from events, and they did not know what to do.

I went on: "You could and should protect Russians here. But there is only one way to do it: by playing a peacekeeping role. That means staying between the conflicting forces and ensuring that they do not violate the dividing line. For that you have to be as sober-minded and evenhanded as possible. I am doing my job. I just had a tough talk in Kishinev; they are on notice that we won't tolerate the use of force in Transnistria. We will also help the parties negotiate an arrangement.

"First there must be a permanent cease-fire, which you will guard, then a more permanent and substantive political agreement. The Moldovans must agree that Transnistria is to be autonomous enough to satisfy the need for self-rule of the Russian and Ukrainian population: a local legislature, Russian-language schools and newspapers, and so forth. The Transnistrians in turn must respect the territorial integrity of Moldova. Both sides should learn to settle their differences through dialogue and compromise, without resorting to violence. The politicians must prove they know how to do their job, rather than ask the army to do their dirty work for them. The democratic government in Russia asks you to stay calm and responsible. We won't leave you alone. You are Russian officers, and we are proud of you."

During the question period I gave them the basics of the reforms in Russia and the situation in the other newly independent states.

One question was direct and painful: What did I think about Rutskoi and his ideas? The vice president was a very emotional man, I responded. He saw people's problems and wanted to help in his own way. And the same was true of me. I was deeply moved too, but as a professional diplomat I could not be guided only by emotions. Just like military officers, politicians and diplomats had to stay cool and look for solutions even in the most difficult circumstances and even under fire. Whatever differences exist, I told them, we would discuss them in Moscow and follow the policies of the democratically elected president. Understand that what I am saying to you is exactly in accordance with this line.

The expression on most of the men's faces changed. As men of discipline and duty to the state, they appreciated this answer.

I believe that was the turning point for the Fourteenth Army. It escaped the real danger of becoming an uncontrolled and destructive bull in the china shop of Eastern Europe. Most important, it was not drawn into the conflict as a direct participant. In practice the army has remained more or less neutral since then, performing peacekeeping duties, separating the fighters of the two conflicting parties.

After the meeting with the officers of the Fourteenth Army, I went to see the actual battle zone. It was supposedly the site where the initial clashes between the Moldovan police and the local militia had occurred. By now the police had been squeezed out to the northern, Moldovan side of the river that stretched out in front of us.

Our car stopped on the corner of a small street. Accompanied by Viktor, my security chief, I left the main party and stepped into an open space to see the square before us.

At that moment Viktor suddenly pushed me back so strongly I struggled to stay on my feet. At the same time, I heard a tiny whistle near my ear and a split second later the sound of a gunshot, followed by two or three more. Both the local authorities and the Russian officers had said there were still enemy snipers in different parts of the city shooting at the Transnistrian militia. Legend had it that there were female snipers, a group that sought revenge for the Soviet occupation of the Baltic states by traveling from one conflict zone to another to fight against the forces that wanted to re-create the Soviet Union. Did I look like a militiaman?

This near escape was just a warning. Right after that I was to meet a hero of the other side, the separatist leader of breakaway Transnistria, Igor Smirnov.

According to journalists, Smirnov and the secession movement he led were part of an unfolding strategy forged by top leaders of the Communist Party and the Soviet KGB during the collapse of the Soviet Union. According to this strategy, the KGB would stir up local minorities in the various non-Russian republics in order to weaken the newly formed governments. The goal was to encourage certain enclaves seeking to break away from their new states and eventually seeking to join politically with Russia for protection.

Transnistria, a Moldovan region that had a considerable Russian and Ukrainian population, was a key target. Abkhazia, a region in Georgia with a majority of ethnic minority Abkhazians, also fit the strategy well. If Moldova and Georgia wished to leave the Soviet Union, according to the logic of this strategy, then they should expect the same kind of secessionist threat to their own integrity. The Soviet leadership regarded this strategy as an effort to restore the Union, which Gorbachev termed the "Great power built over centuries," a euphemism many journalists interpreted bluntly as the Russian Empire. In practice, it both scared the republics and incited separatists, thus contributing in two ways to the disintegration of the union.

The strategy worked all too well. In response to demands for independence by extremist regional leaders, the ultranationalists in the republican capitals responded by rolling back autonomy for the region and using brute force against the agitators, with collateral damage to the civilian population. That response played into the hands of the separatists, who organized militias and eventually their own armies, established political and military control over the would-be independent region, and ultimately established populist regimes of a neo-Soviet character, but based in local nationalism.

Many democrats believed that Igor Smirnov and Vladislav Ardzinba had been recruited to lead the separatist movements in Moldova and Abkhazia, respectively. Both men originated from outside these regions, and one could only wonder what drew them to the problems of the local population, let alone how they managed to generate so much support. Their political agendas were strikingly similar. Prior to the collapse of the Soviet Union, they first demanded a status equivalent to that of the USSR's constituent republics. Once the union collapsed, they demanded independence as a first step toward rejoining Russia. They both had close ties with Russian imperialists who declared that the United States and NATO were responsible for the breakup of the Soviet Union and had set up puppet governments in Moldova and Georgia. These puppet states, they claimed, were charged with destroying the pro-Russian rebellions of secession in order to eliminate any chance for the re-creation of a Greater Russia.

The secessionists were particularly suspicious of the Georgian leader Eduard Shevardnadze, even though he rose to the post of president by leading the forces that overthrew the Georgian ultranationalist government of Zviad Gamsakhurdia, which was responsible for the police brutality in Abkhazia. Clearly, the hard-liners from the Soviet- and then the Russian military-industrial complex never forgave him for cooperating with the United States as the Soviet foreign minister.

Smirnov and Ardzinba actively courted the militarists in Russia, who helped the two men to build up their own security and military forces. Media accounts at the time suspected incredible corruption surrounding the ties between the separatist leaders and their supporters in Moscow, ranging from smuggling to kickbacks on government procurement, to theft of assistance funding.

Unfortunately, the meeting with Igor Smirnov confirmed every expectation I had of him based on his background and sources of support. His presentation was vague on acceptable terms of a possible settlement, and rich in nationalist demagoguery. I encountered the same performance with Ardzinda when I visited Abkhazia.

When both men realized that Russia would not fight on their side, agreements were reached on the permanent cessation of hostilities. An agreement on principles of potential settlement in Transnistria was signed in Moscow July 21, 1992, by the presidents of Russia and Moldova. The key elements were that the integrity of the titular state must be maintained, and that the rights of the local population should be protected and guaranteed by a large degree of political and cultural autonomy. The Russian troops would police the cease-fire under conditions of strict neutrality. These principals could also work for Abkhazia.

The governments in Kishinev and Tbilisi, which had started from a position of aggressive anti-Russian nationalism, began moving toward a more realistic position. But in response to such openings, both Smirnov and Ardzinba pushed for more and more autonomy, all the way up to full independence. The state authorities would then revert back to unrealistic demands. Thus, there was no sustained effort at real accommodation. These tit-for-tat moves ended up accomplishing nothing.

In 2008 Russia launched an armed incursion into Georgia and recognized the independence of Abkhazia and another breakaway enclave, South Ossetia, but the overwhelming majority of the members of the international community, including all the other CIS countries, did not follow suit. To this day, Moldova and its Transnistria region remain mired in a decades-long conflict.

Belgrade: Facing Milošević and War Crimes

The nightmare scenario of ethnic cleansing and other war crimes in the former Yugoslavia, which had been raging since the spring of 1991, preyed on my mind in connection with the breakup of the Soviet Union.

The origins of the crisis in Yugoslavia looked very similar to the situation in the Soviet Union. Yugoslavia was a federation of socialist republics. The death of Josip Tito, the founder and popular leader of the Yugoslav state, in 1980 had led to a greater devolution of power from the federal republic to the constituent republics and autonomous provinces, according to Yugoslavia's constitution. The long-ruling Soviet leader Leonid Brezhnev had also passed away in 1980, allowing his successors to begin a process of slow liberalization of the Soviet Union that paved the way for the more radical events of 1991. With the slow demise of communist authority at the end of the 1980s, both the Soviet Union and Yugoslavia began looking toward democratic reforms. But at this juncture, the two countries went in opposite directions.

As the popular leader of Russia, the major Soviet republic, Yeltsin led resistance to the imperialist-minded coup plotters and led a peaceful transition of the Soviet Union to the CIS.

In contrast in Yugoslavia the Serbian president Slobodan Milošević, who harbored ultranationalist and neocommunist aspirations, took over the central government in Belgrade and, with it, the military and intelligence agencies of the federation. After the republics of Slovenia, Bosnia and Herzegovina, and Croatia declared independence, Belgrade launched armed interventions to punish them. For a long time, the Belgrade regime pursued its policy of dismembering Bosnia-Herzegovina and undermining Croatia by carving out Serbian enclaves.

Russia made the decision to recognize the former Yugoslavia's constituent republics as independent states, following the lead of the European Community.

Europe had not seen such state-pursuing, imperialist, ethnically motivated aggression since World War II. Indignation over the massive loss of life, war atrocities, and large-scale destruction in the middle of a peaceful continent increased daily. Not least among the factors was how unhappy Germany and many other countries were with the growing influx of refugees from the war-torn region. The media, politicians, and diplomats began actively debating how to stop the bloodshed and promote a peaceful solution in the former Yugoslavia.

As a European nation, Russia could not stand apart from those concerns, even though it was geographically removed from the effects of the conflict by thousands of miles. The issue also soon came to the fore in Russian politics. Russian nationalists demanded that Moscow support Milošević in defiance of European and world public opinion under the pretext of a historical affinity between the Russian and Serbian Christian Orthodox Slavic majorities. The Russian Empire, with Orthodoxy as its state religion, had exploited that affinity in its expansion into the Balkans a hundred years earlier and as a result was drawn into World War I. The scourges of that war led to the communist takeover in 1917 and, consequently, to the establishment of atheism as the state policy of the Soviet Union. Nevertheless, modern Russian communists now hailed Milošević as an Orthodox brother. His left-wing populism was an added bonus.

According to its constitution, the Russian Federation is a secular state with equal rights for citizens regardless of nationality. By playing the ethnoreligious card, nationalists threatened to blow up Russia itself, which was and is a multinational federation. Up to 20 percent of its population is Muslim and there is an even larger share of non-Slavic populations concentrated in a number of regions. Unconditional support for Milošević's Serbia could only have isolated Russia from democratic Europe, which was exactly what nationalists and the corrupt bureaucracy behind them had in mind.

Unlike the Russian nationalists, I was interested in Russia's taking an active role in finding a peaceful resolution in Yugoslavia and in developing ties not only with Serbia but with all the other former Yugoslav republics. So, in the spring of 1992, I went on a tour to visit them one by one, starting with Macedonia and Slovenia, and invariably receiving a warm welcome. Serbia was the third stop.

In Belgrade Milošević invited me to lunch and we had a long personal chat afterward. He invited me to taste his brandy and Cuban cigarillos, and I did. Those conversations in a relaxed setting became the foundation for our future contacts. In an hour we started developing a personal rapport that helped us to be straightforward yet human. A known populist in public and a hard-to-deal-with demagogue in diplomacy, he tried to suppress his public persona and be reasonable and pragmatic in private.

I told him that there was a surge of political interest and warm feeling in Russia toward Serbia, which was clearly reciprocated. It was those sentiments that prompted Russia to offer Belgrade a helping hand in forging a peaceful settlement with its neighbors and finding a place in the European community of democratic nations. In that context Russia managed to block the expulsion of Belgrade from the CSCE, despite strong pressure from many Europeans to kick Serbia out. I also made it clear that in spite of the nationalist campaign in the Russian press and parliament, the Russia government would not provide indiscriminate cover for Serbia if it continued waging a crusade against the other republics of the former Yugoslavia. We did it in the hope that Belgrade would come to implement CSCE norms and that there could be no return to the outdated logic of a Russian–German confrontation left over from the world wars. If Belgrade intended to be guided by some warped idea of seeking historical and ethnic revenge, it could not count on Moscow.

Milošević responded that his aggressive policy was an invention of the Germans, who had stirred up anti-Serbian sentiments in the West. "Germany aside, what we want in the former Yugoslavia is to protect the human rights of the Serbian minorities," he explained. "That's the same as you wanting to defend the rights of Russians in the former Soviet Union."

"You can count on us in this effort," I replied. "Though we believe that the use of force is counterproductive, because minorities suffer the most in ethnic conflicts. The solution must be political, not military. It should be worked out within the CSCE framework, and that is why we want Serbia to stay in the CSCE."

He said that the best way would be either to restore Yugoslavia as federation in which minorities were tolerated or, if the other republics did not want to reunite with Serbia, to include the Serbian minority enclaves in a new Serbian Federation, or a Great Serbia. Could it be done without a war? At that stage no, but only because of the stubbornness of the other republics enticed by the West and its slanderous anti-Serbian propaganda.

Listening to his passive-aggressive explanations, I felt as if I were back in Moscow talking to Rutskoi and the other nationalists. None of them cared for the well-being of Russians (or Serbs) in other republics, but simply used their problems, which they actively exacerbated, to advance their imperialist designs. Their dreams of a Great Russia or a Great Serbia could only lead to fratricidal bloodshed. Serbia was going down that path, and I said as much to Milošević many times over the years.

"But why is the West inventing lies and conspiring against Serbia, of all countries?" I asked Slobodan so as to shift the focus of the now heated discussion.

"We are Orthodox, different. The West supports Croats and Bosnians in fighting Serbs, because those nations are not Orthodox. Catholics and Muslims in the Balkans always join in their hatred of Serbia, despite the fact that they hate each other. The West has always hated us and wanted to destroy us, particularly the Germans, historically the enemies of Slavs. And they still do. That's why they undermined Yugoslavia and the Soviet Union."

I was shocked. It was one thing to read about medieval religious wars in history books. It was yet another thing to face a head of state who was in effect refighting those wars at the end of the twentieth century in the heart of modern Europe.

"Of course, I have put it almost grotesquely," Milošević said, seeing my reaction. "But many people here think this way. If you talked to the leaders of the Bosnian Serbs, either the poet Radovan Karadžić or General Ratko Mladić, you would hear the same thing." He was right about this—I did hear this from both of them later on. "The ugliest aspects of Western adversarial tendencies by and large belong to the past," he admitted, but quickly added, "There are still enough of them, even in the modern world.

"The Americans, for example, as winners of the Cold War, are trying to exploit the temporary weakness of Russia by seizing control of the Balkans," he continued, launching into yet another of his propaganda refrains. "Unfortunately, France and other nations that were historically our friends are now too dependent on America to help us. Let's face it, a small country like Serbia is only a testing ground, a first and easy prey for the West. Their real target is Russia with its rich mineral resources," he said. "By the way, my embassy in Moscow reports that many people there share the assessments I've outlined."

"Yes—communists, the opposition . . ."

"And not only them. Many of your colleagues in the administration do too."

I decided to divert the conversation for a while with talk about the history and culture of Europe. Then I came back to the urgent political developments.

"We are under pressure from our European partners for having blocked the UN Security Council resolution imposing sanctions on Serbia for acts of war, especially the shelling of cities." He had been briefed on that and thanked me. I continued: "One of those cities is Dubrovnik, a historic landmark and UNESCO World Heritage Site. I fail to see any military rationale in this barbaric act."

"Many Serbs believe it unfair that the Croats defected from Yugoslavia and took with them almost the entire coastline of the Adriatic, including Dubrovnik. But you are right that it has no strategic significance. I think the shelling should be stopped, but they don't listen to me. Those fighters in Croatia are on their own. They do not belong to the JNA, the Yugoslav People's Army, which is headquartered in Belgrade."

"This goes beyond revenge." I responded. "We are not in the Middle Ages! This should be stopped by all means!"

"OK, I will do something," he said. In spite of everything, I had the feeling he took this seriously.

We went on to repeat many of the same arguments concerning Sarajevo, with the essential difference that this city had significant strategic importance as the capital of Bosnia. Again, Milošević claimed he did not control the fighters, but promised to do what he could to stop them.

I made it clear to him that unless the bombardment of those cities stopped in the next few days, it would be impossible for Russia to continue blocking UN sanctions without taking some share of the blame and responsibility for a barbarism unheard of in modern Europe. We would ask the UN to wait another week or so to give Milošević more time to cope with the situation, but after that the sanctions would be imposed.

After our long conversation, I left Milošević and continued on to visit Slovenia and Croatia. The last leg of my Yugoslavian journey was to Bosnia. To reach Sarajevo, I had to fly once again to Belgrade and take a UN service plane because the Serbs, who had seized the city, wouldn't allow any other flights. Once I was back in Belgrade, I paid a visit to Milošević and thanked him for stopping the bombardment of Dubrovnik—yet the shelling of Sarajevo continued. He said again that he did not control the fighters and that while those in Dubrovnik listened to him, the ones in Sarajevo did not. He was adamant that I should not go there since he could not guarantee my security. I was equally determined to go.

After an hour's flight we touched down in Sarajevo to the sound of explosions. We were advised by the UN peacekeepers to go back, since the Serbian artillery had started shelling again, despite its promise not to do so during my visit. I said that I was used to such tricks and insisted on continuing according to schedule.

Sarajevo looked like a ghost town: no traffic, deserted streets, destroyed buildings. The president of Bosnia, Alija Izetbegović, met us in a heavily damaged city hall. He was tense, suspicious, and restless. He said he had no hard feelings toward Russia, asking only for a more balanced approach. He evidently appreciated my coming since few high-ranking foreign guests dared cross into the war zone.

On the way back, I met Serbian officers in JNA uniforms, and received an unambiguously affirmative answer when I asked whether their headquarters and general staff were in Belgrade. Milošević had simply lied in saying he had no control over those fighters and so had deceived Russia with his promises.

I angrily conveyed my conclusion to the Serbian foreign minister, who came to see me off at the Belgrade airport before I returned to Moscow.

Shortly after my return I received a cable from the Russian permanent representative to the UN, Yuli Vorontsov, saying that the UN observers who had accompanied me to Sarajevo were reporting continuing bombing of Sarajevo by JNA troops. This meant that Milošević, ignoring Moscow and everyone else, had continued waging his ruthless war. Fed up with this one-sided willfulness, a large group of member states of the UN Security Council formally demanded a vote on a resolution imposing sanctions on Belgrade right away, within forty-eight hours. Everybody was voting for sanctions, and a no vote from Russia would isolate us politically and morally. Vorontsov thought our only choices were to abstain or to vote yes. He recommended the latter.

Because of the sensitive nature of the decision, I sent a copy of the cable to Yeltsin and appended a note indicating that Milošević had lied to me and manipulated Russian diplomatic support to provide cover for his sinister policy and war crimes. The next morning, I received Yeltsin's handwritten instruction to "vote yes immediately." Vorontsov did so, and sanctions quickly followed.

After the UN Security Council announced the imposition of sanctions on Belgrade on May 30, 1992, I called Milošević and confirmed Russia's readiness to help him find a diplomatic solution to the problems of the former Yugoslavia. "But you must take our yes vote for sanctions as a warning that we will not provide a cover for warmongering and brutalities. I told you not to rely on those in Moscow who might say differently. Their promises of protection have proven false, and their militant advice counterproductive. We are friends, not patrons. And as friends we offer help in stopping the war and finding a decent compromise solution." Soon he called back and invited me to see him over the weekend to discuss a possible settlement.

Thus, began Milošević's long and painful search for a political settlement instead of a military one with respect to Serbia's neighbors. The fighting and the sanctions dragged on, with additional pressure from Moscow nationalists to support the Serbian separatists. When the UN imposed new sanctions in 1994, Yeltsin, fearing backlash from the nationalists during his upcoming reelection campaign, cast a vote of abstention. Multiple cease-fire agreements were signed, to little effect. An end to the conflict was achieved only after NATO, in its first ever use of force, conducted a serious bombing campaign against the Bosnian Serbs. That campaign enabled the United States to step in to lead the negotiations, resulting in the General Framework Agreement for Peace in Bosnia and Herzegovina (better known as the Dayton Peace Agreement), which was formally signed in Paris on December 14, 1995, by Milošević and the presidents of Croatia and Bosnia. Such an outcome would hardly have been possible, however, had Milošević not known that Russia would not defend his actions inside the UN. We would not be a patron of his war, a point I had repeatedly driven home in frequent meetings with him over a period of three years.

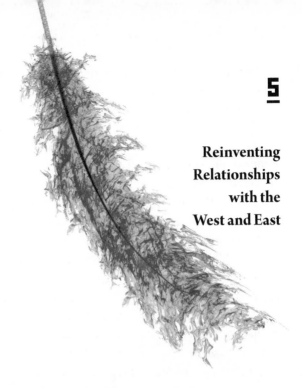

5

Reinventing Relationships with the West and East

MY EARLY DAYS AS RUSSIA'S FOREIGN MINISTER were dominated by establishing benign relations with the newly independent states and putting out fires in hot spots. But I was equally preoccupied with my mission of reforming—indeed reinventing—Russia's interactions with the West and East. Russia was legally the continuation state of the Soviet Union, but if we wanted to pivot from authoritarianism to democracy, we could not pursue the same course in the relationships we had inherited with other countries.

I was convinced that the interests of the democratic Russia were opposite to those of the interest of the Soviets, who defied the democratic West; wasted national resources on the arms race; supported rogue regimes, like Assad's in Syria or Saddam Hussein's in Iraq; and dreamed of restoring an anti-American alliance with communist China. Yet being oppositional was not enough. As a great and sovereign nation, Russia needed a positive international agenda that would contribute to its domestic effort of sustaining democracy and a modern economy. This craving for prosperity and freedom seemed to be as much our national interest as a universal human quest and thus could form the basis for cooperation with other countries.

Because of this I believed that the new Russia had to pursue ideology-free connections with all peace-loving countries, on the basis of parity and reciprocity, earning its proper place as a partner and potential ally among prosperous Western democracies, including Japan and South Korea, and establishing good-neighbor relations with China. It was an unprecedented political course and its implementation required both creative destruction of the old ways and a difficult search for proper new attitudes. Reinventing the policy—and indeed the sense of its place within the society of nations—for a vast state with a thousand-year history was of course a tough, but urgent call.

I said something along these lines of thinking to former US president Richard Nixon in a conversation we had when he visited Moscow in the early 1990s. We were discussing his own bold pivots in foreign policy, such as opening to China. My opponent in the Yeltsin administration, and successor in January 1996, Yevgeny Primakov, later pointed to Nixon's reference to that conversation and openly smeared the notion of reinvention, arguing that the basic national interests of Russia remained the same as they were before: Russia's "traditional" or "historic" interests. That was precisely what the old apparatchiks in the bureaucracy, especially in the military-security apparatus, wanted: to do little more than change the communist red banner to the new tricolor flag over the Kremlin, and then go back to business as usual. Unfortunately, Yeltsin finally succumbed to their pressure.

Windows to Europe

In January 1992 I found myself on a plane to Kaliningrad, capital of the Russian exclave province of the same name. My eventual destination was Germany. Kaliningrad is geographically the most western part of Russia, designed by Peter the Great in the early eighteenth century to open a "window to the West" for Russia on the shore of the Baltic Sea. Ever since, the Black Sea, as a zone of trade and transport, has been the shortest way to reach Russia's Western European partners including the Netherlands, Sweden, and Great Britain.

Kaliningrad, which was part of Germany for seven hundred years, had been among the territories assigned to the Soviet Union after defeat of Nazi aggression in 1945. Yet, forty-five years later it presented painfully striking evidence that though Russia had won the war, it had lost the peacetime competition for high standard of living with Germany and even East Europe. The military presence in Kaliningrad was overwhelming, and most of the territory looked like a fortress under siege dropped in the middle of peaceful neighbors.

In essence, Kaliningrad had been defeated from the inside by the Soviets' aggressive and undemocratic system. The reform-minded Kaliningrad governor, Yury Matochkin, was full of plans to develop the territory as an integral part of democratic Russia, inviting foreign investment on a balanced and competitive basis. I tried to help him and like-minded governors in Northwest Russia. In turn, they tried their best to support our efforts to apply the new policy of partnership to the Baltic Sea area, transforming it from a symbolic Cold War battleground into a business opportunity zone.

At the end of 1991, Russian nationalists started to exploit Kaliningrad's position, alleging that Germany was taking advantage of Russia's economic weakness and attempting to reclaim the province in return for providing financial assistance to Yeltsin's unpatriotic new government, as the nationalists deemed it. I publicly repudiated these rumors right from the start, and assured the Kaliningrad authorities and population, by then more than 90 percent ethnic Russians, that Germany would adhere to the postwar treaties it had signed with the Soviet Union and comply with the CSCE principle of the inviolability of borders in Europe.

In Germany I received confirmation of those assurances, concluding a Russian-German treaty based wholly on previous agreements concerning borders. The new treaty was welcomed in Kaliningrad and Moscow with relief, and Germany soon grew to become Russia's major political and economic partner in Europe.

In 1992 it was Germany's turn to chair both the European Community (EC; now the European Union) and the CSCE (now the Organization for Security and Co-operation in Europe, OSCE). By coincidence, Germany was also slated to be the host of the G-7 meeting in Munich in August of that year, and we reached a preliminary understanding during my visit that Yeltsin would be invited to the gathering as a special guest.

I also obtained assurances of German support for admitting the newly independent states, including those in the Caucasus and Asia, to the CSCE on the condition that they accepted the principles, universally accepted everywhere in Europe, of the inviolability of frontiers and the nonuse of force in international relations. No less important was respect for human rights, including the rights of minorities. I told the German ministers candidly that I wanted the CSCE and individual European nations to make clear to each and every former Soviet republic, from the Baltic Sea to Central Asia, that they had an obligation to observe the rights of the minority Russian populations remaining on their territories.

I was lucky to meet as one of my first colleagues the veteran German foreign minister, Hans-Dietrich Genscher, who kindly shared his diplomatic experience and skill with me. He used his authority and influence within the European Community to help start negotiations on a basic framework for Russian–EC economic and trade relations. A few months later that effort led to the first important agreements on tariffs, and subsequently to a comprehensive agreement spanning a wide range of economic relations in the spring of 1994.

Genscher was also acutely sensible of the competing pressures I faced. During a coffee break at a CSCE ministerial session he mentioned that some of his Western colleagues felt I was paying too much attention to the rights of Russian minorities in the Baltic and the CIS at the expense of the regular agenda. I repeated my well-known position: the issue was a key one for the CSCE as an institution dedicated to security and democracy in Europe. He did not challenge this but, with a smile, took from his portfolio a clipping from a German newspaper. The article, datelined Moscow, was about the election of Yevgeny Ambartsumov as chairman of the parliamentary Foreign Affairs Committee. The new chairman had a majority of only one vote and was under pressure from the communists and nationalists to do their bidding. Ambartsumov, the report went on, had criticized me for traveling to the West and participating in international conferences when the issue of Russian minorities in the former Soviet republics required urgent attention.

"There you have it," Genscher said. "Both sides attack you—that probably means you are doing something right. Just get used to it. I too am criticized both for going to conferences and for not going. If you don't go, critics will say you've missed an important opportunity to promote your country's positions and have weakened the international standing of the homeland, and so on. If you do go, your opponents will accuse you of spending too much time wining and dining abroad instead of working with the government of the homeland on urgent matters. Being under fire from the domestic press and politicians is part of the foreign minister's job. Just keep doing what you think is right, for as long as you can."

I was grateful for his perspective and support.

Genscher was a great wit and gave a piece of advice, which I want to share with future foreign ministers of the world and in fact anyone with foreign exposure: Never try to remember or pronounce the name of a foreigner at the first encounter. Instead, use polite titles like *president, minister, chairman, interpreter,* or simply "my friend," sparing potential confusion or even offense.

With Germany's assistance as presiding chair of the CSCE, important decisions were made on admitting the former Soviet republics. Later, other hot-button issues were addressed at the Prague meeting of the foreign ministers of the CSCE on January 30, 1992. Minority rights were a prominent issue on the agenda. We were especially concerned with the treatment of Russian and other ethnic minorities in the Baltic states. While these states were progressing on a democratic path and working to restore their identity as sovereign nation-states, they were unsure how to deal with the large Russian population within their borders, amounting in some locales to up to 40 percent of the population. We proposed monitoring minority rights with the help of a pan-European high commissioner, which met with agreement. The senior diplomat, Max van der Stoel, former foreign minister of the Netherlands, soon became the first OSCE High Commissioner on National Minorities. He served in this post for eight years, during which he helped to address ethnic conflicts both quietly and ably.

Our ministry continued throughout that year to marshal Western support for ensuring stability in our newly independent Baltic neighbors. On March 5, 1992, the foreign ministers of Russia, Germany, Denmark, Finland, Norway, Lithuania, Latvia, and Estonia met in Copenhagen, where we established the Council of the Baltic Sea States. It was designed as a working forum in which to coordinate policies in the fields of law enforcement, the economy, transportation, energy, the environment, and the development of democratic institutions in general. I also proposed at this meeting the establishment of an ombudsman or high commissioner within the Council of the Baltic Sea States with the mandate to monitor the observance of human rights, including the rights of minorities, in participating states. The office would function much as the same office in the CSCE but was then preoccupied with war-torn Yugoslavia and its resources were stretched thin. In particular, I wanted the new ombudsman to concentrate on the Baltic states.

The Estonian and Latvian diplomats interpreted my proposals as a Russian attempt to exert pressure on their states. Yet on the contrary, my proposals had been formulated with Moscow as well as the Baltics in mind: if Europe ignored Russia's concerns about Russian minority populations outside of our borders, then the Russian neo-imperialists and anti-Western hard-liners would gain increasing political support at home for unilateral actions against our new neighbors under the pretext of defending our compatriots. After a short debate we reached an agreement to establish such an oversight office. Both the CSCE ombudsman and the Council of the Baltic Sea States high commissioner subsequently proved instrumental in aligning the Baltic states' treatment of minorities with European norms.

In 1992 the Barents Euro-Arctic Council and the Barents Regional Council, similar to the Baltic one, were also established, contributing to regional cooperation for years to come. I witnessed the bounties of that framework when I later became a representative to the Russian parliament from Murmansk district. A third cooperation council was soon set up by the Black Sea states, which went on to establish a regional interstate Bank for Reconstruction and Development. That chain of regional organizations for cooperation was vital to Russia's ability to use the seacoast west of the Urals as a modern-day window to Europe.

The United States: START II

Our approaches to the Western democratic states continued on a presidential level with Yeltsin making visits to the United States, Canada, the United Kingdom, and France. The trip to the United States in particular loomed large: it would afford Yeltsin his first opportunity to confirm Russia's succession to the great power role vacated by the Soviet Union.

Yeltsin's debut was to be at the UN Security Council summit beginning January 31, 1991. This was to give him his first full-scale foreign policy and diplomatic exposure. Yeltsin's nervousness and uncertainty over his function at the upcoming UN sessions had me worried. The stress of wrestling with a problem that had no clear dénouement would sometimes drive him to drink. That had happened in Minsk and in Belavezha in December 1991. At that point, he had no clear vision of the outcome and was not sure he would do the right thing. So, he acted erratically, and only reestablished a firm footing when he realized that a peaceful solution to the puzzle of a failing Soviet state and the creation of a new commonwealth was at hand.

With that experience in mind, I concentrated on persuading him that in New York he would encounter no surprises either from the other heads of state or during the sessions. Diplomats had arranged everything well in advance. "Then what's the sense in going if I am to be only a marionette in your hands and those of the other foreign ministers?" he retorted.

This question, put in his trademark guess-if-this-is-a-joke manner, put me on edge. After the unhappy episode in Minsk the previous December I was all too familiar with Yeltsin's desire to appear on top of everything; and his unique penchant for throwing his aides onto the back foot by making a surprise public announcement for which they were wholly unprepared, often on critical policy matters. I started to have grim fantasies about what unknown initiative he might unexpectedly announce.

A few days later, leaving Yeltsin's private office, I ran into a group of space scientists who had an appointment to see him. They began describing a project that entailed using the space station for monitoring military threats on Earth on a global scale. The worrying thought that something like this could lead to a potential ill-thought-through initiative at the UN summit crossed my mind. Unfortunately, I had to run to another meeting and so did not follow up on my hunch, which I would later come to regret. From the few words I did hear about the project, it appeared to be the classic bright idea that would require billions of dollars and decades of hard work to realize. In a word, it was little better than science fiction, but invented by real, first-class scientists and thus in a sense even more thrilling if no less fictional than the *Star Wars* movies I enjoyed watching with my daughter.

So, I cannot claim it was entirely a surprise when, in his formal address to the UN Security Council on January 31, Yeltsin proposed building a "global system of protection of the international community," to be based in outer space and constructed jointly by scientists from Russia, the United States, and other countries. Such a system, he asserted, was needed against the threat presented by rogue dictators.

The initiative was poorly presented and poorly received. The Americans at first took it as a return to the old Soviet habit of coming to UN sessions with totally unrealistic peace-propaganda proposals, such as for complete disarmament, that were intended to score points with the populist press back home and embarrass the West. Yuli Vorontsov, Russia's permanent representative to the UN, and other members of the diplomatic team quickly communicated to the US delegation that Yeltsin's initiative was motivated by idealism and revealed as much of his lack of experience as it did his good intentions in world politics. It was a masterstroke in confidential diplomacy, since the explanation had to be conveyed in a way that would not humiliate Yeltsin. We correspondingly asked the Americans to take the bizarre proposal seriously in public so that Yeltsin would not look stupid back home. Graciously, President George H. W. Bush said that the initiative was worth examining. Nonetheless, I was deeply worried. It was unclear whether Yeltsin could be persuaded to stop playing old-style global hegemony games and start focusing on the hard work of building trust and practical partnerships with the West.

Vladimir Lukin, the chairman of the foreign affairs committee of the Russian parliament and a member of our delegation shared this concern and helped to communicate it to the president in a humorous, but clear form. At a full delegation, it was his job to wrap up the meeting in the evening, and he told a popular joke about a kolkhoz (collective farm) assembly. He said: "There are two items on the agenda—repairs of the pigsty and the triumph of communism in the world. Since we are short of materials and labor for the repairs, I propose to skip the first item and pass directly to the second one." Yeltsin chuckled, pretended to be perplexed but then laughed together with the company. I admired Lukin in those early days for his wit and active role in the pro-democracy movement. Sadly, only his wit endured, and Yeltsin's lighthearted attitude to criticism also proved short-lived.

In that particular time and place in history we needed to overcome the Soviet legacy in both word and deed. And in the beginning was a word. When Yeltsin's aides and speechwriters discussed the draft of Yeltsin's UN Security Council speech, I fought to include certain statements, and was gratified that Yeltsin retained them in the final text of his official address: "Russia regards the United States and the West not only as partners but as allies. This, to my mind, lays the basis for a revolutionary change in the peaceful partnership of the civilized world. . . . The full-scale observance of human rights and liberties in accordance with international documents is of the highest priority for us. . . . This is not the internal matter of a state, but the international obligation of each and every country."

Both statements, on partnering with the West and on human rights as a universal obligation, were forgotten in two to three years and would never be repeated today by the Russian authorities. Yet the fact that the first popularly elected leader of Russia expressed these ideas while addressing the UN Security Council marked a high point in Russian political discourse. Sooner or later, the promise implicit in those words will be realized because it is in the best interests of Russia and the world.

The US response to Yeltsin's interest in a new relationship of parity with the West came the next day. President Bush invited Yeltsin as a special guest to Camp David, where the two presidents signed the Camp David Declaration on New Relations. The document stated that Russia and United States did not regard each other as potential enemies and that their relations would henceforth be characterized by friendship and partnership based on mutual trust, respect, and adherence to democracy and economic freedom. In practical terms, talks on a new joint agreement that would result in START II, a treaty on strategic nuclear weapons reduction, were begun. US secretary of state Jim Baker and I were in charge.

Those talks would take as their foundation the earlier START I, signed by Gorbachev on July 31, 1991, which limited the number of nuclear weapons allowed on either side. From the beginning it was agreed that we should undertake the unprecedentedly ambitious mission of not only limiting the sum of those weapons, but of decreasing their offensive edge and thus the risk of war.

For years the Soviet regime had maintained a first-strike capability with "heavy" land-based intercontinental ballistic missiles (ICBMs) capable of launching multiple nuclear warheads at the United States in forty to sixty minutes. The Soviets had traditionally fiercely defended these weapons against any treaty limitations. War with the United States was considered unavoidable, and thus Moscow believed it needed to be able to strike first when an opportunity or a crisis arose. That thinking passed virtually unchanged from the Soviet military to the Russian Federation military, and my immediate task was to repeal it and replace it using logic rooted in the new political reality of having the United States as an ally, not an enemy.

If the Russian military remained mired in Soviet dogma, then our new foreign policy would fail. Moreover, our national security would be threatened as a direct result of keeping the first-strike weapons, which in the case of a crisis in Russian–American relations, however remote, would tempt the US command to prepare for its own preemptive strike. To make things even worse, the land-based silos of those "heavy" missiles were easy targets, since their whereabouts were well-known to the other side thanks to photographs taken by reconnaissance satellites in outer space. This vulnerability would in turn prompt Russian generals to keep the rockets in a state of launch read-iness and use them whenever there was a risk of potential conflict. Thus, the ever-present danger of accidental nuclear annihilation sparked either by technical failure or miscalculation would remain an unnecessarily elevated risk. US superiority in submarines with ICBMs and strategic bombers also had to be reduced under the new treaty.

I privately discussed the problem with Defense Minister Pavel Grachev. Rather than argue on substance, he said that a climb-down on "heavy" mis-siles would be suicidal for him in the face of the old-guard generals. I then gave an unusually lengthy presentation—about fifteen minutes—to Yeltsin who listened carefully but concluded by calling the issue technical and ask-ing me to make an extra effort to iron it out with the minister of defense. After that I shared my concerns with Gennady Burbulis, Yeltsin's right-hand man, who promised to engage the boss and Defense Minister Grachev on the need to rethink Russia's strategic balance with the United States. This was a weaker response than I had hoped for, but soon thereafter Grachev stepped away from Soviet doctrine on ICBMs. He and the head of the General Staff of Russia's armed forces, Mikhail Kolesnikov (a seasoned and highly respected strategist), publicly acknowledged that these weapons did rep-resent a potential first-strike capability and, in order to make the strategic balance between Russia and America more stable, they *should* be included in negotiated reductions. Yeltsin approved both this revolutionary change in doctrine and the instructions Grachev and I proposed for our negotiating position with the American team.

Yeltsin's decision made possible an unprecedented advance in the arms control negotiations, which culminated in an agreement on mutual reduc-tions in strategic nuclear weapons. For the first time ever, the risk of nuclear war was reduced both quantitatively and qualitatively.

Jim Baker and I achieved this crucial breakthrough on June 9, 1992. I spent that day in Washington, DC with a large team of Russian military and civilian experts ironing out the main points of START II alongside the US team. Baker, a tough, seasoned negotiator, quickly grasped the opportunity created by the new relations between Russia and the United States and ap-proached his task in an open-minded and flexible way. The result was a very high quality, professional job, accomplished by the same people who had spent years negotiating START I. Through that process they had acquired a thorough knowledge of—and a common language for—an impossibly complex issue. I was deeply impressed by the final event that happened on June 9, 1991 in Baker's office, to which he had invited me for a cup of coffee. Suddenly a phone rang on his desk, and he excused himself for a moment to step into a separate room. When he returned, I noticed he was unusually agitated. He told me it was a call from the Pentagon asking him to demand an additional concession from me. He flatly refused to do so. "We've made a fair deal," he said to me, "and I won't play last-minute tricks." It is wrong to say that politics and diplomacy is a dirty business. Some men of honor play the real—honest—game.

On the Russian side the agreement was a historic achievement of the first popularly elected leader. Daringly he had parted with the preconceptions of his predecessors and had acted in accordance with Russian national interests. I pointed this out proudly to Yeltsin when I reported the results of the Washington deal to him.

"Now you see that I am better in foreign policy matters than Gorbachev," he said with the air of an individual who had finally been vindicated and appreciated. But he was still wrestling with Gorbachev's shadow and I think still suspected me of being a Gorbachevite. Yet more signs of his damaged ego were to come.

"Yes, you and Baker did good job. Two professionals! Yet only presidents can make a final decision of that magnitude. Yes, you acted on my instructions, but still the last touch, the concluding confirmation of the agreed numbers of missiles must come out as a result of my handshake with Bush. Please, don't argue. Yes, the text of the agreement should be prepared in advance, but surely a couple of digits could be inserted very quickly. In any case, it's my final decision!"

While Yeltin's resoluteness and ability to seize the political moment was a great asset, some features of his character were a real liability to the country's new foreign policy. In the immediate context of the treaty, his vanity would result in an episode of pure black comedy.

Needless to say, for us to try to follow Yeltsin's "handshake" demand would be a recipe for disaster, since, at least at that time, no president of any state would agree to an on-the-spot deal on such a delicate and highly technical matter. So, I did not stop the negotiating teams in Washington from reaching an agreement on final weapons reduction numbers and preparing the documents for signing. But I had to act boldly at the June 1992 Russian–American summit in Washington.

Upon arriving at the White House with Yeltsin for the usual exchange of diplomatic pleasantries that preceded the signing of agreements, I rushed to President Bush and asked him as a favor to speak with Yeltsin one-on-one at some point before the signing ceremony. I suggested he should ask the Russian president to give him the final numbers, so as to create the appearance of a private agreement between heads of state. I explained that this unusual request stemmed from the peculiarities of Yeltsin's personality and did not represent any hesitation or attempted trick on our side. I assured him there would be no last-minute surprises with respect to the substance of the deal. President Bush took it more easily than I had expected. He seemed to understand Yeltsin well and also appreciated the importance of appearances.

As to Yeltsin, I gave him a pocket-sized sheet of paper with the final numbers, which had been agreed on by both negotiating teams and were already included in the prepared documents. Bush invited Yeltsin for a private walk in the White House South Lawn garden and asked him for the numbers. On their return, both were smiling. Bush gave the sheet of paper that Yeltsin had handed him a moment before to Baker, who briefly looked at the numbers and nodded.

An hour later the document called the Basic Agreement was signed. In his speech at the ceremony Yeltsin described it as the tangible "expression of the fundamental change in the political and economic relations between the United States of America and Russia." The Charter for American-Russian Partnership and Friendship, which the presidents also signed in Washington on June 17, 1992, characterized our new relationship as a "strategic partnership."

Back in Moscow, Yeltin's communist and nationalist opponents excoriated the negotiators, including Yeltsin and myself for entering into a "poorly thought out and hasty" treaty.

The charges, false in every respect, arose from a couple of different sources. The first centered on Yeltsin's pursuit of a fairly rapid turnaround in defense posture, and the requisite revision of Russian military doctrine toward the United States. Yes, Yeltsin wanted badly to strengthen his relations with Bush so they would stand at the same level as they had with Gorbachev. To strike such a historic nuclear disarmament agreement with the United States would overshadow the famous START I signed by Bush and Gorbachev just a year earlier.

Yet the turnaround in strategic posture and attitude to weapon reductions was enacted quickly but not "hastily." It reflected both the groundwork laid by Gorbachev in the preceding year and a new readiness to search for mutually acceptable solutions by an American side that was willing to place a big bet on Yeltsin's bold rejection of Soviet orthodoxy. In fact, the new treaty was better thought out than the fossilized Soviet approach left to us after the Soviet collapse—an approach that had run the nation's economy into the ground.

The second source for criticism of the treaty was, unfortunately, Yeltsin himself. He bragged to his aides of striking the final deal during the one-on-one with Bush, and they promptly leaked it to the Russian press. Rumors that the final numbers had been agreed on during a garden stroll thirty minutes before the signing ceremony were grist for the mills of the opposition and hard-liners in Moscow, who framed it as though Yeltsin had made a spontaneous decision on a matter of national security. As they knew Bush had long experience negotiating on strategic weapons with Soviet leaders and Yeltsin had none, they speculated that the US president had managed to get "unwarranted concessions" from his Russian counterpart.

Despite such attacks and speculation, talks to develop the framework agreement to reduce the nuclear arsenals proceeded for the rest of the year. The negotiations were very difficult and by December seemed on the edge of failure. On December 30, Grachev and I met in Geneva with Lawrence Eagleburger, James Baker's successor as secretary of state (Baker had earlier left office to head up Bush's reelection campaign), to iron out some final differences. I bet Eagleburger a bottle of Scotch that the treaty would be ready for signing before Bush had to turn the Oval Office over to the president-elect, Bill Clinton, in January. It was a joke, not an artificial deadline to be met by all means, as Clinton was briefed on the matter and supported the deal.

START II was signed on January 3, a date that also marked the last encounter between Yeltsin and Bush. Eagleburger, who was always charming and witty, produced a fine Scotch, which I gladly shared with Grachev and other members of the Russian delegation.

That January signing ceremony marked much more than a formal resetting of relations between Russia and the United States on a new, cooperative trajectory. It was also the culmination of our efforts to promote reform in military strategy during the first year of Yeltsin's administration and to conduct the corresponding foreign policy.

Later Yeltsin made some other courageous political decisions in the field of defense policy, including signing agreements with Germany and the Baltic states to withdraw the former Soviet troops from their territories. I was proud to work with him on reaching those results and then in executing them. At each turn, he strongly overruled the opposition in military services.

Back in February 1992 we traveled directly from Washington, DC, to Canada, where Prime Minister Brian Mulroney and Foreign Minister Barbara McDougall received us as old friends. Yeltsin also enjoyed meeting Prime Minister John Major and Foreign Secretary Douglas Hurd at our next stop in London. Hurd had been instrumental in proposing that the Russian Federation pursue continuing state status with the UN after the demise of the Soviet Union. We had a more difficult and more formal meeting with President François Mitterrand of France in the Élysée Palace—though it was balanced by a warm chat with Paris mayor Jacques Chirac, who even spoke a bit of Russian. We signed fundamental treaties or declarations establishing new relations with all three states.

On returning to Moscow, Yeltsin provided a special briefing for parliament stressing the positive results of his visits to the United States, Canada, the United Kingdom, and France. He pointed out that he had achieved the two major tasks he had set out to accomplish: to help Russia join the "civilized community" of nations—his term for the peaceful and economically developed countries of the West—and to secure support for Russia's internal transformation. That was exactly my understanding of how our national interest was to be served by foreign policy. He also reiterated the main point he had made abroad: that Russia regarded the United States and the West not as potential enemies but as friends and allies.

The briefing was well received by parliament. Many times later I urged Yeltsin to deliver a similar briefing, but in vain. Had he continued presenting the new foreign policy to the deputies and the public as highly favorable to Russia internally, the opposition in parliament and the bureaucracy would not have been able to challenge it as aggressively as it did.

Yeltsin felt he had been welcomed by world leaders and proudly called them his friends in private and in public. That summer, he was invited to join the G-7 leaders at a luncheon, which jump-started Russia's affiliation with the group until it became the G-8. Participation in the club of the heads of democratic and market-economy states was a significant impetus for Yeltsin to keep Russia's foreign policy tightly within the framework of international cooperation.

Turkey

Yet another urgent situation our new Russian foreign policy had to address concerned the crossroads of Asia and Europe. From the outset, my concern was to avoid backsliding into the historical rivalry and confrontation between Russia and Turkey. The potential for trouble was enormous and ever present. At the time, the biggest issue was the raging Nagorno-Karabakh conflict, which threatened to escalate into open war between pro-Russian, predominantly Orthodox Armenia and pro-Turkish, Muslim Azerbaijan.

In Russia, the memories of centuries of hostilities gave succor to powerful forces looking for arguments supporting that the source of conflict between Russia and its neighbors (and thus for the fortress mentality) lay much deeper in history than the communist period and would not disappear with the end of the Soviet Union.

The communist and so-called patriotic press in Russia liked to portray Turkey as a monster with two barking and biting heads, one representing aggressive pan-Turkism, the other NATO, since the country was a member of the alliance. And where better to inflame anew the spirit of the Cold War than in the area that had given birth to it? Stalin's meddling in the internal affairs of Turkey and Greece had prompted the Truman Doctrine in 1947—the official call by the US president Harry Truman for the Western democracies to unite in containing Soviet expansion. That is why my policy toward Turkey enraged the communist and nationalist forces in Russia, and I anticipated being attacked by them for going to Ankara.

But my assumption was the opposite of theirs. It was precisely Turkey's NATO membership that gave the best indication of its positive transformation in the preceding decades, and a guarantee that Ankara would maintain its policy within reasonable limits, despite pressure from its own extremists. During CSCE and UN meetings, I had candidly checked this assessment with my American and Western European colleagues and received unanimous confirmation. They promised to use their influence through NATO and other contacts with Turkey to prevent adventurism, but they also emphasized one condition for success: that Russia follow up by sticking to a nonimperialist policy.

I shared my vision of Russian–Turkish good-neighbor relations—and cooperation in stabilizing the Transcaucasus and Central Asia—with the Turkish foreign minister, Hikmet Çetin, whom I had met at an international conference in the fall of 1991 and discovered that we were on the same wavelength. We agreed to pay official visits to each other's countries and instructed our staff members to start preparing a joint document outlining the new relationship and common interests in regional stability.

Having Çetin as my Turkish counterpart in that crucial moment was a stroke of good fortune. He was tough in promoting his country's interests and flexible in searching for solutions. With a different person in his place, it would have been much more difficult, if not impossible, to lay a sound foundation for future Russian–Turkish relations. We were able to address the most sensitive issues and were each aware of the obstacles and pressures that the other faced in defending a cooperative approach.

In Ankara I met with Prime Minister Süleyman Demirel, and we confirmed our understanding that Turkey would not compete with Russia for a sphere of interest, and vice versa. Demirel impressed me as a seasoned and wise politician. He visited Moscow in May to conclude a treaty on Russian–Turkish relations and assured Yeltsin that Turkey would not intervene in the Azeri–Armenian conflict.

The constructive relations that we established between our two countries in the first months after the birth of a new Russia enabled both our countries to weather the storms that would ravage the region. Among these episodes was Azerbaijan's dramatic withdrawal from the CIS, which was intended to punish Moscow for what the Azeris saw as its pro-Armenian position in the summer of 1992. It is also noteworthy that by March 1993, Russia had signed contracts with Turkey for $75 million worth of military equipment, its first weapons sale to a NATO nation.

China: A Communist Neighbor—and Stabilizing Force

Along with establishing new relations with our major partners to the west and south of Russia, we were reaching out to our neighbors to the east. I proposed visiting China and South Korea. Yeltsin was more interested in Japan, believing that cooperation with the region's rich and highly developed "Western" nation held the most promise for the economy of Russia's Far East— which comprises, roughly, the land between Lake Baikal and the Pacific Ocean—and resource-rich Siberia. Theoretically, he was right, but the Soviet Union had left us with a huge stumbling block with respect to our relations with Japan; and I doubted we would be able to remove it anytime soon.

But if I was skeptical about the prospects of success with Japan, he felt the same way about China. The contact he had had with Beijing's leader at the UN meetings in New York was nonconfrontational, but too brief to melt the ice. Yeltsin still felt offended that the Chinese president, in contrast to other top visitors to the Soviet Union the previous year, had declined to meet him and had emphasized the central role of Gorbachev as head of the Communist Party in ensuring good relations between the two socialist states. Grudgingly, the president approved my going both to Japan and China preparing the way for him to visit if things went well.

He also approved the concept of good relations and a potential partnership between Russia and China as the two neighbors sharing the longest land border in Asia. Recalling the Chinese fable about a marmoset that defeated both a lion and a rhinoceros by making them fight each other, we agreed that China should not be allowed to play "the Russia card" against the United States and that we in turn would not play "the China card" in any geopolitical maneuver.

I invited the Chinese ambassador to the ministry and, having outlined our interest in developing ties with China, asked for the nearest opportune time for a visit to Beijing. The following morning the ambassador was back with an enthusiastic response to our offer of putting ideologies aside and forging good-neighbor relations as well as a potential partnership. We set a date for my visit in mid-March later that year. I called Yeltsin and reported that we were on the right track with our giant neighbor.

Red carpet treatment and productive talks awaited me in Beijing. I was impressed by the balanced approach of the Chinese foreign minister Qian Qichen to international issues, and particularly to the CIS. Qian indicated that China had no interest in meddling in either the internal or regional affairs of the post-Soviet space, a position that subsequently enabled China to play a stabilizing role during those turbulent years. For our part, I assured Qian that Russia would continue its One-China policy and develop relations with Taiwan only on nonstate bases in economic and other fields that Beijing did not oppose.

China's Chairman Jiang Zemin received me in the State Palace. He readily agreed that the new relations between our countries should be free of the burden of ideology or troubled history, and also of "third-party play," whether in the form of friendship or conflict, with any other country, particularly the United States. He shared the view that on this basis, Russia and China could develop a very constructive partnership in several fields.

After the traditional official ceremony, Jiang took me to his private office for a friendly chat and continued that practice on every visit thereafter. He treated me in a somewhat fatherly manner, which I did not mind since he was a generation or two older. He spoke a little Russian and liked Russian songs, which he had learned in his youth while studying at Leningrad (now St. Petersburg) University. He also liked Russian black rye bread, and on every visit to Beijing I brought him a loaf of it, which he received with pleasure. He would immediately start to pinch off pieces. In my turn I rather liked Jiang Zemin. His sense of humor and personal warmth contrasted with what might be expected from a *functionary* sitting at the top of a communist regime. Later Yeltsin shared that positive feeling, and a good rapport between the two leaders contributed to the steady progress of the Russian–Chinese partnership.

When I privately asked Jiang Zemin about the events in Tiananmen Square and the crackdown on the liberalization movement, he expressed regret that the showdown had reached the point of bloodshed but was sure that the rally, and indeed the entire process of liberalization, needed to be stopped by all means necessary. "I must first care about feeding and educating one billion people. Other things can come gradually, later," he said. He answered the question calmly and accepted it as a legitimate one. What was most striking was what he didn't do—which was resort to demagoguery or claim the unrest had been caused by foreign subversive influence. It was very different from the usual bombastic and accusatory rhetoric typical of Moscow before and after the 1990s.

We agreed that the top leaders of Russia and China would visit each other at least once a year, starting with Yeltsin's trip to Beijing in 1992, while the foreign ministers would exchange visits at least twice a year. Sino-Russian relations were indeed on track. I also surmised that the Chinese leaders were too well balanced and too experienced to engage in any serious anti-American activity with Moscow even if Russian politicians might try that game at a later stage.

Unfortunately, the temptation to use the Chinese platform to score anti-American points was already in place, and Yeltsin succumbed to it on his first official visit to Beijing in December 1992. Later, public statements in favor of a "multipolar" world and against the "domination" of any one country would become routine for Russian leaders visiting China. In 1994, irritated by US reluctance to support our efforts in searching for solutions on Bosnia, I too made a remark along those lines during a visit to Beijing.

On specific international issues we occasionally took positions close to China's, or even in coordination with China, either for or against certain US views. At the same time, we also discussed Asian issues with the United States and occasionally acted in tandem with the Americans. That is the right of sovereign nations, and both Beijing and Washington accorded Russia that kind of freedom, as we did them. What I deemed dangerous and inadmissible was any effort to set up an alliance between any two of these powers against the third one. I shared this view candidly with both of them, and they concurred.

During the first part of the 1990s, the vague anti-Americanism from neo-Soviet forces that routinely appeared in Russian media had a general and nonaggressive character, and never translated into attempts to offer China anything close to a suggested anti-Western partnership. Yet those neo-Soviet forces grew in power, and my successor Primakov offered just such a strategy to Beijing. I was gratified to see the Chinese administration handle those overtures in the same cool manner I had anticipated in March 1992. Even during the first visit to China by the next Russian president, Vladimir Putin, in July 2000, the Beijing leadership stressed that relations between the two countries were excellent, being "not an alliance, not confrontational, and not aimed at any third country." It is vitally important for both countries to stick to this.

Japan: Treaties Deferred

Despite Yeltsin's keen interest in improving economic and cultural ties with Japan, and despite that country's welcome of the emergence of a democratic Russia, the potential for greater cooperation was solidly blocked by the absence of a peace treaty ending World War II between Russia and Japan and the key problem of the four Southern Kuril Islands, which the Japanese call "the Northern Territories." Japan considers the four islands to have been unlawfully seized by the Soviet Union in 1947 and demands vigorously that they be returned.

This was the most intractable of the disputes Russia had inherited from the Soviet system. While we also had an unsolved territorial dispute with

China, Beijing took a relaxed, long-term view of the matter, and we agreed to calmly look for solutions, as the Soviets had begun to do a few years before. Tokyo declined to do the same, despite the fact that we went farther than our predecessors in demonstrating respect for Japan and its concerns, including territorial ones.

During ensuing contact with the Japanese, we reiterated that Russia as a UN continuation state would honor all the agreements and obligations of the Soviet Union, including the Soviet–Japanese Joint Declaration of 1956, which restored diplomatic relations between the two countries, recognized the "territorial issue," and mentioned the transfer of two islands to Japan after the conclusion of a peace treaty. For tactical reasons, we preferred not to identify the Joint Declaration in public statements, keeping it as a special concession, to be made perhaps at a top level. In the meantime, we tried to address Tokyo's position, offering to keep the issue on the agenda and to set up a working group to look into it and try to find a solution. In return, we hoped for greater economic cooperation, and Russia offered investment opportunities, especially in its Far East sector and in Siberia.

Yet the Japanese chose a more insistent approach (in my view), raising expectations at home and anxiety in Russia. There were reports that Japanese agents tried to take advantage of the organizational weakness and political chaos in Moscow as the Soviet Union was breaking up by offering inducements to some of Gorbachev's closest aides to give Japan control of the islands. That practice was evidently continuing under Yeltsin. Both the Soviet and the Russian officials approached in this manner had no idea of the complexity of the issue or of the diplomatic efforts under way to resolve it, and yet they had made promises, which the Japanese in turn took as official commitments from the Russian Federation. Politically, the nationalists in the Duma made hay of the affair, which often appeared in the news headlines. The communists in particular waved the flag of patriotism, asserting that the whole business of the Southern Kuril Islands merely proved that the integrity of the national borders had been better safeguarded under socialism.

Yeltsin himself fed this witches' brew by failing to take a strong public stand. Typically, he used parliamentary hearings not to explain and promote his administration's policies, but to collect more opinions on a "possible solution." A month before his visit to Japan, which was scheduled to begin on September 14, 1992, Yeltsin publicly admitted having twelve proposals from various sources on his desk. He added that he would reveal his own views to the Japanese prime minister alone. Perhaps the impetus for Yeltsin's statement was again his exaggerated ego and desire to appear in full command of everything, including on delicate matters of diplomacy. The statement only made matters worse. The opposition read it as part of a conspiracy to decide national border issues behind the back of the Duma and the public. On August 25, many deputies, including the moderate chairman of the International Affairs Committee, Yevgeny Ambartsumov, harshly criticized Yeltsin's upcoming visit to Japan and rejected any territorial changes.

With his back to the wall because of his own handling of the issue, the president summoned a special meeting of the national Security Council, a consultative body comprising the leaders of parliament and the government, five days before his planned departure to Tokyo.

There were two ways out. One was to adopt our proposal, which boiled down to recognition of the issue and the need to examine possible solutions in diplomatic talks with the Japanese, based on the legal documents inherited from the Soviet Union, including the Soviet–Japanese Joint Declaration of 1956. The nationalists wanted to deny the issue and the declaration, but their extreme demands could be rejected on the ground that Gorbachev had already recognized both in recent years. However, the Gorbachev factor was probably the reason that Yeltsin did not like our proposal, for it essentially repeated the approach of his predecessor. Thus, he would not be able to make a "historic breakthrough." But there could be no historic breakthrough in any event: indeed, there was no solution acceptable to Japan other than going beyond the 1956 declaration to cede all four islands to Japan. Yet for a nation already deeply wounded by the collapse of a land empire, any further border change would probably be too much.

The second option was simply to postpone the planned September 1992 visit to Japan on grounds of the complexity of domestic developments back in Russia, which required the president's full attention and presence. I had suggested this option in a private talk with Yeltsin two weeks earlier, assuring him that Japan and other countries would understand the context for deferring the trip. I also pointed out that time was running out for a postponement to be seen as normal.

The meeting of the Security Council opened on a somber mood. The discussion amounted to little more than a speech by Vice President Rutskoi denouncing the Japanese "claim to Russian lands." In the middle of the proceedings the president's chief bodyguard, Alexander Korzhakov, suddenly said that "according to secret information," the Japanese could not guarantee the safety of the president of Russia in Tokyo and they had turned down requests from the Russian security service to take various measures to improve the security situation. Under these conditions there was no question of risking the life of the Russian leader, and the visit should be canceled. With no further discussion, the decision was made.

I suggested that we provide a neutral public explanation for the decision and not invoke the ridiculous pretext of a lack of security in Tokyo. Yevgeny Primakov, chief of the Foreign Intelligence Service, supported me, for a change. It was a rare occasion on which I was glad to have him as a colleague.

The next day the press roundly attacked the administration for disarray in its decision making. The additional colorful details depended on whether the outlet was the communist or the liberal press. The liberal *Izvestia* condemned the act of abandoning a state visit in an advanced stage of planning under pressure from the security people as a manifestation of the internal weakness of the administration's foreign policy. I had to respond to this, and did so in an interview denouncing, in my turn, the "unprofessional interference by the bureaucracy in foreign policy." I tried to present the step as not insulting or arrogant to Japan.

A few months later my ministry was able to begin quiet talks with Japanese diplomats on making collateral improvements in the two countries' relationship, which paved the way for a reasonably successful state visit of the Russian president to Japan in October 1993. During his visit, in addition to a positive presentation of Russia's position regarding the islands, he also expressed deep regret for the USSR's mistreatment of Japanese prisoners of war, in wording we had thoroughly vetted with Tokyo to avoid any misunderstanding. His delayed visit did aid cultural and economic contacts between our two countries as he had wished, though the matter of the Southern Kuril Islands/Northern Territories remains unresolved.

South Korea and the ASEAN Countries: New Friends

North and South—presented some unique challenges to our efforts to develop good-neighbor relations with countries in a broad belt around Russia. We had kept diplomatic relations with North Korea, but resolutely removed any remnants of support that the Soviet Union had had with that communist dictatorship. By contrast we wanted the best possible relations with the former Soviet enemy to the south.

Gorbachev had begun normalizing relations with South Korea in the waning days of the Soviet Union. My own meetings in Seoul in March 1992, which moved our relations toward full-fledged cooperation and partnership, paved the way for an official visit by Yeltsin that November. During that visit Yeltsin and his hosts signed a treaty opening up the prospects of cooperation in all fields, from bilateral trade to world politics. These agreements helped turn the page on the hostility left over from the Soviet Union's backing of North Korea in its invasion of South Korea almost fifty years earlier. It also marked an important crossroad for Russia's internal orientation, away from its Soviet past and toward a future of alignment with the democracies of the world and participation in the global institutions of the developed economies.

The door was now open to broach the topic of the Soviet Air Force's downing of Korean Air Lines Flight 007 over Siberia in September 1983.

The wounds from this event had not healed with time in South Korea, especially as the Soviet regime had persisted in denying any responsibility for the tragedy. A public apology and some concrete demonstration of remorse from the new Russian president seemed appropriate. Yeltsin, with his flair for the dramatic, ordered Defense Minister Pavel Grachev to produce the KAL black box so he could deliver it during his visit. Grachev battled his generals to retrieve it, and Yeltsin delivered a warm and meaningful speech at a highly publicized ceremony during which he turned over the black box to South Korea.

This time, Yeltsin's instinct for the dramatic gesture came up short. The South Koreans soon informed us—and the world—that the box was empty. The flight-tracking device inside the box had been retained by the Russian military. Russia's president and commander in chief became a laughing stock on the world stage.

This episode was one of the clearest examples of how the inertial strength of the old structures and the old ways of thinking in Moscow created a drag on the execution of Russia's new foreign policy. But it was not the only episode connected to the Koreas. In March 1992, we learned that the chief of staff of the military forces of the CIS, who had been retained from a similar position in the Soviet Union, had paid a visit to North Korea's Pyongyang in accordance with the old Soviet schedule of planned visits connected to military cooperation. Allegedly this cooperation extended to regular arms transfers to North Korea, though the Soviet/CIS/Russian commanders in Moscow denied it. Yet those involved justified this business-as-usual military partnership by invoking the USSR–North Korea treaty, which was still in effect. Article 1 of the treaty spelled out Moscow's obligation to aid Pyongyang in case of a conflict.

The Soviet Union had spent decades developing close ties with the dictatorial militarists on the Korean Peninsula, as well as with similar regimes in Iraq, Syria, and Belgrade. These relations commanded broad support in bureaucratic, industrial, military, security, and diplomatic circles in Moscow. This network had been enriched and strengthened in the final years of the Soviet Union through corruption—and its grasp of some of the levers of power was more than able to compete with the fragile, nascent groups working to chart a new course for the foreign policy of an independent Russia. The pressure from this network was unremitting, and almost instinctively I wanted to sever their connections abroad as quickly as possible.

Deputy Foreign Minister Georgy Kunadze and I urged Yeltsin to meet with the South Korean foreign minister in June at the Kremlin and, in the presence of the press, to inform him that the treaty between the USSR and North Korea was no longer entirely valid, particularly with respect to Article 1 and provisions for strengthening socialism in both states. It did not bother me to hear Yeltsin phrase the idea less diplomatically. The treaty, the president said, "has lost its effectiveness and exists in name only." He also confirmed that Russia would not continue to provide North Korea with offensive weapons and assistance in developing its nuclear program.

Only when real measures had been taken to stop military and nuclear cooperation between the two countries did I feel ready to restore political contacts with Pyongyang. Kunadze went there in the spring of 1993 and agreed to maintain good-neighbor relations. Of course, our old friends did not want to discuss the debt owed to Russia of about US$3 billion, but instead demanded that we provide more military supplies on the same credit terms of the Soviet era, which would have increased their debt to us—one unlikely to ever be repaid. Our offer to sell them defensive weapons and spare parts on a normal commercial basis greatly lowered Pyongyang's interest. Amazingly enough, the Russian military-industrial complex suddenly felt the same way. North Korea's economically disastrous regime provided an opportunity for corruption only when it was subsidized by Moscow. In observing these aging lobbyists for rogue states clutching to positions of power in Russia's military and security organizations, it was clear that what they had lost in ideological vigor was more than balanced by their enthusiasm for financial rewards. The spectacle might be considered a small step toward a market system, even if taken by such avowed foes of reform.

In July 1992, the twenty-fifth annual meeting of the foreign ministers of ASEAN (the Association of Southeast Asian Nations) was held in Manila. For the first time ever, Moscow was invited to attend a session of that organization as a guest of honor, along with China. I offered a number of proposals for the development of political and economic partnerships between the "Russian bear" and the "Asian tigers," which were positively received by our hosts. Fresh from the Yeltsin–Bush summit in Washington and participating as invited guests at the G-7 session in Munich, I explained that Russia, with two-thirds of its territory in Asia, was seeking a new constructive role in the Pacific. Our goal was to be a power friendly to other big players in the Pacific—the United States, Japan, and China. Following this session, Russia joined as a permanent participant in ASEAN, and also developed bilateral relations with other ASEAN countries. The opening to Southeast Asia was praised in the Russian media.

Ironically, one corner of the Russian media started criticizing me for neglecting the East and concentrating only on the West in my diplomacy. It was an outrageously unfair charge. Throughout my trip to Korea and China in March 1992, and on every subsequent trip to Asia, the governors and members of the Russian parliament from Russia's Far Eastern regions accompanied me. They were consulted on all issues, particularly regional ones, such as border trade and immigration control. We facilitated meetings with government officials responsible for regional cooperation, provincial leaders, and businessmen. Moreover, a pool of reporters from the Russian press traveled with us, and most seemed to understand the goal of renewing relations with Russia's eastern neighbors on a positive footing: "Developing relations with China and other countries in the East is, according to Kozyrev, a priority for Russian foreign policy," said *Izvestia* on March 18.

The charges in the press that we were neglecting the East, in my view, were not targeted as much against me (though I was certainly a target) as they were part of an effort to shift Russia's orientation to the East in a political and ideological sense—meaning against the West. In peddling the "Eastern" direction as a priority, they sought to torpedo any partnership with the West because it ran counter to their interest in upholding the image of the United States and NATO as enemies.

It was disturbing to hear Yeltsin repeating those allegations at the end of the year: he knew their biased character but couldn't resist flirting with the opposition and hard-liners in the Kremlin. Later, when demands to "restore balance" by paying undivided attention to the East became the favorite tune of the opponents of "Western" democratic and market reforms, Yeltsin's joining in the chorus was the best indication that he had started to succumb to their pressure.

In the first months of the Russian Federation's existence as an independent state, we formulated and started to implement a new policy toward the major international players in a large belt around Russia, from the United States to China and from the Baltic to the Black Sea. The framework of emerging relations with them, opening a wide horizon for mutually beneficial cooperation, from border trade to multibillion-dollar investments, was also vitally important as a positive environment for domestic reform and for addressing urgent challenges in the post-Soviet space. Yet progress in domestic reforms in Russia greatly lagged behind those in international relations, and increasingly discordant engagements with parliament undermined the promises of treaties of economic aid and cooperation crafted during this period of nascent democracy.

As the second half of this book will show, the domestic foundation at home for that international framework started crumbling almost from the very start.

6

Shared Fate

Foreign Policy and
Domestic Politics

UPON THE DISSOLUTION OF THE SOVIET UNION in December 1991, the reformist Yeltsin government had a unique opportunity to live up to its billing. After the degrading experience of Gorbachev's indecisiveness (to say nothing of the attempted retreat from the path of reform), the media and public opinion were by and large prepared to give the reformers a chance.

The international environment was also generally beneficial for Russia. The United States and other Western countries, including Japan, presented no threat. To the contrary, they enthusiastically welcomed a democratic Russia and its new foreign policy, seeing—correctly—the enormous potential for mutually beneficial political and economic cooperation. They offered support in the transitional period, starting with supplies of food and medicines that helped alleviate daily hardships. Along the land borders we had good neighbors: China and the Commonwealth of Independent States, the latter on the road to living up to its promise of peaceful coexistence, however bumpy.

Yet the task before the government was formidable. The most urgent problems lay with the economy. Yegor Gaidar, Boris Yeltsin's acting prime minister in 1992, played a major role in Russia's economic transformation.

(He describes the challenges he faced in his memoirs and in an academic book, *Collapse of an Empire: Lessons for Modern Russia*, published in November 2007. My purpose here is not to revisit this subject.)

Like my colleagues, I had to promote reforms in foreign policy, using government structures inherited from the Soviet Union. All of them, including the constitution, required profound remodeling.

In the democracy-oriented climate, the reformers could only succeed if their policies could achieve wide popular support. The president and government should have been vigorously explaining the reforms at every step, correcting their implementation according to feedback, answering critics, and debating opponents. Needless to say, parliament should have been in the forefront of that effort.

The deficiencies of that old-style institution were reflected in its name: the Supreme Soviet. From its inception in 1990, representatives had been split about half and half between those appointed by the Communist Party and those elected by the people in defiance of the party. Nevertheless, this body had elected the rebellious Yeltsin as its chairman in 1990; appointed a number of radical reformers to the government; given the president extraordinary powers in November 1991 to implement Gaidar's program of dramatic reforms (despite its controversial elements); and finally ratified the Belavezha Accords.

Unfortunately, neither laborious structural transformations nor regular communication with parliament or the public were near the top of Yeltsin's agenda. He liked the high drama of politics and hadn't the taste or talent for tedious routine or disciplined and rigorous argument. More significantly, he had a rather vague idea about what the transformation of the society by the principles of democracy and capitalism meant in practice and was not prepared to support reformist strategies either for the economy or in foreign policy in battles he found tiresome. His top aides and the heads of the military and law enforcement agencies, the so-called *siloviki* (men of force), were composed of men personally loyal to him. The military commanders were not particularly reformist.

Yeltsin's great willingness to sign friendship treaties abroad was matched by an apparent reluctance to promote reform at home. For instance, the logic of the change in Russia's stockpiles of nuclear weapons and its strategy for dealing with the United States enshrined in START II meant retiring outmoded military thinkers and promoting officers who could grasp the new reality and bring fresh ideas to the table. Moreover, our government needed to summon the courage to tell the military and security institutions who Russia's strategic friends and enemies were. This kind of courage was critical to our democratic development and national interests. We also needed our state employees—civil servants, diplomats, and military and security officers, to unite behind the government's policy. Yet the president left a vacuum in strategic guidance from the top. Each of Yeltsin's ministers was left to lead according to his conscience. This ranged from my advocacy for radical reform, to the far more neutral Grachev, to Yevgeny Primakov who represented the forces of conservatism. Gradually, the hard-liners regained access to president's ear—and to power.

Thanks to the vacuum at the top of government, Russia's political structures—most of which were inherited from the Soviet system—were inevitably filled with old-style ideas and attitudes, nostalgic for Russia's superpower or imperial status, and with corruption. In their turn young reformers had no appreciation or taste for relentless public campaigning. Moreover, they obviously lacked practical experience of democracy and capitalism. What knowledge they did possess was drawn from Western books, rather than sustained exposure to these types of societies. Most members of Gaidar's team saw themselves as technocrats dedicated to the execution of the leader's program who should not waste their time trying to explain economic magic to the unenlightened. As a result, organizational structures and bureaucracy from the Soviet era were simply reborn, with new names.

Increasingly I found myself in the wilderness, and my voice was too weak to have any effect.

No wonder public opinion was shaken and disoriented. The tremendous costs of the Gaidar reforms fell on the shoulders of ordinary Russians. (That is why we urgently needed serious help from the United States and the West.) Communists and nationalists used the language of populist demagoguery to capitalize on the troubles. Soon they combined forces with the novel "centrists," who sought to decelerate the pace and limit the scope of reforms. The president sought to calm this tempest by replacing key reformers on his team with officials more pleasing to the "centrists." This served only to feed their ambitions and weaken his democratic base.

The Opposition Surge in Parliament

That in turn created an opportunity for Vice President Rutskoi and the hard-liners to advance their agenda. These forces took almost full control of the Supreme Soviet (the Soviet-style parliament) with the help and increasingly active leadership of the parliament's chairman, Ruslan Khasbulatov.

Khasbulatov was a shrewd and ambitious politician, who smoked a pipe continuously. Like Rutskoi, he had played an important role in defeating the coup attempt in August 1991 and wanted to be an equal player to Yeltsin in running the country afterward. Unlike Rutskoi, Khasbulatov and probably the majority of the parliamentarians were initially less extreme in their political views and ambitions and could be dealt with on a relatively reasonable basis. At least my initial experience of him was not so bad. I tried to keep the lines of communication open by dropping into his office at opportune moments to discuss foreign policy issues.

Khasbulatov was more supportive of my requests for appropriations to establish embassies in the newly independent states than the financial officers of the government were. They were sticking to a narrowly circumscribed economic view of priorities and neglected political needs. As urgent as these were, the resulting slowness in opening our embassies because of the lack of financial support from the government not only damaged our ability to address pressing problems in the post-Soviet space but also played into the hands of those who accused the reformers of being too pro-Western and of ignoring Russian interests closer to home.

Khasbulatov was no angel, but no demon either. Indeed, he was almost pushed into the opposition's camp because of the public attacks on him engineered by Yeltsin's new press attaché, Vyacheslav Kostikov. Kostikov had been a little-known journalist who suddenly, at the age of fifty-two, was projected into the front line. He too was intent on playing a political role. Yeltsin rarely read carefully the press releases he authorized, and Kostikov took full advantage of this. His aggressive and often rude remarks began to infuriate not only Khasbulatov but also many of the deputies, who felt humiliated that their leader was being insulted by a second lieutenant in the president's cohort. As a result, by April, Khasbulatov was siding with Rutskoi in leading attacks against Yeltsin and the government in the parliament.

Kostikov's bullheaded tactics had an impact not just on Khasbulatov but also on certain sensitive foreign policy issues. In one statement he explicitly

linked progress in the withdrawal of Russian troops from the territory of the
Baltic states to improvements in civil rights in those states. This was a view
that played into the hands of extremists on both sides and provoked a storm
of indignation in the international community. It also weakened our position
during difficult negotiations with the Baltic states on those very issues, which
could only be fruitfully addressed as separate problems. Though Yeltsin retal-
iated, authorizing the Foreign Ministry publicly to correct his press secretary
as well as giving Kostikov a dressing-down himself, the damage was done.
The episode proved to the opposition's satisfaction that, if it succeeded in
pushing aside the democrats, Yeltsin might be manipulated by aides pursuing
changes in policy to its liking.

With the strong winds of opposition blowing through parliament and
clear vacillation in the president's camp, some deputies started to advance
their own agendas in early 1992. Vladimir Lukin, the chairman of parliament's
Foreign Relations Committee, asked Yeltsin to appoint him as Russia's ambassador to the United States, which would make him the first person to
hold that position. But before leaving for Washington, he wrote a farewell
letter to the parliamentary deputies denouncing what he described as weak
policy toward neighboring countries. Provocatively, he suggested raising
the question of transferring Crimea from Ukraine to Russia. This letter was
enthusiastically welcomed by the opposition, which forwarded a resolution
on Crimea demanding "the return of Crimea to Russia" at the assembly of
the parliament, which convened in late April. By this point Lukin was in the
United States, enjoying the newly minted reputation of being an envoy of
democratic Russia. Part of that role involved making speeches about policy
with respect to international law and cooperation, yet even as he made those
speeches, he would have been aware that the resolution he had initiated had
become a major instrument of the communists and nationalists in their attacks on that very policy.

So parliament became the arena for the first frontal assault on the course
of reform. Correspondingly, it upped the ante for the reformists. When a draft
resolution demanding that the economic reforms be curbed was put on the
table, Gaidar proposed that the members of government should threaten to
resign en masse if the draft was not revised. Yeltsin was not informed of this
particular move. Despite his lack of involvement, in the face of this threat,
most of the deputies retreated from their demand to negotiate a milder resolution on economic policy that limited but did not stop the reforms. It was a

turning point—by acting resolutely, the government had won an important political battle.

As Gaidar notes in his memoirs, "Till that point, the government had been no more than a bunch of technical specialists invited by Yeltsin. After the move taken by the ministers at the congress it became a political player in its own right." Yet the victory was brief, since the reformers in the government never again had the courage to act independently from Yeltsin in the political field. So the whole democratic movement fell into line and led the cheerleading no matter what Yeltsin did.

Yeltsin's reticence in handling the ministers' rebellion was telling. He preferred to do battle with the opposition alone rather than asking for help from political figures in his own camp, who at best might put constraints on his ability to maneuver and at worst could compete with him for Russia's leadership. As a result, the technocratic government was left at the mercy of the opposition.

Beyond this, the media speculated that the ongoing rancorous political debate was providing a smokescreen for infighting among various lobbyist groups in the government and parliament for control of lucrative special licenses and quotas for the export of crude oil and other raw materials. Despite the general liberalization of foreign trade, the system of arbitrary bureaucratic management of the commodity exports—a legacy of the Soviet foreign trade monopoly—was never dissolved. The fortunes of those businessmen, who soon became fabulously rich and influential oligarchs, were therefore mostly built on the foundation of special relationships with the managers of that licensing machine.

In early 1992 I asked Gaidar why this system of distributing favors had to be kept. He told me that it takes time to correct everything. Yet when in April the former Soviet minister of the oil and gas industry and the founding father of Gazprom, Viktor Chernomyrdin, was appointed deputy prime minister, the question became moot. I never asked again.

At the sitting of the April parliament, the deputies requested a special report on the policy toward the former Soviet republics. The opposition was not ready at that stage to challenge the whole foreign policy line, not least because of the successful start of new relations with the United States and other major countries. So, for the time being, the CIS (Commonwealth of Independent

States) was identified as a weak point. Along with the draft resolution on Crimea, the deputies forwarded a motion to annul the agreement that dissolved the Soviet Union and set up the commonwealth. High on their list was the demand that Russia should be able to intervene in the internal affairs of neighboring states of the CIS to "protect" ethnic Russians and separatist movements there.

The hysterical calls of the communists and ultranationalists to "liberate our abandoned brothers" in Crimea or Transnistria were uncomfortably close to what had transpired during Nazi Germany's campaign to "protect" the Sudeten Germans, or German Bohemians, in Czechoslovakia in 1939. Hitler used the problem instigated by his own propaganda as a pretext to occupy the Sudetenland and later the whole country. This dangerous similarity to Weimar Germany was not lost on the democrats in parliament, nor indeed to reform-minded observers in the media. It was a harsh comparison, but, mindful of the outcome of the policy of appeasement of the Nazis, they wanted to fight the red-brown propaganda—fascistic communism—before it could take firm root. I shared and appreciated this vigilant attitude.

I decided to tackle the challenge head on and demanded the floor to explain my policy. I avoided terms like "red-browns" in my speech but strongly rejected the draft resolution on annexing Crimea because of its potential for destabilizing our relations not only with Ukraine but also with Russia's other CIS neighbors, since each of them had predominantly Russian-populated enclaves that could become targets of Russian territorial claims

I began by declaring that the choice was not between the Soviet Union and the CIS but between fratricidal war and peace. The commonwealth was a historic achievement because the Soviet Union had collapsed. Yet again I found myself pointing to the Yugoslav scenario as the only alternative to the CIS, in which Russia would fight with breakaway neighbors as those neighbors fought among themselves to challenge borders, in an ever-escalating cycle of destruction and bloodshed. In contrast to that nightmare possibility, the CIS was busy establishing new cooperative structures and mechanisms for potential integration between the former Soviet republics. That was the signal achievement of the formation of the CIS.

The process, however, was more painful than many deputies had expected because the Soviet system had alienated those peoples so much. Russia's "aggressive patriots," I pointed out, by threatening coercive economic or military action against the country's new neighbors were pushing them farther away and damaging the prospects of Russian-led voluntary reintegration. The idée fixe of re-creating "the socialist camp," the Soviet Union or the Old Russian Empire, even in a reduced state, was both unrealistic and counterproductive. The practical impact of the "heroic" stance of the "hurray patriots" was nothing other than an aggravation of the conditions of Russians and other national minorities in neighboring states, making them look like an alien and retrograde force.

These words had an instant and inflammatory impact on the audience. My speech was interrupted by angry catcalls and shouting: "It's you, democrats, who ruined the Soviet Union and betrayed the Russians!" The democrats among the deputies shouted back: "Heroic provocateurs! Nazis!" The giant hall, filled with more than a thousand angry men and women, looked increasingly agitated and unpredictable. Yet the majority of the deputies seemed impressed by the stark realism of what I had to say and responded to the chairman's calls for order.

I spoke for about forty minutes, and then answered questions for another half hour.

Among other things, I said, "If we want to live in a democratic state with high standards, then we have to set the same standards as the cornerstone of our relations with our neighbors. We should not compromise either in domestic or foreign affairs. This doesn't mean that Russia should not use all methods possible to protect its interests and human rights, including tough measures as a last resort, and even force. On the contrary, we should learn to use every form of protection in accordance with existing norms and standards of international law."

I reiterated my view that building partnerships and potential alliances with the developed economies of the West was not just an option but the single most important element of a successful foreign policy in the former Soviet space. Most CIS countries, I said, wanted to win the respect and economic assistance of the West and Western-based international institutions, such as the International Monetary Fund or the World Bank. If Russia were at odds with the West, those countries would have less incentive to behave in a civilized way internally and in foreign policy.

One question asked by a deputy gave me the opportunity to address a long-standing thorn in terms of Russia's eternal envy of America. "The US secretary of state James Baker has just concluded a trip to the CIS and inaugurated US embassies in some of them. When are we going to open Russian embassies in those countries that are so close to us?" In response I pointed to the lack of funding for foreign embassies in the newly independent states and asked the Assembly Appropriations Committee of the parliament to correct the situation. Thus, a very specific job awaited those deputies, I stressed, who were really concerned with promoting Russian interests and protecting Russian citizens in those countries.

That got the funding ball rolling, though it took a few months more before parliament and the government started to finance the embassies at even a bare minimum.

Like Gaidar, I think I could say that after the congress, I struck out to become more of a political player on my own.

Yet the deputies approved the resolution denouncing the Belavezha Accords that called for the dissolution of the Soviet Union and the establishment of the CIS, and another one claiming Crimea for Russia. The Foreign Ministry immediately prepared a draft statement rejecting the resolution as making a territorial claim to Ukraine. Our statement was approved by Yeltsin and issued as the official position of the Kremlin. It weakened but could not completely assuage the anger and suspicion raised on the Ukrainian side.

The Security Council and the Party of War in the Kremlin

In the aftermath of the April session of parliament, the opponents of reform regrouped, and went to work even more aggressively inside the bureaucracy, even inside the Kremlin itself. They found a home in the Security Council of the Russian Federation, which convened for the first time in June. The council membership included the "political" government ministers of defense, foreign affairs, internal affairs, security, justice, and top representatives of the parliament.

Yuri V. Skokov was an archetypal "red director" and fixer, who was appointed to the new position of secretary of the Security Council. He never expressed his political views, either publicly or in government discussions, and could be regarded as a politically neutral technocrat, like Chernomyrdin and others in the bureaucracy. We were at different ends of the political spectrum but had fairly good personal relations as members of Yeltsin's team.

Soon after becoming secretary, Skokov proposed regulations requiring that any significant draft decision for the president should be signed by all concerned ministers to ensure a balanced character. In case of disagreement, the ministers should try to reach consensus and, as a last resort, bring the dispute to the president for arbitration and a final verdict. There was nothing new in this proposal compared to existing practice. What was new was that the secretary of the Security Council claimed a coordinating role and would prepare drafts for the president in case the latter decided to summon the council to discuss matters at the "round table."

I supported this proposal, which Yeltsin soon signed as a presidential directive, and relied on Skokov's bureaucratic and managerial skills. As far as I know, other ministers initially shared this attitude, though with more skepticism. I remember one of them telling me that while I naively expected Skokov to consult the Foreign Ministry, Skokov expected to use his position and skills to control and command the Foreign Ministry as well as all other ministries.

The skeptics proved to be right.

Soon the new secretary invited me to a private meeting at his office in the Kremlin. He greeted me in a friendly fashion and said he wanted to talk off the record. He was a very cautious man, but behind his affable tone he was clearly trying to warn me that my policy needed correction, testing to what extent I would be flexible in making changes. Essentially, he was on the same wavelength as Transnistria's Igor Smirnov and Abkhazia's Vladislav Ardzindba, whom he referred to as loyal aides. I could also clearly hear themes of reestablishing Great Russia by supporting those loyal leaders and fighting the "international conspiracy" by adopting a tough position in talks with the West and protecting "our Slavic brothers" in Belgrade.

I was shocked. That suggestion was quite opposite to my position and the official stance of Yeltsin's administration.

Skokov was not alone, but part of a clique of like-minded bureaucrats in key organization positions close to Yeltsin. The most prominent figure among them was Yuri Petrov, the president's chief of staff. He was an influential player who regulated large flows of information to and from the president. Both Petrov and Skokov were supposed to use their connections with the communists and representatives of the industrial and military lobby to help the president. They were more experienced in bureaucratic games than I and better positioned to play those games. And both men's personal relationship with Yeltsin predated mine. They had the president's ear on private matters, including, I suspected, some delicate issues of internal intrigue.

Even some allegedly democratically minded of the president's aides schemed against the new foreign policy. I daily faced petty impediments to communicating with the president, such as delayed messages, canceled meetings, and so on. I resorted to the direct telephone line that was supposed to be reserved for emergencies.

All kinds of tricks were used. The morning after the landmark UN vote on sanctions against Belgrade on May 30, 1992, the communist newspaper *Pravda* published the text of a "top-secret cable from the Russian representative to the UN Yuli Vorontsov" and hinted that it was leaked by "patriotically minded" diplomats in my ministry indignant about "Kozyrev's betrayal of our Slav brothers in Belgrade." Yeltsin called me, angry over the leak, and asked me to focus on the work of the ministry. Ten days later investigators reported that the leak had come from the Security Ministry, not the Foreign Ministry. Yeltsin and *Pravda* remained silent.

Feeling growing isolation from the Kremlin, I started to think of measures I could take to safeguard my policy and position. My choices were very limited.

To seek help from my natural allies, Gaidar and the other democrats in the government, was unrealistic and unfair. They themselves were under attack in the media, and even more so inside the power structures because of the economic reforms. Yeltsin had just appointed another conservative industrialist to a top position in government, thus tying Gaidar's hands. And, of course, I had no chance of outmaneuvering my opponents in the bureaucratic corridors.

I had only one option, to appeal to public opinion, which at the time favored the democrats. Yeltsin needed and heeded it in facing Rutskoi and Khasbulatov.

On June 30, 1992, the popular newspaper *Izvestia* published my interview under a headline in large type on the front page: "The Party of War Is on the Offensive in Moldova, in Georgia and Russia: Minister of Foreign Relations Andrei Kozyrev Warns of the Danger of a Coup d'état."

The effect was explosive. The word "coup" immediately grabbed readers. I had been warned about the headline in advance, and my first thought was to ask *Izvestia* to change it. My second thought was that it would not be so bad to hint at Rutskoi's ambitions, which might in fact lead him to a coup attempt (and actually did a year later). He was vice president of Russia, just as Gennady Yanayev, the head of the August coup plotters, had been vice president of the USSR.

But my words were primarily aimed at Yeltsin, whom I wanted to draw to my side using public pressure. If he wanted to change the course of the reforms, I believed he should do so openly, not through bureaucratic decisions made behind closed doors.

I made it clear that the party of war was concentrated in a powerful bureaucracy in the military-security complex. They were pushing Russia into a militaristic and interventionist course of action in the post-Soviet space, just as Milošević was doing in Yugoslavia. No wonder they saw him as an ally. To justify their actions and goals, they were bombarding the president and public with biased information.

The first objective of the party of war, I said, was to create the impression that "our friends" were the separatists and extremists in newly independent states and that they were in peril from "our enemies," the elected governments of those states. The second objective of the party of war was to secretly provide backing to the separatists and extremists in the form of money, weapons, and even "volunteers" recruited from the Russian military and security forces.

In the meantime, their agents and collaborators in the media and parliament were waging a hysterical campaign, demanding unrestrained unconditional support for "our friends" abroad and denouncing the "weak" democrats inside Russia. The ultimate goal of the party of war was to seize the Kremlin, not necessarily by a direct coup, but by converting the president to their faith.

Democracy and badly needed reforms in Russia were incompatible with national-imperialism in Russian foreign policy, I said in the interview. Trying to mix them together or giving ground in foreign policy to the hard-liners would merely strengthen the uncontrolled power of the military and the state security agencies. Ultimately, the responsibility for preventing this catastrophic outcome rested with Yeltsin.

Immediately after the interview appeared, the TV and radio stations picked up on its content as major breaking news. I was pleased to see that the party of war had been brought under the fire of public opinion.

By the end of the day, I had received notice of a summons to an extraordinary session of the Security Council of Russia, to be held behind closed doors. When I arrived at the Kremlin all the other members of the council were already there. They had sorted themselves on two sides of the hall. There were Rutskoi, Skokov, and Primakov talking in a small circle, and a step away from them a group of the ministers of defense, interior, and state security. All of them pretended to be too engrossed in conversation to shake my hand. There was also a smaller gathering comprising Burbulis, Gaidar, and Shakhrai, who gave me a particularly warm welcome.

The meeting opened with a brief statement by Skokov, the secretary of the Security Council, who said that one of the council members had made an unusual and inadmissible public statement that exposed to the outside world his disagreement with the president's political line and also apparently accused other council members of conspiracy to unseat the head of state. This meeting had been convened at the request of the vice president, whom Skokov invited to take the floor.

Rutskoi began speaking from his seat. His language was accusatory and his tone whining. The main problem, he claimed, was not the breach in discipline and confidentiality but the incorrect and "weak" policy in the CIS and Yugoslavia that I had allegedly advocated in the "slanderous" interview to *Izvestia*. He insisted that only his personal intervention in the conflicts in the CIS countries had saved Russia from being humiliated. Yet in Transnistria the foreign minister had made a totally misguided intervention that had prevented the Russian troops there from a decisive use of force. Now, they were limited to a humiliating peacekeeping role.

Within a few minutes he had worked himself into a state of high indignation. He stood up and began shouting.

"You, you listen to me!" Rutskoi pointed his finger in my face. "I will not allow you to make Russia a banana republic!"

"You, you listen to me!" I jumped to my feet, pointed my finger in his face, and shouted back at him. "I will not allow you to draw Russia into a bloody Yugoslavia-type mess!"

The vehemence of my response caught him at a loss for words. He turned red-faced and clenched his fists. Burbulis quickly rose from his seat to my right and made the gesture of a referee separating two boxers.

"It is unfair and not true," Burbulis said to Rutskoi in a low, tense voice. He went on in a more normal tone: "Gentlemen, let's calm down and respect the Security Council. Here is the president, who has the authority to establish the policy. And only the president! So, let's help him with our advice rather than quarrel."

His words were followed by a deep silence.

"Take your seats," Yeltsin said in a muffled voice. "That's enough. I know your points of view."

Once everyone was seated again, he continued, "Yes, only the president sets policy, and everybody else should stick to it. You can make proposals and disagree with each other here, in the council. It is normal that we have different ideas on different subjects. But you should stick to one line in public and stop making your arguments through the media. It is wrong to go to the press to argue with the vice president, Andrei Vladimirovich." With these last words he turned to me, even though until then he was patently addressing Rutskoi.

"Actually, I was the last to go public, Boris Nikolayevich, and I am the first in favor of stopping the media war and following the president's line, as I have always done," I replied. "If some of my colleagues feel hurt by the reference in the interview to the danger of a repetition of the coup attempt, I am sorry, but the whole thrust of the interview is that the danger must be prevented. President Yeltsin is not Gorbachev"—here I turned to the assembly—"and he will not bow to communist pressure and will not transform you into Kryuchkovs and Yazovs. Read what I said, not the commentary and interpretations. Journalists like to overdramatize to draw attention."

"The meeting is adjourned," Yeltsin said, and left the room.

He never mentioned this episode to me again. Only once, answering a reporter's question at a press conference in the Kremlin about a week later, did he say that my statement had been discussed by the Security Council and adjudged harmful. But the journalists present noted that he went on to stress points corresponding to my policy concept: Russians in the former Soviet republics should be protected by peaceful means. As for Transnistria, it should be given a special status, but within Moldova. The Fourteenth Army should be neutral and should play an exclusively peacekeeping role.

The few democrats left in parliament won a special meeting with Yeltsin in Kremlin. The group comprised a number of outstanding personalities with impeccable reformist credentials and credibility in public opinion: Viktor Sheinis, Nikolai Vorontsov, Sergei Kovalyov, Boris Zolotuhin, and Sergei Ushenkov. They also met with Gennady Burbulis, who at that point was still Yeltsin's right-hand man, and had his backing.

Their message to Yeltsin was loud and clear: stay on course with the reforms and keep the military and security lobbies under control. The press reports highlighted the group's concern over the political attacks being directed against me. Viktor Sheinis was quoted as saying that despite some nuances, the consolidated opinion of the democrats was that my ministry and I "wage basically democratic and sound policy in the national interests of Russia" (*Nezavisimaya Gazeta*, August 4, 1992).

From the day of the Security Council meeting, my path for communicating with Yeltsin was cleared of obstacles, and I soon got approval for the Foreign Ministry's approach with respect to handling regional conflicts, including my efforts in Moldova and Transnistria. Yeltsin issued written instructions to all ministries and agencies to follow this line. The document further specified that only the Foreign Ministry was authorized to present the official point of view on those and all other international problems.

It was an important victory but, as I later learned, not a decisive one. Rutskoi was stripped of any authority in military and political matters, though he went on speaking about them freely and very negatively.

The Civic Union

Yeltsin's public rebuke left Rutskoi diminished but not defeated. He was still vice president and in search of a role for himself. Recognizing that public opinion was unfavorable to warmongering or demanding a halt to the economic reforms, Rutskoi decided for the time being to leave those matters to the most militant communists and nationalists. Instead, he once more pretended to be a centrist positioned between the two extremist camps: the radical democrats, on one side, and the communists on the other. In this feigned centrism, he was joined by a loosely linked coalition branded the "Civic Union." Most of its leaders simply pursued a more prominent role in the new movement rather than advancing any particular policy or ideology.

One of them was Sergei Stankevich, a young lawyer who had joined the democratic movement before I did. In 1989–90 he became deputy mayor of Moscow City but was overshadowed by Mayor Yury Luzhkov, who remained mayor for almost two decades (it seemed little coincidence that his wife became a billionaire Moscow real estate magnate in the meantime). Stankevich published an article titled "The Resurrection of a Great Power," in which he demanded the right to consider the former Soviet republics and countries of Eastern Europe to be a special zone of Russian interests where Moscow should dictate its own rules and play a dominant role. Ironically, a few years later he sought refuge from alleged persecution in one of those countries, namely Poland, perhaps appreciating that his demand had not been honored.

Vladimir Lukin also started to promote the idea of a "middle ground," or centrism. While still Russia's ambassador to the United States, he gave interviews to Russian journalists and coined the phrase an "infantile pro-Americanism," which guided "certain young people" in Moscow. Their naive trust in US friendship was simply exploited by the Americans to squeeze unilateral concessions from Russia—unspecified because there were none. The corrective move for Yeltsin evidently would be to replace his young foreign minister with a veteran, Lukin, who was fifteen years older.

In practice the moderate-sounding centrism of the "Civic Union" simply undercut the forces of change midstream. Since the centrists themselves were weak and disorganized, they joined forces with the communists and imperialists in attacking the reformers in parliament. All of them thought that Yeltsin, with his background as a communist apparatchik, had no strategy of his own and was just acting under the influence of the democrats in his entourage. Thus, he could be manipulated, first by the centrists and then by the serious opposition leaders if they had enough representatives at the top surrounding him. This strategy was not entirely without merit: We referred to it as creeping "apparatus revanche."

The Civic Union had held its first meeting on June 21, 1992. A year later, it was gone. The different factions and their leaders, who formed the Civic Union in an uneasy alliance, were never well matched politically and grew increasingly estranged from one another. But for a time, badly advised by his aides, Yeltsin took it seriously and tried to appease it during the run-up to the December session of the parliament. In a move that struck at the morale of the democrats, Yeltsin removed Burbulis from government at the end of November. He also fired some more ministers from Gaidar's team and went on discussing additional personnel moves and policy issues with the Civic Union's leaders.

This misguided tendency to appease the Civic Union also manifested itself when the president visited the Foreign Ministry on October 27 to address the session of collegiums with the participation of as many diplomats as could be accommodated in the conference hall. I had been asking for such a visit since the beginning of 1992, especially after he had visited the Ministries of Defense, Interior, and even the Foreign Intelligence Service (where, he told me, he had been impressed by Primakov's presentation of the history of Soviet spy operations, particularly the stealing of nuclear bomb secrets from the United States).

Yeltsin's Speech at the Foreign Ministry

When Yeltsin arrived, he seemed patently nervous and could not meet my eye. He read his address stumblingly. When he gave speeches, he had personally worked on, he did so smoothly with the air of a prophet communicating important and serious things. If the text was prepared by his assistants without him, he would read it in a constricted voice, halting in mid-phrase and repeating difficult sentences—as he did that day.

The speech sounded like a digest of Civic Union clichés. He asserted that "Russia is seen by the West as a nation that says only yes." He took a witty sideswipe in my direction, labeling me "Mr. Da." Since Andrei Gromyko, the Soviet Union's long-serving and inscrutable foreign minister, had been known worldwide as "Mr. Nyet" for his confrontational policy, the centrists tried to portray me as the opposite extreme, offering a "balanced" candidate, like Primakov, instead.

Listening to Yeltsin's speech, I wondered: How does he know what they think in the West? The answer came a few sentences later: "I personally receive more and better information from intelligence sources abroad than from our ambassadors."

During his speech I took notes and drafted a few points to answer the most disturbing accusations, which I intended to do both emotionally and directly. Yet Yeltsin, a strongly instinctive man, could sense my intentions. As he finished reading the prepared text, he thrust the paper aside and stopped me from speaking with a gesture: "Wait a minute. I haven't finished yet."

He continued by saying that despite some difficulties and errors, the ministry had been doing no worse a job than other government institutions and that "the president supports the foreign minister and his policy." Suddenly his tone changed, and he became more heated, as if arguing with an invisible opponent. He spoke forcefully of the need to continue the radical reforms in the country, despite the tremendous difficulties of the first ten months. "At the forthcoming congress of the parliament we can expect an attempt to reverse the policy of reform by changing the government. . . . This should not happen. . . . By all means, the foreign minister should be preserved, at a minimum . . . and most important is to safeguard Gaidar."

I put the draft rebuttal in my pocket, thanked the president for honoring the ministry with his visit and sharing his wisdom, and adjourned the session.

Despite his last words I was taken aback by the thrust of the text he had read. Oddly enough, I felt that he was too. As we walked to my office, he told me to take it easy. "Most of what I've said, Andrei Vladimirovich, reflects current opinion. Some points are worth thinking about but should not be taken literally. As I said, you are doing a good job here, and now we both deserve a relaxed chat. Let's see your office."

I accepted his explanation, and started telling him about the building, which had been put up in the same year I was born and where I had spent sixteen years, starting as a junior clerk and ending up as head of the department. He was eager to see the room I had shared with sixteen other employees from 1974 to 1984. About the same number of people were occupying it when we dropped in. Though the room was fairly spacious, it was far too small even for six people. This was no exception but a typical accommodation in the Foreign Ministry of the Soviet Union, inherited by the Russian one.

Yeltsin was surprised that the diplomats had to work under such cramped conditions, and even more surprised when I reminded him of the low salary they were paid. My reformist friends in the Finance Ministry had been reluctant to increase the diplomats' wages, even when I pointed to higher salaries for those of the Defense and Security Ministries. This was a lingering reflection of the priorities of the Soviet regime and needed to be changed. Yeltsin asked why, in the face of miserable wages and working conditions in the Foreign Ministry, diplomats had always been considered an elite group in the Soviet Union.

I pointed out that a diplomat posted to a Western country could take advantage of the artificial exchange rate to make himself wealthy back in the USSR. When abroad he could purchase a slightly outdated music set for a trifling sum and sell it for the price of a condominium apartment back in Moscow. That prompted Soviet diplomats to stay on a foreign assignment for as long as possible, but also contributed to the grinding sense of inferiority that sharpened the typical Russian mindset, which combined grudging admiration for the West with an intense hatred.

"That's just so much history now," I said. "But in the new economic conditions, these incentives are not only humiliating—they no longer work. The limited internal convertibility of the ruble has eliminated the gap between the prices of foreign goods abroad and at home. We need to provide diplomats with decent salaries or we will lose the best cadres to the private sector. We lack money to maintain existing embassies, and we badly need funding to establish new ones in the newly independent states. I'm sorry to say this, but the government is not listening to us. We count on your help!"

He promised to look into the funding issue, then added, "From outside, Stalin's skyscraper"—the nickname for the former Soviet Foreign Ministry building that had now become the Russian Foreign Ministry—"always looked like a symbol of glory and might, while inside it hid a humiliating reality. Like Soviet foreign policy, and indeed almost everything in the Soviet Union!"

We parted on good terms. He did not mention the speech again until May 1995.

I carefully went over a copy of the president's remarks with my close aides, searching for clues to what seemed an alarming twist in policy.

Our first guess was that the president's aides had crafted the speech to reflect their own views and he had simply read the text. Though to some extent that was probably true, it seemed too simple an explanation. His aides wouldn't have dared to go that far on their own. And the criticism had implicitly been directed at the president no less than at me, since he had approved all policy and political moves—and his aides knew it.

A much more disturbing clue lay in the president's apparent willingness to throw a foreign policy bone to the Civic Union and to old customers in power structures. Clearly, for now his commitment was only verbal, but he would certainly try to follow with deeds. Vladlen Sirotkin, a professor at the Diplomatic Academy, wrote to the then-liberal newspaper *Nezavisimaya Gazeta* (May 26, 1992) that while the Foreign Ministry was pursuing a "diplomacy of partnership," with the West, the other two Russian government agencies, with their own channels of communication with the Kremlin, were pursuing their old strategy of undermining that partnership. Those "other agencies" were the Foreign Intelligence Service, successor to the KGB, and the GRU, the military intelligence unit of the Ministry of Defense. Their task, Sirotkin said, "remained focused on debilitating a 'potential enemy.'"

If in the spring and early summer of 1992 Yuri Skokov and his aides seemed to be improvising when they argued with me for a revision of Russia's new foreign policy, by late fall, they had achieved a strong consensus, with the support of various factions. Publicly I called this new emerging consensus "neo-Soviet."

In a superficial departure from the Soviet legacy, the neo-Soviets abandoned the main ideological thrust of communist propaganda, which cast the West as a class enemy. In its place they posited the idea of a Western, and in particular a US, conspiracy against Russia. The underlying rationale for this apparent conspiracy echoed what Milošević had explained to me in Yugoslavia: the centuries-old juxtaposition of Western Christianity and Russian (Oriental) orthodoxy, rivalry for domination in the Balkans and elsewhere, and the desire of the West to take control of Eurasia and its natural resources.

Certain correspondents abroad and commentators on international affairs at home publicly promoted this new iteration of the anti-Western doctrine. This group had long been implicated in the Soviet propaganda network closely connected to the KGB. For example, Yevgeny Primakov, the head of the Foreign Intelligence Service, had long served as chief *Pravda* correspondent in the Middle East. Most of these Cold War veterans and their trainees had retained their positions after the collapse of the Soviet system. The president was receptive to those opinions and, especially to the advice and information supplied by Primakov, whom he entrusted to oversee the transition of the KGB to the Federal Security Service (FSB) preserving the old KGB's cadre and capabilities—and mindset.

Yeltsin and many high-level officials with Soviet backgrounds found the conspiracy theory, however hypothetical, far more appealing and familiar than the complex analysis of the kaleidoscopic international reality offered by the Foreign Ministry. Partnership with the West required work, difficult negotiations, and a tough defense of Russian interests. It was the best avenue for building a strong, democratic Russia. But it threatened to leave the bureaucracy with no scapegoat to blame for socioeconomic problems and the security services with no adversary to justify their power at home.

The Democrats' Attempt to "De-Communize" Russia

Immediately after the August 1991 coup failed, the democrats began looking for a way to make the rejection of communism a decisive turning point in the country's mentality. Many realized the need for a focused campaign of "de-communization," analogous to the de-Nazification campaign in Germany after Hitler's defeat in 1945. Shakhrai, Burbulis, and a liberal lawyer, Andrei Makarov, decided to try to have the Communist Party banned through a legal process similar to the Nuremberg trials of the Nazi leaders, which condemned Nazism as a crime against humanity.

I doubted that going through the court system was the wisest option. The task of overcoming totalitarianism was to my mind more a political than a legal one, and needed to be carried out by denouncing the mass repressions and aggressive military adventures of the Soviet state through appropriate media and educational efforts. I wrote an article pointing to a number of UN and Conference on Security and Co-operation in Europe (CSCE) documents denouncing totalitarianism as incompatible with basic human rights and freedom.

After a dramatic opening, Yeltsin's initial enthusiasm similarly became lukewarm, and he excused himself from personal participation in the effort. The process became embroiled in legal arguments and counterarguments, and public attention quickly fell away.

Unlike the Nuremberg trials, the Moscow trial did not focus on personalities, partly because the most recent party leader had been Mikhail Gorbachev, respected by reformers for jump-starting the process of democratization and refusing to authorize the use of force to safeguard the communist system. Evidently, he could not be accused of crimes against humanity as the Nazi bosses were. Nevertheless, he was called to speak as a witness in the case.

One morning in late October 1992, a public statement issued by the Kremlin caught me by surprise, announcing that the Foreign Ministry and other agencies had been instructed to deny Gorbachev exit from the country until he honored the court summons. Clearly Yeltsin was irritated by Gorbachev's criticisms of his policies and was trying to take revenge on his old rival.

It didn't take long for Gorbachev to get in touch on the phone.

"What kind of democrats are you, repeating old practices like this?" he shouted. "I thought I had put an end to most of the Soviet exit impediments as well as surrendering the presidency of the USSR!" I tried to explain to him that it was a temporary measure, which I personally did not like and would try to get canceled as soon as possible. In any case the foreign ministry had nothing to do with the border control supervised by the interior ministry. Also, I added, it was my personal opinion that he could do a great service to the cause of democratization, which he had started, if he spoke to the court as a witness of Soviet totalitarianism.

"I called you because I thought you were different, but I was wrong. You are just one of them, the false democrats! I don't want to know you!" he yelled at me and hung up the receiver. It was a bad day.

Within a week, the shameful refusal to allow Gorbachev to exit was canceled, but not before many damaging media comments had been made, nor indeed without telephone calls to Yeltsin from the leaders of many democratic countries. This incident also permanently halted the democrats' efforts to use the court to outlaw the Communist Party.

Most importantly, de-communization or, perhaps better, a political departure from the totalitarian past, was not formalized and consolidated in society as de-Nazification had been in Germany. Russia still suffers from that today.

The Firing of Gaidar

At the long session of the parliament scheduled to begin on December 1, 1992, the Civic Union had a hit list of key figures of Yeltsin's cabinet. The possible impeachment of the president himself was also much discussed.

Yeltsin's position was weakened by his decision not to form a political party of his own or to affiliate with an existing one, such as Democratic Russia. He insisted he had taken an oath to be president of all Russians and that he needed to stand clear of partisan politics. Though advocating for the Democratic Russia, I halfheartedly chose to agree to Yeltsin's argument in private conversations with him.

On November 9, a large gathering of democrats took place in Moscow with the idea of forming a party to counteract the forces of the Civic Union and the nationalist opposition. Yeltsin addressed the meeting in a speech full of commonplace assertions and generalities. He failed to indicate his readiness to head a reform party. He said only that he was "thinking" of the necessity of such a party. Many participants, who saw no other leader for the party they hoped to form, had expected Yeltsin to lead it and were not prepared to act on their own. The meeting ended with no practical result—a disappointing contrast to the successful mobilization and institutionalization of the opposition factions.

Many staunch democrats challenged Yeltsin's preference of operating "above the parties," stressed the real, practical need for such a party, and felt betrayed when Yeltsin declined to lead it. In retrospect, I think they were right. Sitting above the power structures, however, Yeltsin finally found himself with only one organizational ally left, the state bureaucracy. The bureaucrats were only too happy to offer him unchecked power in the tradition of the Soviet system, along with its backbone—the state security ideology and apparatus. The "bureaucratic choice" actually sustained Yeltsin but doomed the nascent capitalist environment in Russia to cronyism, corruption, and oligarchy rather than a competitive and equal opportunity marketplace.

The disorganization and demoralization of the democrats was evident in the parliament halls. Ahead of congress, Gaidar addressed the Supreme Soviet on the economic situation, indicating willingness to engage in certain compromise measures, such as providing greater support for key industries. And Yeltsin, seeking to soften the agenda of the Civic Union, removed key members of his administration, including Burbulis and Mikhail Poltoranin, along with Yegor Yakovlev, head of Ostankino television. The hard-liners welcomed Yeltsin's concessions, but did nothing to moderate their demands in return.

Proceedings at the congress itself were heavily manipulated by parliamentary chairman Khasbulatov in favor of the opposition, with the help of the centrists. Initially Khasbulatov had cautiously welcomed the birth of the Civic Union, thinking it might play a buffer role between the democrats and communists and help him run parliament, but now he discovered that the "center" was in essence a swamp with no political agenda or power base different from those of the nationalistic and communist opposition. In all important debates and votes the self-styled centrists ended up on the side opposite the democrats.

After a weak opening speech, Yeltsin came under a barrage of criticism. Even though the proposal to impeach him was defeated—along with a number of other resolutions intended to weaken his powers—Yeltsin found himself in almost constant conflict with the Civic Union and parliament. A major point of contention centered on the expiration of his special powers, granted in 1991. Yeltsin indirectly asked for a continuation of those powers while the country prepared for a new constitution according to a referendum he proposed. That proposal was not accepted. The parliament and the president of the Russian Federation were now locked in battle both over economic policy and the division of power.

Yeltsin angrily returned to the session on December 10, and in a short, televised speech from the podium called for a referendum at which the people of Russia would vote either for the president or the parliament. In the meantime, the constitution should be left untouched. That strong move took the dispute between the president and the parliament to the arbitration of the highest authority, the people.

The speech was correctly addressed to the public outside the walls of the assembly. Yet at the end of it, Yeltsin asked his supporters in the hall to stand up and walk out to pass the decision to the voters rather than the congress. Even though most of the democrats had long supported the call for such a referendum, many of them remained seated. They had not been consulted, they were caught by surprise, and they felt detached from their leader. Millions of television viewers saw even the democrats hesitating to follow Yeltsin's lead. The congress continued its deliberations and only a week later made the decision to have a referendum in the spring.

I asked to take the floor to report on foreign policy and rebut personal attacks, as I had done before. This time Khasbulatov denied me the privilege.

Yeltsin replaced Gaidar as prime minister with Viktor Chernomyrdin, the former Soviet minister of oil and gas who in April had accepted the same position with the Russian government. The congress applauded this decision as a clear signal that the strategy of changing the policy by changing the top officials was working. The radical economic reforms slowed and, in many respects, stopped. Yet the new prime minister proved to be a real compromise figure. After some antireformist and populist statements he took a more balanced line, disappointing the opposition even more than the democrats.

I was deeply concerned about Yeltsin's sacrificing his team of radical reformers in the economic field. It was clear to me that the neo-Soviet ideas about managing the economy and government would eventually undermine the foreign policy based on the strategy of integrating Russia into the community of free-market democracies.

I also knew that after Gaidar, I would be the next to be forced out, which made me seriously consider retiring. I discussed the matter with Burbulis and Gaidar. Both were strongly against it, seeing it as an undeserved Christmas present for the opposition. They made public statements in support of Yeltsin as the leader of the democratic movement and thought that my resignation would only weaken this movement at a difficult moment. Each of them remained in contact with Yeltsin as an adviser. Thus, the democratic leaders once again decided to stay with Yeltsin and fight for his ear and heart rather than challenge him openly politically. I agreed halfheartedly to stay on, though it was not clear to me how I could continue executing Russia's foreign policy.

Stockholm Démarche

On December 11, while parliament was still in session, I caught the late flight to Stockholm, where I was scheduled to participate in a general discussion the following morning at the ministerial conference of the CSCE. One of the reporters in the press pool who usually showed up at the airport for a previsit press conference asked me whether I had instructions from Yeltsin to change my speech at the ministerial meeting in order to accommodate the views of the opposition and reflect the points Yeltsin had made while speaking at the Foreign Ministry in October. I replied that I had not.

On the plane I recalled the question and wondered how long it would take for Skokov or someone else to push Yeltsin into signing new foreign policy instructions, and what those guidelines might look like. An article on foreign policy in a newspaper I had picked up, signed by an activist of the Civic Union and a businessman close to Moscow's mayor Yury Luzhkov, Aleksandr Vladislavev, suggested an answer. His coauthor was a research fellow at the State Institute of Europe, Sergei Karaganov, who was the most likely candidate to have written the piece, since he had made it look like a professional essay rather than the collection of bald-faced political slogans that it was. "There's an example of the mild rhetoric of the so-called centrist advocates of policy change," I mused. The authors claimed that by following their proposals, Russia would gain in international status. I knew that Yeltsin was heeding arguments of this sort for the purpose of accommodating the opposition. "How can I prove them to be wrong?" I kept asking myself.

Then the idea of how to use the upcoming meeting—which had been set up just as another polite diplomatic talk session—struck me. I perused the draft of my speech, prepared by my aides, and knew what I should do.

When I woke up, there was a war going on in my head between my diplomatic and political instincts. "Wait! You should not make a major political move, especially abroad and with public consequences, without seeking approval from the political authority," the diplomat said to the politician. "In normal times you would be absolutely right," the politician answered. "But these are not regular circumstances. It is a truly unique time of revolution, or rather counterrevolution, and one has to act accordingly."

"What if Yeltsin fires you for this move?" the diplomat whispered. "And if he did it on the technical ground of violating the diplomatic code? Then you would just be giving up your position to your opponents, to no effect."

"There will be an impact! And it will be a political impact! Nobody pays attention to procedural matters. If Yeltsin is going to fire me, he will do it anyway."

On arriving at the conference, I immediately sought out the chair, Sweden's minister of foreign affairs, Margaretha af Ugglas, with whom I had a very good personal relationship. I asked Margaretha for a procedural favor: to be given the floor to speak twice, with about an hour's interval between speeches. Each minister was usually allotted only one time slot for an address, but after I told her that my unusual request was prompted by some dramatic political developments in Russia, of which she was aware, Margaretha agreed to allow me to give my speech in two parts.

"Today I must announce serious changes to the foreign policy of the Russian Federation," I declared when given the floor, and I paused to allow the translators to deliver the message to the delegates, most of whom were barely listening to their colleagues deliver well-known policy statements. In a minute the noise level plummeted. The tension in the hall was palpable.

I put aside the prepared text of my speech and took a clipping from the article I had read the previous day on the plane. Then I summarized the piece: "While fully maintaining the policy of entry into Europe, we clearly recognize that our traditions in many respects, if not fundamentally, lie in Asia, and this sets limits to our rapprochement with Western Europe.

"First: We see that, despite a certain degree of evolution, the strategies of NATO and the WEU [Western European Union], which are drawing up plans to strengthen their military presence in the Baltic and other regions of the territory of the former Soviet Union and to interfere in Bosnia and the internal affairs of Yugoslavia, remain essentially unchanged.

"Second: The space of the former Soviet Union cannot be regarded as a zone of full application of CSCE norms. In essence, this is a postimperial space, in which Russia has to defend its interests using all available means, including military and economic ones. We shall strongly insist that the former USSR Republics join the new Federation or Confederation without delay, and there will be tough talks on this matter.

"Third: All those who think that they can disregard these particularities and interests—that Russia will suffer the fate of the Soviet Union—should not forget that we are talking of a state that is capable of standing up for itself and its friends."

As I walked to my seat from the podium, I saw with deep satisfaction that the hall, so silent before, was buzzing with activity. Many ministers were hurriedly leaving to telephone their capitals.

The moment I took my seat members of the Russian delegation attacked me. They were no less surprised than the others.

"Andrei, have you just received these new instructions? Of course, you are not going to agree with such a policy, and that's why you've interrupted your speech. I am going to resign as well," Galina Sidorova said, in her honest manner. I had invited her as a gifted journalist and strong voice for reforms in *Novoe Vremya* (New Time), to join our team to help communicate with the media.

"I am resigning too," said the Russian ambassador to Sweden, Yury Fokhin. He was a long-serving professional diplomat, appointed in Soviet times, and I had not expected a veteran of the Soviet Foreign Service to take such a strong political stand. I met his sharp look and shook his firm hand with extra force. "Yes," he repeated with a smile but great determination. "I am resigning too." He paused, and then added softly, "You have at least no less sympathy than skepticism toward your policy among the ranks of the seasoned Soviet diplomats, Mister Minister."

In a moment—to my delight—I found myself the only one ready to advance the new policy I had just announced. So I gathered my team and revealed the game I was playing, apologizing for the need to keep it to myself until that moment. For the greatest impact, the new policy needed to look serious to others, and the obvious surprise and revulsion of my team was adding to that impression.

Larry Eagleburger, the US secretary of state, was gesturing frantically for me to join him outside the hall for a talk. He was a good friend and an understanding person. It would be unfair not to confide in him.

"Andrei, what can I do for you? Are you under threat?" Larry asked the moment we entered a private room reserved for bilateral consultations. He thought that a coup d'état had taken place in Moscow and that I had been forced to make a statement by former KGB agents threatening my life.

"You son of a gun! You almost caused me a heart attack!" he exhaled, relieved at my explanation. "I see your point. You and your friends are going through difficult times back there. And I would be the last to demand diplomatic protocol in a struggle like this!" I expected no less from him. He promised to keep the secret until my next speech except for briefing his president by phone.

"Please, don't keep the suspense going for too long! Make your second speech before another Cold War starts!" said Douglas Hurd, the head of the British Foreign Service, when we met in the lobby. "The Ukrainians and some other delegates from the CIS, not to mention the ministers of the Baltic states, have already asked us what security guarantees NATO could provide for them in the face of Russian pressure."

Galina Sidorova hurried to me with her hands full of fresh cables from the major news agencies. The firestorm my words had ignited was threatening to escalate into an international crisis. Governments and political leaders from the CIS and Western countries were expressing deep concern and demanding explanations.

Oddly enough, there was no inquiry from the Kremlin. One of Yeltsin's press aides later told me half-jokingly that many of his colleagues in the president's entourage initially thought that "Kozyrev has finally started to talk in the right way" and were alarmed only when they saw the international reaction, which surprised them. That's when they considered bringing the incident to the attention of the president.

I asked Margaretha to give me the floor again.

"Yes, Andrei. We deserve a clarification," she said.

"Dear colleagues," I spoke into the deep silence, "in the first part of my speech I presented to you the sorts of changes in Russian foreign policy that are typically demanded by the centrists in Russia. Of course, this is just a pale simulacrum of the U-turn in strategy that the real opposition would make if it seized power. I wanted you to be aware of these demands and I wanted those who put them forward in Russia to be aware of your reaction, which was, I hope, clear enough to cool the hotheads down. I thank you for that, and for your understanding.

"I am happy to tell you loudly and clearly that as long as the first freely and fairly elected president of Russia, Boris Yeltsin, leads the country and I implement his foreign policy, those changes are out of the question."

I knew I was being only half honest. I was not so sure about the first part of my pledge and was not too surprised when it proved wrong a couple of years later when Yeltsin appointed Primakov my successor. I continued, "I am now going to present to you the actual policy of the Russian Federation as defined by the president, and the official text of my remarks will be distributed to the delegates and the press." With those words I read the text of a regular speech that, after the shock of the first, received satisfyingly close attention and was triumphantly reported by the media as evidence that the announcement of a new Cold War had proved to be only a caution.

Most Western observers and politicians understood my message and started to speak of the need to be more attentive to Russia's problems and our foreign policy needs. Some realized that the new cooperative approach we had offered the world came at the cost of an intense political battle inside Russia and even inside the Kremlin and could not be taken for granted. Unfortunately, these conclusions in the West did not have a practical impact and quickly faded from attention.

Many Ukrainian and Baltic commentators seemed to focus on the first half of my speech as representing a real new direction in Russia's foreign policy. Yeltsin had to repeat over and over that he had never considered changing his policy direction. His strong public commitment was exactly what I had wanted to achieve.

The proponents of the reversion to a neo-imperial Soviet-style federation, both in its power structures and in the centrists' headquarters, were forced to backtrack and publicly denounce their own goals by calling the first part of my speech an "invention and exaggeration." They also had to insist that they had never demanded the policy be changed but just wanted it to be less "pro-American." Soon they adopted the unified tactic of portraying the Stockholm event as the sheer hooliganism of the foreign minister, who was much too loose a cannon and needed to be tutored by the president in both conduct and diplomacy.

Amazingly, they found an unlikely ally in Helmut Kohl, the chancellor of West Germany, who on the day of the speech had arrived in Moscow on an official visit apparently in demonstration of support to Yeltsin. I was told that Helmut had expressed indignation at the violation of diplomatic order in Stockholm to his friend. The German foreign minister, Klaus Kinkel, later confirmed that Kohl, like Kinkel himself, was at first struck by the sense of disorder after he learned that the "proclamation of the new Cold War," which caused him so much anxiety, was just a ruse. "But soon," he said, "we recognized the importance of the signal you sent in Stockholm and pressed Yeltsin as to his real intentions. Further discussions of the episode were focused on bringing home to him that the international reaction to the first part of the speech could not be interpreted as other than a clear and strong warning against changing the policy and the minister who so ardently defended it, even if he chose a disorderly way to do it."

When asked about the speech at a press conference at the conclusion of Kohl's visit, Yeltsin said simply, "Kozyrev acted on his own. He probably exaggerated the strength of the opposition as demonstrated at the Congress of People's Deputies and has been too pessimistic about our ability and resolve to promote the new foreign policy and reforms."

So in Stockholm I gained some breathing space, but it proved to be little more. A few days after my speech, Yeltsin confirmed my feeling that despite the strong effect of the démarche, his resolve to fight for fundamental domestic and foreign policy reforms was not unconditional. While on a visit to Beijing he insisted to the press that Russia's foreign policy had been "excessively Americanized" and that Russia would do better to look for allies elsewhere, especially in the East. The Chinese leaders wisely heard this with detachment, and the anti-American overtones did not spoil an important opening with China. Yet Yeltsin's words were an alarming sign. He seemed to be heeding the Civic Union's advocacy of a pivot to China both in foreign policy and in shaping reforms according to a model of the state capitalism.

In 1993 my room for maneuver when defending Russia's new foreign policy narrowed. Yeltsin's increasing reliance on a poorly restructured state apparatus on top of his decision not to stand at the head of any political party, deprived the democrats of strength in the legislature and of a popular leader at the helm of the reforms.

As a result, the great potential that had opened up for Russia, as the democratic nation seemed to wane, alongside the pursuit of the new foreign policy, required a tough struggle— primarily on the domestic stage, though it also presented considerable difficulties in relations with the new US administration.

Boris Yeltsin defies the Soviet coup.

Protestors atop a Soviet Army tank.

Belovezha hunting lodge, where the fate of the USSR was decided.

Representatives of Ukraine, Belarus, and Russia sign the Belovezha Accords.

With my best partner, US Secretary of State James Baker, during US President George H. W. Bush's official visit to the USSR, July 30, 1991. SPUTNIK / Alamy Stock Photo

Visiting local commanders in contested Nagorno-Karabakh region.

Meeting with George H. W. Bush at the White House.

With Boris Yeltsin, Warren Christopher, and Bill Clinton to discuss peacekeeping operations in the Balkans.

With my press secretary, Galina Sidirova.

Meeting with Yasir Arafat.

Signing ceremony for the Oslo Accord. Beside me from left to right are Shimon Perez, Bill Clinton, Yitzhak Rabin, Yasser Arafat, Warren Christopher, and Mahmoud Abbas. ZUMA Press, Inc. / Alamy Stock Photo

Visiting the naval base near Murmansk, a region I represented in the Duma.

7

Balkan
Complications

THE NOVEMBER 1992 US ELECTIONS ALLOWED THE Democratic
Party to consolidate its hold on the White House. But at the same time the
democrats in Russia were on the defensive. The Republican defeat in the
1992 presidential elections along with the transition to a new administration under the inexperienced and domestically focused Bill Clinton dealt
an unexpected blow to the democracy movement in Moscow. We had lost
a devoted partner in a painful reform effort to a friendly but self-centered
administration in Washington.

George H. W. Bush, the outgoing American president, had vast experience
in foreign and especially in Soviet affairs as former director of the CIA. As
the ambassador to China he had seen the true face of communism, and as
US president he had firsthand knowledge of the arcane subtleties of Moscow
politics, understanding well the doublespeak of politicians. The same was
true of his foreign policy crew, headed by hardened veterans such as National
Security Adviser Brent Scowcroft and Secretary of State James Baker.

The US team, despite parting from Gorbachev on friendly terms, clearly
recognized the magnitude of opportunities that were opening up with the demise of the Soviet Union and the creation of the CIS. Fresh from the perils of
the Cold War, they recognized that Russian democratic transformation was a

priority, since it was closely tied to the vital concern of reducing the threat of nuclear war. For the team following in their wake, this threat already looked much more distant, banished to the past by the new regime with whom they had to deal in Russia.

The Bush administration was also well aware of the difficulties the reformers faced. In a speech at Princeton University on December 12, 1991, on the eve of his visit to Moscow, Baker offered his insight into the turbulent situation in the collapsing Soviet Union and called for an appropriate response not only from the United States but also from the West as a whole. At that historic juncture, he said, the world was needed to help channel the current of change in the direction of democracy and economic freedom in Russia, Ukraine, Kazakhstan, and other republics that had started to build their own future. Nobody, Baker warned, should disregard the difficulty inherent in achieving that kind of change and the strength of the "dark forces," representing the legacy of the Stalinist system and extreme nationalism, that were waiting for a chance to reemerge. He concluded by proposing that a coalition of Western states collectively aid the newly independent states with humanitarian assistance, especially food and medicines; help in promoting democratic institutions; and economic aid, aimed at the development of free-market mechanisms.

The United States and other Western countries were also quick to help Russia join the world financial institutions. At the seventeenth G-7 meeting, held in Munich on July 6–8, 1992, with Russia participating as a special guest, a project of increased assistance for the CIS countries was proposed.

But as the prospects for the reelection of the Republican administration faded, we saw ties to Washington wither. Republican attention was caught up with a presidential campaign in which the party was increasingly revealed to be a lame duck.

Once Clinton was elected, his attitude proved to be friendly enough. He even inaugurated the era of "Bill and Boris," a relationship born of both leaders' tendency to personalize foreign policy. Yet however good his intentions, this relationship was unable to disguise the underlying problems. Untested in foreign affairs, Clinton depended on the audiences he was playing to, with Congress and the public expecting him to deliver first of all on his campaign assurances to boost the domestic economy. Subordination of foreign policy to the swinging fortunes of partisan domestic politics prevented him from being the kind of consequential friend President Yeltsin desperately needed. Even the language in which he addressed critical issues such as NATO membership and Bosnia added to the atmosphere of uncertainty that gradually coalesced around his dealings with Russia. Nor did the grandly promised aid materialize in amounts large enough to move the reform efforts forward. The Americans seemed not to understand the dire social situation of the Russian population and the effect on its fledgling democracy, and Russia found it difficult to advance reforms without significant outside support.

Nor were the International Monetary Fund (IMF) and the World Bank prepared to flex their muscles adequately. To be effective, they would have had to directly engage the Russian government and economic actors, helping them make hard decisions and undertake sustained measures at macro and micro levels. The whole process of engagement and support demanded exceptional organization, extraordinary political will, and a substantial budget, which only the governments of the United States and the major Western countries could provide. Without enhanced resources and American guidance, the IMF and World Bank could not do more than they did, which was to wrap disbursement of the funds in conditions. Thus, the Russian authorities were primarily supplied with what felt like schoolbook advice on the basics of a market economy and financial discipline.

The reformers in Russia knew those fundamental principles by heart but needed practical assistance in implementing them despite growing resistance in parliament and even of their old-school president's aides. The communist opposition and the old-style bureaucracy started to criticize those institutions for their disdain toward social problems and their poor management. Criticism of this sort was not unheard of in both developed and developing countries and was not always groundless. Yet in Russia it was marked by a distinctive antiwestern ideology and anti–free-market tone. The economic reformers in Moscow made no more than weak and sporadic attempts to explain the benefits of cooperation with world bodies. Some bureaucrats deliberately added to the confusion in order to cover up their own inefficiency in using the funds, as well as to divert attention from constant accusations of corruption in their distribution. As a result, the World Bank and particularly the IMF became symbols of the West's mistreatment of Russia in a large part of the Russian media.

Yeltsin especially defied the perception that he was being bullied by international bureaucrats. He denounced the IMF's demand that Russia freeze fuel prices and wages, arguing that such a move, besides being a political death knell, would trigger a large general price rise. Because meeting even milder demands, as a condition for receiving assistance, estimated at $24 billion, couldn't be achieved without serious assistance in place to do so, a vicious circle was promptly created, effectively blocking any large-scale material aid. The highly publicized "helping hand" of the United States and its allies in the interest of strengthening democracy in Russia degenerated into little more than empty and humiliating talk and gave the opposition in parliament and the executive bureaucracy an opportunity to gloat over the clumsy failures of the "hapless schoolboys" who were trying to negotiate aid from the West.

This contrast between the initial rhetoric on the part of the West, especially the United States, on the one hand, and the sluggish delivery of assistance on the other was destructive. Critics of the new policy of partnership actively exploited the widespread sense of Moscow's disillusionment with the West and the pursuit of reforms of a democratic and free-market orientation. This happened at a time when Russia urgently needed the support and aid of a new Western coalition, as the reforms in Russia were daily proving increasingly difficult and painful to implement.

Bill Clinton had won the US presidential election having made very few foreign policy statements during the campaign. I hoped and expected he would learn more once in office. One bright spot was that many knowledgeable people, including some well-known experts on Russia, were joining the administration. Among them was my good friend Toby Gati, who had been appointed to the US National Security Council and later became under secretary of state, specializing in the CIS. Her husband, Charles Gati, was a professor of international studies at Columbia University who had fled to the United States after Hungary was forcibly drawn into the sphere of Soviet domination. Whenever I was in New York I would see the Gati family and enjoy informal dinners at their apartment on the West Side.

The Gatis knew Bill Clinton and asked me to help arrange a meeting with Yeltsin when the latter was visiting Washington during the summer of the 1992 election year. At that point Clinton was a candidate of the opposition party—we were working with the Republican Bush administration at the time—and it was quite common for foreign visitors to unofficially meet major candidates for the American presidency. Clinton's request for a meeting had been forwarded through regular diplomatic channels to the office of the Russian president, who flatly rejected it, claiming loyalty to George H. W. Bush and holding firmly to his belief in Bush's reelection. Eventually, however, persuaded by the practical argument of not offending a person who might become the US president, and in keeping with the democratic tradition of meeting leaders from the party that was not in power in an election year, Yeltsin reluctantly received Clinton in a setting he perceived to be as low-key as possible. The interview was scheduled for no more than half an hour in the morning, before Yeltsin started the third and last day of his official visit to the States, and in Blair House, the US residence reserved for visiting dignitaries.

That was the right thing to do, but even though I had lobbied for the meeting it seemed not to have served us well. If Clinton did become president, he would be remembered by Yeltsin as a political puppy who had begged for a handshake from the great president of Russia—the same person who just the day before had addressed a joint session of the US Congress to standing ovations. The setup was a replay of history in reverse. If from the start of his relationship with President Bush, Yeltsin had felt like an underdog, trying to gain points in his rivalry with Gorbachev, with Clinton it was just the opposite: he was now the seigneur and Clinton the untutored supplicant. This meant that any encouragement for Yeltsin, a former provincial Communist Party apparatchik, to rein in his old political habits was significantly diminished when in November Bush, a leader perceived as strong, was voted out and the weak Bill Clinton was voted in.

For Kremlin bosses like Brezhnev and Gorbachev, respect for their American counterparts—Nixon, Ford, and Reagan—as strong and resolute leaders occasionally checked their hand, not only in Moscow-Washington affairs but also in domestic affairs, such as the handling of political dissidents. (Khrushchev, by contrast, generally conducted himself as having the upper hand over the supposedly weaker President Kennedy, especially in the early days of the American president's administration.) I suspect that Yeltsin may have regretted losing a strong counterpart as a balance to his apparatchik tendencies. He knew well that Russia needed substantial assistance from the West for a successful transformation. The availability of such assistance depended crucially on American leadership, and Yeltsin doubted that the foreign policy lightweight and domestically focused Clinton could deliver it where even Bush had failed. That is why in his first call to congratulate the new American president he virtually demanded that Clinton pay a formal visit to Russia as soon as possible, so that Yeltsin could establish a working relationship with him and was frustrated when Clinton demurred.

I fully shared Yeltsin's apprehension about the future performance of the Democratic administration. In November 1992 I published an article in the then leading Russian liberal weekly, *Moscow News*, under the title "Partnership with the West: A Test of Strength." The piece was also published in an English translation and was frequently quoted in the foreign press. It was addressed both to my opponents at home and to the incoming Democratic administration in the United States. I welcomed its broad distribution, for the article marked a signal attempt to warn the West of the stark dangers already forming in Russia, and what Russia needed to surmount those challenges and continue on the path of reform.

In it I pointed out that the greatest danger to Russia lay not so much in a direct challenge to the authorities, such as a coup attempt against Yeltsin, but in the creeping revanche of the apparatus and the *nomenklatura*, especially among the administrative organizations, which were merging with the Russian mafia and joining forces with the nationalists.

From this standpoint, and depending on the ability of Russian democrats to withstand these forces and on the policies of Western governments, I saw three possible outcomes for Russian–Western relations: (1) a return to confrontation, not on a communist basis but under the banners of nationalism and neo-imperialism; (2) alienation and rivalry, especially in conflict zones such as Iraq and Yugoslavia; or (3) a friendly and allied interaction. Although the first two options required no investment from the West, they might subsequently entail enormous costs. The third option was not feasible without serious investment—political, economic, and organizational—but could be expected to yield a good return. Within the frame of cooperation—which meant, among other things, promoting democratic and market-economy institutions—Russia would also need help in finding new markets for exports, including armaments, high technology, and space technologies.

The demand for markets was not a payoff to Russian hard-liners. Rather, it recognized that the Russian military-industrial complex could not just be ignored or dispensed with but had to be reformed and reoriented from an instrument of authoritarianism at home and confrontation abroad into part of a new civil society and cooperative world system. Thus, like Russia itself, it should be given a new place and a new mission in the world.

Many reasonable-minded military and industrial people I spoke to in Russia, while allergic to calls for restoring the Soviet Union or a return to its aggressive foreign policy, argued that there was no alternative to selling to old rogue clients, such as Iraq or North Korea, because the West was stonewalling any chance for fair competition in more legitimate weapons or nuclear energy markets, which it had monopolized during the Cold War. The argument used in these competitions, according to potential buyers, was only a rerun of the old ideological shibboleth: you cannot trust the Russians, and if you deal with them, you'll find yourself on the wrong side of the East–West confrontation.

Neither Washington nor its allies ever seriously responded to my argument for high-tech markets, and especially military ones, preferring to avoid discussing the situation altogether while actively lobbying for expansion of their own industries into Eastern Europe and the former Soviet republics. This narrow-minded and shortsighted attitude backfired, for it consolidated the reflexive anti-Western stance of the influential part of the Russian nuclear and military elite, which stubbornly continued to cultivate ties with rogue regimes, perceived as the only available business partners.

Worse, the American reticence was accompanied by self-congratulatory remarks on having won the Cold War. These remarks made the headlines in Russia and were eagerly latched onto by the opponents of the new foreign policy as proof that Russia was being treated by the United States and the West not as an equal partner in building a new world but as a defeated enemy that had to submit to the victors' intentions. Among those most sensitive to the characterization of Russia as the dog that lost the fight was Boris Yeltsin.

With all that recent Russian history and sentiment in mind, I sought to end my article with a clear message: "By showing the wisdom and good organization displayed during earlier moments of crucial historic choice—in fighting fascism and containing Soviet expansionism—the West could help Russia establish itself as a permanent member of the democratic 'club' of most advanced nations."

I had no illusion that the third option required leaders like Winston Churchill, who in 1946 called for mobilization against the "Iron Curtain" that was falling on Eastern Europe. Now, when the curtain was going up, there was no figure of Churchill's caliber.

Bosnia on the Front Burner: The Vance–Owen Peace Plan

In the meantime, a cease-fire and a political solution were desperately needed in Bosnia, where territorial divisions were continuing, along with ethnic cleansing.

On January 2, 1993, the former US secretary of state Cyrus Vance, acting on behalf of the UN, and the former head of the British foreign service David Owen, representing the European Union, after consulting the parties to the Bosnian conflict and various international actors, including Russia and the United States, forwarded a peace plan for Bosnia. The Vance–Owen peace plan reined in the expansionist designs of the Serbian militants, requiring them to retreat from certain territories they had already seized. It proposed creating ten semiautonomous regions within Bosnia and Herzegovina.

Although the plan represented a complex compromise and posed difficulties in implementation, I decided to support it. Produced by American and British diplomats, the plan seemed likely to receive a positive response in the West. Through associating with it we could manage to avoid a dangerous fracture with the Western powers. By supporting an international peace plan we could also resist the pressure of the Russian nationalists, who were dominating public opinion with demands to protect our "Serbian brothers," whatever crimes they might be committing against Muslims or Croats. Suspicions that the plan was prejudiced against the Serbs calmed down somewhat after the press reported that the Muslims and Croats were reluctant to accept it without significant bargaining. Since this mirrored the Serbian reaction, the plan was finally accepted in Moscow as being evenhanded and fair. Through such arguments I persuaded Yeltsin to actively support the Vance–Owen peace plan and I was proud of his decision.

Russia circulated a draft statement in the UN Security Council calling on the conflicting parties in Bosnia to reach an agreement on the Vance–Owen peace plan without delay. We received a positive response, especially from the Europeans, who saw the plan as an EC initiative.

The emerging international consensus suffered a powerful blow, however, when on January 22, 1993, the day after the inauguration of President Clinton, the *International Herald Tribune* reported that certain comments by the new secretary of state, Warren Christopher, had put America "in the awkward position of publicly supporting a negotiating process, while criticizing—and perhaps undermining—the particular plan that is on the table."

I learned about the article from Yeltsin, who had a report on it the next morning. Certain aides were quick to draw his attention to those facts, believing that they testified to the naiveté of a policy of cooperating with the United States, which would not hesitate to act unilaterally and undiplomatically in pursuit of its selfish interests at the expense of its European allies, not to speak of Russia. I tried to persuade him that this was an exceptional episode caused by the mess of a transitional period.

"I did not realize that it is also in their tradition to throw away everything done by their predecessors," he said. "Do you think they might also challenge START II and the other agreements we've reached with Bush?"

I said that I had had direct assurances from the outgoing US secretary of state Larry Eagleburger that President-elect Clinton had been briefed on the START II negotiations and had publicly approved the treaty. As to other issues, that remained to be seen.

"Cyrus Vance," Yeltsin continued, "was secretary of state in a Democratic administration and his recommendations should be more acceptable to the Democrat Clinton than those of many other appointees of the previous Republican government. It might be, though, that this new man, Christopher, who served as deputy to Vance, now wants to denigrate his former boss."

I was surprised that he had been briefed on details such as Vance's party allegiance and I thought it could not have been done by anyone other than Yevgeny Primakov, director of Russia's Foreign Intelligence Service.

"Some say that we've been too quick to abandon the Serbs and support the Western plan, which is now challenged by the West itself, but you also have a strong point, saying that this plan is the best we have," Yeltsin concluded.

"It is the best everyone has," I said, "and the Americans will come back to it sooner or later. They are probably right in putting most of the blame on the Serbs, but in the end there is no way to settlement other than by getting the Serb leaders on board. The key to the solution lies in Belgrade. Like the authors of the plan I have spent a lot of time with Milošević and believe that he can gradually be induced to recognize the inevitability of a compromise. He is starting to realize that Serbia is losing too much, both because of the sanctions and because of the disgrace of the bloody war and ethnic cleansing waged by fanatics in Bosnia. He accepted the peace plan just a few days ago and recommended that the Bosnian Serbs' leaders—the political leader Radovan Karadžić and the military leader [Ratko] Mladić—do so as well. That is potentially a major game change. The extremists just wouldn't last long without political and material aid from Serbia. Unfortunately, the turnaround will be a painful process and the atrocities and intransigence of the Bosnian

Serbs will continue to provoke indignation around the world, and particularly in the West."

I spoke my mind. Then he spoke his.

"Russian public opinion has the opposite view. It regards the Serbs as victims, and we have to take that into account. If Clinton tries to follow up on his campaign threats to punish the Serbs, we won't be able to swallow it. Air strikes are inadmissible!"

The American team at the UN countered our draft with its own, which would simply "take note" of the Vance–Owen peace plan and call for negotiations basically returning the political process to square one. Unfortunately, the explanation offered by the Americans showed their hand by echoing the Bosnian Muslim leader Alija Izetbegović's criticism that the proposed plan "ratified and legitimized partition of the country and the fruits of Serbian aggression and 'ethnic cleansing.'" That assessment was clearly as partisan and unfair as the one proffered by his opponent, the Bosnian Serb leader Radovan Karadžić, who accused the plan of being tantamount to the genocide of the Serbs in Bosnia and a historic humiliation of Serbia proper.

Lord Owen in his memoirs later revealed that the US State Department had killed off the draft statement we circulated in support of the Vance–Owen peace plan "because it was a Russian initiative, and they were suspicious of Russian motives."

After the American blow to the Vance–Owen peace plan Milošević believed he was trapped, telling me that he had always known the United States was not interested in a peaceful solution but just wanted to establish itself as the supreme arbiter in Europe and force the Serbs to their knees. We, along with the authors of the peace plan, persuaded him to continue supporting it, but his resolve to fight for it with Karadžić and Mladić and risk his popularity in Serbia was slow to return.

Most European governments also felt betrayed and humiliated and tried to argue with Warren Christopher. However, they were not prepared to do anything without US backing, preferring an unhappy Atlantic unity to an autonomous partnership with Russia, even in defending their own peace plan. I in turn felt betrayed by the Europeans, who could not level with me despite my democratic credentials and the sacrifice I had made in confronting the Serbs for the sake of the peace plan.

Despite all this, Vance and Owen continued their effort to keep the peace process alive.

Troubling US Diplomacy

I prepared carefully for my first meeting with the new secretary of state in February 1993. My basic message was that the United States should regard Russia not as a developing country with nuclear weapons looking for American help but as an industrial power undergoing a difficult transition, the direction and outcome of which were taking shape even as we spoke. If we failed to cooperate, the likelihood would increase that Russia would move in a different direction, one advocated by the nationalists in parliament and the neo-Soviet bureaucracy in government, and then Christopher would be speaking to a different foreign minister. To drive home the reality of this danger, I reminded Christopher of Moscow's preparations for the April 1993 session of parliament, at which the deputies were to vote on the impeachment of President Yeltsin, a move aggressively advanced by the hard-line opposition.

In regard to practical matters, I suggested addressing two sets of issues.

The first had to do with financial aid and access to markets. According to the US ambassador in Moscow, President Clinton wanted to put together a financial assistance package for Russia, to be provided by the United States and the other G-7 countries. I urged Christopher to coordinate it with the economic reformers Yegor Gaidar and Boris Fyodorov, who at the time were still in government. I also explained why the legal and political barriers to Russian exports of nuclear, space, and other high-tech goods and services to nonrogue developing countries had to be removed. Otherwise it would be very difficult to argue for the need to drop former clients and to pursue a partnership with the West, with the consequence that the powerful economic forces in Russia would become easy prey for neo-Soviet and nationalistic demagoguery.

My second major point was that as a great power, Russia needed a visible place in world affairs. The country's public opinion would trade the Soviet-style confrontation with the West for a partnership but were not willing to abandon the status itself. This meant that in addressing international problems, from Bosnia to North Korea, Washington should take care to coordinate and consult on its actions with Russia, just as it did with its other allies. Should we find ourselves not in agreement and facing pressure to move in opposite directions because of domestic public opinion or legislative actions, the way to handle the situation would be to give as much advance notice as possible of the next move, which would provide space to review and if possible iron out differences, or at least give the other side time to prepare its case and limit the damage domestically. Early consultation and avoiding surprises should be the name of the game.

Christopher listened politely and nodded at major points, but I felt he either missed the essence of what I had to say or did not care. He seemed interested only in having a friendly meeting and in discussing certain logistical matters of the day, mostly preparations for the first summit between Clinton and Yeltsin, which we agreed to schedule for April 4 in Vancouver.

With this muted response, a strikingly different and terrifying reality began to take shape in my mind. In contrast to Baker and Bush, the new Washington team, it appeared, had no understanding of the reform efforts under way in Russia. For them we were not reformers engaged in the hard work of transforming the Evil Empire into a democratic power, a potential strategic partner of the West, but just strangers to bargain with in pursuit of the Clinton administration's immediate interests, with our interactions dictated by regular diplomatic considerations and domestic political needs. Everything I had said to Christopher about the difficulties of that momentous transformation had become, in his eyes, reduced to a diplomatic trick aimed at collecting additional bargaining chips.

(My suspicion was corroborated by Strobe Talbott many years later. In *The Russia Hand: A Memoir of Presidential Diplomacy*, he recounts Christopher's distaste at my clear warning that I would be sacked if the nationalists gained the upper hand over the reform-minded democrats in Moscow. Evidently Christopher regarded it as an instance of the unsubtle pressure tactic the West often ascribed to Russians: "Do what we say or you'll get somebody worse.")

As a final point, I told Warren Christopher that although we appreciated specific statements in support of the democratic reforms and Yeltsin as the reform leader, the Americans should be cautious about making mega-billion-dollar promises of aid, which so far had been seen as too little, too late, fueling irritation with Yeltsin's foreign policy and anti-American sentiment. We had had enough declarations of new relations from the previous US administration and now needed to move on to the implementation stage. Again, Christopher agreed, but without a commitment. In Vancouver on April 4, 1993, again in Tokyo at the G-7 meeting on July 7–9, 1993, and forever thereafter, Clinton made soaring statements of friendship and promised astronomical aid packages, which never even half materialized. This failure to make good on promises of aid had a disastrously counterproductive effect on both Yeltsin and the Russian public.

Back in Moscow I tried to downplay the difficulties of doing business with the new administration. In a March 7 interview with the then influential weekly *Moscow News*, I spoke firmly of the opportunity for a mutually agreed-upon strategic partnership.

I took my concerns to Strobe Talbot while visiting Washington on March 23, 1993, in preparation for the April summit in Vancouver. Strobe spoke Russian and became known for translating Khrushchev's memoirs, which had been smuggled out to the States; and for years had covered the Soviet Union as journalist. He had been Clinton's roommate as a student at Oxford and was waiting for congressional approval to assume the highest position on Russian affairs in the State Department, second only to Warren Christopher. I hoped that through him we could have an understanding and efficient channel of communication with the new administration. His counterpart on our side was Georgy Mamedov, a gifted young diplomat whom I first got to know when he was in charge of the American desk at the Soviet Foreign Ministry. I promptly promoted him to deputy minister and had full confidence in his ability to find solutions to the most difficult issues, which he subsequently did many times, together with Strobe.

In Washington I met with Strobe in private. I was impressed by his intelligence, and his deep interest in Russian culture and politics. He was evidently a problem solver, which he would later demonstrate many times. It was a big relief after the clockwork-like diplomatic professionalism of his immediate boss, the secretary of state. On the flip side I was concerned that his brilliant ability to quickly grasp events and characterize them in vivid language might skate over the complexity of underlying currents shaping relations between Moscow and Washington and within Russia. We discussed various mechanisms for broadening top-level personal contacts between the two governments and for cooperation in economic matters. I suggested setting up a commission as the mechanism, to be cochaired by Prime Minister Viktor Chernomyrdin and Vice President Al Gore. I thought this initiative would be better received if the American side at the summit proposed it.

Strobe's efficiency was in evidence when Clinton made this proposal to Yeltsin in Vancouver. Yet in presenting it, Clinton described the commission as cochaired by the two vice presidents and almost ruined the deal, since Yeltsin was terrified at the thought of giving his vice president, Rutskoi, any role in important policy matters. Spotting Yeltsin's emotional reaction, Clinton realized his funny mistake and quickly corrected it: "I meant my vice president and your prime minister, Boris. I meant prime minister and nobody else on your side." Reassured, Yeltsin immediately agreed.

That was perhaps the most significant positive outcome of the summit. Otherwise Clinton's tack seemed to be to try to impress Yeltsin and the US Congress—where the Republicans, following the Bush legacy, still wanted to help Russia—with American magnanimity, speaking at length of a grand windfall of dollars that would advance Russian economic reforms. But every project had a footnote stipulating that the money could be disbursed only if parliament passed a balanced budget with certain social and economic constraints. When Yeltsin understood the conditions of the proffered largesse, he was rightly humiliated and angered. Only a week earlier he had narrowly escaped impeachment in parliament, and in two weeks' time he would be putting his mandate to a referendum, all in a desperate bid to overcome parliamentary resistance to budget discipline, passing new laws needed for Russia to fruitfully become a market economy, and other critical reforms. He needed American help, but now, not in some far-off future. And he needed help precisely to overcome the resistance to reforms. As for the future, he and everyone else in Russia knew that after the reforms were implemented, Russia, if only because of its natural resources, would be a wealthy country.

So, Yeltsin cut off Clinton in the middle of the stream of promises and asked whether anything useful was available for aiding the reforms, and available right away. One of the most urgent funding needs was connected to the withdrawal of the former Soviet troops from Eastern Europe and the Baltic states. At the urging of Baltic politicians the United States had pressed Russia to speed up the process, and Yeltsin asked for emergency funds to build housing for returning officers.

Clinton, after conferring with his aides, magisterially offered the trivial sum of $6 million. Yeltsin regained his voice only after a long breath—"That's peanuts, Bill!"—and tried to explain the true scope of the issue. In the end Clinton promised to ask his experts to increase the amount.

Yeltsin also made a pitch to open Western markets to Russia. He explained his need to calm the military-industrial complex by giving it access to Western markets. Success on that front would testify to the benefits of the pro-Western policy and offset the loss of the former Soviet markets, such as Iraq or Libya. In Yeltsin's mind the most natural way to gain access to Western markets was through removal of the trade barriers set in place by US legislation, the legacy of the Cold War. Gorbachev had earlier asked Washington to solve the issue after perestroika had removed the reasons for those barriers, but without success. The conservatives in Moscow interpreted that failure as a sign that the United States would always discriminate against Russia, no matter what reforms Russia undertook or how many concessions it made in foreign policy.

Yeltsin gained plaudits from the West for going much further than Gorbachev had in demolishing communism and forming a partnership with the United States. Nor was he asking for too much: he wanted the US president to initiate in Congress a repeal of the Jackson–Vanik amendment to the Trade Act of 1974, which tied Soviet trade with the United States to free emigration from the Soviet Union, and a couple of other older laws linked to Soviet domination of the Baltic and Eastern European states, which were now free. Clinton agreed that these pieces of outdated legislation should be overturned. Yeltsin took that as a promise of action, while the American diplomats told us that Clinton and his aides thought that the US president should not spend his political capital in Congress on old matters of only symbolic value. Yeltsin's bitter lesson was that Americans would not spend domestic political capital on even the most legitimate needs of their foreign friends.

The removal of other legislation restricting Russian (formerly Soviet) exports, especially high-tech ones, was carried out by Americans on condition of Russia's abrogation of a contract signed by Gorbachev in 1990 with Iran to build a nuclear reactor. Iran was a full member of the international Nuclear Non-Proliferation Treaty, and the contract was under the supervision of the International Atomic Energy Agency. The Russian Atomic Energy Ministry and other experts insisted that the deal was legitimate and flatly rejected American claims that it could endanger the nonproliferation regime by giving Iran a military nuclear capability; US pressure to tear up the contract was seen as an attempt to squeeze Russia out of a lucrative market for its nuclear technology for exclusively peaceful use. The argument between the Soviets and then the Russians and the United States had gone on at an expert level for three years, without any light at the end of the tunnel.

That was one of the most sensitive and important issues to come up at the summit. Knowing that Clinton would raise it, I had privately suggested to Warren Christopher that it be done at a one-on-one meeting of the presidents and in the most serious manner. The US president should come prepared with hard evidence that would justify the American demands. If there were no facts, a convincing political argument had to be clearly spelled out. But the issue should be resolved one way or another, for all time. Clinton spent their private meeting discussing assistance to Russia, which could just as well have been addressed at a plenary session. When the sensitive Iranian problem was raised at the plenary session, it was merely referred to the Russian minister of atomic energy and the US under -secretary of state for arms control and nonproliferation, both veteran participants in the argument and on opposing sides. The summit produced no progress on the problem, and none on Bosnia, where the weight of public opinion in Russia favored the Serbs and in America was against the Serbs.

Thus, the summit brought no tangible fruit in terms of urgent political matters. Instead of taking steps toward developing a strategic partnership or, failing that, seriously addressing issues that concerned both countries, Washington seemed to prefer a friendly summit with lots of window dressing and little substantive action on critical issues.

What Clinton and his team did do well was to present the summit as a success to the world media, including the Russian media—a very useful public relations move on the eve of the referendum on Yeltsin by the Russian people. As it happened, the democratic aspirations of Russians were still strong, and they voted in favor of the reform and the president and against his opponents.

Yeltsin's Peace Initiative for Bosnia-Herzegovina:

The situation in Bosnia continued to deteriorate, prompting the increasing involvement of Western and CIS countries. The Bosnian Serbs tightened the siege of Srebrenica, an enclave declared by the UN Security Council to be a "safe area" according to a French initiative. Now even the French, who, like the Russians, were sympathetic to the Serbs, began to lose their temper. All sides except the Bosnian Serbs seemed to have accepted, however reluctantly, the Vance–Owen peace plan, and the cochairmen (as we called Vance and Owen), with the help of Greece, an Orthodox Christian country traditionally close to the Orthodox Serb faction, Russia, and France, were going the extra mile to meet the Bosnian Serbs halfway.

But if they continued to reject the plan, endorsed even by Milošević,

Russia would not be able to veto a new UN Security Council resolution strengthening sanctions against Serbia, mostly aimed at the Bosnian Serbs, who by now were regarded by the international community as bloodthirsty warmongers. On April 17 Russia voted "abstain" on Resolution 820, which was approved by all the other fifteen member-states of the UN Security Council. The resolution prohibited the transshipment of goods through Protected Areas; prohibited the provision of services, such as banking, necessary to conduct business; and froze the assets of certain Yugoslav entities. The sanctions would be implemented only after Milošević was given additional time to press Radovan Karadžić and Ratko Mladić to accept the plan.

Having survived the April referendum vote in Russia, Yeltsin took a strong stand, saying that Russia supported the peace plan and would not protect those who opposed the world community. Hoping to surf on the success of the referendum, on April 29 I told *Izvestia* that a vote for the president also meant a vote for our foreign policy. Sending the Serbs a warning to accept the peace plan rather than count too heavily on their supporters in the Russian parliament and bureaucracy, I indicated that we had probably erred in not committing to the new sanctions, since the Bosnian Serbs were dragging their feet and Milošević had not pressed them hard enough.

A few days later Milošević publicly urged the Bosnian Serbs to accept the Vance–Owen peace plan without delay, after which he began gradually cutting off supplies to the rebellious combatants. Vance and Owen, joined by the Greek prime minister, Konstantinos Mitsotakis, my deputy, Vitaly Churkin, and a high-ranking American diplomat, Reginald Bartholomew, at a conference with the Serbs in Athens in the last days of May all noted that change in Milošević's attitude and thought it potentially crucial to the success of the settlement.

Earlier in May President Clinton had announced his new policy for Bosnia, which boiled down to the old lift and strike policy, which was supported by US Senate Resolution 341, and passed on September 16, 1992. In May 1993 Secretary of State Warren Christopher took the new policy on tour to Europe. The European countries received it coolly as it was strangely detached from the actual peace efforts ongoing at the time. France's foreign minister Alain Juppé, the embodiment of French manners, style and sarcasm, publicly scorned the "unacceptable division of tasks"—the Americans envisioned themselves flying in planes and dropping bombs, while the Europeans, especially the French, were on the ground, participating in the UN Protection Force, which provided security in the safe havens, the Protected Areas, basically to keep the civilian population alive.

By the time Christopher arrived in Moscow, his mission to sell the lift and strike policy had already failed. I tried to portray the short interview given to him by Yeltsin and my meeting with him as productive with respect to searching for a solution in Bosnia. Relieved of the awkward task of defending the policy, he seemed more open to discussing some down-to-earth alternatives.

Within a few days the Bosnian Serbs, in a more than dubious referendum, had rejected the Vance–Owen peace plan. Milošević reacted with additional measures aimed at cutting off supplies to Mladić's army. At a meeting in Belgrade I asked him why Karadžić and Mladić were so stubbornly pursuing a war that couldn't bring them more gains than they would have achieved under the plan—about 50 percent of the territory of Bosnia, while the Serbs constituted only about 33 percent of population—but that was bringing disgrace and hardship to them and to Serbia. Angrily he started to explain their logic, which he found perverted, then suddenly stopped and looked at me in amusement, as if for the first time realizing that I was not only an official but also just a guy about his own age wrestling with the difficulties caused by the same people who irritated him. He told a popular anecdote illustrating the Bosnian Serbs, called Bosniaks, famous for their stubbornness. A Bosniak finds himself on an uninhabited island for three years and desperately tries to extract some milk from a coconut. Suddenly a young lady appears with a cow and asks what she could do for a companion in trouble. "Help to crack the coconut, idiot!" he retorts.

From my perspective the Bosnian Serbs could not be allowed to kill the peace plan. That would mean not only a continuation of the tragedy in Bosnia but also a division among the major powers as they took sides. The West would back the Muslims and Croats, and Russian public opinion would demand protection of the Serbs despite Karadžić's monstrous ethnic cleansing. That dynamic would be feeding the nationalistic and undemocratic tendencies gaining strength in the Russian parliament.

I shared my concerns with Yeltsin and got his approval for a final effort to secure great power cooperation on the only available basis, the Vance–Owen peace plan, even if it had to be modified and its implementation made gradual. If all the warring parties but the Bosnian Serbs agreed to the plan, Russia would not object to enforcement aimed at obstructionists. The final approval would have to come at a UN Security Council meeting at the level of heads of state.

The strategy was made public under the name of President Yeltsin's Peace Initiative for Bosnia. I insisted on attributing the initiative directly to Yeltsin, despite anticipating more whinnying in Washington, because it would be more difficult for the Bosnian Serbs to say no, and easier for us to punish them if they did.

In mid-May David Owen and the new UN appointee Thorvald Stoltenberg replacing Cyrus Vance came to Moscow. I had become friendly with Thorvald a year earlier, when he was foreign minister in his native Norway, and welcomed him as a dedicated peacemaker. I had always found him to be an honorable person of great integrity and honesty. He and Owen were of the same league determined to save the peace plan and secure international cooperation in pressing the conflicting parties in Bosnia to compromise.

On May 17 I took the Yeltsin Initiative on the road, starting in the former Yugoslavia, where I found an unusual coincidence of opinion among Milošević, Izetbegović, and Croatia's Franjo Tudjman in favor of both progressive implementation and a high-level UN conference either to ratify the compromise or enforce it against obstructionists.

The Europeans were also quite positive. The British and French ministers signaled their readiness to go to New York for a ministerial session of the UN Security Council to affirm a strong resolution in support of the peace plan, with a threat of harsh consequences for any party that chose to stand in the way. Yet our mission to the UN, though it had heard no objections to the initiative, also reported no progress in consultations on the draft resolution. In private, the Europeans singled out Washington as the holdup, but were not prepared to challenge the US leadership, despite Warren Christopher's declaration at congressional hearings after his fruitless European tour that Bosnia was a European problem and it was up to Europe to take care of it. Thus, the fate of our initiative hung on the outcome of my forthcoming meetings in Washington.

I felt I was on thin ice from the moment I arrived in the US capital. I was told that President Clinton was too busy to see me on my first day but that the State Department was trying to squeeze in some time for an interview the following morning before my departure in the afternoon. That was thinly veiled blackmail. Declining to receive a visiting foreign minister at the White House would be a noticeable breach of tradition and a personal affront to the visitor.

Warren Christopher offered me, instead of the UN Security Council meeting to vote on the Yeltsin Initiative, the cosponsorship of a Russian–

210   The Firebird   ·   Andrei Kozyrev

American initiative, to be presented in a joint statement about further efforts to bring peace to Bosnia. It seemed to me far from the worst scenario. Russia would welcome the symbolism of two great powers' leadership, and the Europeans would be grateful we had managed to bring the Americans back. I suggested involving the Europeans and thought the UN Security Council would be the best mechanism to gain international approval.

Christopher demurred, agreeing only to invite the British and French foreign ministers to Washington, instead of the UN, and to present them with a prepared text for approval.

With respect to the substance of the proposal, he tried to downgrade the Vance–Owen peace plan, even though there was nothing better on the table. The best I could get was a reference to the Vance–Owen process. In contrast, he surprised me with a U-turn in his position on the map of Bosnia: whereas before he had criticized the Vance–Owen peace plan for giving too much territory to the Serbs, now he thought it unrealistic to demand so much rollback from them. Under the new plan, the Bosnian Serbs had to retreat from about 20 percent of the captured territory to meet the limit of 50 percent of the total of Bosnia. Even Milošević had not asked for additional territorial concessions to the Bosnian Serbs. I seized the moment to argue for the northern corridor that the Bosnian Serbs wanted—not unreasonably—and were prepared to negotiate through swaps of other pieces of land with the Bosnian Muslims. Izetbegović also thought it feasible, so the amendment we were preparing would be very helpful for achieving a compromise.

By the end of the day the statement was ready, and the following morning Clinton received me. I briefed him on the situation in Russia, pointing out that despite the clear message delivered by the referendum supporting his friend Boris, the parliament was continuing to block constitutional and other vital reforms, which left the president no choice but to dissolve parliament by decree in order to open the way to new elections and a popular vote for a post-Soviet constitution. Clinton nodded understandingly, then turned to Bosnia and the Middle East. I envied Warren Christopher's good luck with his boss, when Clinton revealed a detailed command of foreign policy subjects.

At the State Department I found Christopher in the company of European ministers we had jointly invited the previous day: Douglas Hurd of Britain, Alain Juppé of France, and Javier Solana of Spain, currently chair of the EC. They tried to argue for giving the Vance–Owen peace plan more prominence in the communiqué and signaled their willingness to approve it in the UN

Security Council but were flatly rebuffed on both points, as I had been the day before. With minor changes the Big Four (powers) plus one (the EC) approved the draft statement.

So the semblance of unity between the great powers was restored, and the statement was presented to the public as a major achievement. The cochairmen and Russia redoubled efforts to encourage Milošević to increase pressure on Karadžić and Mladić to accept the Vance–Owen peace plan. Soon Milošević had gained control of the Serbian-Montenegrin border with Bosnia, preventing delivery of weapons, spare parts, and munitions to the rebellious Bosnian Serbs, and had even agreed to an international verification of this blockade, which the UN confirmed. (These and similar actions against the Serbs caused Milošević serious difficulties with the nationalist opposition, which had a strong influence on the military forces.) And because Milošević had to be able to demonstrate to the Serbs both in Serbia and in Bosnia that meaningful steps on the road to peace would bring tangible improvements in the socioeconomic situation, I thought it important to assure him that the severity of the UN sanctions imposed on Serbia would be mitigated in proportion to the verifiable measures he took against the militant Bosnian Serbs.

In promoting this commensurate approach, I came under growing criticism in the Russian parliament, which demanded that all sanctions against the Serbs be lifted without any delay or conditions. At the other extreme, the United States was stonewalling even a serious discussion of a gradual reduction in sanctions, insisting that the international community could not trust Milošević. The Americans turned a deaf ear to my argument that we were speaking not of someone's soul but of material measures, checked against delivery.

Milošević Takes an Unlikely Role Model, Arafat

An international event in another quarter soon provided another argument for working more closely with Milošević and granting him some relief from sanctions. Like Milošević, the Palestinian leader Yasser Arafat had long been denounced as an untrustworthy villain. Yet in the fall of 1993 he was welcomed in Washington and praised for his readiness to sign the Declaration of Principles on Interim Self-Government Arrangements, better known as the Oslo Accords, with Israel's prime minister, Yitzhak Rabin. Why shouldn't we encourage Milošević, who had already moved much farther, in recognizing the right of Bosnia not only to exist, but to exist within its legitimate borders—whereas Arafat still wanted to negotiate the exact borders of Israel. Like Arafat in the Middle East, Milošević was a key player in the Balkans, and no opportunity to engage either of them in a peace process in those regions should be missed.

The Declaration of Principles had been negotiated confidentially between the Israelis and the Palestinians during long talks held in Oslo. The United States and Russia were official cosponsors of the Middle East peace process, and when the declaration was ready for signing, Russia expressed interest in equal participation with the United States in the high-profile ceremony, to take place in Washington. The Americans agreed that Warren Christopher and I would participate equally, while Clinton as head of state would play a much more prominent role.

I flew to Washington from Central Asia, making a brief stopover in Moscow to change planes. Images of war-torn Afghanistan and Tajikistan, the voices of local politicians promising peace contrasting with the incessant sounds of machine gun fire and artillery shelling not far away—all that was still alive in my eyes and ears. On reading the text of the declaration, I could not escape the apprehension that this landmark document still awaited translation into binding agreements laden with details and the devils lurking therein. Would the real settlement follow?

The ceremony on September 13, 1993, was more than impressive. TV stations all over the world broadcasted images of Clinton encouraging Rabin and Arafat to join in a historic handshake, with Christopher and myself flanking the group, smiling and applauding, along with thousands of other viewers on the South Lawn of the White House.

On the afternoon of the ceremony I briefly saw Toby Gati at a cocktail hour in the Russian embassy where we had a joking exchange.

"Some people in the State Department feel that you could have done better at the ceremony," Toby said.

"Why? Did I say or do anything wrong? Like Christopher, I followed the protocol and saw to it that my brief speech echoed those of other speakers in exuding both solemnity and optimism. Didn't I?"

"Yes, your remarks were excellent. Yet people noticed they were off the cuff, not read from a written text. The interpretation could be that you did not come prepared and sort of took the whole thing lightly." We recalled that ailing Soviet leaders had been ridiculed for always reading slowly from notes, and we laughed—lightly.

On the long flight back, I shared that anecdote with my party, to everyone's amusement. Yet much more serious thoughts were on our minds. Clearly, in contrast with the Middle East, Washington had no interest in Tajikistan and Afghanistan. Along with all the other messy conflicts in our vicinity, we would have to deal with them on our own. Bosnia, on the other hand, was a headline-maker. But for now, it was put in diplomatic "freeze" until such time as the Europeans, pressed by the ongoing bloody fighting, dropped their objections at least to the second part of the American formula of lift and strike. Without a clear, united policy approved by the UN Security Council, the air strikes on Serbs would be seen in Russia as a triumph of the American diktat. If the strikes were conducted under NATO auspices, every bomb dropped on the Serbs would add another building block to the image of NATO as enemy, an image that was quickly rising up again not only in Russian military and security circles but also in the media.

NATO—Not a Tea Only Party

Unlike other Western institutions, NATO was a military-security alliance. For decades Soviet propaganda had demonized it more than any other Western institution. Hard-liners in Russian military-security continued to cultivate an adversarial attitude toward NATO as the last line of defense of the privileged position they inherited in the state power structures. If NATO were recognized as nonthreatening, what else could be portrayed as a real and present danger hanging over Russia from abroad? If it was no danger, there could be no justification for these defenders of the motherland to keep their exceptional powers. That's why maintaining the enemy image of NATO was—and remains—indispensable for the Russian military-security apparatus.

The alternative to that attitude was for the military and security forces of democratic Russia to become the strong and valuable partners and allies of their Western counterparts in fighting common enemies—terrorism, drug trafficking, and so on. Of course, that would require a deep reform of those institutions, for which cooperation with NATO would be helpful. And it could be achieved only under robust and determined political leadership.

I spoke with Yeltsin about it more than once, but he preferred to retain personally loyal yet politically neutral ministers of defense and police and a conservative chief of the Foreign Intelligence Service, who entertained the usual prejudices against NATO.

NATO's potential entanglement in Bosnia and the subsequent fallout for Russia's efforts to build contacts and partnerships with the West was one reason that I used every opportunity to privately urge Western colleagues to speed up the development of direct contacts between NATO and the Russian military organizations. Such contacts would help break the ice accumulated during the Cold War and give both sides a sense of partnership. It was no less important to find a formula for political cooperation between Moscow and Brussels, to remove the suspicion coalescing in Moscow that it was being excluded from European decision making.

I believed that until Russia and NATO worked out a firm partnership or better mutual alliance, no new members should be admitted to NATO. Instead, countries that were applying should engage in a process of political and military cooperation preceding full membership, which would be expected to take several years. Thus, the idea of Eastern European countries joining NATO, as advocated by Clinton during his election campaign, should be viewed in a long-term perspective and within the broader European context.

I raised that issue with Christopher. Without addressing the political considerations, he indicated that nobody in Washington had the time or interest to give any practical thought to the future of NATO, much less to possible new members. He was certain that the idea of enlargement would not be on the agenda anytime soon. We arrived at an informal understanding that the NATO issues should be handled with special care and agreed to go on discussing them while avoiding any surprise moves.

Unexpectedly, Lech Wałęsa, the president of Poland, blew this "slow-movers" agreement to pieces. Like Havel, he was an outstanding leader who came out of the anticommunist opposition, though unlike his Czech colleague, the Polish president did not have the background of an intellectual but of a worker. In dealing with Yeltsin he preferred to adopt the straightforward if not rude manners of a simple but earnest guy, foreign to bureaucracy and diplomatic intrigue. He sensed a kindred soul in Yeltsin, who for his part liked to be seen as the "Russian bear," who at times compensated with decisiveness for a lack of political consistency and diplomatic sensitivity.

Thus, Yeltsin detected no problem when, on a visit to Warsaw on a hot

August day in 1993, Wałęsa invited him to a private dinner in a "simple and friendly" format: one-on-one. Well after midnight a call from the president woke me, which was unusual. When I walked into Yeltsin's apartments it was clear that he was almost unable to speak. He finally said that he had agreed with Wałęsa to insert a new paragraph into the prepared text of a political declaration scheduled for a signing ceremony the following morning. He handed me a piece of paper with ragged handwriting on it but was not in any condition to discuss anything.

Apparently, the Polish leader had resorted to a trick played by Kazakhstan's president Nursultan Nazarbayev and some other CIS bosses, who used to drag Yeltsin to private tête-à-têtes. Between friendly toasts they would persuade him to make promises and sign papers on concessions, mostly on trade and financial matters. By the time Wałęsa tried the technique it had largely been abandoned by others because we had learned to sabotage or reverse those decisions after Yeltsin had had time for sober reflection. In the end, such practices left only a residue of bitterness and were counterproductive. Wałęsa did not know that.

When I read the new paragraph, I was of two minds. The passage committed Russia to support Poland's intention to join NATO as soon as possible. In principle, I could only congratulate Yeltsin on such a straightforward approach. But it was dangerously premature.

In practical terms, Russia, Poland, and other former Soviet states were at a very early stage of learning to work together with NATO in the framework of the North Atlantic Cooperation Council, which was formed in 1991 to give potential candidates some idea of how NATO worked and its mission, and those states could not jump over certain stages anyway. Some time would be needed to ease the transition for the military, especially in Russia, and to demonstrate to them and to the Russian public the benefits of cooperation with the former enemy. A statement like the one Wałęsa proposed would wake the sleeping dogs, to no practical purpose. I was also convinced that in the case of NATO, Russia as a major military power and former adversary should be the first to establish a solid framework of new cooperative and alliance relations.

The following day at dawn I spoke to Defense Minister Pavel Grachev, and together we went to Yeltsin, who appeared to need Alka-Seltzer more than anything else. After a brief discussion he agreed to a more general formulation, saying that Russia recognized the right of Poland, like that of any sovereign nation, to join any multilateral bodies it chose, including NATO. But Yeltsin felt awkward in going back on his word with the Polish leader. We pointed out that the declaration had been negotiated and approved by both sides at the highest level in advance, as is normal practice in international affairs, and that this cowboy-style of taking aim at a sensitive issue would only impede its solution in future. After some bargaining, Wałęsa also accepted the milder formulation, but then started to tell everybody how I had tried to sabotage Poland's joining NATO.

The midnight formulation was leaked to the press, and soon the matter of the new Eastern members joining NATO, known as NATO enlargement, became the most explosive and damaging issue in relations between Russia and the rest of Europe. Though it did not happen at my initiative, I felt obliged to offer Christopher my regrets over the Warsaw statement at our next Washington meeting. Most important, we lost all ability to discuss the matter calmly and find a solution without politicized domestic pressures, which immediately heated up in Russia. The Warsaw "Not a Tea Only Party" should be included in history books as a classic example of bad timing as well as the unexpected fallout of late dinners.

Unfortunately, the statement did let the dogs out. Poland, the Czech Republic, and Hungary immediately demanded unambiguous responses from the United States and NATO on whether the alliance was open to the new democracies. That amounted to an offer neither Washington nor Brussels could refuse. Extremist critics of "slow movers" accused the West of betraying the countries still faced with a Russian threat. On the opposite side, the Russian hard-liners made hay by quoting references to "the Russian threat," accusing me of failing to see that NATO remained an alliance aimed at Russia. Yet from the fall of 1993 into the spring of 1994, Washington apparently saw no immediate reason to engage in the difficult and potentially expensive process of enlargement. As I gathered from the traditional December meetings of the Euro-Atlantic organizations, from the CSCE to the North Atlantic Cooperation Council, the NATO allies, to the regret of the Eastern Europeans, still largely shared this slow-moving attitude.

To avoid the political firestorm igniting almost overnight in Moscow around the issue of NATO enlargement, I worked strenuously to decouple the criticism of hasty enlargement from hostility toward NATO itself. "Hasty" was the key word. Once the question of the speed of the process came into play, opposing enlargement was a mere tactical disagreement with a friendly

alliance on how and when best to accommodate its potential new participants. Without this as a focal issue, Russia's opposing enlargement became a
strategic confrontation with an enemy trying to advance to our very borders.
As I told NBC's *Meet the Press* on September 26, an expanded NATO would
not be against Russia's interests. But if it expanded without Russia, that might
create tension in Europe.

In the meantime, I redoubled efforts to promote military contacts between Russia and the United States and NATO. This effort culminated in
the official visit of Russian defense minister Pavel Grachev to Washington
in early September. Grachev was impressed by the quality of the US military
forces and their status in society. He also seemed more receptive to the idea
of Russian armed forces being proud partners with and perhaps allies of the
best armies in the world. Even democratic control of the military institutions,
accompanied by adequate, reliable financing, started to look more attractive
to him. The nascent relationship between the militaries was gaining traction, though it was likely too fragile at that stage to withstand rough political
moves, such as hasty NATO enlargement (on the part of the United States
or NATO) or linking the process of withdrawal of former Soviet troops to
the rights of Russian speakers in Baltic states (on the part of the Moscow
opposition).

Grachev was surprised and gratified to discover that US deputy secretary
of defense Bill Perry and other top Pentagon officials were on the same wavelength as their Russian colleagues with respect to two extremely sensitive
issues. They opposed any military ground operations in Bosnia and were very
cautious about air strikes. As for NATO, they definitely preferred developing
military contacts and working at joint peacekeeping missions to enlargement.

Yeltsin Is Served Only Half of Clinton's Message

In mid-October, Strobe Talbott informed my deputy, Georgy Mamedov, that
after some debate with advocates of speedy enlargement, he and the other
realists had gotten Clinton to propose to the Eastern Europeans that they
should wait on the question of enlargement and instead work with NATO on
individual programs of cooperation, particularly in the military field, along
the lines of the Pentagon's thinking. Unlike NATO membership, which at
that early stage could not be extended to Russia, the cooperative program ap-

proach was inclusive; that is, Russia would also be invited to have an individual program. The Partnership for Peace (PfP), as the overall program would be called, would serve as a sort of anteroom to NATO membership. Candidates interested in a future with NATO could participate in limited projects of cooperation, but the NATO security arrangement would not cover them. If in the near future the Partnership for Peace removed enlargement from the political agenda, in the long run it would not substitute for actual membership. Rather, potential candidates would do a lot of preparatory work, and at an unspecified time some might be invited to become full member-states.

The possibility that the Partnership for Peace might become a stepping-stone to NATO membership drew stiff opposition from the conservatives in the Kremlin, who wanted the very possibility of enlargement to be rejected as a condition for dealing with NATO. They countered my formula of "no" to hasty enlargement, "yes" to partnership with one of their own: "No partnership, no enlargement!" I argued that the double-no formula was the equivalent of retreating to the Soviet position of confrontation with NATO and dictating to the Eastern European states. In practical terms it would provide ammunition to those who wanted to isolate Russia and speedily enlarge NATO.

The Foreign Ministry proposed: (1) to support the Partnership for Peace idea and work out a program with NATO of cooperation for Russia, particularly in the military field, and (2) to firmly tell the United States, NATO, and the Eastern European states that enlargement could be discussed only on completion of a substantive stage of the Partnership for Peace program, which would be expected to positively change both NATO and its partners, including Russia. Thereafter the "new" Russia might consider joining the "new" NATO, along with other potential candidates, or might just have a special treaty of alliance with NATO. In any case, once Russia was in an advanced stage of partnership with NATO, the admission of new members to NATO would not bother the allied Russia.

This proposal won the approval of Grachev and many reasonable people in his ministry, as they wanted to explore cooperation with NATO in practical ways. Yeltsin, overruling the opponents of the plan, approved it.

It was fresh from that internal fight that on October 22, 1993, I welcomed the visit of Warren Christopher and Strobe Talbott, who came to Moscow specially to present the Partnership for Peace concept to the president. Yeltsin's response to the US president's special message, delivered at a high diplomatic level, was calculated to put an end to the infighting in the Russian (and American) bureaucracy and ratify the two presidents' joint understanding on a sensitive issue.

Yeltsin was hunting outside Moscow, in Zavidovo, when I phoned him to tell him of their arrival. He was pleased to hear that Christopher had brought exactly the message we were expecting. He asked me to tell the US secretary of state anything appropriate under the circumstances but declined to see him personally. Yeltsin had just survived a bruising battle in parliament to retain the presidency and was now relaxing with a small group of good friends. He did not want to see Christopher, whom he disliked anyway. "Just finish with the guy and come here, but alone." With that the connection was broken.

The urgency and high level of the message required that a meeting take place nonetheless. I called the president's chief bodyguard, Alexander Korzhakov, and he was able to persuade Yeltsin of the necessity of granting at least a short interview to Christopher. After some further ado, Korzhakov called to say that a helicopter would take Christopher and myself to Zavidovo, with one aide on each side—I chose Mamedov and Christopher chose Talbott— but I had to promise that the interview would not take more than ten minutes of the president's time. "I'll do my best to get him in the right place to deal with this by the time of your arrival," he said. "But please, no more than ten minutes. He just won't last longer, you know." Oh, yes, I knew . . ."

After we landed, a protocol officer took the three guests on a tour of the large hunting lodge, built ten to fifteen years earlier for the Communist Party elite and now the favorite retreat of the president. In the meantime, I went around to the back to have a chat with the host.

"I am doing this for you, Andrei Vladimirovich," Yeltsin said, inviting me to sit down in an armchair next to his in the Winter Garden. "Otherwise Clinton might refuse to see you next time in Washington. But I really don't envy you having such a counterpart. Of course, Clinton himself is no match for Bush, but your guy just cannot stand anywhere near Baker! He has no voice of his own, so what's the sense of discussing anything with him? And after all, Grachev and their—"

"Bill Perry."

"Yes, Perry, also Bill, they agreed to developing ties instead of enlargement. I instructed Grachev to actively pursue this line, and he seems to like it. You wanted the military to cooperate. Now they are, right?"

"Sure, Boris Nikolayevich, you've done your job and Grachev is doing his. Unfortunately, my job is to bring you this envoy from the US president. My only excuse is that he is the US secretary of state and bears an important message from his president to mine. And, of course, I want him to convey to Clinton a reply that he has heard from you firsthand, especially on not proceeding hastily with regard to new members. You should be aware that Strobe Talbott, who is accompanying Christopher, and my deputy Mamedov helped substantially in shaping this new NATO approach as a substitute for enlargement. But this arrangement is only for now: let's face it, your friend Wałęsa and the others in Eastern Europe won't be satisfied with anything less than membership, and in the long run the West won't be able to resist. That's why it is important for Russia to use this time to forge new relations with NATO. Of course, the Foreign Ministry will do everything to help our military colleagues in that task."

"*Khorosho, khorosho,*" Yeltsin said. I saw that he was getting tired, and I needed him to be in a good mood for the official meeting. I told him a little joke; he laughed and we headed for the meeting.

Strobe Talbott has described the conversation that then took place in his book, *The Russia Hand: A Memoir of Presidential Diplomacy.* The account reveals both Strobe's talent as a journalist and the problems that arise when American diplomats, overly keen to get along well with the Russian president, try to sweep potentially inflammatory issues under the rug. In his words:

> Chris laid out our decision on NATO: we would not proceed immediately with enlargement but concentrate instead on developing the "Partnership for Peace."
>
> Without letting Chris finish, Yeltsin spread his arms and intoned, drawing out the words, "Genialno! Zdorovo!" (Brilliant! Terrific!). "Tell Bill this is a wonderful decision!"
>
> After a brief review of other issues, Kozyrev and Yeltsin's other aides virtually booted us out the door. They had a happy president, and they didn't want any further discussion. As we were saying good-bye, Yeltsin gave me a military salute and, dropping his voice to a stage whisper, thanked me personally for the good news.

Strobe also recalls that he tried to give me the full message—"PfP today, enlargement tomorrow"—in the chopper on the way back to Moscow, but that I had closed my eyes, apparently napping.

In fact, I had closed my eyes, to avoid giving in to the temptation of opening my mouth and telling both visitors what I thought of their performance: they had just failed to do their duty, which was to convey the message of their president to the president of Russia.

Warren Christopher in his memoir, *Chances of a Lifetime*, provides essentially the same description of the meeting. "My first reaction [to Yeltsin's cheerful interruption in the middle of the presentation] was that it just couldn't be this easy," Christopher recalls frankly.

His guess at an explanation is no less telling and brilliant than Talbott's: "Had Kozyrev, Russia's foreign minister, deliberately failed to alert Yeltsin to the full scope of Clinton's decision, or was Yeltsin simply relieved that NATO's expansion would not be immediate? A third pretty obvious alternative also occurred to me—that perhaps Yeltsin was having what we euphemistically described in North Dakota as a 'bad day.'"

As Lord Owen recounts in his *The Balkan Odyssey*, he had noticed on various occasions that "scapegoating was a hallmark of the new administration's style." Had the message been passed through regular diplomatic channels it would be my job to carry it to my president. But Christopher came specifically to deliver it in person, and I could not have done his job. My job was at the side of my president, who did convey his message: PfP today "Genialno! Zdorovo!"

The US envoys had enough time to alert Yeltsin to the full scope of Clinton's decision. Both admit in their memoirs that Yeltsin, after his euphoric outburst, did not walk away. Moreover, there was a brief review of other issues. Christopher was a seasoned diplomat sensitive to rules and customs. Even in his capacity as secretary of state he could and indeed should have insisted on presenting the full scope of his president's policy. Much more so as he came as a special envoy and the PfP was the whole purpose of his visit—especially if he thought that Yeltsin was selectively registering only one part of the message. Yet the envoys made no attempt to return to the unfinished business of the PfP. So Yeltsin had solid ground to assume that the topic had been exhausted, and that Clinton was intent on the Partnership for Peace instead of NATO enlargement as his new policy.

The Russian foreign intelligence sources scorned Christopher's presentation as little more than a smoke screen. They regularly reported to Yeltsin and leaked to the press that despite the (deceptive) message delivered in Zavidovo, the Partnership for Peace was in reality just a trap staged to draw Russia into a program whose sole function was to trigger NATO enlargement. Thus, the United States and NATO could not be trusted as strategic partners, and Russia needed to be very cautious in considering any kind of participation in a Partnership for Peace program. Nevertheless, Boris relied on Bill's word.

8

The Battle for the Kremlin

IN THE SPRING OF 1993 THE INTERNAL battle for the president's ear intensified.

As well as representing hard-line and imperialist forces, Yuri Skokov freely let them into the bureaucracy. Yeltsin knew about this and let Skokov do what he wanted. In his memoirs Yeltsin referred to Skokov as "my 'shadow' prime minister."

Yeltsin's predilection for establishing rival bodies with competing visions for the same external or internal matters reflected his own hesitation and uncertainty over the way forward rather than a true striving for balance, as he often claimed. In practice, ignoring his alleged task of improving coordination at the top of the government, Skokov did not consult me about Security Council activities. He knew that many decisions made under his auspices ran counter to Yeltsin's declared foreign policy goals and would have been challenged had he asked me. I returned the favor in-kind, ignoring Skokov and seeking support from the ministers most directly concerned, often Defense Minister Pavel Grachev, before presenting my proposals directly to the president.

Nonetheless, in practice the office of the secretary of the Security Council and the structures behind it had an impact on developments in the conflict regions and especially on the behavior of the Russian military and intelligence services. Leaders of the breakaway separatist regions in Moldova and Georgia had kept close informal ties to the power centers in Moscow. This had allowed them to build strong military and police forces to support their regimes and uncompromising policies.

My opponents at first denounced the notion of peacekeeping in the neighboring Commonwealth of Independent States (CIS) as too weak, but they soon subscribed to it as a useful cover for intervention. They began to insist that peacekeeping operations be conducted exclusively by Russian troops, which should be given a free hand in imposing law and order in trouble spots in neighboring countries. Moreover, they demanded that the UN and other international bodies ratified that interpretation and gave Russia an "umbrella" mandate for its execution. In early 1993, with the help of the president's aides, they succeeded in inserting a demand for a UN and Conference on Security and Co-operation in Europe (CSCE) umbrella mandate into one of Yeltsin's speeches.

I countered by insisting on conducting peacekeeping operations in accordance with the UN model of impartiality. These operations, unlike imperial interventions, required a separate mandate in each case. Asking for a blank check was both unrealistic and provocative, I said, while requests to share the peacekeeping burden on the basis of individual decisions made by the UN Security Council or the CSCE were quite legitimate and we should insist on them, despite Western countries' reluctance. The president agreed, and authorized the Foreign Ministry to assert individual operations, but also, consistent with his preference for maintaining a "balance" by keeping two different ideas in play, kept occasionally reverting to the blank check notion in public statements.

Unfortunately, the United States and some European governments grabbed on to the talks as an umbrella mandate, downplaying the official requests made from Russia to the UN in the usual form as orders.

The April Referendum

The beginning of 1993 was marked by the Constitutional Court decision to hold a referendum in April allowing the people to be the supreme arbiter in the dispute between the executive and legislative branches of the government.

In advance of the referendum, a small army of Yeltsin's supporters took to the streets to garner support for it. Gennady Burbulis, Yegor Gaidar, and many democratically minded deputies—Galina Starovoitova, Sergei Yushenkov, Viktor Sheinis, Petr Philippov, Nikolai Volkov—worked day and night fine-tuning the political messages and coalitions, mobilizing activists, and organizing rallies. Mikhail Poltoranin, a key Yeltsin aide in relations with the media, held weekly meetings with a large group of journalists, briefing them on our strategy and answering questions. I reduced my foreign trips in order to participate in that effort and I used my wide media exposure to advocate for the slogan "Say yes to 1, 2, and 4, no to 3!"

The April 25 referendum contained four questions, each worded and intended by parliament to reduce Yeltsin's authority and credibility.

1. Do you have confidence in the president of the Russian Federation, Boris Yeltsin?
2. Do you support the economic and social policies that have been carried out by the president and the government of the Russian Federation since 1992?
3. Do you think it necessary to hold early elections for the presidency of the Russian Federation?
4. Do you think it necessary to hold early elections of the people's deputies of the Russian Federation?

The outcome of the referendum, with more than 50 percent yes votes on questions 1, 2, and 4, and a similar percentage of no votes on question 3, was favorable to Yeltsin and his policies. The democrats urged Yeltsin to redouble his efforts to consolidate popular support and forge ahead with the reforms, starting with writing a new, post-Soviet constitution that would put an end to the games of the existing parliament, which kept modifying the old constitution in order to challenge the government's institutional legitimacy. The new constitution should provide a firm basis for state institutions and for early elections of the people's deputies in accordance with the will of the people, as expressed in the yes vote on question 4 of the referendum. The parliament especially disliked that fourth point and did everything to sabotage the constitutional reforms.

To be sure, Yeltsin bore a degree of responsibility for parliament's attitude. He selected the first question answered at the referendum as the most important, whereas in the campaign waged by his supporters the second question was inseparably bound to the first. So instead of building a broad-based political initiative on the support received for the economic and social policies that had been carried out by the president and the government of the Russian Federation since 1992, he tried to reap the fruits of the referendum to augment his own personal power. I realized that this was going on, but counted on the positive impact of the referendum on the political climate in the country and on my ability to use it to promote the foreign policy I was pursuing.

However, Skokov's cohorts rushed to undercut me. They launched their next attack on the independence of the Foreign Ministry in early May 1993. This time it was not limited to the conflict zones but was aimed at Yeltsin's entire foreign policy. The Interdepartmental Foreign Policy Commission led by Skokov produced a draft statement titled "Foreign Policy Concept" that emphasized difficulties in relations with the West, particularly the United States.

By then Yeltsin, bruised by the recent battle over the referendum, in which he suspected Skokov of sly dealings with parliament behind his back, had had enough. On May 6 he publicly accused Skokov of disloyalty and dismissed him within a few days. Yet many of Skokov's people remained in the security and power structures and continued to implement his agenda.

The President's Club

If my position in the bureaucracy was improved by Skokov's departure, it was soon significantly elevated. On June 12, Yeltsin invited a close circle of top officials to a casual dinner to commemorate two events that had happened on that date: in 1990 the Supreme Soviet of the Russian Republic, still part of the USSR, had approved the Declaration of State Sovereignty, and in 1991 a leader—Yeltsin—was popularly elected for the first time in Russia's history. Only nine other people were there: Viktor Chernomyrdin, the prime minister; Mikhail Barsukov, minister of security; Viktor Erin, interior minister; Pavel Grachev, defense minister; Viktor Ilyushin, chief assistant to the president; Alexander Korzhakov, Yeltsin's chief bodyguard and the person closest to him other than his immediate family; Vladimir Shumeiko, deputy chairman of the Supreme Soviet; and also Yeltsin's tennis coach, Shamil Tarpishchev, and a journalist who wrote Yeltsin's memoirs, Valentin Yumashev. At the dinner Yeltsin announced the formation of the President's Club, with the present company as its founding members.

Thus, the president's inner circle of top aides was brought together. He also treated us as personal friends. We met each other in an informal atmosphere almost daily at dinner, occasionally at lunch, and in the early morning on the tennis court (giving rise to the moniker "the presidential tennis club"). The club functioned as an unofficial advisory board to the president, and hence its influence was much bigger than that of any other official, no matter what his position.

As a known ardent and outspoken democrat, I felt somewhat politically adrift in this group. Four members were military and security men. They had no particular political agenda and based their advice on their instincts and on the information and analysis provided by the staffs of their respective agencies. Viktor Chernomyrdin, a rare guest at the dinner table and not a tennis player, espoused a similarly technocratic approach in the economic and managerial spheres. Viktor Ilyushin, a good tennis player, kept a low profile, never expressed any political opinion, and enjoyed a position of power, controlling the president's working schedule and paperwork. Vladimir Shumeiko, the only political figure with a democratic orientation, was occasionally my tennis partner in doubles. Shamil Tarpishchev, a brilliant tennis coach, kept out of political matters. Valentin Yumashev, having no official position, enjoyed a growing ability to influence Yeltsin privately—I suppose at that stage in favor of the reformist group, but very cautiously. The characteristics shared by members of the President's Club could be summarized as successful survival at the top, pragmatism, and personal loyalty to Yeltsin.

The club met in a big government villa in Vorobyov Hills, about twenty minutes' drive from the Kremlin. Surrounded by a tightly guarded tall wall and a beautiful park, the villa had a restaurant, a winter garden, an exercise room with equipment, a large swimming pool, and three tennis courts. While Yeltsin enjoyed relaxing in the company of close friends, in part to relieve his self-imposed isolation, the members of the club got to know each other better. Many went there to work out and swim in the mornings. Since Korzhakov was the chief bodyguard, the guards on duty would call him when Yeltsin was about to leave his residence for the Kremlin. At that signal we would rush

to be in our workplaces when the boss called from the Kremlin. Yeltsin had
a habit of picking up a direct line and calling the private direct lines of our
offices. Sometimes those calls seemed aimed at checking up on our physical
presence rather than discussing anything of substance.

Unlikely Friendship

Sport helped me break the ice with some of the powerful ministers who
had taken me for a foreign policy nerd, far removed from them socially and
culturally. In particular, I became closer to Grachev, Yeltsin's confidant and
closest minister. After receiving such a call Grachev and I would immediately
alert each other, since Yeltsin would usually check on more than one of the
ministers. Such communications strengthened our personal relationship
and soon allowed us to confirm each other's impressions of Yeltsin's mood.
If his voice sounded clear and vigorous, we would consider we had a good
working day ahead, and then compete for the president's time to report on
pending issues. If his speech was thick or blurred, we would avoid discussing
any serious matters with him.

Since most of my proposals needed at least an element of coordination
with the military, we worked together almost daily. Gradually I learned some
of the logic of the military technocrats and Grachev became more attentive to
the foreign policy implications embedded in military decisions. On the basis
of respect and cooperation, we developed a good personal rapport that later
progressed to friendship as we played tennis and traveled together to conflict
zones. Those trips assured us both of at least one cultural feature we had in
common—a disdain for cowardice.

While those efforts paid off, they were not without complications. In
August 1993 Grachev and I vacationed in the Black Sea resort of Sochi,
occupying neighboring state villas near the dacha where Yeltsin was also
vacationing with his family. There were growing rumors that the separatists
in the breakaway republic of Abkhazia, just a few miles from Sochi, were
preparing to violate the cease-fire guarded by Russian troops and attack the
Georgians in order to seize the major regional city of Sukhumi. I suggested
to Grachev that we hold a meeting with Vladislav Ardzinba, the leader of the
separatists, and informally advise him to seek a political settlement to the

long-running armed conflict in Abkhazia. Grachev agreed, and I invited him and Ardzinba to my villa for an informal dinner.

It was a beautiful evening. We enjoyed a rare moment of relaxed, casual dining featuring typical Abkhazian and Georgian dishes and local wine on an open-air terrace overlooking the sea. Ardzinba and his wife seemed little different from the Moscow intellectuals of my acquaintance. Both held PhDs and had formerly worked in research institutions. As we recalled moments from our lives in Moscow, I could scarcely believe this man was heading up an army of fighters, some of them fire-breathing ultranationalists and cold-blooded mercenaries, who were mobilizing for another mass killing.

After dinner Ardzinba promised us as his friends that he would not be the first to violate the cease-fire on the ground. In the tradition of the Caucasus, a promise given on one's word of honor carries special weight.

Yet just three weeks later on September 16 Ardzinba's commandos began an assault on the Georgians. The surprise attack had more than a trace of assistance from Russian forces, since the bolts of heavy weapons, especially the artillery of both sides were in the custody of the Russian peacekeepers. Without a bolt a shot cannot be fired. Yet the attackers alone had had their bolts returned and met no resistance when they crossed the dividing line, which was policed by Russian buffer forces. With such a one-sided advantage they quickly captured a large amount of territory and drove the Georgian population away, destroying Georgians' property and killing many people.

So, it was that they took control of the entire territory they had previously claimed to be independent Abkhazia and ensured their ethnic domination there. Before the attack, Georgians had constituted about half the population. Grachev denied authorizing this unilateral assistance but as far as I knew he never reprimanded the commanding officers on the spot.

I flew over the region by helicopter. The devastation reminded me of the horrific scenes of ethnically cleansed areas I had seen from a low-flying plane in Bosnia—even the animals had either fled or were dead. On my way back, I made a brief stopover in a town where both Russian peacekeepers and the separatists had their headquarters. There I spoke only with Russian officers and servicemen. I felt depressed and personally betrayed and refused to shake hands with Ardzinba.

The Georgian president Eduard Shevardnadze also flew to the battle zone and was almost captured by Abkhazians in Sukhumi. On Yeltsin's order

Russian paratroopers rescued him and escorted him to the Georgian capital of Tbilisi. Shevardnadze also asked Russia to maintain its peacekeeping force along the new dividing line. There was no other choice.

One dimension of the tragedy in Abkhazia on which I had little impact was the West's refusal to authorize UN peacekeeping operations in the conflict areas of the post-Soviet space and to share with us the burden and responsibility of guaranteeing the cease-fire arrangements. At the time of the Abkhazia attack, for instance, only eight international observers were in the area, instead of the eighty-eight who had been envisaged by the UN Security Council planners but had never been dispatched. And those were observers, not real peacekeepers.

When I spoke to the UN General Assembly on September 28, 1993, I emphasized that Russia had made a serious contribution toward establishing and maintaining cease-fires in four conflict zones in the post-Soviet space, and toward normalization and the beginning of a national dialogue in Tajikistan. The problems Russia—and not Russia alone—faced in those conflict zones were far too important for the West to try to compete for a sphere of influence or to fail to act out of a baseless assumption that Russia had neo-imperial plans. Moreover, Russian diplomats had expended enormous energy trying to get a consensus inside the Russian bureaucracy and Yeltsin's approval for direct UN operations in areas regarded by many in Moscow as a Russian backyard, and thus exclusively under the purview of Russia. Yet the West preferred to stand back and criticize rather than participate.

My opponents in Moscow wasted no time in seizing on my speech as a sign that I was making unnecessary concessions to the West and encouraging the UN to interfere in the traditional Russian sphere of influence, for which I was also charged with naiveté. The West, they insisted, would never help Russia but rather would take advantage of any opportunity to create political trouble for Russia in the post-Soviet space.

The October Mutiny

Even at the point on September 28, when I was addressing the UN General Assembly on the necessity of international peacekeeping efforts in the conflict zones, I was preoccupied with the political crisis unfolding inside Russia, which threatened to escalate into civil war.

After the people made their voices clearly heard when the April referendum went in favor of Yeltsin and the continuation of the reforms and new elections, the Supreme Soviet remained defiant. Many democratically minded deputies had left the parliament and moved to positions in the executive branch of the government. Thus, the majority of the Supreme Soviet memberships now belonged to communists who had last been appointed by the party in 1990 and were now intent on keeping their jobs by blocking Yeltsin's every move forward.

They tried to continue business as usual, and even to increase legislative powers at the expense of the president. In fact, the parliament degraded into a reactionary body, blocking constitutional and other reforms and supporting Vice President Rutskoi in fighting the president for power. The old body, a holdover from the Soviet era, trampled over the people's will and lost legitimacy.

On September 21, just a few days before I flew to New York for the UN session, Yeltsin had issued a decree ending the activities of the Supreme Soviet. Instead Yeltsin decreed that there should be a referendum in December to approve a new constitution that would establish a normal, as opposed to Soviet-type, parliament. He also envisaged a simultaneous ballot to elect the members of the new legislative authority. Until then, the president had reserved for himself the right to rule Russia through presidential decree. Essentially, all legislative and governmental authority would be temporarily vested in one person, the president of Russia.

In response, a number—not even all the communist and ultranationalist members of the Supreme Soviet, led by parliamentary chairman Rulsan Khasbulatov, voted to outlaw the president and appoint Vice President Rutskoi as acting president. Rutskoi immediately ordered the army and police forces to report to him. According to press reports, he issued warrants for the arrest of Yeltsin and certain well-known democrats, including me.

Defiantly, the members of the Supreme Soviet gathered in the Russian White House, the same building from which Yeltsin, Khasbulatov, and Rutskoi had spearheaded the resistance to the August putsch just two years earlier. The tragic irony of this turn of events was particularly poignant, and I felt especially sorry for Khasbulatov, who despite once having told me he feared communists and nationalists more than democrats as potential destroyers of Russia, now found himself leading exactly those forces of destruction.

Fateful Delay

The content of Yeltsin's decree was not entirely news to me. On September 11, I had been invited to a luncheon at Yeltsin's state-provided country house, not the usual meeting place of the President's Club. Also in attendance were Pavel Grachev, Viktor Erin, Alexander Korzhakov, and Acting Security Minister Nikolai Golushko. Yeltsin asked each of us to read and comment on the draft of the decree banning the Supreme Soviet.

I spoke last, after everyone else had expressed support for the text, and what I said took everyone by surprise. "I have a serious objection, Boris Nikolayevich." Yeltsin looked at me in bewilderment. So did the ministers present. I was the only one among them known to be a radical democrat, eternally engaged in open polemics with the communists and nationalists in the Supreme Soviet.

"Such a decree should have been issued long, long ago."

I meant it. The referendum held in April of that year had clearly demonstrated support for the president. It was a renewed mandate for Yeltsin, but it was also a specific mandate: to continue the reforms. The mandate was especially valuable since it been given by the people, who were paying very high social and economic costs for the reforms. At the core of the people's verdict lay the desire for new elections and the approval of a new constitution to replace the outdated Soviet one. A draft constitution was prepared by top legal minds and, on July 12, almost unanimously supported by a representative assembly of well-known and respected people. The reforming impetus of the referendum gained momentum. Yet inexplicably Yeltsin decided at this point to go on vacation for about a month. His long absence from the public eye and the silence from his government in response to the ongoing battles in parliament left an unsustainable vacuum. Yeltsin only started to assert himself politically in September, by which time the opposition had regrouped and gained reinforcements, leaving no space for compromise solutions.

It was in this context that I informed Yeltsin and the ministers that the decree was long overdue.

"OK. We gave them [parliamentary chairman Khasbulatov and his team] more than enough time to come to their senses. And we cannot afford to wait any longer. The country needs to move forward, not back to the old system, as the Soviet-style parliament wants," Yeltsin said, to general approval.

Yet in the days following the decree, the police and military displayed a conspicuous hesitancy to follow the president's lead, and the opposition took advantage of it. Rutskoi surrounded himself with high-ranking officials who until recently had formed part of Yeltsin's entourage, including the director of the FSB (Federal Security Service). With the encouragement of the opposition leadership, an armed militia started to gather around the Russian White House. This armed force was composed mostly of ultranationalist and criminal gangs, joined by paramilitary forces coming from Abkhazia and Transnistria to fight in the final showdown with the "traitors" backing Yeltsin's policies of compromise rather than confrontation in those breakaway republics. Since there was almost no resistance from the police, these armed mobs grew more aggressive by the day.

At about 10:00 p.m. on October 2, while at an official UN dinner with delegation heads and the UN secretary-general Boutros Boutros-Ghali in New York, I received an urgent phone call from the Russian mission. A group of Rutskoi's and Khasbulatov's partisans had just erupted in violence on Smolenskaya Square, in front of the Foreign Ministry in Moscow. The tiny police line had scattered, and the protestors had easily overwhelmed the single security guard and stormed their way inside the ministry. Many of the mobsters were drunk and armed with machine guns and hand grenades. After shouting radical slogans and cursing the West, democrats, and Jews, the mob moved on. The police presence was nonexistent.

The following morning the news from Moscow was even more alarming, and in the afternoon, CNN showed Rutskoi shouting commands to a crowd of armed men brandishing communist-red banners and wearing armbands with the Nazi-type insignia to overtake the government offices and the Ostankino TV broadcasting center. There was no doubt that the Rutskoi–Khasbulatov gang had initiated an armed uprising against a popularly elected president. At night Gaidar spoke to a rally of Yeltsin's supporters and called on the people to meet force with force. The country was on the brink of civil war, and only resolute actions from the government to suppress the mutiny could—and in the event, did—finally prevent this development. I said as much to the media at a press conference.

My calls to Yeltsin over the next thirty-six hours went unanswered. "It is Sunday, you know," Yeltsin's secretary told me after one such fruitless call, "and the president asked not to be disturbed during his family dinner." Yet the TV screen left no doubt that it was far from a relaxed Sunday afternoon in Moscow. My other contacts there seemed to be truly alarmed and deeply concerned by the lack of information and guidance from the country's leadership when the opposition apparently had begun a wide-scale and violent offensive.

Though I held back from making an abrupt departure from New York while Yeltsin was trying to demonstrate a relaxed attitude in the face of armed protesters, I decided to fly home on the afternoon of October 3. The news from Moscow had reached such a pitch of tension that reporters from the Western press agencies were openly discussing whether Yeltsin or Rutskoi was in charge in Russia and who would address the nation the next morning from the Kremlin.

It was in the face of such unresolved questions that we then spent nine hours in the air. I did not talk to anyone and soon fell asleep. My last thought was calming: Whatever awaits me in Moscow, it's my destiny and my choice. My daughter was safe. I had left her in the States in a boarding school near New York with the clear instruction that she could leave the area only in my presence or, under special circumstances that would be evident from the news, in the custody of a designated person. No Russian diplomats or Russian officials of any kind could talk to her or remove her from the school. The memory of the Soviet practice of holding children hostage as a means of grabbing their fathers was only too fresh for my generation.

I landed in Moscow around 9:00 a.m. on October 4 and was cheerfully informed by Viktor, my chief bodyguard, that the solders with machine guns on the ground remained loyal to our government despite the orders issued by Rutskoi. I went directly to the Kremlin. The security officer let me into Yeltsin's council room. "Just for a handshake, nothing more. He is tired."

"You did well to return earlier," Yeltsin declared. "Last night was difficult. But things will be better now. I'll see you later to discuss business. Go and join Chernomyrdin. I have put him in charge of the operation." With one handshake he simultaneously welcomed and dismissed me. At the same time Grachev went to personally command the squad of motorized paratroopers that had been summoned to crack down on the insurgents.

I found Chernomyrdin in good shape and in a fighting mood, surrounded by key ministers. I was on the point of speaking to him when an aide approached him with news: "Sir, I've just had a call from Khasbulatov's closest assistant. They are ready to make concessions, resume the talks."

"They stopped the talks and started the bloody fighting. They are criminals and will be judged, not negotiated with. Tell them to surrender—the sooner the better!"

I was impressed by this answer, and greeted him with a full heart: "Mister Prime Minister, the minister of foreign affairs reports on his return from the UN and assures you that our partners abroad, indeed all democratic nations, understand the logic of the president's decree, are worried and indignant at the mutiny, and will be on our side should it be necessary to restore order by force."

"Welcome home," he said with a smile. "We are on top of the situation now. Go to your ministry and continue explaining to our partners that we have no choice but to use troops."

"Tanks are shelling the White House!" several people shouted at once. Everyone rushed to the TV monitors.

Thirty minutes later those occupying the Russian White House began surrendering. None of the parliamentarians died, even though hundreds had been killed or injured in the street protests in the preceding days. Khasbulatov, Rutskoi, and their followers were arrested and sent to Lefortovo Prison. The troops began clearing other sites of fighting, and the rebel gangs were on the run. Late at night I saw luminescent bullets pierce the darkness of the sky from the windows of my apartment in the center of the city and heard sporadic machine gun fire in streets nearby.

The Price of Victory

Many democrats, though celebrating the defeat of the mutiny, were worried that Yeltsin would now depend on the military and security forces and rely on them as his power base. I was more optimistic. The lesson he should have learned was how fragile and hesitant those forces were in maintaining law and order. He had only succeeded in making them act at the very last moment. And they had demonstrated an inability to do anything better than fire on the parliament building in the heart of Moscow with a tank cannon. Now, I hoped, he would realize how much the military and security forces needed reform and modernization. The moment was ripe, since the opposition had suffered a major defeat, while the democratic forces were mobilized and united around Yeltsin.

Skeptics thought that Yeltsin, despite the promise of democratic development, would rule with an even heavier reliance on the bureaucracy and the police. I, on the other hand, was sure he would govern through greater reliance on both the results of the upcoming elections and a new constitution. Oddly enough, both forecasts were right.

On October 15 Yeltsin issued a decree confirming the holding of new parliamentary elections, at which time the draft of the new constitution would also be put to a referendum. The vote was scheduled for December 12. Like most of the democrats, I saw it as a chance to finally turn the page on Soviet history and lay a solid foundation for the reforms and a modern foreign policy. We devoted a lot of time to helping the lawyers polish the draft constitution and, after the text was published, promoting the vote as the most important decision to be made by the people. I suggested a few amendments, some of which were accepted, some not, on good grounds.

A few days before signing the final draft and sending the new constitution to the judgment of the populace, Yeltsin called me on a direct line.

"I have just read your last amendment, on the need to consult parliament on candidates for ambassadors to foreign countries," he said. "I know that there is a procedure for congressional approval in the United States, and at times it causes the US administration considerable trouble. I have doubts on this point but will leave it to your judgment. If you want it, you'll have it. But don't blame anybody else in case it becomes a pain in the neck."

I said I wanted the clause for the sake of the principle of the balance of power. Later, when I had difficulties getting parliamentary consent for my candidates, I considered the author of that amendment too impractical and idealistic, but I never thought he was wrong.

My Campaign in Murmansk

In the early years of democratization, I admired and envied the deputies elected by popular vote of the people. They held a direct mandate, and many of them dared speak their minds candidly in public, which was unheard of in the Soviet Union and contributed greatly to the Union's demise. Among the elected deputies were such outstanding individuals as the human rights advocate Andrei Sakharov; the liberal lawyer, later elected mayor of St. Petersburg, Anatoly Sobchak; Gennady Burbulis; Sergei Shakhrai; and Boris Yeltsin himself. I had always taken an active part in public political debate, which led journalists to dub me a "political minister," as opposed to the "technocratic ministers," those members of government who maintained a strictly professional profile. With the upcoming elections I had the opportunity to enter the political fray for real, inspired by the example of people I admired and to help them in their fight.

I felt it necessary in particular to test at the ballot box my conviction that a policy of close partnership with the West would best help Russia advance out of the self-isolationism and militarism that had doomed the Soviet Union. It would also help it to become a strong country again, but on the basis of cooperation rather than misguided attempts at domination. Though I could dismiss the daily criticisms that I was a traitor, selling out Russia to the West, one point did bother me: the claim that even if my policy was correct, the Russian people would not be able to understand it and share my beliefs. That claim, I knew, represented a knuckling under to the pressure of Russia's military-industrial-security lobby, especially when uttered by veteran Soviet apparatchiks such as Yevgeny Primakov and analysts such as Sergei Karaganov and Andranik Migranian.

Still, a bit of doubt crept in when elected deputies such as Vladimir Lukin and Sergei Stankevich, who were not part of the complex, articulated this so-called people's argument. Of course, many elected democrats said the opposite, and supported my efforts. Nevertheless, it began to seem important to check this point and to gain firsthand experience in presenting my political views and indeed my policy to the judgment of the voters and hopefully to obtain a mandate of my own.

Yeltsin in his memoirs speaks of the almost unbearable moral pressure and daily discomfort of living under the slanderous accusations of the communists' propaganda. His opponents called his leadership an "occupation regime" and him the "number one enemy of Russia." After Gaidar left government I inherited the rank of "number two enemy of Russia," which I considered a promotion. I usually said I was pleased to be called that by the communists and nationalists, taking it as recognition of my contribution to democracy and openness to the world. As long as they were furious with me and my policy, I could be sure I was doing something right. That is still true today, when I hear invectives in Kremlin propaganda directed toward my policy as "weak" or "subservient to the West."

I recall a pleasant Sunday afternoon in mid-summer 1992 when the leading democrats of the first Russian government had gathered for a convivial lunch. We had these meals on a rotating basis at the homes of the participants, and it was my turn to host. We were discussing urgent matters and almost shouting when someone asked us all to calm down for a moment. In the sudden silence we could clearly hear my eleven-year-old daughter reading aloud the questions from the crossword puzzle in *Pravda*.

"'Who is the gray cardinal of the occupation regime?'" she read, not noticing that the room had fallen silent and everyone was now listening to her.

"No doubt it's Burbulis," she continued. "Let's see. Yes, it fits all right.

"Next question: 'Who ruined the economy of Russia?' Gaidar should be the right answer. Yes, it is!

"Now, 'Who is selling out Russia to the West?' That's easy—Kozyrev. It fits again. And they call that a puzzle! It's so simple."

When, surprised by the bursts of laughter that followed, she looked up to see the smiling faces of those whose names had just fit so well in the puzzle.

The opposition's propaganda campaign was so unsubtle and pervasive that even children had become familiar with its clichés. Winning the popular vote would be the best answer to that campaign and a strong blow to its organizers.

Facing the Grassroots

The first post-Soviet electoral race started in earnest on November 1, with the formal three-week election campaign due to begin November 21. By that time, I was already among the top ten of the list of candidates and founders of the democratic Russia's Choice party, and thus was virtually guaranteed to be in the lower house of the new parliament, the Duma. But that wasn't enough for me. So, I registered in Murmansk on an independent ticket. In the state Duma, half of the 450 seats would go to nationwide political parties, and half would go to candidates whom the majority of the local constituency would vote for directly. The voters, receiving two ballots, had to choose among parties and among individuals. Individuals in turn could either belong to a party or run as independents, which was my choice.

Russia's Choice was formed in mid-summer 1993 by the same group of democrats who had helped Yeltsin win the referendum in April, led by Yegor Gaidar. A little earlier a different group of democratically minded politicians, led by Grigory Yavlinsky, had established their own party, Yabloko (Apple). Yeltsin again declined to endorse any party, and none of those leaders had enough popular appeal and daring to substitute for him at the top of the democratic movement. Though I was ideologically closer to Gaidar's radical team and regarded Yabloko as opportunist, I tried my best to provide a bridge between the two groups. This endeavor proved naive. Soon I became disillusioned with what I perceived to be an elitist attitude that was infecting both the management and the public campaign of our party.

My friends recommended running in one of the central Moscow regions, typically a stronghold of the democrats. But I wanted something less obvious than Moscow and chose the Far North city of Murmansk, where I had occasionally stopped on my way to Finland. Governor Yevgeny Komarov, showing me around the city, had never concealed the difficulties and hardships the population there faced on a daily basis. Despite being far to the north, Murmansk, because of the warm Gulf Stream current arriving from Norway, has a major year-round open-water port, which was used in the Soviet economy for fishing and as the base for a heavy-cargo transportation fleet. It was here that the American and British ships had discharged the vitally important supplies transferred to Russia under the US Lend-Lease Act of 1941 to help fight the Nazi aggression. There was also a considerable mining industry. Everything had been heavily militarized since the Soviets regarded the place as a stronghold from which to confront NATO. A nearby "closed" city (entrances and exits by civilians had to be authorized by military security), Severomorsk hosted the Russian Northern Fleet. The most modern surface battleships and nuclear-powered submarines, carrying a large part of the country's strategic nuclear weapons, which were aimed at US and NATO targets, were stationed there; its opposite number was supposedly the naval base in San Diego. Together, Murmansk and Severomorsk would form a constituency to elect a representative to the Duma. That would be a challenge for any candidate!

My sources in Murmansk were straight with me: the communists and nationalists, exploiting the social costs of the economic reforms, which were particularly high in that remote area, were very active and had a good chance of getting their candidate elected. Also, the competition would be stiff. Already about seven national and two local political groups had announced their intention to register candidates.

The next day I went to Yeltsin and told him I intended to run for a seat in the Duma as an independent in Murmansk. The campaign would require me to spend more time away from Moscow. I assured the president that the ministry would do its job as always. While ill-wishers accusing me of negligence and too much travel—as if I had a choice in those stormy times!—

complained to Yeltsin that the ministry was poorly administered, in fact it
ran like clockwork in my absence.

I also told Yeltsin that if I were not elected, I would resign as foreign minister on ethical grounds, for I would not have a mandate for my policy in this
test case.

"In this I try to follow your example, Boris Nikolayevich. You went
through more than one personal election campaign and have a national
mandate, on which we all rely. Yet it would be fair if your political aides and
supporters also submitted themselves to the people's judgment and obtained
their own mandate. At least I feel that way."

"Khorosho," he said after a while.

"I see your point, and it is your right to run. Let me just say this: you don't
have to. I know that you are under pressure, but you have my support and
can count on that in future. The most important thing is to get the people's
approval for the new constitution. That would open up a new era in Russian
history and give us a new legal and political basis. So, speak on behalf of the
constitution in Murmansk."

From then on, my life changed. Every week I flew two hours and landed
in a different much more provincial world. My local assistants would start
briefing me on recent local events, socioeconomic problems, the maneuvers
of rival politicians, and so on right in the airport. Those men and women were
local volunteers who came to me after they learned I was running. None had
been a political activist before. They were just open-minded people sympathetic to my policy. Their number included two doctors, one nurse, three
teachers of local schools, three entrepreneurs, and a naval officer with the
rank of major. They also significantly contributed to the success of my second
campaign, two years later.

The competition was tough. My twelve rivals, even as they argued with
each other, joined in playing the same card against me: I was the outsider,
foreign to the region and its specific needs. Local patriotism was very strong,
and I had to pay attention to it. I visited factories, schools, hospitals, small
shops, and dozens of other workplaces so that people could see the Moscow
candidate in the flesh, check my knowledge of their circumstances, and assess
my readiness to address their needs. And how difficult those circumstances
were, and how numerous the needs!

Once, after a long day of meetings and tough questions about what I
intended to do to help people, I sat down for my usual dinner with two or

three assistants and turned on the TV news. Right after the news the national channels reserved time for advertisements by the political parties. My friends saw right through the populist promises of the communists and nationalists. Then an ad for Russia's Choice came on. It showed the spacious residence of a well-off couple about to leave in the company of another well-dressed couple, and a small boy telling his status-breed dog: "What a pity, pooch—we are too young to go with the others to cast a vote for the democrats!"

"That dog," commented one of my assistants, who had just spent the whole day with me talking to people barely able to provide for their wants, "eats more meat daily than most of the people we've met in a month." After the experience of that day I also felt shocked and offended by the ad.

A few days later I met Gaidar and asked him how the advertisement for the election campaign had been chosen; its quality and effect were just awful. But it continued to air after the national news in the evening, and I had to explain over and over to my future constituents that though Russia's Choice had initially been my party, I had nothing to do with the ad and was running on an independent ticket. Though the ad probably did little to influence the vote—which was a poor showing for the democrats, who expected a greater majority in the Duma but were outnumbered by the communists and nationalists on most votes—it did symbolize the inability of the democrats to communicate with the people outside a few large cities.

Making Myself Clear

As I campaigned in Murmansk I had to learn to present my views simply and concisely. That was particularly difficult where foreign policy matters were concerned. Traditional diplomatic language, which is highly nuanced and somewhat evasive, relying more on hints and suggestions than on straight talk, just wouldn't work.

Some observers said that my campaign language had become more nationalistic. In speaking to a national electorate, one naturally emphasizes national interests, yet I never departed from my political principles for the sake of populism. For example, when speaking at an international conference I would emphasize the necessity of close cooperation with the West to resolve global security issues such as the nonproliferation of nuclear weapons, whereas in addressing a preelection rally I would stress the need to have the United

States and other Western powers on our side in persuading Ukraine to give up its nuclear ambitions. The policy was the same.

A meeting with the officers of the naval base prompted a major and decisive explanation of my foreign policy. Initially the hall, filled with a thousand military men, was neutral to unfriendly. Just before speaking I learned that the only newspaper readily available on base was the Communist Party organ, *Pravda*.

Looking out from the podium, I saw faces of a type familiar to me from my meetings with Russian servicemen in Tajikistan and other hot spots: brave, honest, disciplined, intelligent. In particular I recalled a similar hall full of skeptical officers in Transnistria and decided to use the same straightforward approach that I had used there.

"Officers, I know that some call me a 'pro-Western' politician. I am sure that alliance with the West is in Russia's best interests—which of course are different from the interests of the nomenclature that ruled the former Soviet Union. Thus, I am 'pro-Western' because I am 'pro-Russian.'"

The hall was silent. Men of war, they appreciated open combat in argument as well as on the battlefield.

"But what matters is the essence, not words. And the essence of my concept is to pursue our national interests through increasing cooperation and building alliances with the Western countries—that is, those that are called Western, though the major country of that group, the United States, is, like Japan, our eastern neighbor. And it is obvious that these two nations, not to speak of the European ones, are very different and have their own way of doing things. What unites them under the "Western" rubric are democracy and a market economy, which support a high standard of living for their peoples. I want Russia to continue with its radical reforms on the path to democracy and a market economy, and in this sense, I am 'pro-Western.'

"As you know better than anybody, America and NATO have first-class military forces. Your opposite number is the naval base in San Diego, California. I have lobbied for a program of exchange visits of groups of officers between that base and this one. Those of you who have been there will have noticed the striking difference in standard of living between the city of San Diego and the city of Severomorsk. I am proud that in the contest of service skills, your team recently scored higher than the Americans. I dream of a day when we could also take pride in comparing the living conditions of your families and theirs. That's what being 'pro-American' means to me."

First laughter and then applause rippled through the audience. Even as a dream, an American standard of living seemed unrealistic to them. But they liked my point.

"In a word, I want Russia to be equal to those countries in both the well-being of our people and the quality of our military forces. I want Russia as a great nation to be a member of the club of the most developed nations of the world and not remain isolated from them as the Soviet Union was. In that sense I am 'pro-Western.'"

The media quickly reported such confessions of "pro-Westernism," without the explanatory context, and fervidly used them against me in nationalist propaganda. They were also reported to Yeltsin by his staff or by Primakov as "another political mistake of the very young Kozyrev," he told me later.

The audience had warmed to me, and my offer to answer questions and hear what they had to say seemed to please the officers as an example of the sort of openness and democracy-in-practice they were not used to.

The first question concerned the social cost of the reforms. I answered that the cost was doubled by slowdowns, not by the fast pace of the economic transition. The costs could be reduced somewhat by a better performance from the government but mostly by removing the political obstacles to changing from a command economy to a more competitive model. The Supreme Soviet blocked legislation—here I gave specific examples—that would have aided small and medium-sized businesses and thus have provided jobs and services in cities like Severomorsk.

One officer said that the new foreign policy alienated the traditional allies and friends of the Soviet Union in the third world countries that were important geostrategically and also as markets for weapons exports.

My answer was straightforward: those were allies only in the context of the Cold War, which was aimed at irritating the West and fighting "American imperialism" on a global scale. This purpose suited the interests of the Soviet regime, which needed to sustain the image of the West, especially the United States, as an enemy. The new Russia had to look after its economic interests so as to improve living standards on its own shores.

I then told them a true anecdote. About a year earlier I had visited Syria, which used to be one of the Soviet Union's closest allies and a top arms recipient. While speaking to that country's veteran leader, Hafez al-Assad, I raised the issue of the multibillion-ruble debt owed to the Soviet Union that now had to be paid to Russia.

The aging leader's answer was to the point. For decades Andrei Gromyko, the former foreign minister, had told him to stay firm on the road to socialism and against US imperialism and the US ally in the region, Israel, each time offering inducements in the form of shipments of more sophisticated weapons systems so that he could fulfill that mission.

Then, he said, a young Andrei arrived on the scene to say that his name-sake grandpa of Russian diplomacy and all the former Soviet leaders had been wrong. Socialism did not bring prosperity to Russia or anyone. Also, the former Moscow leaders had mistakenly put Syria on guard against America and Israel, and Russia now wanted to be paid back for the weapons Moscow had provided for that misguided mission.

I told the officers, who were laughing at the anecdote, "We will continue negotiations with the Syrians, but the chances of collecting on the debt are not particularly good, and in any case, it would be largely discounted. One reason for this is that the debt is counted in so-called foreign rubles. This denomination was arbitrarily made equal by the Soviet government to more than the US dollar, which was absurd from a market point of view. No wonder the Syrians are challenging that equation and surely would win in arbitration if we did not offer a huge discount! That's one more example of the cost we pay for isolation from the Western markets and institutions. Even worse are our chances in Iraq. That illustrates the simple fact that most Soviet allies were regimes with as disastrous foreign and economic policies as the Soviet Union itself had. And deals that were called arms exports to them were in effect the giving away of weapons and other goods produced at the expense of the Russian people. I am proud that this practice has stopped."

The meeting lasted more than two hours and ended on a friendly note. Thereafter I visited the base frequently to speak with the servicemen. Some of them became dear friends. I loved being on the ships, looking out onto the gray, ice-cold waters of the northern sea, the piercing salty wind in my face.

The Right Answer to People's Anger

The first ten days of December were particularly difficult with respect to the campaign. I felt I was swimming upstream. Everywhere I met angry people demanding to be paid salaries that were two to three months in arrears. Most of them worked in government-owned enterprises, including schools and hospitals. The latter were supposed to be strongholds of the democrats, yet the workers were suffering from payment delays even more severe than in some factories. The teachers and doctors were paid poorly anyway, and delays in receiving the salaries owed them hurt them even more. And though the factories might have a production sideline they could sell on the open market, they could not do so openly and completely legally, since most of them belonged to state-owned and government-run military-industrial enterprises put up in the days of the Soviet Union and not reformed.

So teachers and doctors, factory directors and workers, were all saying the same thing: "If we are to operate under market conditions and compete for consumers, let us do so on a private basis. Yet the schools, hospitals, and factories, particularly those attached to military organizations, are neither privatized nor allowed to conduct private business. Thus, they are on the payroll of the government, which fails to pay in time. This means that the democrats, who are in power, have neglected their duties and don't care about the people."

I took the matter back to the democrats in government responsible for finance and budget matters. Their answer was that they were trying their best to curb hyperinflation and hoped to end the year with better numbers. Guided by this priority, they planned to pay the overdue salaries in late December.

I was as indignant as the people in Murmansk and told them so. First, it was unfair to put the burden of anti-inflationary measures on the shoulders of ordinary people. Second, the narrowly focused, bookkeepers' approach of the reform-minded economists had once again ignored the political reality, which was that elections were scheduled for December 12, when Russia's Choice, with some of those very economists at the top of the party list, could expect to feel the anger of the electorate. Alas, my voice, like the voices of millions of voters, fell on deaf ears.

My Opponents Mobilize

The opposition meanwhile had capitalized on the economists' anti-inflationary policy to the utmost. Vladimir Zhirinovsky, the founder and leader of the Liberal Democratic Party of Russia (LDPR), was busy visiting the regions of Russia and promising to pay the past wages as soon as he was elected to the Duma. Unlike the hundreds of other promises, he made to the electorate, that one in fact was fulfilled. The wages were paid by the end of the year, after Zhirinovsky led his hitherto minuscule party to victory in the party-list elections. He also professed the old Soviet militarism and anti-Americanism packaged in new ultranationalist and populist rhetoric.

No one had paid attention to the quiet rise of the LDPR. Most democrats were convinced that Zhirinovsky had roots in the KGB, which at the end of the 1980s had tried to deal with the newly awakened democratic aspirations of the people. A powerful group of KGB bosses wanted to build a national-istic regime combining state control of the most important segments of the economy with the small and medium-sized businesses in consumer-oriented fields. This idea of partial economic liberalization could well justify the word "liberal" in the name of the KGB-created party, while removing the outdat-ed control of the communist ideologues provided the grounds for the term "democratic." Thus—perhaps—the new party was called Liberal Democratic not only to mock liberalism and democracy, as many people thought after Zhirinovsky's performance, but also in accordance with the interpretation of these concepts by the KGB bosses. This explanation seems realistic in the light of developments in Russia in the late 1990s and the 2000s. Zhirinovsky, sometimes called a clown, sometimes a neofascist, is still (at the time of writ-ing) deputy chair of the Duma.

In December 1993 Zhirinovsky arrived in Murmansk specially to chal-lenge my candidacy. His was also a leading voice among those demanding that I be fired, and Russia's foreign policy be changed. His allies and patrons wanted to make their presence felt, and not only behind closed doors. On November 25 Yevgeny Primakov, head of the SVR (Foreign Intelligence Ser-vice) held a press conference. He presented some "research" on NATO that his service had conducted and, as he expressed, it had been "met positively" by the military.

The major conclusions of Primakov's presentation contradicted the official statements of the Foreign Ministry and President Yeltsin. Most prominently, while our position was that NATO posed no threat to Russia, Primakov thought the alliance was insufficiently reformed and by implication did present a danger to Russia, just as it had to the Soviet Union. Thus, if the Foreign Ministry said that Eastern European countries were free to join NATO and that their accession should be coordinated with the participation of Russia, the SVR insisted that NATO expansion should be discussed only after the alliance had become something different. Both NATO and its potential new members would see this unrealistic demand as a warning that Russia was reverting to a Soviet anti-Western strategy and thus was an additional argument for the enlargement.

The authors of the anti-NATO policy did not worry about the counterproductive effect of their stance. It was far outweighed by the expected domestic victory, which would restore the legitimacy and authority of the security and military institutions that had stood against this foreign enemy in the days of the Soviet Union and would stand against it again in the new Russia.

I said as much to Yeltsin at our meeting the next day, and also showed him documents he had signed that contained explicit approval of my policy and authorized the Foreign Ministry to publicly promote this policy as the one and only official position of Russia. I also showed him evidence that the policy had been worked out in coordination with the military and security services, which had officially consented to it, before it was presented to Yeltsin for final approval. Yet the statements made by Primakov at the press conference had not been discussed with the Foreign Ministry, which as a clear violation of both ethics and established procedure.

Yeltsin in turn told me that Primakov had briefed him on some conclusions of the research done by his agency, and they deserved further examination. It was not a new policy approved by the president, he said, but just a contribution to public debate. (Primakov had said the same when I called him after I heard about the press conference from my bewildered assistants.) Yes, it was unusual for a secret service to take that step, Yeltsin went on, but we were in new times. After all, Primakov had been a scholar and he liked academic exercises. As a democrat I should welcome arguments and not overdramatize differences of opinions.

It was the first time I felt that Yeltsin was not being straight with me. On some occasions he had changed his mind on certain issues after listening to somebody else, but he had always said so straightforwardly. Then I could argue the case either right away or later, and he might agree or disagree, but the final decision was clear enough, and he stuck to it. In that sense I could rely on his word and act according to an agreed-upon position. This time I had the feeling that although he had reiterated his administration's policy toward NATO, from then on, I would have to pursue that policy on my own, without his backing. I knew it would be an impossible act to sustain in the long run, but I hoped that the reality of the international situation and more contacts with Western leaders would help him get back on the track of a sound policy.

Meanwhile, I had to concentrate on my campaign in Murmansk. It was thrilling—going places, addressing rallies, shaking hands, speaking to old and young . . . I had expended so much time, effort, nerve, and eloquence that I felt deeply committed to the region and the people. I could not sleep the night after the vote while waiting for the early returns.

I Am Elected! The New Parliament

The preliminary results of the vote for the political party lists came in from the eastern parts of the country well in advance of vote tallies for independents in Murmansk and other western regions. Along with millions of other Russians I watched a big cocktail party in the Kremlin on TV, where many of Russia's Choice leaders and top government officials had gathered in anticipation of victory. They were so confident of success that they had described the banquet as a celebration of the new political year. Yet the early returns from the Far East, ten hours ahead of Moscow time, left no doubt: the democrats had not attained top standing in the party-list voting. The final figures for the party lists confirmed that Zhirinovsky's LDPR was the winner, with 22.7 percent of the votes, and, together with the communists, would be a force to contend with in the new parliament. By dawn the celebration party looked more like a funeral, and the live feed was turned off.

The vote tallies for the independent ticket in Murmansk came in around 5:00 a.m. and confirmed my win, at almost 70 percent of the vote. I was gratified that my hard work at outreach and explanation had paid off.

Russia's Choice won 30 constituency seats. The combined total of seats won through party-list votes and independent (constituency) votes gave Russia's Choice the largest representation in the Duma, at 70 seats (15.6 percent of the 450 seats), while Zhirinovsky's LDPR came in just behind, at 64 (14.2 percent). However, it did not give Russia's Choice—or even the combined democratic forces in the Duma—a mandate or sufficient power to control the parliamentary agenda or push through their interests.

The new constitution was approved by 57 percent of the voters. That marked a clear rejection of the Soviet system and quest for democracy.

Yet the elections also demonstrated the weakness of those forces that had to implement the people's will. On the same day of the vote the democrats won a basic legislative victory but failed to achieve a leading position in the new parliament. Voters punished them for arrogance and the inability to choose a leader different from Yeltsin with his "above the parties" stance. Unfortunately, the lesson was not learned. From that moment, democrats continued to neglect the crucial importance of articulating and promoting a clear vision of their policies that could justify the hardships civil society would have to bear in the course of the reforms. They also continued as Yeltsin's cheerleaders, relying on the success he had had at the April referendum and in adoption of the constitution. In rejecting the Soviet system, voters expected to be led to a better future. Yet in the absence of a reformist strategy and a resolve on the part of the president, the certified leader of the democrats, to support and protect reformers, people were succumbing to populist and nationalist demagoguery. The few remaining democratically oriented journalists were becoming more reticent in their comments, while nationalistic and anti-Western overtones dominated the public discourse not only of the opposition but of most of the moderate media as well.

In that environment, despite feeling more self-assured, having been elected a deputy to the new parliament, I did not expect much understanding and support from the floor in the Duma. Nevertheless, I shared a consensus among the president's aids on the need to cooperate with the Duma.

As a practical measure, Yeltsin allowed me to meet privately with a former communist deputy, Ivan Rybkin, who had been escorted from the Russian White House by the president's guards after the shelling, but released within a few days rather than imprisoned and put on trial. I had known him as a moderate. He had been reelected again on the party-list ticket and had privately signaled his readiness to cooperate. After a one-on-one lunch with Rybkin I reported to Yeltsin that he might be a good candidate for mediating among the various factions of the new legislature and as a go-between for the government. Soon Rybkin was elected speaker of the Duma.

I differed with most of Yeltsin's entourage not so much on the need to lend an ear to the conservative and patriotic sentiments of the new parliament majority but on the nature of the compromise with them. To my mind we should not have given up key reformist positions but modified the tone and emphasis of the arguments to make them more acceptable to the public. Yeltsin felt dif-

ferently. After Rybkin's election, the president practically separated himself
from both the Duma and civil society by a wall of entrenched bureaucracy
that was essentially on the same wavelength with the conservative deputies
and good for nothing more than opportunistic maneuvering.

I Won, but We Lost

By the end of 1993 I knew that the chance to radically transform Russia into
a modern democracy with an open-market economy could well have been
missed. The political and economic reforms had become stuck midstream,
probably for a significant period, and the new foreign policy would inevitably
be hamstrung. A half-reformed Russia would be tortured by its double identity. The communist legacy, burdened by neo-imperialist and anti-Western
complexes, would doom the neo-Soviet state to being at odds with the United
States and Europe. It would also alienate its new neighbors. The new freedoms and market forces, on the other hand, even though only partly realized,
would push in the direction of Western markets and increase national interest
in being part of the modern world.

    This dilemma suggested I needed to adjust the goals I had set for myself
and Yeltsin for Russia's foreign policy. Though it might be impossible to
achieve a radical transformation, there was still room for maneuver aimed at
minimizing the neo-Soviet legacy and strengthening the outward-looking
dynamics of the previous two years. Thus, I needed to make my policy more
palatable to the pragmatists of the neo-Soviet elite and try to pull the rug out
from under the populists.

    The alarmist talks in Washington about the "new Kozyrev," the nation-
alist, illustrated only unwillingness or inability to grasp the reality. I simply
subordinated an emphasis on the commonality of interests with America to
a "Russia-first" position and the need for Moscow to chart its own course,
which, I kept insisting, nevertheless led to the club of Western democracies.

    On the last day of 1993 I made some quick notes in my diary: "From now
on compromise will be the name of the game. OK, let's play it, but only as
long as the balance is satisfactory—that is, as long as the old-style reflexes
of society and Yeltsin do not take over by more than 60–70 percent. To participate in a truly neo-Soviet experiment would be too disgusting. It would
also be difficult even if I wanted to, since the old customers would never

accept me as one of them. More important, crossing the line would damage my place in history as the first foreign minister of Russia who both openly advocated and put into practice the bold new policy of cooperation with our neighbors and alliance with the West." This mental shift in direction marked the hard-won acceptance of the results of a year of turbulent change and many disappointments.

Over the course of two years the CIS had peacefully replaced the Soviet Union. Russia had emerged from the political infighting of 1992–93 with a new, democratic constitution; a developing private business sector, forbidden under the Soviet system; and a new foreign policy. I was gratified to have been elected a representative to the new parliament and to be among Yeltsin's closest circle of ministers.

Nevertheless, my optimism about the future had almost disappeared. If two years earlier I had worked to advance a policy of peaceful cooperation with the West and neighboring states, now my ambition was more modest—to prevent its retreat. There were ominous forces regrouping against the disorganized and disenchanted defenders of the good. The fast vanishing hope for a helping hand from outside—from the West—added to the frustrating picture.

9

Opportunities
and Anxieties

IN EARLY JANUARY, NATO APPROVED THE AMERICAN proposal to establish the Partnership for Peace (PfP) as a mechanism through which countries interested in joining NATO could cooperate with the bloc and be prepared for potential future membership. The Russian ambassadors in the NATO capitals reported that the Europeans who were eager not to alienate Moscow had taken into account Yeltsin's enthusiastic support of the PfP concept as reported by Warren Christopher and Strobe Talbott. The wording of the communiqué, though somewhat ambiguous, suggested that the PfP was approved in place of enlargement, at least for the present. That allowed time for the parties to calm down and engage in a substantive Russia-NATO dialogue, which I hoped would start during Clinton's official visit to Moscow in mid-January.

When, just two days after the NATO decision, Clinton said in Prague that it was not a question of whether NATO would enlarge but of when and how, his words were immediately reported to the Russian president and commented on in the media as proof that all those NATO debates and communiqués had been nothing more than a diplomatic show to cover up Washington's aggressive NATO enlargement strategy. Yeltsin was furious. He felt it as a political blow and as if he had been betrayed and outfoxed by his friend. "Why has

Bill done this to me?" he asked. "I start thinking that Primakov is right that Americans are not trustworthy. He is more experienced in foreign affairs . . ."

The next day Clinton flew to Moscow from Kyiv together with the Ukrainian president Leonid Kravchuk to meet with Yeltsin. The three presidents signed an agreement of two basic commitments. Ukraine agreed to transfer the nuclear warheads on its territory to Russia, where they would be eliminated. In return Ukraine would receive security guarantees (later codified in the Budapest Memorandum on Security Assurances); compensation for the highly enriched uranium, useful in a variety of industrial applications; and technical assistance from the United States in dismantling the nuclear infrastructure and missiles on its territory.

I was relieved that the ordeal of denuclearizing Ukraine was coming to an end but disturbed by the inability of Ukraine and Russia to resolve the matter no outside help. This uneasy feeling was shared by everyone from Yeltsin to the media in Russia. It was also in evidence on the Ukrainian side. Whereas the Ukrainians had wanted third-party guarantees of the agreement, especially of the inviolability of their national borders, they also wanted to be seen as an equal participant independent of either Russian or American protectorate.

Insensitive to such feelings, Clinton, his diplomats, and the press attaché went out of their way to stress Clinton's role in concluding the agreement. The pomp and fanfare no doubt boosted Clinton's image back home, but it harmed us in the court of Russian public opinion, fueling anti-American prejudices.

Yeltsin in particular was displeased by Clinton's attempt to impress his domestic audience and score points with the media at Russia's expense. George Bush had never engaged in such antics, Yeltsin said, even toward the end of his troubled reelection campaign. To balance that negative impression, I drew Yeltsin's attention to the substance of the American contribution. There were not many examples in world affairs of a play as fair and robust as that of the Clinton administration (and before that of the Bush cabinet) in such a sensitive matter. In the best tradition of realpolitik, I said, the Americans could have used the problems between Russia and Ukraine to divide and rule, using the issue of Ukraine's nuclear weapons as the opening gambit for a tug-of-war. After all, only recently Russia had been considered a strategic adversary that had tried to create a nuclear menace in Cuba, the US "near abroad." The prudent American attitude toward denuclearizing Ukraine was a vivid demonstration of the vital importance of Russia's new partnership with the United States. Yeltsin nodded, but I felt that his agreement with this line of thinking was only halfhearted.

To escape further embarrassment, Ukraine's president quickly left Moscow. The bilateral Russian–American summit started with a big dinner. Clinton was given a gold-plated saxophone, which he played after the whole company had consumed enough caviar and vodka. The next morning's review of agenda items by the presidents followed the by now familiar scenario: nothing was scrutinized in any depth; all problems were referred to the Chernomyrdin–Gore, Kozyrev–Christopher, and Mikhailov–Davis duos as appropriate, to be discussed in the interim and reported on at the next summit.

In both private discussions and public pronouncements in the preceding months, Clinton had careened from position to position in connection with NATO expansion. His disquisitions on the matter ranged from "PfP now, enlargement somewhere in the future" to "PfP and enlargement should go hand in hand" to, suddenly, "The process of enlargement has been initiated," which might in turn be followed by, "Don't worry—all this is just thinking out loud" or "Nothing will be done against you or without your knowledge." These chimerical, off-the-cuff remarks left no room for meaningful discussion of the issue—an agreement was out of the question.

I had been unsuccessful in urging Yeltsin to hold a serious meeting with the American in which both sides would present clearly formulated positions. Instead of trying to put the brakes on Clinton's roving verbalizations, Yeltsin responded in the same casual manner, following the game of doublespeak— soft for foreign consumption and tough for domestic audiences. This kind of mutual duplicity nurtured suspicion as to Yeltsin's intentions on the part of the anti-Western traditionalist contingent in the Kremlin and sowed confusion among the Russian public.

At the press conference following the summit both presidents put on a show of bonhomie, disguising how little had actually been accomplished.

Last Achievements

In the meantime, following their success in the December elections, Zhirinovsky and the nationalists wanted to translate their victory into action. The most immediate danger was that the situation of the 25 million ethnic Russians in the newly independent states who had become "foreigners" overnight might be converted into an excuse for military intervention. As an immediate pretext for intervention some top military commanders, including Lieutenant General Alexander Lebed, pointed to ethnic tensions in the neighborhood, which had been exacerbated by the warmongering of politicians on the Russian side. This was essentially the thrust of a manifesto published as early as 1992 by Andranik Migranian, one of the most outspoken critics of my policy including in the President's Consulting Group.

The course opposite to interventionism was escapism, a choice expressed by other top generals in Moscow, who, partly in defiance of the imposition of internationally accepted guidelines for peacekeeping missions and maintaining bases on foreign soil and partly out of weariness from handling the burden of peacekeeping without UN assistance, sought the immediate withdrawal of all Russian troops from abroad, refusing even to consider participating in peacekeeping operations in the former Yugoslavia.

Whatever prompted this escapism, it was tantamount to blackmail. Give us a free hand or face floods of refugees, escalating armed confrontations on Moscow's periphery, and out-of-work servicemen joining the ranks of the nationalists in Moscow. On such grounds, the generals' desire to stand down from peacekeeping duties had as much calamitous potential as interventionism did. Our relations with neighboring countries, uncertain of Moscow's intentions, were suffering from their deepening mistrust.

In this situation, conveying Russia's new foreign policy was becoming a high-wire act. Both publicly and in private discussions with Pavel Grachev and my counterparts abroad, I explained that under certain circumstances Russian troops were indispensable for protecting human lives in trouble spots under a peacekeeping flag. In exceptional circumstances they might even be asked to act without a peacekeeping mandate, as the Americans had done in the 1970s in Grenada and Panama.

As for the Russian (formerly Soviet) troops that were stationed outside areas of direct conflict, I insisted on either moving them to Russia or negotiating formal basing agreements with those governments that were willing to retain a Russian military presence, as a few were. All that was said and done in unambiguous opposition to imperial designs and within the framework of international law.

At the annual gathering of Russian ambassadors in early February 1994, I repeated the call for a peacekeeping presence plus agreements on the basing of Russian troops in the areas of the former Soviet Union "vital to Russia's interests." The response to my remarks in the West and particularly in Eastern Europe was of some concern.

Kicking off the rumpus, a Latvian correspondent reported that I had threatened to use force against the Baltic states and had refused to withdraw the Russian troops. Washington issued an official statement deploring Moscow's return to the old politics. Though we rebuffed the overly hasty Washington criticism, it was interpreted in Moscow as confirmation of the view, long held by the opposition, that the United States continued to regard Moscow through the lens of the Cold War, despite my "pro-American" policy.

Yeltsin in his first State of the Nation address to the new parliament, on February 24, made an effort to bend his pronouncements on policy with respect to the CIS to the reality of the opposition majority, saying that Russians abroad would be protected "in deeds, not only in words." The opposition interpreted it in its favor, but I was rewarded too, for within a few days the president signed a decree requiring the Ministry of Defense and the Ministry of Foreign Affairs to begin negotiating basing agreements with neighboring countries on terms consistent with international law, keeping only the agreed-upon contingents and withdrawing the rest.

An early beneficiary of the decree was Latvia, which for years had been petitioning Russia to remove combat troops and military technicians servicing the early warning radar facility in Skrunda. The two radar devices at the site had been important to the Soviet Union for tracking possible incoming ICBMS and listening to satellites. Since the two sides found themselves at an impasse in early 1994, strong pro-Baltic sentiment in the US Congress pushed the Clinton administration into acting. The US State Department's Strobe Talbott facilitated the Skrunda compromise, signed by Latvia and Russia in April 1994.

The Russian Federation was allowed to continue operating the station for four more years, after which it was required to dismantle the station and withdraw the servicemen. The agreement thus also assured Latvia of a way to remove Russian troops from its soil. The agreement was observed: in September 1998 the Organization for Security and Co-operation in Europe (OSCE) verified through an investigative team that the facility had ceased operations, and troop withdrawal began.

The Sarajevo Hills

Though Russia in early 1994 was deep in an economic crisis, with skyrock-
eting inflation and a frustrating slowing of the economic reforms, the newly
elected Duma, in one of its first sessions took time to discuss the rather
remote crisis in Bosnia. I thought the priority misplaced and considered that
the Duma might be using foreign policy matters as a pretext for avoiding
difficult matters of internal reform. My concern grew when the debate turned
into an exercise in anti-Western and nationalist rhetoric. The Duma almost
unanimously passed a resolution indiscriminately protective of the Serbs,
including the Bosnian Serbs.

Despite strong political opposition from Russia, NATO gave the Bosnian
Serbs an ultimatum: to withdraw their heavy weapons from around Sarajevo
within ten days or face air strikes. The ultimatum had been prompted by
horrible images of a mortar explosion in a crowded Saturday open-air market
in the center of the Bosnian capital—the latest in an apparently endless series
of crimes against humanity committed by the Bosnian Serbs.

If the Duma, most of the media, and the political elite in Russia were
openly demanding a strong response from the Kremlin to the threat of air
strikes as inadmissible in principle, Yeltsin chose a more nuanced position.
His public comments the morning after the ultimatum were focused on
the inadmissibility of a NATO decision of such gravity on a matter of deep
concern to Russia without consulting Moscow. The belated phone calls from
Washington and other Western capitals to Yeltsin and me asked only that
Russia exercise its influence over the Serbs and persuade them to withdraw
so that NATO would not be forced to live up to its threat. In this way the West
implicated Russia, as part of NATO's strategy but without being consulted
on the actions the alliance was about to undertake.

As I had expected—and had accordingly warned our Western colleagues—their failure to include us in decision making pertinent to Russia's
interests ignited another round of apprehension in Moscow concerning
the alliance and the PfP. After the ultimatum the prospects of benign
Russian–NATO and even Russian–Western relations depended on the ability to quickly establish an "early warning" system, under the PfP or another
umbrella, with respect to NATO's actions.

I equally disliked Russia's protection of Bosnian Serb warmongers and our
exclusion from equal participation in decision making by the world powers.

I had devoted considerable time and energy to persuading the president not to veto the UN resolutions authorizing the use of NATO air strikes should UN peacekeepers in Bosnia come under attack. It was unfair to send men and women in uniform, including hundreds of Russians, on a noble international mission and leave them unprotected. Now NATO pointed to those resolutions as justification of its action. Yet that was not precisely correct. First, under the ultimatum, the air strikes would be conducted not in an immediate response to an attack on UN personnel but as a punishment for noncompliance with NATO's other demands. Second, according to the UN resolutions, the authorization to strike could be given only in response to a specific request from the UN military commanders on the ground and only by the UN secretary-general in consultation with the permanent members of the Security Council—which included Russia.

UN secretary-general Boutros Boutros-Ghali, whom Yeltsin highly respected, insisted that the strikes were necessary and said he had asked NATO to deliver them. Basically, he and NATO were in the right: a strong response to Serbian savagery in the heart of Europe was needed. Nonetheless, the unambiguously unilateral character of NATO's decision and its frivolous handling of the UN, of which Russians proudly considered themselves an important part, were interpreted as a deliberate offense by public opinion and exploited by anti-Western forces in Russia. Thus, in taking a step to contain aggressive Serbian nationalism, NATO had exacerbated nationalism in the much more powerful Russia. The consequences of that choice are still playing out in Russia's internal politics and foreign policy today.

I dwell on these details both as a corrective to some versions of events as they played out in that critical moment and to draw out their stark lesson. In situations of this sort, it is better for the United States and NATO not to have a UN mandate at all and to act on their own than to reach a compromise with Russia and then dodge its unacceptable aspects. An openly unilateral operation has the benefit of honesty and clear rationale on moral and political grounds, while a fig leaf inadequately concealing a twisted UN decision prompts suspicions, disdain, and grudges.

My deputy, Vitaly Churkin, Yeltsin's special representative to the talks on the former Yugoslavia (he would later become permanent representative of the Russian Federation to the UN), had already spent some time traveling between Belgrade and Sarajevo, trying to persuade the Serbs to withdraw their artillery. Vitaly felt that after the NATO ultimatum, Milošević had redoubled pressure on the Bosnian Serbs to pull back, but the military commanders insisted that removal of the artillery would pave the way for the superior infantry forces of the Muslims to overrun the Serbian positions and that the UN peacekeepers would do nothing to prevent this operation. They told Churkin they trusted no one but Russia, especially after the threat of air strikes.

"If our peacekeepers could come to protect the Serbs," Vitaly said in a telephone conversation, "there might be a chance for more reasonable behavior on the Serbian side. Yet it is totally out of the question"

"Why?" I asked. "I can talk to Boutros-Ghali about this matter."

"The problem is not on the UN side but on ours," Vitally replied. "Just yesterday [February 14] the UN asked our general if the Russian troops stationed at the peacekeeping mission in Croatia could be moved to Sarajevo. After consulting the Ministry of Defense in Moscow the good commander flatly refused. He explained to me that Grachev always considered the Sarajevo sector too dangerous and that after the NATO ultimatum he does not want any association with the bloc."

"Wait a minute!" I cried, jumping up from my chair. "Vitaly, please check whether the Serbian officers would indeed agree to withdraw under Russian protection. Also ask their political leader and, perhaps, Milošević to guaranty that. For my part, I will do my best to persuade Pasha [Grachev] and the president to send the troops from Croatia."

Both of us sweated blood over the next two days, but we succeeded. On February 16 the Russian military command informed the UN it would agree to move troops to Sarajevo, and then did so quickly. Immediately after their arrival, the Bosnian Serbs started to withdraw their artillery and, on February 20, the expiration date of the ultimatum, the UN announced that it was satisfied and there was no need for air strikes.

The media in both Russia and the West spoke of a great victory for Russia, hailing its return to the world political scene as an important and independent player. The public at home was euphoric: Russia had proved its influence on the world stage.

This influence, I kept telling my Western counterparts, could work against them or to their benefit. For a benefit to ensue, Russia being in the throes of an extremely difficult process of determining its new identity needed understanding and sensitivity—indeed, even a helping hand—from our new partners in the West. Despite assurances of cooperation given at summits, however, in daily practice we faced competition and thinly veiled hostility from Washington.

The UK's David Owen in his memoirs, *The Balkan Odyssey*, confirmed this impression: "Most Europeans were fulsome in their welcome for the Russian troops coming into Sarajevo. In Washington the reaction was more reserved. They appeared to fear that the presence of Russian UN troops . . . would inhibit air strikes and were most reluctant to involve the Russians formally with NATO decision-making."

The US response was to caution Russia not to take uncoordinated actions in "sensitive" areas—which meant not taking action at all. In other words, we were told to sit calmly in a corner and wait for the Western morning news to arrive to learn that Russia's role in sensitive areas had been abrogated. The subordinated relationship sought by Washington was the equivalent of a death sentence not only for the new foreign policy I was trying to sustain but also for trust between Russia and the United States. As a result, the relationship was demoted to crisis management.

An Interlude with the US Secretary of State

On March 14 in Vladivostok I shared my concerns with the US secretary of state Warren Christopher regarding the exclusion of Russia from important decisions. I suggested that the choice between two models for the US–Russian relationship lay before us: either tight coordination, with decisions made jointly, or a looser partnership involving coordinating strategies but with each country free to act on its own in pursuit of agreed-upon targets. However, the option that had apparently been chosen by Washington—the first mode for Russia (the requirement that Russia tightly coordinate its actions) and the second for the United States (free to pursue its own means)—had to be rejected.

To illustrate my concern, I offered as an example the two countries' diplomatic outreach to the Middle East. I did not question the primary role of the United States, which annually gave hundreds of millions of dollars in aid to Israel and to key Arab countries such as Egypt. Yet Russia had historically played an important role in the region and retained considerable interests there.

We had worked hard to improve relations with countries the Soviet Union had deemed to be enemies, in particular Israel, and had no intention of resurrecting the role as protector of their opponents. Yet the Palestinians might still be more willing to listen to us as traditional friends. Just recently Russian diplomats had brought Yasser Arafat and Yitzhak Rabin back to the negotiating table after an incident involving civilian deaths had terminated peace talks. I was a known factor, and my pro-Western credentials should have been enough to reassure the West of Russia's peaceful intent. Yet I had heard from the Israelis that they were constrained in exploring the potential benefits of our initiatives because of negative reactions from Washington.

Just as had happened a year earlier, I got the feeling that Christopher was barely listening. Later I learned from an American friend that the US secretary of state had been bored by my "lecturing on generalities" and did not consider there to be any inequality in the US–Russian relationship—at least not one he would acknowledge to me. We did not return to either of the options, tighter or looser coordination, I had posed earlier.

Roadblocks to NATO Partnership

Russia's signing of the PfP framework agreement, a standard document initiating joint work on a substantive program of cooperation, was tentatively scheduled to take place at a meeting with the NATO foreign ministers on April 21. I was invited to attend for specifically that purpose. But a heated political fight in Russia preceded the event.

The head of the Foreign Relations Committee Vladimir Lukin compared our joining PfP to acquiescing to a political "rape of Russia," because the alliance disregarded Russian objections in Bosnia and felt free to do what it pleased elsewhere. Andranik Migranian, chief adviser to the Committee on CIS Problems in the Duma, said that with the PfP Russia was "not joining a security system, but just rendering recognition to NATO as the one and only security system." Konstantin Zatulin, a prominent deputy in the Duma, made this point more trenchantly: the PfP, he said, was intended to isolate Moscow not only in Europe but also in the former Soviet space. This last point illustrated the perverse logic of the imperialists: all newly independent states were already cooperating under the PfP, and by joining the club Russia would "legalize" their isolation from Moscow as an imperial center.

Not only the foreign ministry but also Grachev and his officers defended the PfP in the press and during the hearings in the Duma. Once again, the president's spokesperson, Vyacheslav Kostikov, who would later be fired, stuck a knife in our back. On March 31 he announced that in light of the differences of opinion in society and in parliament as to the merits of joining the PfP and NATO, there was no hurry, and that the process would take at least six to seven months. This, he said, he had concluded from a conversation with the president.

Grachev and I rushed to Yeltsin, who said that despite the pressure that had been brought to bear, he was not changing his decision to sign the PfP framework document in April. The next morning, amid much speculation in the foreign and domestic media on Moscow's true intentions, I confirmed the decision to sign the document on April 21, and the Defense and Foreign Ministries pressed ahead with preparations for the signing.

It was NATO that delivered the knockout blow to the plan on April 11. Without consulting Russia or providing advance notice of its intentions, the alliance conducted air strikes on Bosnian Serb positions. Although we publicly deplored the actions of the Serbs, who had intensified the siege of the Muslim enclave Goražde, at the same time as striking UN personnel deployed in the city, we were distressed by the arrogant disregard of the United States (the planes used in the air strikes were American) and NATO to our requests to be consulted or at least informed in advance. (Clinton's phone call to Yeltsin once more came several hours after the strikes had been executed and had been reported by the media.) Reporters beset Yeltsin in the airport when he was leaving on an official visit to Madrid. "I insist that decisions as important as air strikes should not be made without consultation between Russia and the United States," he said, with obvious indignation. The ensuing discussion that he conducted with Grachev and me was emotional. We concluded that we would not join the PfP unless there was a solid provision for consultation between NATO and Russia in cases of this sort.

The overwhelming reaction to unilateral NATO strikes in Russia was succinctly expressed by the reform-oriented politician Sergei Shakhrai, who headed the small centrist Party of Russian Unity and Accord group in the Duma. "The bombing of Serb positions without an iota of notice is a slap in the face of Russia that strengthens nationalist-patriots like Zhirinovsky." "It seems," an observer, Georgy Bovt, concluded in *Kommersant* on April 16, "that had the strikes not happened, they would have had to have been ordered by Moscow [hard-liners], since ... the vague anti-Western sentiments took the clear form Russians had been used to from childhood: 'They are against us!'" Signing the framework document in April was no longer on the table.

My chief concern was to thwart a wholesale frame shift: to prevent indignation over the arrogant behavior of the United States and NATO from framing them as hostile entities in principle while the Bosnian Serbs were depicted as their innocent victims. Friction with NATO arose not from the substance but from the execution of partnership, I said. NATO had a lot of trouble securing consensus among its member-states and now had to learn to consult an outside partner, a non-NATO member. Thus, a provision for political consultation should constitute the core of an addition to the standard PfP agreement that would apply to Russia. The agreement plus an addition was dubbed "PfP Plus."

That was a hard sell, both domestically and internationally. To Yeltsin and the public, I stressed that there was no other way to avoid isolation—a majority of Eastern European and even some CIS countries had already joined or were in the final stages of joining the PfP. In that I had support, however halfhearted, from the military and the moderate parliamentarians, who, though offended by NATO's unilateral actions, were still attracted to the potential of partnership with NATO in some fields. Yet the same people were also receptive to the skepticism expressed by the Foreign Intelligence Service about NATO's readiness for substantive political and military coordination with Russia.

The Kremlin and Duma hard-liners, already celebrating a victory over the PfP, were furious with the proposal of an even more far-reaching PfP Plus. Toying with ideas of a PfP or PFP Plus, they argued, was tantamount to legitimizing NATO with its expansionist urges.

At the final closed-door conference with key ministers, Yeltsin listened to both sides. He seemed responsive both to my argument about Russia's potential international isolation and to my opponents' argument of a likely negative domestic reaction to NATO expansion. The international concern weighed more in his calculations; the domestic concerns could be addressed later: the next Duma and presidential elections were not until December 1995 and June 1996, respectively. Concluding the meeting, he asked the participants to cooperate in preparing a position paper based on the Foreign Ministry's concept and sent me off to try my luck with NATO: "We want a partnership that reflects our superpower status and no expansion of the alliance." After an extensive argument I succeeded in inserting the word "hasty" into this formula, so that the final version of the position paper approved by the president spoke of "no hasty expansion."

It was no less painful getting NATO to accept the PfP Plus idea. Again, I had to make clear that there was no alternative if the allies wanted to have Russia on board. Unlike other partners, Russia would have to negotiate and sign with NATO not only the standard framework agreement but also an additional protocol defining its special status. Warren Christopher was horrified by the idea. He was haunted by the fear of being accused by the Eastern European states and their expatriate populations in America of caving in to Moscow's pressure at their expense. Two issues were in question: giving Russia special status as a privileged partner and, more important, the ability to constrain smaller countries' membership in NATO even if they tried to join "without haste."

The British foreign secretary Douglas Hurd performed brilliantly as intermediary between the American and Russian diplomats. With Hurd, we worked out formulas that finally satisfied everybody. As the only non-NATO European nuclear weapons state and a member of the UN Security Council, Russia was eligible for special treatment without offense to other PfP participants. Soon Russian and NATO diplomats and military experts began working on the text of the additional protocol, to be signed together with the framework agreement at an opportune moment after the dust of the NATO strikes had settled. Though powerful forces in Washington and Moscow were digging in their heels through mutual suspicion and regarded the PfP Plus as nothing more than a face-saving measure, I still entertained the hope that in the end we could indeed work out a true partnership with a tight political link. It was greatly in the interest of both Russia and its partners!

Important Steps Forward

The Bosnian Serbs had responded to the NATO strikes, which were limited, by escalating their military operations. While the pro-Serbian faction in Moscow went out of its way to stir up hysteria over the NATO bombings, the Foreign Ministry made a special effort to brief the more balanced parts of the media on the real situation. Soon some newspapers such as *Izvestia* and

Kommersant started publishing reports critical of the Bosnian Serb artillery shelling, sieges, and ethnic cleansing in Goražde and other UN Protected Areas.

Vitaly Churkin, returning to Moscow from a marathon of shuttle diplomacy in the former Yugoslavia, leaked to the press his frustration with the endless cheating by Bosnia's Serbian leaders, who, by playing off Russia against the West in the interests of pursuing a strategy of aggression, were reducing Russia's role to that of a "banana republic." This charge made headlines all over the world, prompting a backlash against the Serbian nationalists in the Russian press as well. Of course, the Russian nationalists characterized it as further proof of the Foreign Ministry's treachery toward the Slav brotherhood and complacency with NATO's "anti-Serbian" campaign.

Churkin's remarks were delivered to Yeltsin with astonishing speed, along with a correspondingly negative interpretation. At 8:45 a.m. Yeltsin's direct line to my office sprang into life. Why were deputy ministers talking to the press about the results of their missions before briefing the president? Were other parties in the Bosnia conflict angels? Was Churkin losing his ability to communicate with the Serbs and maintain a balanced posture toward the conflict?

I had to admit that the remarks were unusually blunt for a diplomat but probably could be attributed to exhaustion. Churkin had been in the region for a long time, doing an excellent but draining job. In fact, the Bosnian Serb leaders deserved even stronger language for their ongoing massacres. Not only the European politicians but also Milošević deplored them. By contrast, all of them praised Churkin's efforts. Treating Churkin harshly would damage our image. After a tense pause, Yeltsin said that it was my job to ensure that Russian diplomats behaved properly.

After this conversation with Yeltsin, as a first step I issued a statement to the press that we were in the process of assessing the situation in Bosnia. A few days later I took a second step, telling the media that the Bosnian Serbs should not underestimate the resolve of the international community, including Russia, to stop the war and rein in the warmongers by all means, including enforcement. Yeltsin also delivered a public warning to the Bosnian Serb leaders not to cross the line.

In the West these statements were welcomed as an overture to resuming cooperation on Bosnia after Moscow's angry reaction to the air strikes.

Since the strikes had proved counterproductive in stopping Bosnian Serb aggression, first Europe and then the United States began looking to Russia in search of a political solution. One after another my Western colleagues asked that we exercise our influence on Milošević and if possible, on the Bosnian Serbs, promising to consult Moscow in future.

Douglas Hurd again demonstrated his diplomatic brilliance, quickly convening the foreign ministers of Russia, the United States, France, Great Britain, and Germany for informal talks in London. Thus, the Contact Group on Bosnia and Herzegovina was born. In July it set up a new peace plan envisaging that the recently proposed, American-brokered Croat-Muslim Federation would have 51 percent of Bosnian territory and the Serbs would receive 49 percent.

This plan, based largely on previous drafts of the defunct Vance–Owen peace plan, was to be presented to the conflicting parties as a peaceful ultimatum, accompanied by a predetermined set of incentives, including the gradual lifting of sanctions on Serbia and Montenegro if Milošević supported the plan, and penalties, including enforcement and NATO strikes, if compliance was not forthcoming.

Over the next three months the Contact Group worked hard on the plan, despite the Americans dragging their feet on incentives and the Russians doing the same on enforcement. The united front of the world powers forced Milošević to announce his support for the plan, officially deplore the resistance of the Bosnian Serb leaders to it, and declare a sealing of the border between them, which UN monitors confirmed. After that the United States agreed to suspend some sanctions against Serbia and Montenegro. When after years of siege the first international flight landed at the Belgrade airport, the Serbs were ecstatic. Milošević told me at our weekend meeting in early October—by that time we were meeting at least once a month—that he finally had cause to doubt the theory of a US- and German-led international conspiracy to suffocate the Serbs whatever they did. His pressure on the Bosnian belligerents tightened.

When in November NATO again delivered air strikes on Serbian forces attacking the UN Protected Areas, even though it was again done without previous notice to us, Yeltsin took it much more calmly, directing his criticism instead toward "those who rejected the peace initiatives of the international community and provoked the air strikes through their irresponsible actions."

This was a courageous statement, for it flew in the face of the almost unanimous Duma resolution condemning the NATO action as unwarranted.

After the earlier difficulties, progress was also achieved on the NATO-Russia dialogue. On June 22 I signed the PfP framework document and the PfP Plus protocol, affirming, "Russia and NATO have agreed to prepare a wide-ranging individual program of partnership, in keeping with Russia's size, importance and potential."

Yeltsin and his Western counterparts solemnly endorsed both the Contact Group and the PfP Plus at the G-7 meeting in Naples in mid-June, to which Yeltsin had been invited for the first time as a full participant in the debate on political matters. Clinton had apparently urged this elevated status with the tacit understanding that it represented compensation for Russia's adherence to the PfP and to troop withdrawal from the Baltic states by August 31, 1994. I saw signs of hope in Yeltsin's decision to fix the date of the troop withdrawal from the Baltics despite opposition in the Duma and in his own administration. It was achieved after painful negotiations in which Estonia agreed to respect the civil rights of the Russian military pensioners who had chosen to continue living on Estonian territory.

The importance of Russia's entry into the elite political club of the G-7 was symbolized by a funny detail, a change in the dress code for the Moscow delegation. Always constrained in the past by a false communist puritanism and wanting to represent himself as a revolutionary figure fighting for reform, Yeltsin had flatly refused to follow the black-tie requirement at official G-7 dinners. It was because of this that approving glances and smiles followed us when we marched through the magnificent hall of an Italian palazzo in Naples in luxurious Trussardi tuxedos. Yeltsin even wore a bow tie, something he had formerly denounced as particularly unacceptable. Perhaps his garb indicated that Yeltsin was beginning to feel comfortable in his role as a world leader among equals.

Though I had advocated wearing tuxedos as a sign of willingness to follow the code of the club of the world's democracies, I had mixed feelings. Well turned out in his tux, the president of Russia was indistinguishable from the heads of seven democratic states, six of which were NATO member-states while the seventh, Japan, was a close ally of the United States. Yet back home in Moscow he listened to the men in gray suits, the old Soviet guard, which still regarded NATO as a certified evil and preached authoritarianism. To which club would he be loyal?

Bill Promises Boris

The next Russian–American summit, held in Washington in September 1994, showed signs of adhering to the established pattern of deferring any discussion of substantive matters. Thus, it came as a surprise that at the presidents' private lunch, NATO expansion was addressed in some depth. Yeltsin reported that Clinton had promised to stick to "three nos" in handling the expansion: no surprises, no hurry, and no exclusion. Although this formula provided no clear guidance for practical diplomacy, it did imply there would be enough time to sort out the issue. The "no exclusion" part of the formula opened up the possibility of concentrating on the key issue: the inclusion of Russia in a practical partnership or, better, alliance with NATO. Clearly there would be a process, and it would take time, but as soon as Russia's inclusion became substantive, enlargement would cease to be a problem.

Back in Moscow Yeltsin agreed that I should quietly and informally sound out our Western colleagues and the power players in Moscow as to the various options for the inclusion. I used my briefings to him on the results of those tentative discussions to discover his own thinking on the matter, which proved to be rather ambiguous.

Almost everybody's immediate prescription was Russia's membership in NATO, at least as an ultimate goal. Getting the United States and other NATO member-states to concur on that possibility posed the crucial problem and would also be the litmus test of whether the alliance was fundamentally against Russia's interests. I put this question to Christopher in a confidential meeting with the secretary. A positive answer came at the beginning of 1995: yes, Russia could be a member of NATO.

Some of those I spoke to, however, were skeptical about the chances of Russia's full membership because of Russia's Eurasian geopolitics. Many Russians were concerned not to alienate China, and again I got authorization from Yeltsin to cautiously test the waters with my Chinese counterpart. The answer, as hypothetical as the question, was that most likely it would pose no problem. Membership in NATO would not preclude Russia's having a separate treaty with China on nonaggression, noninterference, and other confidence-building measures along the border, but even that might not be necessary.

Despite those encouraging hints, I was not sure that full NATO membership should be our goal, at least in the near future. The magnitude of the task made it seem more a fantasy than a practical goal and would paralyze any attempts at implementation. I am sure Putin knew this when in the early years of his presidency, he toyed with idea of joining NATO. It had the effect of distracting and placating America and the West, while domestic propaganda was making additional efforts to promote authoritarianism and anti-American foreign policy.

To prevent an irreparable rift with NATO, practical steps would have to be taken. I hoped to do most of the job in 1995, before elections in Russia and the United States, and clear the way for the Eastern European states to join NATO in 1996–97. What would be faster and more immediately practical would be an agreement on an alliance between Russia and NATO, which could later be converted into membership if need be. Operationally, I concentrated on the main provisions of the new relationship, whether it was to be future membership or some kind of alliance. And that, of course, was the most difficult task, since the devil is in the details.

Along with finding an alliance with NATO I was advocating strengthening the CSCE (Conference on Security and Co-operation in Europe), in which Russia had full and equal membership, as did all newly independent states. The CSCE promoted democratic norms that put human rights and civil liberties ahead of the principle of noninterference in the internal affairs of member-nations. Those and other provisions enshrined in CSCE documents had proven very helpful in defeating the totalitarian Soviet Union and were still of practical use for reformers striving to overcome the Soviet legacy in Russia and other post-Soviet states. At the same time, member-states were required not to challenge existing borders by force or threat of force.

For a long time, we tried to engage other European states and the United States in defining the new role of that important institution. We believed that along with its unique contribution toward stabilizing and democratizing Europe and part of Eurasia, the CSCE could be an umbrella organization for the coexistence and cooperation of NATO, the European Union, the Council of Europe, the Western European Union, and the CIS. Those organizations would be deemed more acceptable by countries that were not member-states if they were seen as elements of a broader system of cooperation in which everyone had a stake and was guided by the same principles. It could help the CIS catch up to the European standards already promulgated by the other organizations. The CSCE was not a challenge to NATO, as the Americans suspected from our proposals. The CSCE had been erected on the same values, but it bore no resemblance to a military bloc even hypothetically able to compete with or interfere in NATO's sphere of competence. The Americans particularly disliked our idea that the CSCE could serve as a coordinating center for the efforts of various organizations in the areas of stability and security, peacekeeping, and protecting the rights of national minorities. Contrary to American suspicions, carrying out those functions would not impinge on the independence of the other bodies or impede their efficacy. And in fact, such coordination did happen. For example, the NATO bombing forced the Serbs to stop the ethnic cleansing in Bosnia, and the OSCE, the CSCE's successor organization, provided assistance in building and monitoring institutions that prevented the Bosnian Serbs from sliding back into ethnic bloodshed.

My opponents used the US negativity toward the CSCE as evidence that the Americans were reluctant to enhance any European institution other than NATO, because that alliance was working without and against Russia. While criticizing US objections to the CSCE, I did not hesitate to counter the anti-NATO positions of the Russian hard-liners. I felt badly though, when their demands to substitute NATO with or at least subordinate it to the CSCE were picked up by the United States in its critique of the idea of the CSCE as a coordinating body, as if the hard-liners' demands and complaints were official elements of Russian proposals.

At the Washington summit in April, Clinton had promised Yeltsin that he would focus on an interim agreement between Russia and NATO and would attend the Budapest CSCE conference in December, at which they and the other European leaders would inaugurate a new era in building a true all-European security system, of which NATO would be a key but not the only instrument. Yet little changed in the diplomatic negotiations of the CSCE: the Americans still effectively blocked Russia's efforts to upgrade the CSCE. Yeltsin felt deceived on this account by his friend Bill and lent an ear to those in the Kremlin and the Duma who claimed that Americans did not care for anything but NATO enlargement.

By November the reluctance of the Americans to discuss any meaningful strengthening of the CSCE had become irritating not only to us but also to many Western countries, which shared our perception of a narrow-minded NATO-centrism and understood the point in prioritizing CSCE principles. At the Budapest summit in December the heads of state and heads of government agreed to rename the CSCE the Organization for Security and Co-operation in Europe, or OSCE, to reflect its actual work, and set out to strengthen a number of OSCE institutions. The promising Budapest summit declaration, "Towards a Genuine Partnership in a New Era," which identified the OSCE as "the security structure embracing States from Vancouver to Vladivostok," was approved, but in practice, owing to continuing US resistance, the new organization was more like the old CSCE than like the foundation of an enhanced partnership in post–Cold War Europe.

Baghdad and the Iron Lady

On October 11 and 12, 1993, Washington announced that according to its intelligence sources, the Iraqi dictator Saddam Hussein had ordered his troops to march dangerously close to the border with Kuwait. Clinton ordered American reinforcements into the Persian Gulf and pledged to act no less decisively than President George H. W. Bush had in Operation Desert Shield in August 1990, when the United States led a coalition of nations in repelling Iraqi aggression against Kuwait.

I reported these developments to Yeltsin, emphasizing that we should not hesitate to join the international community in support of Kuwait. He agreed, and the Foreign Ministry spokesperson issued a short statement that in case of real danger, Kuwait could count on protection from Russia, while prudently stressing that more information on Hussein's action and motives was needed.

We were unsure where to turn for accurate information. Our intelligence "sources" at first reported no unusual military activity in Iraq. About a day later, when Iraq had confirmed the troop movement, our sources said that yes, "Saddam's guards" were conducting "routine exercises." That was followed by an acknowledgment that the exercises were a bit larger than usual and involved tanks and artillery.

The need to operate on the basis of world media reports, without factual and unbiased information of our own, was distressing, and I shared my concerns with Yeltsin. Though defensively dismissive of my criticism (were our sources not good enough?), he proved receptive to the political commentary provided in abundance by the sources, according to which the crisis was little more than an invention of Clinton's people on the eve of the US congressional elections. The hawkish Republicans were poised to gain seats, and Clinton wanted to outflank them with a show of American military force in Iraq. This assessment was leaked to the Russian press and gained currency. Democratically minded observers differed from their nationalistic colleagues not in harboring skepticism about American motives, which was generally shared, but in their dislike of a Saddam dictatorship.

Hussein's stated casus belli was that Kuwait, which Hussein considered only a breakaway part of Iraq rather than an independent state, was siphoning off crude oil from the Al-Rumaylah oil fields along their common border. In diplomatic circles a different consensus opinion emerged, namely, that Saddam had ordered the provocative exercises not for the purpose of threatening Kuwait but to demonstrate his defiance of what he considered excessive American pressure. Iraq had been cooperating for some time with the UN inspectors, who had confirmed progress in compliance with some of the disarmament conditions imposed on the country after its 1991 defeat in the Persian Gulf War. French, Chinese, and Russian diplomats spoke of the need to recognize that progress at the level of the UN Security Council and to demonstrate to Iraq that further compliance would result in the gradual lifting of sanctions. These developments were followed very closely in Moscow because they made repayment of the Iraqi debt of about $7 billion more likely: Saddam needed access to the world markets for Iraq's oil exports. The Americans, however, adopted a very rigid position, virtually ignoring any positive changes in Saddam's behavior.

Chief of the Foreign Intelligence Service Yevgeny Primakov, who openly professed that he was a personal friend of Saddam, claimed that Hussein was prepared to retreat in response to "friendly advice"—but not American threats. The door was now open for Russia to try to temper both sides' behavior while demonstrating its capabilities on the world stage and safeguarding prospects for the repayment of Iraq's enormous debt. Primakov offered to use his personal ties with Saddam and the Iraqi foreign minister Tariq Aziz to ensure that whatever Moscow decided to offer Bagdad would go straight to the top leader and be received in the right way.

Initially Yeltsin was skeptical of this option as he did not want to repeat Gorbachev's humiliating attempt to prevent Desert Storm by sending Primakov to talk to Hussein when both aggression and the preparation for a military response to it were proceeding at full speed. By contrast, I thought that the opportunity, however tiny, was worth exploring. I argued that dialogue with Saddam could be productive only if conducted from a position of strength (in this case, the threat of force from the United States) and with clearly defined, stringent conditions requiring compliance with international law.

I asked Igor Ivanov, my first deputy, and Viktor Posuvaluk, the former Soviet ambassador to Iraq, to visit Bagdad and assess how far Saddam could go in extricating himself from the trap of his own making. Their report was encouraging. Saddam called back the exercises and promised to make a public statement to that effect.

I persuaded Yeltsin to demand official recognition of Kuwait's sovereignty and existing borders from Saddam, thus removing not only the immediate military pressure on that country but also Iraq's main political and legal pretext for attacking it in the future. That should prove a turning point in Iraq's policy toward Kuwait and a major step toward compliance with the UN resolutions, thus clearing the way to the partial lifting of sanctions.

While the president liked the idea, he wondered whether it was too much to ask. I answered that we had to deploy all our silver bullets: I would fly to see Saddam, making the first visit by a top official from a UN Security Council member to Baghdad in ages, and carry a personal letter from the president of Russia asking the president of Iraq to make an important step toward peace. Putting that plan in place required first obtaining an assurance from Saddam through a reliable back-channel that he would do his part in the trade-off. Tariq Aziz, whom we allowed to make a secret visit to St. Petersburg for that purpose, gave this pledge to me.

Within a few hours we had informed the UN Security Council of my intention to fly to Baghdad, which required special permission, since the airport was closed by the sanctions. After a closed-door briefing of the Security Council by Russia's permanent representative to the UN Sergei Lavrov, who outlined our plan, the chairman of the council, the British ambassador to the UN David Hugh Alexander Hannay, issued a statement on behalf of the council publicly endorsing our initiative. I also briefed Warren Christopher by phone, and Yeltsin placed a call to Clinton. Both of them were surprised but wished us well. They were prepared to repel aggression by force if need be but would welcome a peaceful resolution. "Andrei," Christopher said, "I wish you success, but can you trust a guy like this?" "It is not a matter of trust," I said, "but of hard evidence and verifiable moves: the return of troops, public and binding recognition of Kuwait, continued cooperation with the UN monitors, and so on." What mattered was not trust but Hussein's actions.

Arafat was my trump card with Milošević, and it played well with Saddam also. The two had a lot in common: strongmen covering their dictatorial rule with nationalist posturing of "not bowing to American diktat," but being cornered by unexpectedly strong international pressure. Of course, they wanted most of all to safeguard their power, but if it could be done Arafat-style, by changing their image from one of an international outlaw to that of a respected leader, they certainly would explore that possibility.

There was, however, one point when I felt déjà vu in my conversation with Saddam, but this was in connection with the last communist Tajik boss with whom I had dealt, rather than Milošević. He stressed that his potential concessions concerned only foreign policy. "You, people, think that my iron fist could be substituted with a democracy, only because you don't know Iraq. The country would be torn apart by conflicting tribal and religious groups and foreign forces." After my experience in Tajikistan, I chose not to argue on that point and to return to the foreign policy.

The UN's demands, I explained, were merely the standard norms applicable to any country. Iraq's old friend Russia, a great power and a permanent member of the UN Security Council, would help make Saddam's compliance with those demands look not like defeat but like the achievement of a sensible politician. We would expect an oil-rich Iraq to become a key player in the world economy and Middle Eastern politics, just like its competitor, Saudi Arabia.

At first Saddam listened with a somewhat sarcastic smile playing about his face, but soon his expression changed to one of real interest and he waved his hand to dismiss his staff. His body language betrayed that he was an emotional and perhaps unstable human being, rather than suggesting, as I had seen earlier, that he was a great and confident leader. At the end, he called his aides back, and his demeanor mimicking his golden statue mounted in the middle of the central Bagdad square returned. He instructed them to prepare a communiqué stating that after receiving the foreign minister of Russia and a letter from the Russian president, the president of Iraq now ordered his troops to complete the return to their initial positions. He had also made the historic decision to recognize Kuwait and its international borders. All that had been decided in response to a goodwill request from Russia, long a friend of Iraq.

The communiqué was seen as almost offensive by Washington. Clinton and Christopher at first tried to say they had not been informed of my trip and its purpose. Then the Pentagon challenged whether Iraqi troops had been withdrawn, reluctantly acknowledging the fact a few hours later. Finally, Washington implied that the communiqué had been ill-conceived because it mentioned a possibility of lifting sanctions, thus "rewarding the aggressor."

I made a public rebuttal indicating that a hasty negative response was hardly consistent with partnership, claims that Washington had not been consulted in advance were not factual, and the communiqué's reference to the possibility of sanctions being lifted if and when Iraq complied with the UN resolutions was nothing more than a reiteration of those resolutions approved with US consent. Yeltsin, with whom I was on the phone every few hours, shared the view that later dominated Russian press coverage, namely, that Clinton was jealous of Russia's diplomatic success, which he had simply discounted when agreeing to my trip. Also, Clinton likely felt robbed of an opportunity to score as a resolute commander in chief, especially on the eve of the US congressional elections. The Republican leaders, among them the World War II hero Bob Dole, were skillfully playing on Clinton's image as a peacenik for his repeated deferrals from service during the Vietnam War era.

But the leaders of Kuwait, to which I flew from Baghdad, welcomed the results of my mission. Unlike the Americans, they appreciated the recognition of Kuwait's sovereignty as vitally important to the peaceful future of their country. The US response confused them most of all. They did not want to be caught up in disputes between great powers.

The US ambassador to the UN Madeleine Albright started to push for a Security Council vote on a draft resolution on Iraq, refusing to wait the twelve hours it would take me to fly to New York from the conflict area. According to the Russian embassy, many diplomats in New York were uneasy with the US attitude, which they attributed to Madeleine personally. She wanted to succeed Christopher and used the opportunity to play an "iron lady." If that was the case, the posturing was done at the expense of favorable conditions in which to change Saddam's aggressive behavior (which could have spared America from a costly protracted war a decade later) and in an affront to Russia's intent to play a positive role in a Middle Eastern conflict. I seriously considered vetoing the draft and voting for a resolution only after I had had an opportunity to address the Security Council, per usual diplomatic procedure. I called Yeltsin, and after discussing various scenarios, he said it was up to me to decide how to vote in the UN.

I was torn. My own star would rise in Russian public opinion if, through resorting to the power of veto, I taught the Americans in the UN a lesson, and it would be fair. But a dramatic break with Washington on an issue as sensitive as Iraq would certainly play into the hands of the anti-Western forces in Russia, which were striving to abolish any notion of a partnership with the United States and looking for reasons to restore Soviet-style alliances with Iraq and other rogue regimes on an anti-Western platform. Nor could I disregard the appeal of Kuwaitis who asked that the resolution be passed despite American truculence. They relied on American aid and did not want it to be jeopardized because of diplomatic quarrels prompted by the political ambitions of certain individuals in the United States.

Just before boarding the plane for New York, I sent our UN representative Sergei Lavrov instructions to vote for the resolution. Sergei was a gifted diplomat, whom I first had appointed my deputy and had recently moved on his request to be assigned to the UN post. In a few hours before voting he succeeded in substantially improving the resolution with a couple of amendments. From a semi-hysterical, bellicose manifesto it became a more balanced document combining a warning to Iraq to refrain from provocations and an indication of conditions for pursuing the peace process. The document noted the declared recognition of Kuwait, indicating that to be legally binding it should be ratified by the Iraqi parliament, which Saddam promised to take care of soon.

Saddam was in a less cooperative mood at our second meeting a few weeks later. He was frustrated by the UN reluctance to commend his recognition of Kuwait, which he saw as a fundamental reversal of his policy, and something that had always been a key point of the Security Council resolutions. Nevertheless, I persuaded him to stick to the new course and make another attempt to overcome the accumulated mistrust of some UN members. So he lived up to his promise and completed the process of recognizing Kuwait as a sovereign state. The law to this effect was passed by the Iraqi parliament. To make the procedure look different from a rubber stamp he asked me to address the deputies, which I did. It was quite a show. There were even some doubts and objections expressed, despite the decision already made by the national leader. After ratification, Saddam agreed to take one more step and form an international expert group to trace the Kuwaiti prisoners of war who, according to the Iraqis, had disappeared after the 1990 invasion. It was difficult to explain to him the significance of this humanitarian problem. He seemed bewildered that anyone could really care about the fate of ordinary individuals.

However, the Americans refused to include even a hint in the next UN resolution of easing of sanctions in response to those positive moves.

According to our embassy, Saddam had mentally retreated back into aggressive defiance and isolation. Russia and its young foreign minister, he said, had done its best. But, as he, Saddam, had foreseen, the Americans would not agree to anything but the humiliation of Iraq and its leader. This belligerent mentality riddled with clichés was familiar to me from encounters with Serbian and Russian nationalists.

The media at home on the one hand celebrated our bold diplomatic moves in Iraq, but on the other, shared Saddam's mood, adding Russia to Iraq as a target of humiliation. In that context many comments also referenced the US bargaining with North Korea, where Americans cynically demanded that the international consortium buy an American-made nuclear reactor for that country, which violated the terms of the Nuclear Non-Proliferation Treaty (NPT) and its monitoring mechanism, the International Atomic Energy Agency (IAEA). Yet Washington at the same time had vociferously argued against Russia's offering a similar reactor to Iran, a full member of the NPT and IAEA. As to Madeleine Albright, she was promoted to secretary of state and her pictures swept twice through Russian media: once visiting North Korea and once dancing with Primakov in the UN hall and singing something like "NATO enlargement" while he vocalized "No enlargement."

In the face of perceived American hostility, further dealing with Saddam would be too burdensome. Russian public opinion was susceptible to US arrogance and, once offended, nurtured an indiscriminate anti-Americanism. So Iraq was being seen more and more in the old Soviet light: an enemy of America is our friend.

Because of this I let relations with Saddam subside. We never met again. He resumed his defiance of the UN, but he never took back his recognition of Kuwait or threatened that country. That alone made my trips to him worth the trouble.

Even today I believe that Washington demonstrated a lack of strategic vision and political courage and missed a potentially historic opportunity to change its zero-sum game with one of the most important countries in the Middle East. Had this potential been explored, perhaps there would be no costly, protracted, and in some ways disastrous American invasion a decade later. At that juncture, unfortunately, Washington demonstrated the same basic approach that it had with Russia over the problem of NATO expansion.

A Cold Peace

The US midterm elections in November 1994 helped clarify to Moscow the effects for Russia of the struggle for power in the United States. We watched with growing concern as the Clinton administration bowed to the pressure of the Republicans, who gained congressional seats on a platform that included speedier NATO expansion and lifting of the arms embargo in Bosnia.

Nevertheless, I had quietly welcomed the return of the Republicans, remembering the Bush–Baker team and an article in the *New York Times* by former president Richard Nixon, who upon visiting Moscow urged the United States to be candid with Russia instead of trying to drown differences in champagne toasts at "feel-good" summits. Where straightforwardness might have cleared the air and made relations between the two countries more productive, the outfoxing maneuvers only fed suspicions. The Clinton administration though went on dodging an unpleasant face-to-face with the Kremlin while toughening its positions under congressional pressure.

The moment of truth arrived in December. First the Contact Group on Bosnia learned that the United States, reversing its position, was once again pressing for a lifting of the arms embargo on Bosnia, a move seen by us and by the Europeans as dangerous adventurism damaging a promising collective work. The popular question in the Kremlin those days was why the United States should be the one and only country allowed to accommodate its internal political needs at the expense of other nations. I was deeply concerned by what it was suggesting. In Russia we were under no less heavy pressure from the Duma, but we stayed the course.

The second surprise awaited me in Brussels at the NATO foreign minister's session, where I was invited to fully sign Russia into the Partnership for Peace program (in June I had signed only a short statement on that matter, because the complete program had to be elaborated by experts afterward). It was understood that the work on our program, as well as that of other countries, would be allowed to proceed at a steady pace, in contrast to the speedy admission of new members to NATO for NATO enlargement. My opponents in Moscow were up in arms, pointing to alarming rumors from NATO's headquarters that were being leaked to the press. The diplomats in Brussels and the other European capitals had been speaking openly of deep divisions within the alliance over Bosnia and the future of NATO. With just a few days remaining before the PfP signing, I was increasingly concerned that last-minute decision making at the ministerial meeting could present me with unpleasant surprises.

Shortly before the session the American side informed Russian diplomats that the specific wording of the NATO communiqué would not be forthcoming until the last minute because further discussion among the ministers was expected, with the implication that the document might be changed to reflect some nuances. That was not reassuring. To be on the safe side, I asked Vitaly Churkin, who at his own request had been appointed Russian ambassador to Brussels, to make a statement on the eve of the NATO ministerial meeting with a strong caution against any surprises with respect to NATO expansion, which he did.

Christopher assured me that the American ambassador would give Vitaly a "blueprint" of the communiqué as soon as an agreement was reached, which would give me opportunity to analyze and discuss it with Yeltsin before it was published, and in advance of my arrival at the NATO headquarters.

I arrived in Brussels the evening before the scheduled ceremony and dined with Vitaly, who was a bit nostalgic for the crazy Bosnia marathon but appreciated the composed ambassadorial life, which gave him the opportunity to see more of his family. We waited until midnight for the call from Vitaly's American colleague, and Vitaly then kept his external line on alert through the night. In the morning he reported that his colleague had called and promised to call again a bit later since the session had gone late into the night, and the blueprint was not ready. We spent the morning playing tennis in the embassy garden and waiting for the call, which never came.

Our game was abruptly terminated when I was summoned to the embassy to take an urgent call from Moscow. The Russian news agency ITAR-TASS, according to Yeltsin's assistant, had reported that the communiqué, just published by NATO ministers in Brussels a few minutes earlier, contained a new initiative aimed at speeding up NATO enlargement. Yeltsin's assistant asked whether he should wait for my cable with an analysis of the communiqué or just report the news to the president, who had already inquired a few times about what was happening in Brussels. I asked him to give me fifteen minutes, and hung up. In the meantime, the BBC and the local radio stations had announced that the NATO communiqué had been made public and apparently contained new provisions on NATO expansion. Even when he was dealing with the Bosnian Serbs, I had never seen Vitaly so frustrated.

Within a few minutes we were able to gather pieces of the section of the

NATO document related to expansion. There was no doubt that it contained important new elements. Within a year the minimum membership requirements were to be discussed in preliminary fashion with three potential candidates, Poland, Hungary, and the Czech Republic.

Vitaly was able to reach a European colleague. The poor guy picked up the receiver right in the corridor of the NATO building and, surprised by his Russian friend's questions, he answered with indignation: "But Christopher assured the session that you, the Russians, were fully briefed and satisfied! The American proposal wouldn't have passed otherwise."

The Moscow line rang, and the assistant said that Primakov had just walked into the president's office. A moment later Yeltsin came on. His scorn flowed through the line. "Now, Andrei Vladimirovich, what do you say of your beloved Americans? The 'sources' you have always been so skeptical of knew better: Washington is pushing a new plan for speedy NATO expansion! I had a report on that already yesterday. And you called after the press report came out! Where is your friend Christopher? He had promised to give you advance warning if there were any new elements in the communiqué, hadn't he? Does he say there are none? What do you make of the alliance's decision?"

"I am sorry to be late. It looks like a long and complicated document, which we were not briefed on despite Christopher's promise. The communiqué certainly points to the start of preparations for enlargement, but not enlargement itself."

"But they want to start negotiations with the new members—Poles, Hungarians, Czechs!"

"In preliminary fashion."

"Who cares for your diplomatic subtleties—politically it is the beginning of admitting three new members! Don't be in a hurry to sign anything."

I agreed and promised to demand explanations from NATO and particularly the United States, which had promised us "three nos" and now presented with exactly the opposite: surprise, haste, and exclusion.

"What happened to Bill? How could he have done this to me again?" Yeltsin screamed. "Make your own decision, Andrei Vladimirovich, but don't hurry to sign."

Forty minutes later I went to the meeting. After exchanging greetings, I loudly asked Christopher if he had the text of the communiqué. He turned to the NATO secretary general, Willy Claes. Many eyebrows rose. Claes handed me the communiqué with an awkward smile. Then he pointed to a document placed before my seat. "This," he said, "Andrei, is the PfP program for Russia. We all worked on the partnership agreement long and hard, and here it is, ready to be signed by the two of us."

"Yes," I said, "this is an impressive, substantive, and promising agreement that envisions broad-scale cooperation between Russia and NATO. It should and will be signed." I paused. "Yet unfortunately, it cannot be signed right away, even though I came here, to Brussels, to do exactly that. The reason for the delay is that I haven't had an opportunity to familiarize myself with the decisions you adopted a few hours ago. According to the media they are significant and, in particular, envisage new steps for the expansion of NATO. Before signing the PfP I need to understand these new elements and report to my president," I said, fingering the communiqué.

Christopher whispered something to Willy, who quickly asked the press to leave.

Behind closed doors, Claes apologized for the failure to provide me with the communiqué in advance, because, he explained, right up to the last minute the ministers had been discussing formulations to express the delicate compromise of new and old. How, then, I asked, could they expect me to proceed without reading the text, not to mention discussing it with my president? Was Russia indeed a partner-to-be?

Later, every effort was made to blame me for what happened. The US State Department spokesman, Mike McCurry, characterized my statement as a theatrical performance meant for domestic political consumption. What duplicity! I had spent months arguing in public and inside the government for the PfP and for long-term cooperation with NATO. How could it have been my choice to be defeated at the last moment? But defeated I was. And not by Zhirinovsky but by Christopher!

My comments to the Russian press that the episode was only a bump on the road to cooperation with NATO were scarcely heard amid the cries of indignation that NATO had again snubbed Russia. The dismay in Moscow was exacerbated by reports that in the move toward expansion, Washington was trying to bring into the fold the allies who had been distressed by its lift and strike policy toward Bosnia. In other words, NATO unity was shored up at the expense of Russia and Russian interests. This conclusion was almost unanimous in the press and in the Kremlin.

I tried to persuade Yeltsin to play his hand coolly. Yes, there was no doubt that Washington had tried to restore the alliance's solidarity at the expense of Russia, and we had strongly objected to it. I had caused a scandal in Brussels, I told Yeltsin, so that he could appear presidential in Budapest at the forthcoming summit of the OSCE. After a while he calmed down and asked me to outline the major points of his upcoming speech. "I'll talk to Bill about NATO in Hungary," he concluded.

Speaking first at the CSCE summit, Clinton described NATO as the centerpiece of the European security system, effectively thrusting the CSCE, the host of the gathering, out of the picture. "No country outside NATO will be allowed to veto its expansion," he said, throwing the gauntlet down at the feet of Yeltsin, who had only spoken against surprise, haste, and exclusion.

Speaking after Clinton, Yeltsin robotically read passages with our vision of a new Europe guided by the CSCE principles. His roaring bass returned when he came to the few sentences devoted to NATO that had evidently been inserted at the last minute; they were not in my draft of the speech. If that alliance was to overshadow all other organizations and to enlarge its membership, the new Europe would be thrown back, if not to the Cold War, to a cold peace. The word "haste" in the formulation of his objection to NATO enlargement had been stricken through in a bold red hand.

Yeltsin had been offended not only by Clinton's remarks but also by his decision to limit his attendance to just a few hours, leaving no opportunity for any substantive exchange. The two presidents could do no more than pose for a handshake before the cameras. The happy American had intended to deliver his speech and leave as the winner of the day. Yeltsin was simply furious. And rightly so! He made sure that "friend Bill" had no easy escape. The "cold peace" epithet was on the wires of the world news agencies before Air Force One had left the runway.

From then on, I was the sole voice in Moscow speaking against a hasty expansion of NATO, while all others, including the president, had dropped the word "hasty." I continued the old song on the ground of official written instructions, duly approved by the president and never changed. Yet I knew that de facto, those documents, constructed out of hope for a partnership and alliance with the West, already belonged to the past.

Inside and outside the Kremlin, Yeltsin's "cold peace" was taken not as a warning to NATO expansionists but as an official declaration of the end of the foreign policy that Russia had pursued, with immense effort and to certain good ends, in 1992–93.

Tragedy in Chechnya

In mid-December 1994 the president called for an extraordinary meeting of his Security Council to discuss the situation in Chechnya, a small autonomous republic in the northern Caucasus. Member after member reported that the Chechen government under the former Soviet general Dzhokhar Dudaev had acted in violation of the Russian constitution and laws. Dudaev had even put together his own armed forces and threatened to use them against the independent state of Georgia.

"Other speakers have proposed giving Dudaev an ultimatum: if in ten days he does not return to observance of the Russian constitution, we will use coercion. Do you think that's a good idea?" Yeltsin asked me.

"Russia as a sovereign state is obliged in accordance with international law to exercise control of its territory and bear the responsibility for any troop movements or military actions inside or beyond its borders," I said. "So, we have the right and indeed the obligation to take all measures, including the use of force, to ensure control over the whole territory of the country, including Chechnya. This we can explain to our foreign partners without difficulty. So, there are two questions on my mind: whether other means have been exhausted and whether we can take effective action if the ultimatum is rejected. The worst policy is to issue empty threats."

The president turned to other ministers. They gave affirmative answers to my questions, and I joined the rest in a unanimous yes vote.

Ten days later the Security Council met again. Dudaev had rejected the ultimatum.

At this second meeting, Defense Minister Grachev said that according to the recent estimates carried out by military specialists, the operation against Dudaev's forces would require more time, troops, and firepower than had previously been contemplated. It did not look like a limited and quick police action, and he felt inclined to provide more opportunities for negotiation. But this word of caution was too weak and it came too late. Intercepting a quizzical look from the president, Grachev quickly said that the army was of course ready to do the job.

The decision to use force was again approved unanimously.

But it divided the democrats. Gaidar denounced the decision on behalf of Russia's Choice. I was irritated that he had not consulted me and, I suppose, other interested politicians. I had also just returned from my constituency in

Murmansk, where many regarded the military option as tough, but necessary to preserve the integrity of Russia. In a TV interview I said something about leaving Russia's Choice—words I later regretted, since it weakened the fragile liberal party and injured my relations with Gaidar, whom I respected.

What was contemplated and approved by the Security Council as a limited, high-precision police action against a defiant gang rapidly turned into a protracted war in Chechnya, with massive destruction of the lives and property of the local civilian population. The army's "sledgehammer approach," as a January 10, 1995, editorial in the *New York Times* put it, "dishonored the important principle that Moscow has the right to maintain the cohesion of the Russia Federation and, in extreme cases like Chechnya, may use limited military force." It would strain relations with our Western partners for years to come.

Here is my thinking at the time: The heroic epoch of the good democrats fighting the bad communists has reached the point that both are sitting in the same Duma with the president playing off each side against the other to maintain stability, but not to continue the aspired to—and badly needed—reforms. Yet on balance, we have succeeded in moving the country ahead economically and politically. Not only did Russia avoid the Yugoslav scenario in the space of the former Soviet Union, we have continued to develop benign relations with all of Russia's new sovereign neighbors. Moreover, despite pressure from the nationalists, we have kept a balanced policy toward the former Yugoslavia through our work as a member of the Contact Group on Bosnia and by staying close to the position of the European powers.

So why not try to play by the new rules: not as the hero-protagonist making history but as a team player? Only if the course were to turn very bad—back to the Soviet way, say—should one think of abandoning the team and its leader. I was under no illusion that this meandering thought process was simply a cold-minded analysis of reality. It was partly motivated by the comfort of my personal position in the inner circle of the president's men—a position that I would most probably be unable to use to change the negative trend in foreign policy.

PART III

The Downward Slope,
1994–1996

10

The End of the
Beginning

NATO DOMINATED THE AGENDA RIGHT FROM THE beginning of 1995. Many sought to draw lessons from the high-drama clashes, mine in Brussels and Yeltsin's in Prague. The lessons were not congruent.

Intriguing Proposals

In early January the Russian press was full of pessimism as to the future of relations with NATO. Only a few comments in *Kommersant* and *Izvestia* expressed regret for the rift and urged Russia to try to meet the alliance halfway, for NATO was seen as a difficult but still valuable strategic partner. It was consistent with my evaluation and encouraging. Yet the public mood was drifting overwhelmingly in the opposite direction. There could be no more illusions as to the true anti-Russian nature of the alliance, and particularly its plans for enlargement. The strong stance in Brussels and Budapest was correct, if overdue; there was no room for compromise in the future—these were the conclusions prevailing in the Russian media.

Anti-NATO feelings dominated not only in the public sphere but also in the Kremlin. The military and security agencies began redrafting their operational and long-term projections on the assumption that the United States and NATO were inherent threats—a view only too familiar from the Soviet era.

That political dynamic did not escape the attention of Western observers. On January 3, 1995, John Thornhill reported in the *Financial Times*: "The political mood in Moscow has changed markedly in recent weeks. President Boris Yeltsin is growing more isolated and unpopular, distancing himself from his former liberal supporters, and increasingly relying on his own administration and the 'power ministers' of defense, interior, and counterintelligence." Reading this characterization of the president's behavior, I wondered whether it was a result or a cause of both the brutality in Chechnya and the anti-NATO drive. The chiefs of the power agencies, most of the president's aides, and individuals from the President's Advisory Council on Foreign Relations competed in depicting to Yeltsin the nightmarish prospect of facing an outraged electorate during the Duma elections in December, and especially in the run-up to the presidential elections in the spring of 1996, as a result of Washington's and NATO's sharp turn on expanding the alliance.

The next moves of the Americans suggested that they had picked up on the election-year argument from their Kremlin sources. It made perfect sense to them as it was consistent with their own priority of salving domestic public opinion before tending to foreign policy interests. The Russian refusal to sign on to the Partnership for Peace (PfP) was seen as a defeat of American diplomacy, and Washington wanted to vindicate itself. Thus, early in 1995 Washington made an offer the election-obsessed Russian president could not refuse: the United States would not take any public steps toward NATO enlargement during the election year of 1996. In exchange for this and perhaps some other concessions Russia would sign the PfP program. Yeltsin wanted a full price for that as Americans needed the signature now, whereas his election was only the following year.

I was appalled that a rug-merchant type of bargaining over how soon Russia would sign the PfP protocol had replaced the substantive decision making. And the currency in which the price would be denominated no longer lay in the domain of national interests but in Yeltsin's calculations as a politician tuning in to the nationalists' interests in his desperation to prolong his power.

From that point onward, for me it was not a question of whether to resign, but when and how. I quietly wished to make my resignation politically significant, a public act of defiance and protest against the Kremlin's turnaround from cooperation to Soviet-type acrimony with the democratic West. So I started to look for an opportune moment to gain the maximum attention through my move.

Two unexpected offers that I could not refuse stopped me from resigning immediately. One was from Yeltsin, the other from the United States.

Yeltsin's offer came during our return flight from the Pskov region, in Russia's Northwest, on the border of Russia and Latvia. The region had changed hands at different times in its history and was now claimed by Latvia on the basis of the 1920 Treaty of Riga. I contended that the principle of respecting existing borders on which the independence and security of the post-Soviet states were founded meant that such a claim, made on historical grounds, could not be countenanced. Yeltsin's rejection of it helped boost his ebbing popularity. On the flight back to Moscow Yeltsin was in a good mood and we discussed Russia's internal politics, which was increasingly dominated by the nationalists and communists. The democrats, meanwhile, were holding back, waiting for Yeltsin to decide whether he would run in the next presidential election and, in the interim, they were losing their dynamism and appeal.

I decided to open the discussion of his candidacy on a positive note. After carefully introducing the need to start preparing for a presidential run, I suggested he assign a close aide as his campaign manager. If the last Duma elections were any indication, the battle would not be easy. So the campaign organization and messaging should start as early as possible and be handled professionally.

Yeltsin considered my words, then said: "You know that I did not want to run again. There should be someone younger, with a fresh mind . . ." I recognized the Soviet-speak for what it was, a trick used by Stalin and other Soviet leaders to test the loyalty of aides. "Yet you are probably right: it will be a tough fight, and there is nobody I can trust to be able to win. People like [Boris] Nemtsov, a young democratically minded governor of a Volga region, or [Grigory] Yavlinsky, the leader of the liberal 'Yabloko' party, are still too young and inexperienced to face old wolves like [Gennady] Zyuganov (communist) or [Vladimir] Zhirinovsky." He sighed and paused again.

I swallowed the objections that sprang to my lips. Those he had mentioned were young but already seasoned politicians, and there were others. Why not give the "young people" a chance to hone their leadership abilities at an early stage in the campaign preparations, and choose one a year later?

"I don't see any alternative to your candidacy," I said cowardly.

"You are a professional, Andrei Vladimirovich, in everything you do. Why don't you run my campaign? You can combine this with the Foreign Ministry for the preliminary stage, and when the official campaign starts, in February and March of next year, we'll see how best to proceed."

I was pleasantly surprised by the offer and promised to do my best. Later on, I tried to salve my conscience, thinking that perhaps this appointment would allow me to craft a new reform message for presidential candidate Yeltsin, reviving his democratic agenda of the previous election campaign. Yeltsin's entourage resisted this approach, and, sensing my intentions, he avoided discussing the political thrust of the campaign as premature. All in all, my activity in this new area of responsibility was received without enthusiasm.

However, a second major reason for staying on as foreign minister for the duration of 1995 came in the form of an unexpected offer, this time from Warren Christopher.

An Offer Too Late

I had met Christopher in early January in Geneva, and after an unusually cordial discussion was left with the impression that he was finally prepared to address my concerns about NATO. We agreed to start an exploratory dialogue on a strategic partnership that might develop into a true alliance, one that could weather political storms and make the enlargement of NATO not only acceptable to but welcomed by Russia, because in the new equation each new member of NATO would be a new ally for Russia too. I was delighted to be able to inform Yeltsin of these developments. His reaction was much more reserved and skeptical. Nonetheless, he agreed we should not turn down the opportunity to test American goodwill and asked me to put together a specific proposal in coordination with the Defense and Security Ministries, the usual process for preparing documents on such matters.

Both ministries, however, insisted that Washington could not be trusted, and any dialogue on a partnership with NATO would be dangerous and counterproductive to the foremost task of restraining NATO expansion. The entrenched red generals, especially in the security apparatus, were unwilling to drop the image of NATO as the enemy they had worked so hard to reinstate, providing a strong base for restoring the power and perks they had enjoyed under the Soviet regime.

Recognizing that I would be on my own in pursuing Christopher's opening, I decided to adopt the roundabout course of taking the proposal to the president without confirmatory signatures, counting on the reformist instinct he had demonstrated in difficult situations in the past. To avoid procedural difficulties, I formulated the new position statement as a follow-up to my previous year's assignment to explore the means of achieving a possible compromise with NATO. I suggested responding to Christopher's opening with a tentative offer to enter into a partnership with NATO on the basis of four points.

1. Engagement in genuine joint work on a new structure for comprehensive European security in which NATO as a military alliance would be an important player, along with the OSCE, the EU, the CIS, and other bodies with different profiles and memberships operating for the benefit of the countries from the Canadian West Coast to the Russian Far East. Neither NATO nor any of the other organizations would pretend to exclusivity and dominance; rather, all would contribute to security and socioeconomic cooperation in their own field of competence.

2. Establishment of a permanent mechanism for political consultations that would exclude mutual surprises and vetoes but ensure joint decision making.

3. Establishment of the same in military matters. The two military machines should learn to cooperate in an increasing number of arenas on a daily basis and at different levels of interaction in order to overcome their historical alienation and become allies. Clearly, this process would be much more complex and of much longer duration than setting up a political mechanism. For that reason, a transitional period should be contemplated, perhaps accompanied by guarantees from the military on both sides that they would not move their bases or weapons, particularly nuclear ones, toward each other during the transition period.

4. Military-industrial cooperation in creating, producing, and trading modern weapons and equipment on an open and enlarged NATO market.

Yeltsin thought it worthwhile to explore Washington's intentions on the basis of those four points.

Christopher's response was equally positive. All points were acceptable in principle, though considerable work would be needed to endow them with practical meaning. Encouraged, I told Yeltsin that now our consultations should also gradually engage other NATO members so that the Americans could not backtrack later on the pretext that they could not speak for the entire alliance. He read the points through once again, and, after I had confirmed positive signals from Christopher, shrugged, and uttered his famous "khorosho," OK.

In mid-February I attended the Foreign Policy Committee of the Duma as a member and used the opportunity to outline the four points in a brief speech. The response was neutral, and I felt rather encouraged.

More encouraging were the early responses from the European NATO allies. All four points were recognized as important building blocks for a Russia–NATO partnership. Many of them, including the UK, France, and Germany, surprised us with their seriousness in the new dialogue, which focused on the political consultative mechanism as a relatively simple and quickly achievable goal.

By March we and the NATO allies had started to discuss in practical terms how to wrap up the four points and other elements of the new relations in an agreement. I wanted a Russia–NATO treaty of alliance. Washington preferred a declaration or a charter that would have the same content and be equally binding but would not require a long and painful procedure of ratification by sixteen NATO members and the Russian parliament. At their meeting in Carcassonne in mid-March, the European ministers forwarded a preliminary proposal for a treaty between NATO and Russia.

As a result of enormous effort, we had finally succeeded in Russia's being taken seriously and positively by the West. But the better developed our dialogue with NATO, the more resentment flowed from the Kremlin. My close aides in the ministry sensed it daily. We were also concerned that Warren Christopher might face a similar if less severe opposition from the hardliners in Washington. That prompted us to engage our American partners in preparing an exchange of letters between our presidents that would "ratify" the progress already achieved on the Russia–NATO equation and open way for the continuation of our effort.

Our opponents in Moscow had good intelligence on my ministry and were busy persuading Yeltsin that Washington was simply practicing deception to cover NATO enlargement and to gain our signature for the PfP program. Unfortunately, the United States provided grounds to support this interpretation. In parallel with exploratory talks on the substance of a Russia–NATO future, American diplomats continued to insist that Moscow sign the PfP framework agreement and to bargain over the price it was prepared to pay Yeltsin for this formal act.

Yeltsin, however, wanted to sell directly to Clinton, to get the best deal. Clinton for his part apparently understood that he had to meet Yeltsin to secure his signature, and it strongly swayed his decision to accept our invitation to attend the May 9 VE Day observance in Moscow. His advisers naively assumed that the very fact of his coming to Moscow, a city distracted by the Chechen War, would be payment enough for Yeltsin.

My efforts were concentrated on keeping Yeltsin focused on the substantive consultations on Russia–NATO relations. This fundamental issue I hoped would be discussed between the two presidents while Clinton was in Moscow. The VE Day celebration marked the occasion of Moscow and Washington having worked together as allies sixty years earlier to rid the world of the Nazi nightmare; it was time to contemplate a new alliance after the nightmare of the Cold War. I was encouraged to read Robert D. Novak in the *Washington Post* on April 17, 1995: "The most important advice for Bill Clinton from his professional diplomatic advisers for his May 9 summit in Moscow is: Don't hug Boris! The public spectacle two weeks ago of Defense Secretary William Perry seeming to fawn as he toasted Russian Defense Minister Pavel Grachev, the butcher of Chechnya, appalled State Department officials. They do not want a repeat performance."

Christopher asked me to come to Washington for talks on the subject of preparations for the forthcoming summit. After an attempt at light blackmail—I was denied the usual courtesy of a meeting with the US president unless Christopher could report that we had agreed on the PfP signing in Moscow—I saw the US president only after Yeltsin had finally authorized me to endorse the idea, with the proviso that the final touches to it would be concluded in a phone call between the two presidents.

To my deep disappointment, in my talks with Christopher and Clinton the substantive goals of crafting new Russian–American and Russia–NATO relations were sidelined. Clearly, this was about to be repeated in Moscow, and my recently renewed optimism as to the possibility of a real Russian–American partnership was quickly melting.

The Pathetic Deal

Playing on a field of backdoor dealings and power intrigues instead of working toward substantive engagement, the Americans stood no chance against the former Soviet apparatchiks. This made me cheer for Yeltsin, who had drunk heartily at dinner before the scheduled phone call with Clinton and hung up when the American president tried to dwell on the PfP.

The careless choreography of the main public appearances at the VE Day celebrations in Moscow, though perhaps inadvertent, had Clinton following in the footsteps of his radiant host, giving every appearance of a country cousin waiting for promised largesse. After my recent New York–Washington experience I did not care about Clinton's embarrassment, but I worried that it was not just the Kremlin coterie feeding the Russian president's bad habits. The day's antics proved just a foretaste of the clowning in Hyde Park, New York, on October 23, the last summit I attended, where Clinton doubled over in laughter at the crude jokes of his drunk friend at the post-summit press conference, having earlier begged him to send Russian peacekeepers to Bosnia so that the operation there would look less risky to Clinton's critics on the Hill and in Europe.

In Moscow, the Americans again tried to corner me into executing their responsibilities and helping them achieve what I considered their ill-thought-out goals. Right after the public ceremony in Red Square, Strobe Talbott whispered to me that the PfP formula worked just fine and that now I should announce my intention of joining the NATO foreign ministers at the end of the month to sign the protocol. I pointed out that even if Yeltsin had dropped a hint of agreement, as Talbott claimed, it could not be taken seriously in such a casual social setting. No, I would not ask the president on my own initiative because he was busy doing his job—which, at the moment, was to be the host for the world presidents he had invited.

This scene played out again after the presidents met one-on-one, accompanied by Talbott and Dmitry Ryurikov as note-takers; I was not present. I advised Talbott to check his notes concerning the PfP with his Russian counterpart, who, as Yeltsin's foreign policy assistant, was the person who conveyed instructions from his boss to the Ministry of Foreign Affairs. Apparently Talbott had done so and was in a panic: Ryurikov was being evasive. Talbott rushed to Clinton, who had to try again to get Yeltsin's attention.

Reluctantly, the Russian president gave Ryurikov instructions to ask me to sign the PfP agreement by the end of the month.

The price Clinton paid was impressive. First, Yeltsin announced a speedy upgrade to effectively full-scale participant status at the post-summit press conference at the next G-7 meeting of most developed democratic countries. The pro-Western democrats could not ask for more. Their opponents were also satisfied: during his speech Clinton had indicated that the treaty on Conventional Armed Forces in Europe would have to be modified to address Russian concerns and that NATO's internal deliberations on expansion were not yet at the point of agreeing on procedures or the timing of accession of new members. The hard-liners saw in Clinton's ingratiating tone confirmation that instead of seeking a strategic agreement with NATO, the Kremlin could just play hardball.

Clinton was promised that the PfP program would be signed on May 31, at the NATO semiannual ministerial conference in Noordwijk, the Netherlands. Even after his handshake sealing the deal, however, Yeltsin tried to duck and delay its execution. In search of a further stumbling block to signing of the PfP, Yeltsin decided the Russian Security Council, which had been dormant for months, under the supervision of its executive secretary, his friend Oleg Lobov, would be convened on May 24 for a full-scale decision-making session devoted to relations with NATO.

Lobov, a good-natured (if simpleminded) apparatchik, and I had been friendly since August 1991, when we were sent—he to the East and I to the West—to represent the Yeltsin government outside Moscow. Now he felt awkward helping the neo-Soviet hard-liners dump me, though his sentiments had gravitated toward their side. Most important, he sensed that Yeltsin did not have a clear vision of the outcome of the session, so Lobov was careful to maintain a neutral stance. It was from Lobov that I learned about the inclination of the military-security group of Security Council members headed by Primakov. It could be summarized as decidedly revengeful and revanchist, but also liable to change rendering to Yeltsin's mood and wishes in accordance with the old apparatus modus operandi, "Come to the boss with your opinion and leave with his." Skillfully using bureaucratic motions, they put me on the firing line for refusing to coordinate my presentation draft of the session's resolution with them—though to be on the safe side, they also refused either to make known their objections to my resolution or to present their own resolution. In keeping with his coordinating function, Lobov as secretary of the Security Council tried to correct the situation, but in the end, he just reported to the president that my presentation had not been coordinated with the other members.

When I mounted the podium to begin my presentation, Yeltsin said: "Somehow everyone in this room is against your approach. Chernomyrdin recently spoke firmly against NATO expansion, and [also] the PfP, if it is just an anteroom for the new members. This seems to be a consensus opinion."

The edge of theatricality in the gathering and in Yeltsin's behavior swayed the immediate thought that rose to my mind—to tell them that a neo-Soviet policy toward NATO would harm Russia, and then to resign. That thought did not go away.

Yeltsin's reference to Viktor Chernomyrdin suggested that he was open to reason and only wanted to blow off steam before making an unpopular decision, a pattern of behavior with which his closest aides were acquainted. Though Chernomyrdin was the prime minister, his job did not entail coordinating foreign policy or security decisions, and Yeltsin usually strove to keep him out of politics; the writ of the prime minister and his cabinet was limited to managing domestic socioeconomic issues. By calling attention to Chernomyrdin's statement on NATO, Yeltsin was obliquely criticizing his prime minister and, by extension, cautioning all others who thought they had won the day.

Matching my tone with his, I said that of course, my approach was aligned with Chernomyrdin's, since both stemmed from the same source, namely, Yeltsin's previous directives.

Most of the Security Council members expected me to insist on signing the PfP and were surprised when I said I did not consider signing an important end in itself but was prepared to do so on May 31 if the president wanted it done, in accordance with the agreement he had apparently reached with Clinton during the VE Day celebrations in Moscow. This reminded Yeltsin that what was at stake was his word, that the signing was not my initiative, and that I could hardly be challenged for not coordinating a presentation on the PfP with the Security Council.

"Andrei Vladimirovich," the president turned to me, "sit down with the other members and incorporate their views into a final report for me to make the decision. Don't be capricious or jealous. There are a lot of interesting ideas that should not be lost."

Reviewing this episode in the car on my way back from the Kremlin to

the ministry I came to a sober conclusion: for the time being I could continue managing Russia's foreign diplomacy as an advocate of cooperation and
partnership, but a policy change was clearly in the works. And it was only a
matter of time before those two conflicting lines collided, and the change
would win, leaving me no choice but to resign.

One logical solution lay before me. The summer vacation was coming,
and everything would probably go smoothly until early fall. With the start
of the fall election season I could start my own campaign for reelection to
the Duma. According to the new Russian constitution the Duma mandate
could no longer be combined with a cabinet membership, which dictated my
resignation from the Foreign Ministry by December.

I wanted the signing of the PfP program to stimulate substantive work on
Russia's relations with NATO as a potential ally. But Yeltsin blocked that
option. Shortly before I was to leave for the Netherlands the president came
to the ministry to meet my top aides, mostly deputy ministers, for a televised
handshake and a brief overview of the current state of affairs in the ministry.
On the day before, we had talked over the event, and he gave no indication
that his visit would be substantive. So I was taken by surprise when in the
morning he stormed into the room where the participants had gathered, and
after hasty formal greetings, dismissed the press and addressed me directly.

"Why are you, Andrei Vladimirovich, conducting negotiations on the
conditions under which we could accept NATO membership or NATO
enlargement? Who authorized that? I did not. Nor could it have been coordinated with other agencies. That is a precipitous step and it is in the wrong
direction."

"In accordance with your directives we are conducting preliminary and
confidential consultations not on the conditions of enlargement but on an
alternative to hasty enlargement: that will put the new Russian–NATO
relations first. I will report to you on this matter later," I said, taking note of
the pale faces of my deputies.

"I don't know what kind of alternative you are talking about. Our opponents in NATO take your overtures simply as a sign of weakness in our
position and an offer to bargain over the price for enlargement," he said,
calming down. Seeing my raised eyebrows at his last words, he added, almost
defensively: "There is unambiguous information on that matter from reliable
sources very close to those people you are talking to in Washington. We'll talk

about it later one-on-one, but for now I want everybody here to remember that Russia—the president of Russia—is against NATO, against its enlargement, and we are not going to negotiate any terms or conditions of our agreement since we just don't agree."

At his mention of sources, I knew where the outburst had come from. During my Monday morning reporting sessions, he often challenged me with contrary "information from other sources," usually proving wrongdoing of the US State Department or my Foreign Ministry. Most of these "surprises" turned out to be an inaccurate account of events and a misrepresentation of their political significance. Once I learned that Yevgeny Primakov's thirty-minute Monday session with Yeltsin preceded mine, the mystery source became clear. I had some difficult exchanges with the president over the biased character of the information, and eventually he agreed to my proposal that Primakov and I have regular meetings to compare notes in advance of the interviews each of us had with the president. Primakov also agreed, and we then alternated visiting each other's offices on Fridays for a working lunch to share information. He was friendly but frugal about sharing information and coordinating.

Yeltsin's agitation and his bearing down on "reliable sources" that disputed my position during his visit to the ministry inadvertently disclosed Primakov as the main source of the amendments to the NATO position paper, which had been handled by Oleg Lobov. I did not want either to directly associate me with those additions or the West to miss the warning of an inevitable change in Russian policy they hinted at.

At the signing ceremony on May 31 in The Hague, I limited my remarks to a few protocol niceties while handing the position paper to the NATO secretary general for distribution. The paper made for tricky but, for the West, urgent reading.

My formula for Russia–NATO relations had always been "cooperation yes, hasty enlargement no." The position paper amended after the Security Council discussion looked, on the surface, similar: "conditional cooperation yes, enlargement no." It read: "A decision about the enlargement of NATO to the East would create for Russia the need for a corresponding correction of its attitude to the Partnership for Peace." Since NATO was not going to drop the idea of enlargement, in effect, Russia's position paper had to be read as saying no to both cooperation and enlargement.

A more fundamental message lurked in the position paper's call for the alliance to change its nature "from a military alliance to a political organization." It was simply ignored by the NATO ministers. Yet it had a deep significance, for it clarified the Russian hard-liners' strategy of saying no to NATO's very existence in accordance with Cold War logic: if the Warsaw Pact had been dispensed with, so also should NATO. This line of thinking only hardened in the Kremlin and in military-security agencies in the years to come. It underlies the present-day strategy of undermining and breaking up NATO by any means possible, while Russia's occasional overtures to NATO and complaints about its enlargement are little more than a smoke screen.

In private, I drew the attention of Christopher to those points and again stressed the urgency of a serious, substantive meeting between the two heads of state to discuss NATO and its relations with Russia. Otherwise, I said, the signing of the PfP framework document would mark not the start of a new chapter in the relations but an end to the whole story of partnership. Washington ignored my private warning. On the surface, Clinton appeared to have delivered on his promise to begin the process of NATO enlargement while also securing Russia's adherence to the PfP. That was enough for the domestic electorate, the US Congress, and Washington's European allies. The ticking bomb of Moscow's hostility and revenge was for the time being ignored.

The controversial aspects of the signing did not escape the Western media. The May 31 *International Herald Tribune*, quoting an Associated Press report, said:

> The US secretary of state Warren M. Christopher led NATO officials Tuesday [May 30] in hailing Russia's decision to participate in the alliance's Partnership for Peace as the "beginning of a new era" in relations with Moscow. His Russian counterpart, Andrei V. Kozyrev, warned NATO that the new cooperation agreements would be threatened if the alliance went ahead with plans to take on new members in Eastern Europe. Mr. Christopher however addressed the good news. "An enhanced NATO–Russia relationship is the next important element in our overall strategy for European security." But Mr. Christopher [also] said, "NATO enlargement remains an essential part of our strategy."

The last part Christopher's statement, so divergent from Russia's position paper, and divergent as well from various previous utterances by the Clinton administration, were widely reported in the Russian media and interpreted by the Kremlin as deeply offensive. In securing the signature of Moscow to the PfP framework document while at the same time ignoring its objections to enlargement, Washington, it was said, was demonstrating once again its disregard of Russia and that country's interests. I came under special criticism for signing the PfP despite American arrogance.

A group of Yeltsin's Kremlin aides, including their informal leader George Satarov, in their book *The Epoch of Yeltsin* published in 2000, describe the United States in the early 1990s behaving as if it were the winner of the Cold War, "eligible for trophies: significant expansion and even hegemony in the world." This reality manifested itself most acutely in "two problems dominating Russian foreign policy." The first was NATO enlargement, an American mechanism of trophy collection. The second was the crisis in Bosnia, also the West's enlargement, "only by military actions and under cover of peace-making." They accuse me of complicity in both cases. This perspective, of which I was aware in 1995, left me alone in the Russian corridors of power. Nevertheless, I continued challenging this view as an opportunistic betrayal of Russia's fundamental national interest in forging an alliance with the West, despite the difficulties and the mistakes made on both sides. However, given the Clinton administration's approach, I also felt awkwardly quixotic resisting the rising tide of anti-Western sentiment.

With the signing of the PfP framework document the crucially important subject of Russia–NATO relations was reduced to PR doublespeak on both sides. Diplomatic niceties, especially at Bill–Boris summits, were used as cover for divergent real politics defined for domestic consumption. The successors to Christopher and myself—Yevgeny Primakov and Madeleine Albright—elaborated the next stop on this track after Yeltsin and Clinton had won reelection in 1996. On May 27, 1997, the Founding Act on Mutual Relations, Cooperation and Security between NATO and Russia was added to the PfP agreement that had been implemented as halfheartedly as it had been signed. Upon returning from the portentous signing ceremony at the NATO summit, Yeltsin, in his radio address to the Russian people on May 30, described the act as an effort "to minimize the negative consequences of NATO's expansion." It sounded like a founding act of controlled hostility, rather than cooperation.

Back in 1995, after the NATO controversy had been swept under the rug of the PfP, the events in Bosnia came once more to the front burner.

The Sarajevo Massacre and Yeltsin's Complicity

In early 1995 the Contact Group on Bosnia proposed a modernized plan for peace negotiations. The Bosnian Serbs rejected the offer and carried out attacks on UN Protected Areas. In response NATO executed a couple of air strikes in late May. But hundreds of Muslim civilians and even UN peacekeepers were taken hostage and used as human shields by the Bosnian Serbs in a successful attempt to dissuade NATO from further actions. This contributed to a hardening of the European states' political disposition toward the Bosnian Serbs.

No doubt the Serbian extremists heard Moscow ringing neo-Soviet bells and hoped to be protected by their "Orthodox elder brother" from repercussions for their brutality in Bosnia. There was ample evidence, both in press reports and in the gossip in the Kremlin corridors, that not only messages and messengers but also some military-related materiel was being channeled to Serbia and Bosnia behind my back by unconventional means. In hindsight I tend to believe that Yeltsin at least was aware of these "hybrid" operations and perhaps even authorized them on condition of being able to deny them. Putin has simply continued and expanded this type of interference.

On both sides the anti-NATO warriors were counting the days to the moment of liberation from the bonds of a pro-Western foreign policy in Moscow, when Russia could stand firm against the United States' and NATO's Balkan and world domination strategy.

Despite this, until mid-summer 1995 I was able to keep Milošević in a constructive mood. He held firm to the blockade of the Bosnian Serbs, limiting their aggression. That strengthened our role in the international Contact Group on Bosnia and in European politics in general, and I tried to squeeze as much benefit out of it for the continuation of my policy as I could.

The high point in this endeavor came in early June in London when I met with Prime Minister John Major and Foreign Secretary Douglas Hurd. They agreed to try to return to search for substantive agreement on NATO. Hurd also emphasized the need for Russia and the West to work together in Bosnia because they could not hope to succeed alone. He brought up the necessity for Russia and NATO to have a mechanism of consultation whereby they would not just keep each other informed but could work closely together on security problems, of which Bosnia was only one.

Back home in Moscow, Yeltsin seemed unimpressed by the opportunity that had started to take shape in London to lay the groundwork for a serious partnership with NATO. He was also rather cool to my argument that the alternative to the "London option" was a confrontation with NATO and its impassioned potential new members—most of the Eastern European states. This anemic reaction prompted me to produce the most straightforward argument in my portfolio. Unable to block the enlargement—at best we could rely on Clinton for a pause in 1996—Russia, however much fist-pounding it engaged in, would gain nothing from isolation and stubbornness and could lose much.

The ensuing national humiliation would be exploited by the neo-Soviet nationalist and militarist forces and could not be acceptable to the first elected president of Russia. Those forces would always hate Yeltsin for destroying the Soviet empire and would not be appeased by anti-NATO rhetoric. They would simply pocket the concessions, applaud the reversal of policy as proof of their long-held position, and continue fighting for power and for revenge.

Intercepting a strange look from Yeltsin, as if he were disconcerted by my aggressive tone, I concluded on a more diplomatic note. The president would be joining the G-7 in Halifax in a few days, and positive dialogue on a NATO-Russian future would serve him better than defiance of the Western alliance.

"You are probably right," he said, "but it would be good for both of us to hear other opinions too in preparation for the Halifax conference. Come tomorrow at 11:00 a.m. and join me at a meeting with leading members of the Presidential Council. My assistants say there are important fresh ideas."

In essence, the meeting was a replay of the May 24 Security Council meeting. Andranik Migranian, a known authoritarian nationalist, was the main speaker. (I was not surprised when years later, in 2014, he defended Putin's annexation of Crimea. He conceded that there were similarities between that act and Hitler's seizure of Austria and parts of Czechoslovakia in the 1930s, and implied that the Nazi dictator had acted as a "politician of the highest order" and "gatherer of German lands" prior to 1939 [https://www .rferl.org/a/russia-crimea-and-the-good-hitler/25322600.html].) The fact that either Yeltsin or (more likely) his assistants had chosen someone like this to oppose me was symptomatic of the mood prevailing in the Kremlin.

Migranian opined that Russia had made a serious mistake by signing the PfP framework agreement. It might have made sense had the partnership been a substitute for enlargement, yet NATO's decision to enlarge was now known, so what was the sense of signing the PfP? Second, NATO was building a rapid deployment force for use in the former Yugoslavia, circumventing the UN Security Council. The United States had conducted air strikes without consulting Russia. It was therefore a surprise to hear the Russian foreign minister say in London that Russian troops might join the rapid deployment forces in the former Yugoslavia.

"Perhaps I will have to refute this statement in Halifax. My statement will say that we are against applying pressure through the use of force!" Yeltsin exclaimed, looking at Migranian, then immediately added, turning to me: "Our position on Bosnia remains the same."

The president was playing tough with me for an audience, and for that I was about to explode. Yet he was also clearly signaling to me that he did not intend to change anything in reality, at least in the immediate term, emphatically reiterating the position he had approved before. This, as we both knew, included the possibility of Russia's participating in an international force in Bosnia, as it was the only alternative to being excluded from the most important political process in Europe, the search for a solution in Bosnia.

"We will analyze the situation and only then make a decision," I said calmly but firmly.

After a few more objections from Migranian, Yeltsin brought the meeting to a close. Then he turned to me in the most business-as-usual manner with a routine question about whether there was any news he needed to know to prepare for Halifax. Before I could answer, he added, "I am disappointed with this session. They were almost blistering me and made me irritated. But in fact, there were no fresh ideas, nothing practical for the forthcoming meeting. Was there?"

"It was not my idea to invite them," I said dryly. "As you know, I listen to these guys regularly in the Foreign Policy Consultative Council in the ministry, and they never say anything new. If in Soviet times NATO was called the 'instrument of aggression of American imperialists,' now it is denounced as serving 'American domination.' It is so convenient to all trained in Soviet propaganda, and so much easier than trying to figure out how to cooperate with the West. Of course, there are difficulties and disagreements with America and NATO, but denying them as strategic partners and demonizing them in the old way leads us nowhere but to the neo-Soviet policy of self-isolation.

Nothing else can be expected in Halifax if the president of Russia follows the recommendations we've just heard."

"Relax," he said, rubbing my shoulder. "Let's go to the club for lunch." I was disarmed, my personal rapport with the president restored. I was sure that in Halifax he would follow the line acceptable to me. I also knew that the winds of change were tilting that line in a direction I could not accept.

A few weeks later the Bosnian Serb army overran the UN Protected Area in the Muslim enclave of Srebrenica, pushing the Dutch peacekeepers aside and killing many civilians. The tragedy was widely reported in the world media, with outrage at the Serbs expressed in the West but sympathy for them in Russia, where the atrocities were minimized and the Muslims were accused of having provoked the attack. Amid alarming reports that the Serbs were about to overrun another UN "safe area" in Goražde and increase pressure on Sarajevo, John Major called an international conference in London for the purpose of reaching agreement on the wider use of NATO air power, and as a last resort ground forces to stop the Serbian warmongering. Like other countries, Russia was represented by its foreign and defense ministers.

The conference was a chaotic gathering. After a brief joint session, the foreign ministers were asked to wait for recommendations from their military colleagues, who gathered separately, tasked with assessing the situation on the ground. After a long coffee break I began to hear talk of a consensus reached by the defense ministers on a tough military response to any Serbian attack on Goražde, Sarajevo, or any other safe area. Beyond this, the conference's decision to adopt that consensus was about to be announced at the press conference to be held soon, called by John Major as chairman. I ran to my British colleague and told him that no decision could be supported by the Russian delegation without Pavel Grachev consulting me, and both of us reporting to our president. I was told that apparently Grachev did not object to the conclusions of the military session and had reached an important understanding with his American counterpart, Bill Perry. In any case, I was promised a draft decision "based on the military session" momentarily. It never came.

Soon I met Grachev, who said that he had just finished a very productive get-together with his friend Bill Perry, the US secretary of defense, and was waiting to be connected to Yeltsin on a mobile line. In a few minutes he picked up the receiver, and from his expression I could tell he was speaking to the president. I did not hear what he said or what the president answered, but Grachev lost the confident look he had had just a few minutes earlier. He handed the phone to me, and I briefed the president on what I knew, which was very little, while emphasizing that the British had promised to provide me with a draft decision, the normal procedure for an international conference. Only after that would we be able to report the full picture and ask for instructions on whether to support the document. "Yes, of course; you have to obtain the draft, and we will discuss what to do with it. Please be sure that Pavel Sergeevich, who has less experience in diplomacy, acts accordingly. You are one delegation and should speak with a single voice on my instruction, as usual. In any case we do not agree to NATO military actions. This is my instruction to both of you."

I reminded him that according to his previous decisions, Russia had already agreed that NATO could be used to provide close support to UN peacekeepers in case of a specific request by the UN secretary general in consultation with the Security Council. "Yes, he said. That position remains unchanged, but no additional powers should be given to NATO, and there are to be no air strikes on the Serbs. No air strikes." The last words signaled a retreat from the previous position he had confirmed in the first part of the sentence.

"Strange," Grachev murmured with a puzzled look. "In Moscow he told me not to be confrontational, to avoid isolation . . ." His voice trailed off, then he turned to me. "Everybody in our group supported tough action; blamed the Bosnian Serbs. I gave them factual arguments to the contrary, but they remained unimpressed." I had to admit that despite some reservations from the Greek and Spanish foreign ministers, the mood was the same: the Serbs had gone too far and had to be stopped; there was no other force to do so but NATO. So John Major decided to air the sentiment in the chairman's statement without formal approval at a plenary session. Grachev and I informed our British colleagues of Russia's objections to using coercive force against the Bosnian Serbs.

Grachev and Bill Perry traditionally had a good rapport, so both the Kremlin and the White House expected them to produce a miracle in London. Grachev had also counted on his special relations with Yeltsin to get approval to an agreement with Perry. The moment of truth came when he received his final instruction from the president, which left no room for joining his American friend and other colleagues. I was glad he had come to

London and appreciated his genuine effort to harmonize the new Moscow stance with the European mood. I knew it was impossible and thought it important that the president also had no illusions to that effect.

When the failure of the diplomatic reconciliation became clear, Grachev jumped the track. Thereafter the Russian Defense Ministry positioned itself as a staunch opponent of NATO, NATO's interference in Bosnia, and the use of coercive force against the Bosnian Serbs.

The *Guardian* reported on July 22 that at a joint press conference in London with Pavel Grachev, I had said that the meeting "failed to reach a general consensus," and that General Grachev, "in full military uniform, told the press-conference: 'We rejected the delivery of air strikes. . . . The proposal on the rapid reaction force was also rejected by our side.'"

Oddly enough, Strobe Talbott in his memoirs writes, "The Russians had in effect signed away their rights to prevent the strikes at the London conference in July." Perhaps Strobe, who was not at the conference, had relied on premature expectations of Grachev–Perry cooperation. Also, Washington was desperate to present the decision to bomb the Bosnian Serbs as the "London consensus." The participants knew better. The *Guardian* article left no room for interpretation: "The Russian veto was highlighted by Klaus Kinkel, the German foreign minister, who told reporters bluntly: 'The Russians rejected military action.'"

I Make Up My Mind

The *Guardian* article's lead—"Moscow's line tends to encourage the Bosnian Serbs to think they can get away with anything"—spurred my final decision to leave the ministry. Though I detested Western intrigues no less than domestic ones, Moscow's policy had become unacceptable to me.

On returning from London I looked for an opportunity to have a frank talk with Yeltsin in a relaxed setting to be sure we understood each other and could make the decision either to continue working together—there seemed to be almost no chance of that—or to part on decent terms. Seemingly sensing what was afoot, Yeltsin avoided one-on-one encounters with me, yet was friendly and even warm when at his invitations I joined the group dinners of the President's Club.

That summer Yeltsin vacationed in a state-owned dacha in Sochi with his large family of two daughters and several grandchildren. Grachev and I with our families occupied dachas on either side of Yeltsin's. That was the best summer vacation of the four I spent in those Soviet-era luxury facilities on the Black Sea, enjoying an abundance of tennis and swimming. Learning to windsurf on the water near the shore I narrowly missed colliding with Boris Nemtsov then the young reformist governor of Nizhni Novgorod who was trying to water-ski. It so happened that each one of us was good at the skill the other was trying to learn, and we had a fantastic time together as he taught me to windsurf and I helped him with the skis.

Ten years later Nemtsov fearlessly campaigned against Putin's authoritarianism. He opposed the intervention in Ukraine and was killed by an unknown assailant near the Kremlin on February 27, 2015. Thousands of Muscovites marched in protest and mourning under the prophetic slogan "Heroes do not die!" A few days later the *Washington Post* published my op-ed commemorating my friend and denouncing the aggressiveness of the Kremlin regime.

In that summer of 1995 Yeltsin invited Grachev and me two or three times to join him for a family dinner, and my daughter Natasha spent a lot of time playing at his dacha with his grandchildren, falling in love with "Grandpa Boris" and particularly "Grandma Naina," who were quite generous to the children.

The separation had to be broached gently with my family. One night after Natasha had returned from the Yeltsins' we went for a walk in the darkened park. "We've had a good time in this resort place these last four summers," I began. "We've lived through a very exciting time when I did my best for the country and the man whose family you've been with." Sensing what was about to come, she interrupted: "He's just great! This summer I've gotten to know him better. He looks very tired and much older than before. They say he is ill. But he is so kind to us! And he likes you. I can see by his attitude toward me and by the way he speaks of you, Daddy. Of course, he doesn't mention politics. . . . I know there has been a change in outlook; I've read about it in America [where she went to school] . . . but you always said that he is to decide, being the first elected president." She spoke from the heart, a girl just leaving childhood behind.

I addressed her unasked questions frankly, "Yes, he is a historic figure, and he deserves my unreserved respect as Russia's first elected leader, but apparently he has made decisions—and as you've said, it is for him to decide—that

I disagree with and thus cannot in good conscience help implement. We will discuss it with him at an appropriate time later, and I still have some hope to persuade him to change his mind. Yet it is my feeling that this whole chapter of my life has come to an end. It is our last summer at this dacha in Sochi. It's a bit of a pity, but it is natural to turn pages in one's life. So we should not be downhearted about it. There will be a new page, and a new chapter—and a new sea resort, for that matter. I don't know what it will be like but change and facing the unknown add a thrill to life." Of course, that was easier said than done, but I also spoke from the heart.

A few days later we said farewell to the dacha in Sochi and took our separate flights, Natasha to New York to catch up with school, I to Manila to attend the annual ASEAN ministerial meeting, thence to return to Moscow. Yeltsin remained in Sochi; I was still waiting for a chance to speak with him. There was no urgency, but the clouds were gathering. We had reports that NATO had finished its study of potential expansion and had started focusing on preparations for admitting the first three candidates. Though actual membership was not envisaged for a few more years, the news was greeted in Moscow as tantamount to an immediate challenge to the nation's security. Yet for a time being the military-security analysts' bells were not tolling loudly in the summer twilight.

On August 30 vacation ended and the course of European and indeed Russian politics swerved onto a new trajectory when NATO started large-scale bombing in Bosnia, triggered by the second mass massacre in a "safety zone." This was the beginning of an air campaign that within a month or so had forced the Bosnian Serb hotheads to cool down, lift the siege of Sarajevo, form a joint negotiating team with Belgrade, and, under the leadership of Milošević, start peace talks based on the Contact Group's proposal. Despite Russia's significant role in making Milošević see reason and eventually causing him to be a key factor in the Bosnia settlement, all the glory and the credit went to the United States and its special negotiator, Dick Holbrook. Moscow had virtually isolated itself by vigorously opposing the air strikes and NATO involvement. The operation was portrayed by my opponents in the Kremlin and in the press as an American-led offensive that, in the final analysis, was aimed at Russia itself.

From Sochi, Yeltsin denounced NATO's actions as the "execution of the Bosnian Serbs," thus sending the wrong message of support to the warlords. The Chernomyrdin government issued a special statement accusing NATO of genocide. The Duma then approved a statement demanding that the president take immediate action to forestall NATO aggressiveness, and in particular that Russia not participate in any of the remaining UN sanctions against Serbia. No parliamentary faction, including Gaidar's and Yavlinsky's, refrained from unconditionally condemning NATO and expressing solidarity with the Bosnian Serbs as victims.

In the best Soviet tradition, the Kremlin and the Duma blamed world public opinion and media, driven by the US–NATO conspiracy, and went looking for a scapegoat. As John Thornhill wrote in the September 13 *Financial Times* in an article titled "Kozyrev May Be Balkans Fall-Guy," "[Kozyrev] has played a skillful diplomatic role as the acceptable face of Russia abroad and the benign face of Western interests at home. But as the gulf between Western and Russian interests has widened, he has found it difficult to straddle that divide." The correct word was not "difficult" but "impossible," I thought, reading this somewhat flattering analysis.

A few days after the air strikes began, I was summoned to Sochi. In the foyer of Yeltsin's dacha I met Grachev and the ambassador to Britain, my former deputy, Anatoly Adamishin.

Yeltsin got down to business immediately, starting with Yugoslavia.

"The NATO bombing of our Serbian friends has created a new challenge for Russia, and apparently our reaction has been late and weak. Anatoly Leonidovich Adamishin, one of the most seasoned diplomats and our ambassador to London, witnessed there the recent session of the so-called Contact Group and was outraged by the fact that the participants ignored our demand to stop the strikes now. I am indignant too, as is the Duma and everyone! Russia should not be reduced to the status of a helpless poor nephew in Europe!"

This start to the day was consistent with the morning news I had heard on the radio: according to sources, the president was to hold a landmark meeting in Sochi on Yugoslavia. Kozyrev, who had proved unable to stop NATO's bombing campaign, might be replaced with Anatoly Adamishin, a veteran of Soviet diplomacy accustomed to the tough talk that the West understands.

Yeltsin invited Adamishin and Grachev to address the group first. Both speakers expressed indignation at NATO for bombing the Bosnian Serbs and ignoring Russia. It was high time for Moscow to put an end to all this, if need be by tough measures! Yeltsin looked at me triumphantly: "What do you say, Andrei Vladimirovich?"

Following instructions from the president, I said, at the London conference Grachev and I, and at the London session of the Contact Group I, with
the help of our able ambassador to Britain, did exactly what had been suggested: we had made clear to NATO that the air strikes were unacceptable,
and that Russia could not allow its position to be ignored. Yet our voice was
an isolated one. European public opinion did not share the view that NATO
was by nature aggressive. All the new democracies and the CIS countries
participated in the PfP with NATO. Although some had reservations concerning the air strikes, most of them sympathized with NATO's resolve to
stop what world public opinion regarded as barbarism in the heart of Europe.
All the warring factions in the former Yugoslavia had committed crimes.
That was understood, but unfortunately, the Bosnian Serbs were seen as the
worst perpetrators and Russians as their protectors. This negative perception
would only soar with Russia's repeated public threats to hamstring NATO's
efforts.

"It's a universal law that empty threats are particularly counterproductive to stop anything. So are empty promises to promote something. So far,
I've heard two suggestions of practical measures that could be taken. Pavel
Sergeevich [Grachev] hinted at some steps of a military nature, which need a
detailed analysis from the political angle as well. On the surface, though, what
comes to mind is that the former Yugoslavia is separated from Russia by other
countries, some NATO members and others knocking at the door of NATO
for early membership. They would be able to block any movement of troops
or large supplies over their territory or airspace. So even if those military steps
were considered desirable, they are hardly feasible. The ambassador proposes
withdrawing from the Contact Group to protest NATO policy. That to my
mind would only help the world ignore Russia. If there are forces that want
to squeeze us out of European politics, they will be helped. The same could
be said of the Duma's demand to withdraw from the PfP."

As I spoke, Yeltsin's expression changed from one of defiance to irritation
and finally puzzlement.

"Are there any other ideas for what could be done in practical terms?" he
looked around. After a pause he declared the meeting a productive brain-
storming session and adjourned it. On his way out of the room he asked
Grachev and me to stay for private interviews, which turned into the usual
friendly luncheon.

When Yeltsin reappeared, he invited us to join him in an aperitif; lunch was served. I was in a panic: there would again be no opportunity for a substantive discussion. I considered the most concise way to say what was on my mind. As we stood in a small convivial group with glasses of scotch in our hands, I simply told the old man—for I suddenly realized he was old and tired—that I wanted to run for reelection for my Duma seat in Murmansk that fall.

He did not miss the meaning of my words: because positions in the Duma and in government could no longer be combined, my intention to run equaled a request to resign by the end of the year. "Why?" he asked, in the tone of a teacher challenged by a favorite but stubbornly rebellious student. "I thought you appreciated working with the president. Of course, it's up to you. But do you remember that once you promised to make this kind of decision only after consulting me?—Anyway, it's too early. We'll talk about it later, closer to election season, which will be announced in October." He turned away to take his seat at the head of the table.

When it was my turn to offer a toast, I proposed to Grachev that we raise our glasses to the honor and privilege of a lifetime of working with the first elected president of Russia.

I had come to Moscow with a light heart: my relations with the president were robust. Our deal had held through thick and thin: if he wanted to get rid of me, he would tell me first. On my side, I had made my intentions clear. If he were irreversibly on the new, neo-Soviet slant to foreign policy, I would run for a seat in the Duma and automatically vacate my ministry position.

So, I was not seriously concerned when at a press conference on my return to Moscow Yeltsin criticized the Foreign Ministry for its inability to block the NATO strikes and a few minor things. "Correct your mistakes and find a peaceful solution in the former Yugoslavia," he said, addressing the ministry and me.

I read it as a face-saving attempt to blame the diplomats for a mistake the president had made by fist pounding against the air strikes and earning for his trouble Russia's being ignored as the Atlantic partners sought a resolution to the senseless war. From the Burbulis-Gaidar era on there was general agreement among members of Yeltsin's team to take on themselves as much of the burden and criticism directed toward Yeltsin as possible because of his unique role in leading the country through extremely turbulent times and toward a democratic future. For that reason, the reformers usually did not talk back to the president publicly even if attacked or fired unfairly.

Two days later, at our regular Monday morning meeting in the Kremlin, he did not even mention his harsh remarks, concentrating instead on the prospects of a Balkan settlement. That confirmed my guess as to the face-saving nature of his public comments. Before leaving I told him that although it was OK to make the Foreign Ministry shoulder some responsibility for Russia's diplomatic troubles, it would also be fair to hold the aides and agencies responsible that had tried to push policy in a predictably hazardous direction. For instance, at the same press conference at which he had denounced the Foreign Ministry, the president had referred to the possibility of Russia creating a military bloc to oppose an expanding NATO. Yet in fact there were just too many applicants either for membership in or cooperation with the alliance, including all the former socialist states and the Soviet republics. China and India, the favorite alternatives raised by Primakov, had balanced but conflicting policies; it would be ridiculous even to suggest a political-military bloc to either or both of them. And who else was there for an anti-NATO?

"You know why all that has been said," he replied, irritated. "As to the criticism, you should not take it either too much to heart or arrogantly."

Recalling that conversation in the Kremlin in subsequent days, I thought that Yeltsin would soon tire of such discussions and make a decision about my future. In the meantime, I felt freed of responsibility for executing Russia's foreign policy and settled into daily caretaking tasks.

During this time, I enjoyed very good personal relations with Yeltsin, frequently sharing meals in the President's Club, but he carefully avoided any discussion of either policy strategy or my standing for a seat in the Duma. So, on October 1, I sent him an official letter requesting consent to my absence from the ministry two days a week in order to wage my Duma reelection campaign in Murmansk. A registered candidate had a legal right to absence from work for this purpose but was required to coordinate the dates with the employer. I did not wait for a reply but went to Murmansk on October 6, officially starting my campaign, while still bound by my private agreement with Yeltsin.

Who Will Be the Next President?

The governor of Murmansk area, Yevgeny Komarov, a reform-minded local leader, surprised me with an idea that had never before crossed my mind. "Why don't you think of a larger election campaign? I am sure you have a lot of sympathy, and not only here. There are still many democrats and reformers in the country. It is true that they are on the defensive, but a strong leader would have a good chance to mobilize them and win.—I am speaking of your own national campaign, not Yeltsin's."

"It is too farfetched to think of it. First, I am bound by my agreement to be coordinator of the president's run. Second, I am running for the Duma. Let's see how both issues end up."

When I was in Murmansk again, a week later, Komarov returned to the subject, but suggested we get out of the car and get some fresh air while discussing it. Clearly, he was concerned that the car was bugged. I waved my hand in dismissal. After the fall of communism, legislation was passed banning undercover surveillance unless it had been set up by court order. It would be even more outrageous if an elected governor and an elected Duma deputy were the people being bugged! This would have marked a return to Soviet practices, which some security veterans certainly dreamed of but would not dare attempt in democratic Russia. At least not yet, I thought. We went on in the car.

"I've spoken to some of my colleagues, governors, at an assembly we had a few days ago, and their preliminary reaction has been encouraging: they could see you as their candidate."

"That sounds almost too good to be true" I replied. "But what I said last time still holds. I shall concentrate on my Duma campaign here and after that weigh up other options."

Three hours later, on landing in Moscow, I waited at the airport for the president, who was also about to land after visiting a distant city in Russia. After the usual handshakes the president invited me along with a group of about eight top officials, some of whom had accompanied him on the trip while others had come to welcome him at the airport, to a small room where drinks and canapés were traditionally served on such occasions. He was tense, quickly downed a few glasses of cognac, and proceeded into a boasting mood. The participants tried to cheer him up and ease the atmosphere by

making jokes and telling funny stories. Suddenly Yeltsin stopped laughing
and fixed a steady look on me.

"Why won't we drink to the new president of Russia, Andrei Vladimirovich?" he said in a tense voice that immediately brought the noisy
drinking party to a dead silence.

"We do have a president," I said, caught by surprise. "And I propose to raise
a glass for him to stay!" All rose, ready to drink.

"No!" Yeltsin roared like a wooden bear. "I mean the new president, the
one that will be elected next year!"

"That's what I meant to say too," I quickly replied. "We have a president,
and there is no need for a new one. The elections will certainly only confirm
this conviction, shared, I believe, by all present." There was a roar of approval
and cheers as the guests thought that the incident had spent itself. Yet Yeltsin
pushed on.

"I have different information." Again, there was dead silence. "The new
president will be Kozyrev!" he said weightily. Nobody moved, seeing that he
was not joking. For a second, I was paralyzed too.

"Usually I don't argue with the president," I said, managing a smile. "But
this time I do, and I propose a bet for a bottle of whiskey. Is it a deal, Boris
Nikolayevich?"

"It's unfair; it's a sure bet for Andrei! If you take this deal, Boris Nikolayevich, I want to bet too. I also like whiskey," Grachev said. Now there was
laughter, and many voices proposed a bet for Yeltsin's victory. After more
drinks Yeltsin rose and walked away unsteadily on the arm of Grachev, who
helped him find his way out.

"What a strange fantasy! Why did he speak to you that way?" asked Chief
of Staff Sergei Filatov, not seeking an answer but expressing sympathy. I
shrugged. When Yeltsin first spoke about a new president, I was puzzled too.
Then a memory of Komarov's worry over the possible bugging of his car
crossed my mind. Thinking Yeltsin's outburst over, I came to the conclusion
that the governor had been right, despite there being no proof of it.

About a week later a stranger, his face obscured by a scarf, caught my arm
on a street in Murmansk and said, "You have my respect, Mr. Kozyrev, and
deserve to know the truth. This is a copy of a cable Yeltsin received from a
security agent from Murmansk on October 6." He handed me a piece of paper,
barely waited for me to read it, and quickly snatched it back. "Familiar text,
isn't it?" With these words he disappeared. It was familiar indeed: a transcript

of the two conversations I had had with Komarov in the car. In a few places there were omissions in the text filled with the usual observation, "sound hindrance." The largest such hindrance occurred exactly where I had replied concerning my obligation to Yeltsin's campaign. Not only had the agents bugged a popularly elected politician, they had altered the recordings to their liking. Now there was proof that Yeltsin received and heeded an increasing amount of politically biased, fiddly intelligence, not only from abroad but also from inside the country.

My worst worries concerning the evolution of the regime and the president found new ground.

In a contest with such hidden and unscrupulous opponents I had no chance. So I decided to resort to the same tool I had used in 1992—public opinion, though this time I had little hope for a significant response. Nonetheless, I invited a gifted, democratically minded young reporter, Vladimir Abarinov, to aid in this quest.

The October 20 edition of the liberal daily *Segodnia* (Today) published an extensive interview with me.

Q. At the beginning of 1992 you warned of "revanchist apparatchiks." There is an impression that by now they have already won.

A. The forces that profiteered from the arms race and confrontation with the West are still here and constantly try to get revenge and regain power through the bureaucracy, political parties, and the Duma. Confrontation leads nowhere but fits narrow corporate interests.

Q. In two days the presidents of Russia and the US will meet in America. This would be the first summit accompanied by the unprecedented tide of an anti-American and anti-Western campaign in Russia. Are you concerned?

A. Yes, we are under pressure. . . . I continue to insist that the West is as natural an ally of democratic Russia as it was an enemy of the Soviet Union. . . . There are no "two Kozyrevs." If in 1991 I wanted the CSCE observers to be allowed to go to the Baltic Republics [which had been attacked by the Soviet troops], now I advocate for the OSCE observers to be allowed to go to Chechnya, because the observance of human rights is not an exclusively internal affair.

Three years ago my warning of revanchist apparatchiks trying to force Russia onto the neo-Soviet path had made the headlines almost as soon as it was published. This time even the liberal *Segodnia* did not try to make it a top story, putting the interview on page 9, devoted to international politics.

Also, in contrast to the earlier situation the opposition forces struck back without delay, and openly.

The Covenant Turns into a Trap

The afternoon the interview appeared in *Segodnia* Yeltsin held a press conference on various issues, which I watched on TV at home, since it was Sunday and I was packing to accompany him to the United States the next morning. When asked whether he was more satisfied with the foreign minister than a month ago, when he had criticized how Russia's foreign policy was being conducted, he said in an especially aggrieved and strident voice that on the contrary, he was even more dissatisfied. The foreign minister had not mended his ways. He was not up to his job. He had lost authority in the foreign capitals, which didn't pay attention to Russian concerns, and also among his colleagues in the Russian government, who refused to coordinate foreign policy positions with him. The task now was to find a proper successor.

I carefully watched the evening news. The coverage of the president's press conference was malicious and spiteful: again, and again the TV channels replayed the brief scene of him entering the hall and pinching from the back a nice-looking middle-aged woman stenographer who was sitting at a small table prepared to take notes and who jumped up from her chair with a horrified look. Also, the camera operators made no attempt to hide Yeltsin's awkward gestures and blurred speech, while the commentators were guessing whether he was drunk or ill, or both.

The remarks concerning me were reported in the same manner. Ignoring any political context, including the looming summit in America, most reporters relished the rough wording, and gloated over the dressing-down delivered to one of the president's favorites. The few substantive comments were limited to brief remarks that a change in foreign policy and a change of minister had been in the air for some time already.

Going to bed, I weighed my options. I could choose not to go to the airport the following morning and instead call a press conference and publicly resign, giving as my reason disagreement with the neo-Soviet reversal of foreign and domestic policy. Though this approach would position me at the top of the liberal agenda politically, the press was sure to interpret the move cynically, and it would only contribute to a further weakening of the already fragile democratic movement, while also weakening the Russian president on the eve of an important summit. The voice of the professional diplomat could not be denied: address your personal problems and argue your case after appropriate diplomatic action.

That rumination led to consideration of a second choice: going to the airport and talking to the president. He looked high at the press conference and probably said more than he would have said under normal conditions, as so often happened. If he publicly backtracked—there would be a lot of press there—it might be possible to postpone the showdown until after his return. Also, there would be time to gauge the reaction of the electorate in Murmansk and take it into consideration in choosing a future course of action.

I returned to my first choice. Suppose I was successful and became an instant hero of the remaining democrats and the large part of the population irritated with Yeltsin's erratic behavior. What would come next? Competing for the leadership of one of the marginalized liberal parties debilitated by the ambitions of their current leaders? The prospect was not too appealing. A meaningful return could only come from a race for the presidency. If the retired General Alexander Lebed, formerly head of the Fourteenth Army in Moldova, was gaining strength as a potential candidate for the presidency under nationalist and law-and-order banners, a dissident from the very top of the power structure with years of daily national TV exposure could be a serious contender on the less militaristic but reasonable side of the spectrum. But it would not be me. A not inconsiderable consideration was the prejudice stirred up by my appearance, as described at the beginning of this book. I chose option two, perhaps gutlessly.

At the airport Yeltsin shook hands with me in the ordinary manner, as he did with the others.

"I hope you didn't take too much to heart what was said yesterday, Andrei Vladimirovich. My words yesterday were prompted by irritation caused by other reasons."

"Oh, yes, I did—and I am in doubt: should I fly or stay and ask for retirement? And if I am to accompany you, I ask you to report it to the press here."

Yeltsin turned to the reporters and repeated what he had just told me, pointedly half-turning to my side to let me hear. "Of course, Kozyrev should fly with me. This is a very important mission and he is the foreign minister." Then he turned to the opposite side as if to address a different subject and another group of reporters. I did not hear it when he added the words "... for now," and learned about them only the next morning watching the news on CNN in New York where the delegation had flown to from Moscow.

I think Yeltsin was high for the entirety of the trip. In his memoirs Strobe Talbott provides an account of his erratic behavior and of Clinton's playing up to Yeltsin's boasting at the post-summit press conference. It was a way of avoiding the showdown that might otherwise have arisen over the unpleasant question of who lost Russia on the eve of Clinton's reelection campaign. As well as this, the Russian president had agreed to contribute some troops to the peacekeeping operation in former Yugoslavia as a part of the NATO-led operation, but formally under American rather than NATO command. Participation in the operation was, of course, in Russia's interests: Russia should be seen to have a role in the peace settlement in the Balkans instead of engaging in self-isolation from mainstream European politics. Yet the American president almost begged for Russian participation as a favor. I felt a twinge of satisfaction at not being the only one having to tolerate my boss's mischief-making and public rudeness for the sake of the success of the summit and international cooperation.

After returning to Moscow, Yeltsin fell ill—he was subsequently diagnosed with a heart attack—and was hospitalized before we had a chance to talk. Left with no choice, I registered my position in a TV interview. For months, I said, we had been drifting toward a confrontation with the United States—I was against it—and then, after meeting the American president, the president of Russia had delivered a heartrending protestation to the press: "No, partnership is not dead; we are determined to continue it!" Had we indeed stuck to building a partnership, such a scene would have been unnecessary, and we could have achieved more at the summit.

I was prepared to stay on as foreign minister if this course could be restored and followed steadily not only at summits but on a daily basis.

On November 9, I was allowed to visit Yeltsin in the hospital. He was physically weak but sounder in his judgment than he had been in a long time. Suddenly the charismatic personality I had dealt with in 1991–92 reappeared, speaking the almost forgotten language of the reform-minded leader. He agreed that now, after the devastating effect of the Yugoslav crisis on European and domestic Russian politics was finally diminishing—a peace settlement seemed to be within reach—we could return to partnering with the West on a wide range of issues, including NATO. This political exchange was very brief, but I felt encouraged. After this warm conversation of two longtime accomplices, it seemed almost irrelevant to raise the awkward question of my immediate future. When I did, he calmly and warily said that he did understand my feelings. So many times in his life there had been tough situations caused by unmerited criticism or offenses.

While he was speaking, I took out two pieces of paper and placed them on the small coffee table that stood between us. I handed one to him. I left the other, my request for retirement, on the table so that he could see it. He read the first document through, signed it in his famous calligraphic hand, "Approved. Boris Yeltsin," and returned it to me.

"Take that away," he ordered, pointing to the second document on the table, with a shrewd look. "It's over now, isn't it?" he said, with a piercing look straight into my eyes.

"Almost," I said, then cut myself off, seeing the fatigue of illness return to his eyes. "I have already taken too much of your time today. I am very grateful for your attention and understanding, Boris Nikolayevich. I am just happy to have seen the president, the same president I have known and loved since 1991."

He seemed pleased by these last words and was smiling when I left the room, to be reprimanded by his doctor for exceeding the time allowed for interviews.

The paper signed by the president said that he reiterated the course of foreign policy and expressed support for me "in conducting policy and coordinating its implementation with other government structures." I gave it to the president's chief of staff, Viktor Ilyushin, and also to my press attaché. It immediately made the headlines in the Russian media.

My euphoria soon dissipated. Ilyushin did not pass the endorsement paper with the president's autograph to the Kremlin's spokesman, who subsequently could neither confirm nor deny its existence when asked by journalists. Yeltsin spent most of the time in the hospital, and unlike most of the other officials who sought visiting privileges, I was not allowed to see him. In the meantime, business went on as before: my proposals rarely reached the president, being stopped by his staff, who requested that I coordinate with the other agencies—which was not possible on important issues concerning partnership with the West.

The Americans and other NATO countries, particularly Britain, continued sending signals of readiness to proceed in exploring deeper cooperation with Russia, and I felt it my duty to make clear to the public that these overtures were being blocked on our side. At least it seemed important for the record, since a favorite argument of my opponents was that only Moscow wanted partnership, whereas NATO was giving us the cold shoulder. I decided again to turn to the press to expose the situation. On December 1, *Izvestia* published my interview with the gifted journalist and writer Leonid Mlechin, which contained to-the-point statements: "Right up to the present we don't have a decision on a fundamental question: Are we looking for partnership or confrontation with NATO? My answer is clear: while objecting to the expansion of NATO, [we need to] go on building a partnership with it. What is our biggest objection to the alliance? That it fails to consult us. Yet it is we who reject building a consultative mechanism and mutual trust!"

I also left no doubt as to my intention to resign, and the political reasons for it. Professionally, I told Leonid, I faced a catastrophe, being a career diplomat. A builder or an engineer who engages in politics can return to his core profession afterward. My profession was too political for that.

What I did not say in the interview was that I was bound by my word to Yeltsin.

My 1995 campaign in Murmansk for a Duma seat was even more difficult than in 1993. There was tangible political indifference. Despite the president's criticism of my pro-Western line, which made headlines in Moscow and in the world press, I received only occasional questions on foreign policy. Evidently Yeltsin's approval rating was so low that his words were not taken seriously. A lot of skepticism was expressed toward the liberal Russia's Choice party, which was seen as part and parcel of the social injustice of nascent oligarch capitalism sprouting in Moscow. So, my independent status as a nonparty candidate again played well. Most questions related to my ability to lobby on behalf of regional interests in Moscow agencies for the purpose of distributing budget transfers, getting subsidies to offset difficult life in a hard northern climate, and so on. In that sense, people were alarmed by the president's negativism and they were anxious about my future role. For that matter, I found it convenient to keep a bit of mystery about my future position. Like observers in Moscow, many folks in Murmansk believed that anything was possible in our homeland, including violation of the Russian constitution at the Kremlin's convenience.

With respect to capitalizing on the lobbying potential some thought I had, I was asked why I refused to join a new party, Our Home Is Russia, headed by Prime Minister Chernomyrdin and associated with Gazprom, the state-owned company and monopolist of the natural gas market famous for its wealth in an otherwise poor country. The party nicknamed "Our Home Is Gazprom," was in fact a reincarnation of the bureaucratic core of the Communist Party of the Soviet Union, with red Marxist banners exchanged for nationalist ones. My intense dislike of Soviet statism and my revulsion at the neo-Soviet comeback meant I could never affiliate with such a party. I resigned myself to being ridiculed for not capitalizing on my lobbying potential and for not joining the oligarchs.

Despite an overwhelming victory in Murmansk, the outlook for my parliamentary future was gloomy. Only one of the democratic parties, Grigory Yavlinsky's Yabloko, crossed the 5 percent threshold needed to achieve representation in the Duma, which was dominated by communists and Vladimir Zhirinovsky's ultranationalist Liberal Democratic Party of Russia. Almost out of desperation I remained defiant. Speaking to reporters on December 19, I argued that despite a weak showing by the liberal faction, neither our foreign partners nor we should panic or lose hope. My own victory in a single-member constituency in Murmansk, a region with a large naval base, showed that Russians did not reject either the idea of partnership with the West or domestic reform. As to my future, I promised to discuss it with the president in the next few days.

Good-bye Yeltsin

December 25: Yeltsin, at his state dacha, looked bad—a sick old man. The house slippers and pajama-like outfit he had donned accentuated this impression. Everything from Naina opening the door and giving me a welcoming kiss to Yeltsin's attire bespoke an informal, friendly, and intimate atmosphere.

"Let's just talk as old friends," Yeltsin said warmly.

"I appreciate the offer," I answered eagerly, "and will be frank with you, Boris Nikolayevich. Despite the Duma election results I still believe there is room for continuing the policy of cooperation with the West and the internal reforms. This agenda would also be a winning one for your presidential campaign, which should start soon. As much as I admire you and appreciate your friendship, clearly, I am not the right person to help implement a different policy approach, as was made painfully clear to the domestic public earlier this year. Now, as I am elected to the Duma, it would be easy: I need only stick to the people's mandate, without much explanation. I don't want to damage your position vis-à-vis those crazy communists and nationalists. In leaving the government I would not be betraying you, Boris Nikolayevich."

"I have no doubt of that!" he exclaimed, then, after a pause, said, "Tell me what is bothering you. After all, it is the president's policy; I am the president, and I am still the same."

Everything about the encounter was beginning to suggest an opening: if I admitted some technical error, asked for a little favor, like one more deputy or a better car, and, most important, signaled compliance with a new policy course, I could most likely retain my position as some of my colleagues believed and advised.

So, what was the problem? I had made a successful diplomatic career in the Soviet system. Nothing would have been easier for me than to step back into a Soviet-style distrust of the West. If the old system was balanced on the brink of war with the United States and NATO, the new one would be balancing on the verge of political confrontation with the same enemy. Yet the scenario would make me too much of a Frankenstein for comfort. I knew the rules of the new-old game but could not trample on the dream of radical change to play by them. After chasing the firebird, it would be unbearable to catch an old hen. In making the compromises I had already made, I had probably tarnished my place in history as the first non-Soviet foreign minister of Russia and was afraid of downgrading it further to neo-Soviet status.

These thoughts had dominated my mind for the past year, and now they crossed it like lightning. I went on.

"What worries me, Boris Nikolayevich, is strategy." His face darkened, but I continued on the treacherous path. "It should target a comprehensive agreement on an alliance with NATO. Yet the anti-NATO rhetoric has exploded. That damages the domestic political climate to the advantage of the neo-Soviet forces and sets the stage for the humiliation of Russia in 1997, when NATO expansion will resume regardless of Russian objections. Enlargement has become inevitable, like 100 percent forecasted rain, and we can either provide ourselves with an umbrella—an umbrella agreement on the alliance—or get wet."

He half-listened to the last part of my exposé: NATO was not a disputable issue for him. I took a breath; he said, as if thinking aloud: "We made mistakes, didn't we?"

I nodded energetically in the frantic hope that he was referring to our anti-NATO strategy.

"I guess we were just inexperienced," he continued. "How else could we have voted in the UN for sanctions against Serbia in 1992?"

My crazy hope vanished.

"I still believe, Boris Nikolayevich, that vote sent a sobering signal to Milošević. I spoke with him a few days ago at the peace conference in Paris and he greatly appreciated our role. I told him that soon there would almost certainly be a different foreign minister, more 'pro-Serbian,' but that he should not be tempted to brutalize Kosovo. Keeping him under control will be the most challenging task for our diplomacy in the next few years. Again, it can only be achieved in cooperation with the West."

I was under no illusion. Nobody dared lecture Yeltsin, and anyone who tried did not get away with it. But it was my last chance to tell him what I thought was right.

"Is there anything positive in your arsenal for the elections?" His voice was tense.

"There are some highly visible and simple things. The G-7 is all set to officially become the G-8, welcoming Russia as a full member in the summer, but it will be announced in the spring; also, the members of this prestigious club have agreed to your invitation to have an extraordinary spring meeting in Moscow on nuclear energy, which will demonstrate not only respect for Russia and its president but also recognition of our high-tech achievements. The Council of Europe will finally welcome Russia as a full member in spring. Last but not least, the CIS heads of state have asked you to preside over the Commonwealth for the next year; there will be some important bilateral events with those nations with which we share a common past."

I saw that he was impressed but did not want to show it. A bizarre thought crossed my mind: all those positive results of the cursed "pro-Western policy" would be pocketed by that irreproachable patriot, Yevgeny Primakov, my successor, who argued that toughness was more productive in relations with the West. And indeed, the Western democratic clubs would be welcoming a

Kremlin ruler just after he had abandoned a desperate attempt to establish democracy.

Signaling that the time recommended by the doctors for a business meeting was up, Naina joined us for a cup of tea and small talk about my daughter Natasha, whom she seemed genuinely fond of, and their grandchildren, who were about the same age as Natasha.

Shaking hands good-bye, I asked Yeltsin to answer my question on the future job as soon as possible.

"Yes, I remember and will honor our agreement. Give me some more time. In any case, we will speak again before any decision is made."

The next morning I sent the president's office a request for open-ended vacation time and gave my retirement request to an aide, asking that he be ready to send it to the Kremlin. Then I waited until January 7, when the president called by phone and said that perhaps it would be better if I served in the Duma, though, of course, we would remain friends. "I cannot agree more, Boris Nikolayevich," I answered with almost impolite enthusiasm: the suspense had lasted too long. After that I called my office, asked the aide to dispatch the request, poured a glass of Scotch, and tried to think about the next stage of my life.

And for the hundredth time, I recalled the tea party at the dacha. As I had suspected, it was the final meeting. I was depressed by what I had seen—a sick old man, hardly able to perform even limited official functions yet dreaming of an election campaign and another four-year term at the helm of one of the most troubled countries in the world, a country desperately in need of a dynamic leader determined to carry out comprehensive reforms, which were now stuck at the halfway point.

In exasperating contrast to the past, Yeltsin's political agenda had been reduced to survival at the top of a bureaucratic pyramid. This awkward construction had been assembled from the odds and ends of the system he once wanted to destroy but one that ran too strongly in his blood, as well as new elements he had brought from the West, which proved too alien for him to trust. In that he was genuinely representative of large part of the bureaucracy and the people: caught between two worlds, exhausted, and unwilling either to turn back or to move forward. Oddly enough, despite his physical weakness Yeltsin could win their hearts again, especially if a serious contender did not challenge him. And he certainly had seen to it that there was no challenger around him to do so.

The Yeltsin pages in the book of my life had turned. He was not in the habit of coming back to retired aides, especially close ones, as if he needed to tear them out of his heart once and for all. I was also not prepared to accept this Yeltsin for the democratic leader I had once allied with for the great cause he had now abandoned.

The Duma promised little better, being dominated by communists, the populist Zhirinovsky gang, and Chernomyrdin's lobbyist-centrists. The only democracy-oriented party, Yavlinsky's Yabloko, was not my choice, though I had long known Yavlinsky as a devoted reformer. Yet his rivalry with Gaidar and other democratic leaders, also infected by the mania, had pushed him into an alliance with the semiliberal *shestidesiatniki*, men of a 1960s intellectual bent, such as Vladimir Lukin or Anatoly Adamishin, and some strange characters not of my preference. If I had to choose a party, I would have preferred Russia's Choice, but it did not cross the 5 percent threshold. Elected on an individual nonparty ticket, I decided to take a backseat, joining a politically mixed and disorganized group of independent deputies who had little say in deliberations.

Soon I received a painful confirmation of my pessimism concerning not only political influence but also the financial horizons of a Duma deputy, which further limited my options. Unlike in America, ex-government officials in Russia have no market for speaking engagements or book publishing. The offers I had received from some oligarchs were for jobs requiring me either to leave the Duma, thus throwing away the popular mandate, or to lobby on behalf of private interests, abusing or corrupting my parliamentary status. None of that was to my liking. Nevertheless, for some time I maintained friendly relations with and enjoyed the philanthropic support of a few of them, who entertained pro-reform inclinations, notably Oleg Boyko and Vladimir Gusinsky.

In speaking to the oligarchs, I was surprised that most of those young and successful bankers had such a simplistic vision of politics. They thought that money could buy everything, including politicians, generals, and voters. So, they decided—the final point in consultations was reached at a dinner in Davos in late January 1996—to support Yeltsin for reelection, and appointed

Anatoly Chubais to manage the campaign. Both choices were emblematic of the logic of the rich "new Russians." They hardly concealed their expectations that the weak and ill Yeltsin, if elected with their financial backing, could be managed to suit their business interests, and that Chubais, just fired by Yeltsin in an angry tirade of recriminations, would be so grateful to them for his political comeback that he would help manage the president.

I told those among them who asked my opinion that I thought the strategy wrong. First of all, Russia needed continuation of the radical democratic and market-oriented reforms to the point that private property rights were guaranteed and the Soviet legacy of bureaucratic and security-police arbitrary rule was broken. Otherwise their fortunes would be short-lived and uncertain. For this task a young reformer, not an exhausted veteran—with all due respect to Yeltsin—should be found. That could be Yavlinsky, most suitably, or Nemtsov, or somebody else. If there was a chance to improve the disastrously low rating of public support Yeltsin had at that moment, there undoubtedly was a much better chance to promote a younger and more vigorous candidate.

The response to this argument was that for the midterm future it was better for big business to have a manageable president and acquire more wealth than to install in the Kremlin a devoted reformer who might insist on free market competition, the rule of law, serious limitation of corruption, and other measures harmful to oligarchy almost as much as to bureaucracy.

My second argument was that there was no guarantee that either Yeltsin or the bureaucracy as a whole would play by the rules of the oligarchs. There would always be powerful groups and individuals, especially in the military-security complex, who would choose to become oligarchs themselves instead of serving the existing ones. That argument was met with laughter and disbelief: the security generals were on the oligarchs' payrolls, and the bureaucracy as a whole, like the old man himself, was too disoriented and debilitated in the post-Soviet environment to generate anything but corruption, never mind dynamic and self-guided leaders or groups.

My turn to laugh, but not with joy, came in December 1999 when Yeltsin resigned, handing over power to the chief of the Federal Security Service, the former KGB colonel Vladimir Putin, who was determined to be a czar and to have oligarchs of his own choosing running Russia's business cartels. Recently declassified records of the Bill–Boris conversations suggest that Clinton accepted this appointment easily.

After fulfilling my term in the Duma in December 1999, I recused from running again and reinvented myself, turning into a businessman. Ever since I have done everything from co-owning and comanaging a medium-sized retail firm, sitting on boards of Russian banks, consulting international corporations active on emerging markets, and giving paid speeches on Russian and world affairs.

EPILOGUE

**Can Russian
Democracy
Rise Again?**

BY NOW THE READER WILL OF COURSE have noticed the disappointing dynamics during the period of democratization in Russia. Although the reform movement could ride a big wave of popular support in the early 1990s, by the middle of the decade it had lost energy and had even gone into reverse.

Why?

I wrote this book to provide a candid and accurate account of events that I participated in or was directly affected by and I hope it will help to answer this question. I am aware of course that some readers will come to different conclusions. Even direct participants in historic events often differ in their perspectives. (This happened before my eyes when most of the signatories to the Belavezha Accords, which replaced the Soviet Union with the Commonwealth of Independent States, differed on some key details at an event to mark its twenty-fifth anniversary at Harvard University.)

Accounts differ, but it is also true that history does not have a subjunctive tense. There are no alternatives to the past; there is only what actually happened. As Shakespeare pointed out, "What's done cannot be undone." And what's done is done by flesh-and-blood men and women. There is something mysterious about how those individuals, me included, make their way to the decision-making positions and make decisions. This alchemy is a combination of passions and abilities mixed with contingency and twists of fortune.

If Fate or History does drive events, it does so through people. From my experience, those people have to make choices that affect and occasionally drastically change the course of events in intended or (as it frequently turns out) unintended ways. The coup attempt of August 1991 is one particularly dramatic example. The hard-liners vowed to save the Soviet Union but instead consigned it to the dustbin of history.

With that in mind, I have tried to provide a detailed firsthand account of the decision making I witnessed by President Yeltsin and other key players.

My first conclusion is that the failure of the reforms was not inevitable. Burdened with Soviet concepts and habits, Yeltsin, after an initial effort to enact profound change, in many ways retreated to the old habits of governing. His flaws were matched by the inability of the democrats to act without him; to overcome their personal rivalries; or to nominate a younger leader. This was our major error, and the key reason that Russia's democracy failed. My reformist friends and I share responsibility for that failure.

The Russian people were exhausted by economic hardship and failed by politicians who were unwilling or unable to move ahead. The power structures were usurped to benefit an entrenched bureaucracy, security services, and a growing crony bourgeoisie, not ordinary struggling Russians.

At no point in those years was democratic civil control over the KGB ever established. The KGB, like other key elements of the old system that were carried over to the new Russian state from its infancy, underwent bureaucratic reorganizations and a name change (it is now the FSB and SVR, meaning internal and foreign services). But its essential character survived. This was overpoweringly evident to me anytime I dealt with the agency or its representatives, despite its rebadging. The same thing happened to the army and police, also viewed by Yeltsin as key tools of protection for his power.

Hopes that capitalist entrepreneurs would be a new positive force in the country's modernization and development were fading fast. Many in this class were former government officials and Soviet factory directors who had capitalized on Gorbachev's policy of creating proto-capitalist corporations that controlled Soviet industrial assets. Bureaucratic control of the economy had been the hallmark of the Soviet state and remained dominant in the new Russia. The Yeltsin government's efforts to introduce a market economy changed very little in that regard. Unfinished reforms benefited primarily those with positions in the state, or connections to them. Among the new recruits to capitalism, the most prominent and successful were the young entrepreneurs who could find a network of powerful elders and seize the moment.

The controversial program of privatizations enabled the old elite to expand their holdings and capture state assets for themselves but, most important, to seize the revenues from these huge state enterprises. Together with the newcomers they acquired astounding wealth. Most of those businessmen particularly profiteered from the shady trading of natural resources, especially oil. The asset holder would sell the commodity at low domestic prices or in barter swaps to some affiliated middlemen, who would then export the goods to Western markets for much higher prices and kickback to the source. Even when they gradually started to take control of production, they felt far from assured of their property rights and preferred to stick to quick black- or gray-market profits rather than build modern well-governed corporations. Former KGB and police officers took an active part in such businesses by providing protection, which gave them a new economic and financial base.

What followed was the emergence of the Russian oligarchs and astounding economic inequality, while any positive economic effects lagged far, far behind. The rise in the opulent wealth of the few contrasted with the hardships of the many. In the popular mind, this change had occurred under the banner of capitalism, democracy, and a pro-Western foreign policy. The rise of the oligarchs did untold harm to these concepts in the eyes of ordinary Russians.

By 1993, the corrupt security and military bureaucracy intertwined with the new oligarchy achieved enough critical mass to commence a step-by-step takeover of all aspects of public life. On the one hand, the new ruling class depended on trade with the West and preferred to keep its money in Western banks, but on the other, it was desperate to thwart foreign competition to its domestic assets. It saw the West as a threat not only because of its support for human rights and democracy but also because of its much higher levels of competitiveness and transparency. Russia's new businessmen wanted petrodollars and high-quality goods from the West, luxury real estate in London, New York, and Paris, and at the same they rejected Western "interference" and values.

In 1996 Yeltsin assigned the chief of the SVR (foreign intelligence service), Yevgeny Primakov, to succeed me as the foreign minister in order to reverse my "pro-Western" foreign policy. Later Primakov was promoted to prime minister. In 1999 Yeltsin appointed the head of the FSB (Federal Security Service), Vladimir Putin, as head of the government and as his presidential successor. Many democrats in Russia believe that these appointments were made with the aim of protecting Yeltsin and his cronies at the top of the oligarchic regime. Then more former KGB officers were placed in influential positions and the resurrection of Soviet-style power structures gained new momentum. Today the Kremlin controls all the most important sectors of the economy: exports of oil and other natural resources and military production. It also retains the ability to violate the rights of any individual, including property rights, through an acquiescent legal system. It harasses and intimidates private businesses and brings them to heel. And, of course, it controls the media, including many news- and opinion-making sources that publish on the internet.

The country increasingly depends on exports of oil and gas. In 1999 these accounted for a little less than half of Russia's export proceeds but today they account for 68 percent. The aggregate wealth of Russia totals $1.1 trillion, on a par with that of oil-exporting Mexico and Norway, but those countries have smaller populations. The average Mexican is actually twice as wealthy as the average Russian, while the average Norwegian is thirty times wealthier. Russia is in first place among thirty-eight countries in one respect—inequality. One percent of the population in Russia possesses 75 percent of the country's wealth. According to opinion polls, if Russians had an opportunity to choose, they might once again attempt to build socialism by stripping the rich of their assets and divvying them up among the poor.

Yet state propaganda stirs up Soviet nostalgia. It helps to justify the resurrection of neo-Soviet power structures and to redirect the anger of ordinary Russians over the unfair socioeconomic situation from the present regime to the reformers of the early 1990s. This hypocritical allocation of blame ignores the fact that Putin has been at the helm of power for two decades, which is ample time to correct whatever old mistakes might have existed and to set up a better system.

The Soviet legacy weighs on Russia's foreign policy, which is in essence a continuation of Cold War stereotypes. The main sources of conflict are basically the same as those during the Soviet period that I sought to exclude from the new Russian foreign policy of the early 1990s: anti-Americanism, rejection of NATO and in particular of its enlargement, meddling in neighboring countries, and support of anti-Western authoritarian regimes all over the world from Cuba to Syria and North Korea.

For the Russian rulers, as for their Soviet predecessors, hostility to America and NATO provides critical justification for their power. When European nations, led by the United States, founded NATO on the principles of democracy, individual liberty, and the rule of law, they created a major multinational political pivot in modern history. Parting from centuries-old efforts to gain territory and domination, they found their national interests in peaceful cooperation and prosperity. That's why emerging democracies want to join NATO. And that's why the totalitarian Soviet Union opposed it, and now authoritarian Russia along with undemocratic politicians elsewhere try to subvert it. Had there been no NATO enlargement, they would have found another pretext for anti-American and anti-Western propaganda. Even if NATO had dissolved itself, there would still be a Pentagon and a CIA that could be held up as the enemy.

The events of 2008 and 2014 and thereafter, when Russia waged so-called hybrid wars against Georgia and Ukraine recalled the memories of Stalin's annexations of the Baltic states. They were essentially a reprise of the party of war's stance I had confronted during the showdown in the Kremlin in the hot summer of 1992. The main difference now is that the perpetrators are not acting in conflict with the nascent democracy as they had in the early 1990s but as part and parcel of the belligerent authoritarian regime that embodies aggressive nationalism and militarism. Aggression, both covert and overt, became a means of holding on to power rather than seizing it. Yet in recent years the same old-style Kremlin incursions into Crimea and eastern Ukraine came as a surprise to and have been heralded as something new by American and European governments, which were slow to recognize the uncomfortable reality of the resumption of the Cold War.

Using old and new tools of subversion, including cyber and information warfare, against democracies in America and Europe and the aspiring democracies in Ukraine and Georgia, the Kremlin has unapologetically rushed down the path toward a new Cold War. But equally, it is desperately eager to stop the West from returning to the strategy of containment, which integrated political, informational, economic, and military means.

My career in the Soviet foreign ministry coincided with Ronald Reagan's presidency, and I witnessed firsthand its effect on Kremlin leadership. Reagan made America, and indeed Washington–Moscow relations, great. He stood firm. First he confronted the USSR politically, as an "evil Empire" and backed these strong words with the deployment of Pershing II missiles to counterbalance Soviet SS-20 rockets, which the Kremlin advertised as unbeatable. In response, the new communist leader Gorbachev signaled a pivot from threats to dialogue. Under pressure, he curbed not only aggression in Afghanistan but also the Soviet Union's iron grip on Eastern European satellites. These changes opened the way for productive dialogue, and the two sides negotiated significant disarmament treaties. The Berlin Wall fell. Firmness proved effective.

In contrast, President Donald Trump, at least at the time of this writing, has avoided personally and directly criticizing the undemocratic nature of the Kremlin's regime and its foreign policy. Serious observers regard Russian elections as a sham, designed to confirm the unalterable rule of the present political elite. One of the two major opposition leaders, Boris Nemtsov, was killed in front of the Kremlin; the other, Alexei Navalny, has been locked up many times and is excluded from the list of candidates in any elections. No wonder Putin deigned to participate in debates with the remaining actors during the presidential election season in 2016. Government-sponsored candidates in every corner of every election race enjoy overwhelmingly positive coverage from the state-controlled media that dominates the public space. No wonder the country has a rubber-stamp parliament.

Betting on guns before butter—and militarism, the Kremlin implies that America has been responsible for most of the troubles in the world and for the economic problems in Russia itself. On state TV its propagandists constantly brag about a Russian nuclear arsenal that is capable of turning America into a "radioactive desert." Announcing the government's plans to build new missiles and bombs, they repeat, "Now they [the Americans] will talk to us," making it clear that the nuclear scarecrow is meant to intimidate the United States and extract concessions. In fact, Kremlin strategists are far too gluttonous to be suicidal, but brazen enough to resort to blackmail.

The Kremlin's immediate wish list is well-known: America should (a) repeal the Magnitsky Act that bars Russian officials suspected of human rights abuses; (b) lift the sanctions imposed for Russian incursions into Ukraine; (c) drop objections to the Kremlin policy of subjugating neighboring countries and supporting dictators in Syria and elsewhere; and (d) tolerate cyberattacks in America and Europe.

The Kremlin's champs and chumps in the West argue for a "grand bargain" that would give Moscow a green light to do whatever it wants in the space of the former Soviet Union, while cooperating with the West in other trouble spots. Such a policy would be not only a betrayal of millions of people in those regions but also a shortsighted replay of the policy of appeasement that has proved so disastrous many times in history. The Kremlin's ambitions are far from confined to the former Soviet borders. Only one of the five top recipients of Russian foreign aid in the past ten years was within those borders. The other four were Cuba, Venezuela, Syria, and North Korea. And the anti-democracy operations, especially cyber activities, are global.

Brandishing a nuclear stick, the Kremlin is betting on boosting its fading image. The country's economy has stagnated and is now less than one-tenth the size of that of the United States; despite this, the Kremlin claims to be talking to Washington from a position of strength. If under communism the Kremlin's slogan was "Proletarians of all countries unite!" today it would be "Autocrats everywhere follow me against the free world!" While many in the West are confused, every Russian knows from their middle school literature textbooks the trick that the Kremlin is exploiting. The famous Russian fabulist Ivan Krylov described a dog's justification of his fierce barking at an elephant: "It raises my rating. Without a fight, I can become a big bully." The Kremlin bully will go as far as allowed.

The favorite canard of the Kremlin apologists and their Western friends is that America humiliated Russia after the demise of the Soviet Union, and NATO expansion broke the naive hope of the early Yeltsin administration to overcome the Cold War animosity of the West toward Russia. That is a distortion. The Clinton administration *did* fail to give Yeltsin sufficient help in making the transition to a free-market economy and to properly engage with him on crucial foreign policy issues, particularly that of NATO enlargement. Yet Washington was far from humiliating or rejecting Moscow. On the whole, the United States and the West provided considerable economic and political assistance to Russia and offered the former adversary a partnership with NATO, based on shared democratic values. Moscow rejected this and turned its back on the partnership, using as a pretext the mistakes made by certain politicians and diplomats in Washington.

This book should help the reformers who will follow us in Russia and their American friends avoid past mistakes and do better. It is also testament to the fact that those Kremlin authoritarians are wrong.

The other false idea that is touted regularly to explain the Kremlin's aggressiveness today is that Russia and Russians are fated to be undemocratic and imperialistic in order to live up to their historic obligations and national interest.

Right after they seized power in 1917, the Soviets began shifting the emphasis from world revolution to traditional patriotism, which in their view boiled down to the cult of an omnipotent state opposing "Western" liberal ideas of individual rights and freedoms. Now again the Kremlin is valorizing this kind of patriotism as "the national idea" that animates the Russian "national interest." More precisely, though, it is the traditional credo or interest of autocratic regimes in Russia.

Some say that Russians are different from Europeans and inherently antagonistic to democracy. This denigrating characterization is promulgated by Moscow propagandists who deliberately conceal it under the guise of Russia's "own and separate path," which they claim the country should follow. They like to accuse the West of Russophobia as an alleged explanation for the sanctions imposed on Russia, despite the fact that the sanctions were a response to military incursion in Ukraine and other unlawful international acts. In fact, those very claims about Russia's "own and separate path" and assertions that other nations hate Russians are what epitomize the worst Russophobia. The path of democracy is chosen not only by European countries but also by growing numbers of other countries on all continents, none of which have lost their unique identities, languages, or cultures. On the contrary, freedom and the rule of law boost national pride and prosperity, and cooperation with peers benefits those peoples even more. Russians are in no way inferior to other peoples. It is the autocratic regime and its aggressive foreign policy that makes Russia an outcast among most developed countries.

In fact, Russian culture and self-identity have always been attached to Europe. A dream of someday "living like other people" is deep-seated in the Russian soul. And those model relatives are not—with respect—Asian or African but European, the same Europeans who live in democracies that enjoy better standards of living. The Janus-faced Russian elite has chosen the Western universe as a safe and comfortable haven for their money and their families. The Kremlin kingdom is divided against itself.

The regime is aware of that. Instead of the Soviet claim of superiority it is guided by an inferiority complex relative to the more prosperous West, though it still takes every opportunity to denigrate the West. It also uses the old tools of anti-American foreign policy and propaganda, fostering in the Russian people a false sense of a besieged homeland.

Today the interests of the regime more than ever contradict the real national interest of Russia. The latter consists of catching up with the other European nations that after the Second World War rejected outdated historical interpretations of their national interests. For example, Germany and France dropped the quest for superiority and other territories in Europe. Instead, like other European states, they found that their national interest lay in building cooperation and open societies. The new democracies in the former Soviet-dominated central European states followed suit.

Sooner or later Russia will do the same. I have once witnessed the Russian people rise up for democracy. It happened at the end of the 1980s when they elected Yeltsin and many democratically minded representatives to parliament with the popular mandate to introduce European-style reforms. They stood in a living wall around the Russian White House in August 1991 against tanks and won. On the shoulders of that victory Russia successfully pursued its real national interest of cooperation with neighboring and most developed countries, first of all America, in the early 1990s. I am proud of that policy and of the fact that it still exists in the national memory as a promise for the future. In that context I feel some sense that I am on the right side of history whenever one of today's Kremlin rulers attacks me and my concept of national interest. Almost twenty-five years have passed, yet they are still haunted by that experience and fear its return.

The freedom Russians wanted and fought for in the early 1990s has subsequently been sneered at as a fairy tale invented by delusional democrats. As one of those democrats, I chased the Firebird. Maybe it was a fantasy. But I have no regrets. The quest for the better world it symbolizes in Russian popular fairy tales is real. The Firebird of Russian democracy has arisen many times—in 1905, 1917, and 1991. Sooner or later the Russian people will rise up again and reclaim the Russia they deserve.

ACKNOWLEDGMENTS

THIS BOOK COULD NOT HAVE BEEN WRITTEN had I not had the privilege and honor of working with and learning from people who shaped the historic events that I try to describe here as accurately and honestly as possible. Among those particularly memorable and important for my understanding of Russian and world politics are the first popularly elected leader of Russia, Boris Yeltsin, devoted Russian democrats such as Gennady Burbulis, Sergei Shakhrai, Sergei Kovalyov, and Viktor Sheinis, and my colleagues Andrei Kolossovsky, Galina Sidorova, Georgy Mamedov, Vitaly Churkin, Sergei Lavrov, and Vladimir Lukin. Leaders of America and other countries, including George H. W. Bush, James Baker, Douglas Hurd, François Mitterrand, Alain Juppé, Hans-Dietrich Genscher, Klaus Kinkel, Václav Havel, and Carl Bildt.

This memoir would be merely a heap of recollections put on paper at various times but for the friendly encouragement, advice, and help I enjoyed as a fellow at the Wilson Center in Washington, DC, led by the admirable Jane Harman. The center's Kennan Institute, its director Matthew Rojansky, an enthusiast and deep researcher of Russia, and its staff along with the superb company of other fellows provided a stimulating environment and support for my work on the manuscript. My special gratitude to Joseph Dresen, whose editing and smart counsel was indispensable as I completed the manuscript. It is an honor to count Matt and Joe among my friends. My friendship with Herman Pirchner Jr., president of the American Foreign Policy Council, and his colleagues has also contributed to a better understanding of history and current trends in Russian–American relations.

Last but not least, I am grateful to my wife, Elena, with whom I have shared my life for more than twenty-five years, for her love and support. I also want to express my respect and gratitude to my former spouse, Irina Kozyreva, who provided support to me and cared for our daughter Natalia in the stormy years of the early 1990s. My life and career would not be complete without them.

INDEX